Compañeros

Spanish for Communication
BOOK 2

Ruth A. Moltz, M.A.
Chair, Foreign Language Department
Southfield High School
Southfield, Michigan

Thomas A. Claerr, Ph.D.
Professor of Spanish
Henry Ford Community College
Dearborn, Michigan

AMSCO SCHOOL PUBLICATIONS, INC.
315 Hudson Street/New York, N.Y. 10013

Ancillaries

A cassette program (with script) to accompany **Compañeros,** Spanish for Communication, Book 2 is available separately from the publisher (ordering code **N 635 C**). It is designed to reinforce the skills presented in the textbook and in the accompanying ancillaries. The voices are those of native speakers of Spanish.

To order other ancillaries, please specify:
Teacher's Annotated Edition **R 635 TH**
Cuaderno (Workbook) **R 635 W**
Test Package **R 635 TP**

When ordering this book, please specify:
R 635 H *or* **Compañeros,** Spanish for Communication, Book 2 (Hardbound Edition) *or*
R 635 P *or* **Compañeros,** Spanish for Communication, Book 2 (Softbound Edition)

ISBN 1-56765-457-6 (Hardbound Edition)
ISBN 1-56765-458-4 (Softbound Edition)

NYC Item 56765-457-5 (Hardbound Edition)
NYC Item 56765-458-3 (Softbound Edition)

Printed in the United States of America

1 2 3 4 5 6 7 8 9 10   05 04 03 02 01 00 99 98

Photo Credits

Literary Graphics
page 219

J. Antonio Méndez
pages 63, 91 (top), 91 (left), 113, 115 (left), 117 (bottom), 133, 177, 178, 181, 203, 207, 210, 237, 238, 247, 263 (left), 290, 295 (right), 405

Tourist Office of Spain
pages 245 (both), 417 (right)

United Nations
United Nations (UN Photo 97525): page 51 (left)
United Nations (UN Photo 64957): page 58
United Nations (UN Photo 155939): page 76
United Nations (UN Photo 155947): page 81
United Nations (UN Photo 97355): page 86
United Nations (UN Photo 33376): page 204 (left)
United Nations (UN Photo 98124): page 204 (right)
United Nations (UN Photo 126082): page 259 (left)
United Nations/J. Frank (UN Photo 143391): page 111
United Nations/Milton Grant (UN Photo 155127): page 257
United Nations/John Isaac (UN Photo 154240): page 122; (UN Photo 155214): page 437 (left)
United Nations/Seltzer (UN Photo 33403): page 263 (right)
United Nations/I. Solmssen (UN Photo 145734): page 249 (top)

Visuals Unlimited
R.F. Ashley: page 51 (bottom)
Bill Beatty: page 435
Hal Beral: page 139 (bottom right)
Bayard Brattstrom: pages 110, 201
Francis/Donna Caldwell: page 295 (left)
A.J. Copley: pages 131, 249 (bottom), 471

John D. Cunningham: pages 422, 433 (left)
FCF Earney: page 425
R.W. Gerling: pages 230, 251, 311
Audrey Gibson: page 363
Mark E. Gibson: pages 297 (right), 299, 301 (both), 329; 437 (right)
Mark J. Goebel: pages 36, 119, 124, 134 (both), 258, 306
Jeff Greenberg: pages 29, 30, 51 (top right), 64, 65, 91 (bottom), 104, 105, 106, 123, 217, 233, 256, 259 (right), 289, 337, 361, 391 (left), 399 (both), 400, 417 (left), 453 (left)
Hedaerow: page 327
Arthur R. Hill: page 432
Corinne Humphrey: page 391 (right)
Max and Bea Hunn: page 239
C.P. Hickman: page 139 (top right)
Leslie Lockely-Brattstrom: pages 345, 350
George Loun: page 297 (left)
Steve McCutcheon: page 187 (left)
Arthur Morris: page 428
Bob Newman: page 187 (right)
Erwin C. "Bud" Nielsen: pages 445, 453 (right)
Nick Noyes: page 347
Charles Philip: page 139 (left)
G. Prance: page 117 (middle)
Leonard Lee Rue III: pages 117 (top), 126
L.S. Stepanowicz: page 341
Richard Thom: page 115 (right)
Bernd Wittick: page 433 (right)

Acknowledgments

Cover design by A GOOD THING, INC.

Text design and composition by A GOOD THING, INC.

Cover art by Luis Domínguez

Text illustrations by Susan Detrich, Luis Domínguez, Denman Hampson, Chuck Melvin

Colorization by A GOOD THING, INC.

Dedication

*To my husband, Mort, and daughters, Kathleen and Cyndi,
for their encouragement, patience, and love . . .
and to my students, who challenged me to "go for it."*

R.A.M.

*To my wife, Christine, and daughter, Amelia,
without whose support and patience
this project could not have been completed.*

T.A.C.

¡Bienvenidos estudiantes!

Welcome to **Compañeros, Spanish for Communication,** Book 2. If you used Book 1, this book will look very familiar to you. If your class did not finish Book 1 or if you are a student who did not use Book 1, don't worry: everything you need to know to do the activities is presented in each lesson. At the beginning, each student will find something to review and something that is new.

Most of the vocabulary from Book 1 is reintroduced in Book 2. Vocabulary new to Book 2 is indicated by a large dot in the vocabulary lists. All the Book 1 structures are reintroduced in Book 2, along with new structures. The dialogues and readings continue the story of Paulina and her mostly Hispanic friends **(compañeros)** as they attend high school in the United States and have experiences similar to yours. Of course, you will continue to learn more about the culture of Hispanic people.

As in **Compañeros, Spanish for Communication,** Book 1, at the beginning of each unit you will find the ***Tools*** section that contains all the words *(Vocabulary)* and grammar points *(Structure)* for the entire unit. They are given to you at the beginning so that they will be available as you need them. As you go through the lessons, you will learn how the use *Vocabulary* and *Structure*. However, if you find some vocabulary or structure in the ***Tools*** section that you want to use before it has been formally taught in a lesson, give it a try! (The lesson in which the use of a tool is taught in indicated in parentheses, so look ahead if you need to. And there is a dictionary at the end of the book for you to look up additional words.) Don't be afraid to "make a mistake." You'll eventually learn to say it right.

You will discover that more Spanish is used in Book 2 and that the level of the language is a little more sophisticated—but we know you can handle it! We will revisit some of your favorite topics (such as food, shopping, and parties) and you will learn to talk about some exciting new topics, such as cars and driving and the environment. By the time you have finished Book 2, you will have studied all the vocabulary and basic grammar you need to carry on a conversation with your Spanish-speaking *compañeros.*

¡Buena suerte y comencemos de nuevo!
(Good luck and let's begin again!)

Ruth A. Moltz   *Thomas A. Claerr*

Paulina

Santiago

Rosita

Inés

Raúl

Pablo

Sean

LOS COMPAÑEROS

v

Table of Contents

⤜Unidad I⤛

⪡Unidad II⪢

⇒Unidad III⇐

⋙Unidad IV⋙

⇒ Unidad I ⇐

Unidad I
Tools

Vocabulario

Words preceded by a dot (•) indicate that they are new to **Compañeros, Book 2**.

Los saludos *Greetings*
(Lección 1)

Buenos días.	*Good morning.*
Buenas tardes.	*Good afternoon.*
Buenas noches.	*Good evening, Good night. [after sundown]*
Hola.	*Hello, Hi.*

Las despedidas *Farewells*
(Lección 1)

Adiós.	*Good-bye.*
Hasta la vista.	*See you later.*
Hasta mañana.	*See you tomorrow.*
¡Chau!	*Bye!*

Expresiones de cortesía *Courtesy expressions*
(Lección 1)

¿Cómo estás?	*How are you? [informal]*
¿Cómo está usted (Ud.)?	*How are you? [formal]*
¿Y usted (Ud.)?	*And you? [formal]*
¿Qué tal?	*How's everything? [informal]*
¿Y tú?	*And you? [informal]*
Muy bien.	*Fine.*
Mal.	*Bad.*
Así, así.	*So-so, OK.*
Regular.	*Fair, OK.*
No muy bien.	*Not very well.*
Lo siento.	*I'm sorry.*
¡Qué lástima!	*That's too bad!*
Por favor.	*Please.*
• Favor de + *infinitive*.	*Please + verb.*

Expresiones de cortesía   *Courtesy expressions* (continued)
(Lección 1)

Gracias.	*Thank you.*
De nada.	*You're welcome.*
Con permiso.	*Excuse me. [before doing something]*
Perdón.	*Pardon me. [after doing something]*

Instrucciones del profesor   *Instructions from the teacher*
(Lección 1)

• Abra(n) el libro.	*Open the book.*
la puerta.	*the door.*
la ventana.	*the window.*
• Cierre(n)…	*Close . . .*
• Ponga(n) los libros aquí.	*Put the books here.*
allí.	*there.*
en el pupitre.	*on the desk.*
en el suelo.	*on the floor.*
• Saque(n) la tarea.	*Take out the homework.*
• Vaya(n) a la pizarra.	*Go to the chalkboard.*
• Escriba(n).	*Write.*
• Repita(n).	*Repeat.*
• Conteste(n).	*Answer.*
• Silencio, por favor.	*Quiet, please.*
• Siénte(n)se.	*Be seated.*

Los pedidos del estudiante   *Student requests*
(Lección 1)

Repita, por favor.	*Repeat, please.*
Más alto.	*Louder.*
Más despacio.	*Slower.*
• ¿Puedo ir al baño?	*May I go to the bathroom?*
usar un lápiz?	*use a pencil?*

Preguntando cómo se dice   *Asking how to say*
(Lección 1)

¿Cómo se dice… en español/en inglés?	*How do you say . . . in Spanish/in English?*

Otras expresiones   *Other expressions*
(Lección 1)

Yo (no) sé.	*I (don't) know.*
Yo (no) comprendo.	*I (don't) understand.*

Conociendo a alguien *Meeting someone*
(Lección 1)

¿Cómo te llamas?	*What's your name? [informal]*
¿Cómo se llama Ud.?	*What's your name? [formal]*
Me llamo… *[first and last name]*	*My name is . . . , I'm called . . .*
¿Cuál es tu/su nombre/apellido?	*What's your first name/last name?*
Mi nombre/apellido es…	*My first name/last name is . . .*
¿Cómo se llama el muchacho/la muchacha?	*What is the boy's/the girl's name?*
Se llama…	*His/Her name is . . .*

Los títulos *Titles*
(Lección 1)

señor/Sr.	*Mr.*
señora/Sra.	*Mrs., Ms.*
señorita/Srta.	*Miss, Ms.*
doctor(a)/Dr., Dra.	*Doctor*
don + *first name*	*[title of respect: male]*
doña + *first name*	*[title of respect: female]*

Presentando a alguien *Introducing someone*
(Lección 1)

Quiero presentarte a…	*I want to introduce you to . . . [informal]*
Quiero presentarle a…	*I want to introduce you to . . . [formal]*
Mucho gusto, señor/señora/señorita.	*I'm pleased to meet you, sir/ma'am/miss.*
El gusto es mío.	*The pleasure is mine.*
Igualmente.	*The same here, Likewise.*

Las letras del alfabeto español *The letters of the Spanish alphabet*
(Lección 1)

a (a)	g (ge)	m (eme)	q (cu)	v (uve)
b (be)	h (hache)	n (ene)	r (ere)	w (double ve)
c (ce)	i (i)	ñ (eñe)	s (ese)	x (equis)
d (de)	j (jota)	o (o)	t (te)	y (i griega)
e (e)	k (ka)	p (pe)	u (u)	z (zeta)
f (efe)	l (ele)			

¿Cómo se escribe… ? *How do you spell . . . ?*
(Lección 1)

¿Qué letra es?	*What letter is it?*
¿Cómo se escribe… ?	*How do you spell . . . ?*
Se escribe…	*It's spelled . . .*

Los números hasta los millones *Numbers to the millions*
(Lecciones 1,4)

0 cero			
1 uno	11 once	10 diez	100 cien(to)
2 dos	12 doce	20 veinte	200 doscientos
3 tres	13 trece	30 treinta	300 trescientos
4 cuatro	14 catorce	40 cuarenta	400 cuatrocientos
5 cinco	15 quince	50 cincuenta	500 quinientos
6 seis	16 diez y seis	60 sesenta	600 seiscientos
7 siete	17 diez y siete	70 setenta	700 setecientos
8 ocho	18 diez y ocho	80 ochenta	800 ochocientos
9 nueve	19 diez y nueve	90 noventa	900 novecientos
10 diez	20 veinte	100 cien(to)	1.000 mil
	21 veinte y uno	101 ciento uno	2.000 dos mil
	22 veinte y dos	102 ciento dos	*etc.*
	etc.	*etc.*	1.000.000 un millón (de)
			2.000.000 dos millones (de)
			etc.

- los números pares   *even numbers*
- los números impares   *odd numbers*

Las funciones aritméticas *Arithmetic functions*
(Lección 4)

+ y, más	*and, plus*
− menos	*minus*
× por	*by, times*
÷ dividido por	*divided by*
= es/son	*is, equals*

Preguntando la edad *Asking the age*
(Lección 1)

¿Cuántos años tienes?	*How old are you? [informal]*
¿Cuántos años tiene Ud.?	*How old are you? [formal]*
Tengo… años.	*I'm . . . years old.*
¿Cuántos años tiene tu padre?	*How old is your father?*
Tiene… años.	*He is . . . years old.*
¿Cuántos años tienen tus hermanos?	*How old are your brothers?*
Ellos tienen… años.	*They are . . . years old.*

El calendario   *The calendar*
(Lección 1)

LOS DÍAS DE LA SEMANA	*THE DAYS OF THE WEEK*	LOS MESES DEL AÑO	*THE MONTHS OF THE YEAR*
lunes	*Monday*	enero	*January*
martes	*Tuesday*	febrero	*February*
miércoles	*Wednesday*	marzo	*March*
jueves	*Thursday*	abril	*April*
viernes	*Friday*	mayo	*May*
sábado	*Saturday*	junio	*June*
domingo	*Sunday*	julio	*July*
		agosto	*August*
		septiembre	*September*
		octubre	*October*
		noviembre	*November*
		diciembre	*December*

Preguntando el día   *Asking the day*
(Lección 1)

¿Qué día es hoy?	*What day is today?*
mañana?	*tomorrow?*
pasado mañana?	*the day after tomorrow?*

Preguntando la fecha   *Asking the date*
(Lección 1)

¿Cuál es la fecha de hoy?	*What is the date today?*
Hoy es el (primero) de enero.	*Today is the (first) of January.*
(dos)	*(second)*
(tres)	*(third)*
¿Cuándo es tu cumpleaños?	*When is your birthday?*
Mi cumpleaños es el *[date]* de *[month]*.	*My birthday is the [date] of [month].*

La hora   *Time*
(Lección 1)

¿Qué hora es?	*What time is it?*
¿A qué hora es… ?	*At what time is . . . ?*
Es mediodía.	*It's noon.*
Es medianoche.	*It's midnight.*
Es la una.	*It's one o'clock.*
Son las dos.	*It's two o'clock.*
Son las dos y cuarto.	*It's a quarter after two, It's 2:15.*
Son las dos y media.	*It's half past two, It's 2:30.*
Son las dos menos cuarto.	*It's a quarter to two, It's 1:45.*

La hora   *Time (continued)*
(Lección 1)

Son las dos y cinco.	*It's five minutes after two, It's 2:05.*
Son las dos menos cinco.	*It's five minutes to two, It's 1:55.*
Son las seis de la mañana.	*It's six o'clock in the morning, It's 6 A.M.*
Son las tres de la tarde.	*It's three o'clock in the afternoon., It's 3 P.M.*
Son las diez de la noche.	*It's ten o'clock at night., It's 10 P.M.*

Las personas   *People*
(Lección 2)

el hombre	*man*	él novio	*boyfriend*
la mujer	*woman*	la novia	*girlfriend*
el joven	*young person [m.]*	• todo el mundo	*everyone*
la joven	*young person [f.]*	• la gente	*people [in general]*
el muchacho	*boy*	• el chico	*boy, teenager*
la muchacha	*girl*	• la chica	*girl, teenager*
el niño	*small boy*	• el compañero	*friend [m.]*
la niña	*small girl*	• la compañera	*friend [f.]*
el bebé	*baby boy*	• el vecino	*neighbor [m.]*
la bebé	*baby girl*	• la vecina	*neighbor [f.]*
el amigo	*friend [m.]*	• los habitantes	*inhabitants*
la amiga	*friend [f.]*		

La familia   *The family*
(Lección 2)

el padre	*father*	el tío	*uncle*
la madre	*mother*	la tía	*aunt*
el padrino	*godfather*	el sobrino	*nephew*
la madrina	*godmother*	la sobrina	*niece*
el hijo	*son*	el primo	*cousin [m.]*
la hija	*daughter*	la prima	*cousin [f.]*
el ahijado	*godson*	el padrastro	*stepfather*
la ahijada	*goddaughter*	la madrastra	*stepmother*
el hermano	*brother*	el hermanastro	*stepbrother*
la hermana	*sister*	la hermanastra	*stepsister*
el hermano menor	*younger brother*	el esposo	*husband*
la hermana menor	*younger sister*	la esposa	*wife*
el hermano mayor	*older brother*	el suegro	*father-in-law*
la hermana mayor	*older sister*	la suegra	*mother-in-law*
el gemelo	*twin brother*	el yerno	*son-in-law*
la gemela	*twin sister*	la nuera	*daughter-in-law*
el abuelo	*grandfather*	el cuñado	*brother-in-law*
la abuela	*grandmother*	la cuñada	*sister-in-law*
el nieto	*grandson*	• el hijastro	*stepson*
la nieta	*granddaughter*	• la hijastra	*stepdaughter*

Las carreras y los trabajos   *Careers and jobs*
(Lección 2)

el/la abogado(a)	*lawyer*	el/la periodista	*journalist*
el actor	*actor*	el/la policía	*police officer*
la actriz	*actress*	el/la profesor(a)	*teacher*
el/la agente	*agent*	• el/la secretario(a)	*secretary*
el/la agricultor(a)	*farmer*	• el/la albañil	*bricklayer, mason*
el ama de casa	*homemaker*	• el/la aeromozo(a)	*flight attendant*
el/la arquitecto(a)	*architect*	• el/la ayudante	*assistant, aide*
el/la artista	*artist*	• el/la barbero	*barber*
el/la banquero(a)	*banker*	• el/la cajero(a)	*cashier*
el/la bombero(a)	*firefighter*	• el/la camarero(a)	*waiter, waitress*
el/la contador(a)	*accountant*	• el/la carpintero(a)	*carpenterr*
el/la criado(a)	*servant,*	• el/la cartero(a)	*mail carrier*
	housekeeper	• el/la científico(a)	*scientist*
el/la dentista	*dentist*	• el/la cocinero(a)	*cook, chef*
el/la dependiente	*salesperson*	• el/la conductor(a)	*truck driver*
el/la enfermero(a)	*nurse*	de camión	
el/la estudiante/	*student, pupil*	• el/la electricista	*electrician*
alumno(a)		• el/la embajador(a)	*ambassador*
el/la farmacista	*pharmacist*	• el/la jardinero(a)	*gardener*
el/la gerente	*manager*	• el/la jugador(a)	*player*
el hombre de negocios	*businessman*	• el/la obrero(a)	*construction worker*
el/la ingeniero(a)	*engineer*	de construcción	
el/la mecánico(a)	*mechanic*	• el/la payaso(a)	*clown*
el/la médico(a)	*doctor*	• el/la peluquero(a)	*hairdresser*
el/la mesero(a)	*waiter, waitress*	• el/la pescador(a)	*fisherperson*
la mujer de negocios	*businesswoman*	• el/la plomero(a)	*plumber*
el/la músico(a)	*musician*	• el/la soldado(a)	*soldier*
el/la obrero(a)	*laborer, worker*	• el/la vaquero(a)	*cowboy, cowgirl*

Las características físicas   *Physical characteristics*
(Lección 2)

fuerte	*strong*	rubio(a)	*blond*
débil	*weak*	moreno(a)	*dark-haired, brunette*
grande	*large, big*	canoso(a)	*gray-haired*
pequeño(a)	*small, little*	pelirrojo(a)	*redhead*
alto(a)	*tall*	guapo(a)	*handsome, good-looking*
bajo(a)	*short*	bonito(a)	*pretty*
gordo(a)	*fat*	feo(a)	*ugly*
mediano(a)	*medium*	viejo(a)	*old*
delgado(a)	*thin*	joven	*young*
calvo(a)	*bald*		

Las características de la personalidad   *Personality characteristics*
(Lección 2)

interesante	*interesting*	ambicioso(a)	*ambitious*
aburrido(a)	*boring*	perezoso(a)	*lazy*
feliz	*happy*	trabajador(a)	*hardworking*
alegre	*cheerful*	hablador(a)	*talkative*
triste	*sad*	callado(a)	*quiet*
egoísta	*selfish*	• chistoso(a)	*funny*
generoso(a)	*generous*	• cortés	*courteous*
sincero(a)	*sincere*	• curioso(a)	*curious*
fantástico(a)	*fantastic, great*	• descortés	*rude*
inteligente	*intelligent*	• divertido(a)	*fun-loving*
listo(a)	*clever*	• estúpido(a)	*stupid*
tonto(a)	*foolish*	• famoso(a)	*famous*
tímido(a)	*shy, timid*	• hipócrita	*hypocrite*
amistoso(a)	*friendly*	• intelectual	*intellectual*
popular	*popular*	• loco(a)	*crazy*
simpático(a)	*nice*	• paciente	*patient*
antipático(a)	*not nice*	• serio(a)	*serious*
atlético(a)	*athletic*	• sociable	*social*
amable	*kind*	• tacaño(a)	*stingy*

Otras palabras   *Other words*
(Lección 2)

muy	*very*
bastante	*quite, enough*
un poco	*a little*

Las palabras interrogativas   *Question words*
(Lección 2)

¿Cómo?	*How?*
¿Dónde?	*Where?*
¿Adónde?	*Where (to)?*
¿Quién(es)?	*Who?*
¿Qué?	*What?, Which?*
¿Cuándo?	*When?*
¿Por qué?	*Why?*
¿Cuánto(a)?	*How much?*
¿Cuántos(as)?	*How many?*
¿Cuál(es) + *verb*?	*Which?, What?*

El cuerpo   *The body*
(Lección 3)

el cuerpo	*body*	la pierna	*leg*
la cabeza	*head*	la rodilla	*knee*
la frente	*forehead*	el tobillo	*ankle*
el cerebro	*brain*	el talón	*heel*
el cuello	*neck*	el pie	*foot*
la garganta	*throat*	el dedo del pie	*toe*
el hombro	*shoulder*	la cara	*face*
el pecho	*chest*	el pelo	*hair*
los pulmones	*lungs*	el ojo	*eye*
el estómago	*stomach*	la nariz	*nose*
el hígado	*liver*	la oreja	*ear*
el corazón	*heart*	la mejilla	*cheek*
la espalda	*back*	el bigote	*mustache*
el brazo	*arm*	la boca	*mouth*
el codo	*elbow*	el diente	*tooth*
las nalgas	*buttocks*	el mentón	*chin*
la mano	*hand*	la barba	*beard*
el pulgar	*thumb*	• la ceja	*eyebrow*
el dedo	*finger*	• el oído	*inner ear*
la uña	*nail*	• el labio	*lip*
la muñeca	*wrist*		

Estados físicos y emocionales con «estar»   *Physical and emotional states with* estar
(Lección 3)

estar aburrido(a)	*to be bored*	estar tranquilo(a)	*to be calm*
estar agitado(a)	*to be upset*	estar triste	*to be sad*
estar cansado(a)	*to be tired*	estar bien	*to be well, fine*
estar celoso(a)	*to be jealous*	estar mejor	*to be better*
estar contento(a)	*to be happy, content*	estar así, así	*to be so-so*
estar enamorado(a)	*to be in love*	• estar mal	*to not be well*
estar enfermo(a)	*to be ill, sick*	• estar peor	*to be worse*
estar enojado(a)	*to be angry*	• estar asustado(a)	*to be frightened*
estar loco(a)	*to be crazy*	• estar casado(a)	*to be married*
estar nervioso(a)	*to be nervous*	• estar entusiasmado(a)	*to be excited*
estar ocupado(a)	*to be busy*	• estar orgulloso(a)	*to be proud*
estar preocupado(a)	*to be worried*	• estar cómodo(a)	*to be comfortable*

Estados físicos y emocionales con «tener»   *Physical and emotional states with tener*

(Lección 3)

¿Qué tienes?	*What's the matter?*
tener catarro	*to have a cold*
tener tos	*to have a cough*
tener fiebre	*to have a fever*
tener la gripe	*to have the flu*
tener dolor de…	*to have an ache/pain in . . . , . . . hurt(s)*
tener infección de…	*to have an infection of . . .*
tener (mucha/poca) hambre	*to be (very/not very) hungry*
tener (mucha) sed	*to be (very) thirsty*
tener (mucho) calor	*to be (very) warm/hot*
tener (mucho) frío	*to be (very) cold*
tener (mucha) prisa	*to be in a (big) hurry*
tener (mucho) sueño	*to be (very) sleepy*
tener (mucha) suerte	*to be (very) lucky*
tener (mucho) miedo	*to be (very) afraid*
tener razón	*to be right*
no tener razón	*to be wrong*
• tener (mucho) cuidado	*to be (very) careful*
• tener celos	*to be jealous*

Los adjetivos que cambian significado con «ser» y «estar»   *Adjectives that change meaning with ser and estar*

(Lección 3)

ser aburrido(a)	*to be boring*	estar aburrido(a)	*to be bored*
ser listo(a)	*to be clever*	estar listo(a)	*to be ready*
ser seguro(a)	*to be safe*	estar seguro(a)	*to be certain*
ser rico(a)	*to be rich*	estar rico(a)	*to be delicious*
ser malo(a)	*to be bad*	estar malo(a)	*to be ill*
ser nuevo(a)	*to be brand new*	estar nuevo(a)	*to be like new*
ser vivo(a)	*to be lively*	estar vivo(a)	*to be alive*
ser verde	*to be green*	estar verde	*to be unripe*

El cuarto   *The room*

(Lección 4)

el frente	*front*		la luz	*light*
el techo	*ceiling*		la parte de atrás	*back*
el lado	*side*		la fila	*row*
la puerta	*door*		el suelo	*floor*
la pared	*wall*		• el rincón	*corner*
la ventana	*window*			

Las cosas en el aula   *Things in the classroom*
(Lección 4)

la pizarra	*chalkboard*	el pupitre	*student's desk*
la tiza	*chalk*	el diccionario	*dictionary*
el borrador	*eraser*	la cartera	*briefcase*
el estante	*bookshelf*	la mochila	*backpack, knapsack*
el reloj	*clock*	la papelera	*wastepaper basket*
el armario	*cabinet, closet, locker*	el sacapuntas	*pencil sharpener*
la bandera	*flag*	las tijeras	*scissors*
el calendario	*calendar*	la regla	*ruler*
el cuadro	*picture, painting*	la computadora	*computer*
el tablero de anuncios	*bulletin board*	la calculadora	*calculator*
el mapa	*map*	la grabadora	*tape recorder*
el globo	*globe*	la cinta	*tape*
el libro	*book*	el cuaderno	*notebook*
el retroproyector	*overhead projector*	el papel	*paper*
la videocasetera	*VCR, videocassette recorder*	el lápiz	*pencil*
		el bolígrafo	*ballpoint pen*
el casete	*cassette*	la goma de borrar	*pencil eraser*
el archivador	*file cabinet*	la silla	*chair*
el escritorio	*teacher's desk*	la mesa	*table*

La existencia   *Existence*
(Lección 4)

había	*there was, there were*
hubo	*there was, there were*
hay	*there is, there are*
habrá	*there will be*

Las formas y los tamaños   *Shapes and sizes*
(Lección 4)

grande	*big*	bajo(a)	*low, short (in height)*
pequeño(a)	*small*	largo(a)	*long*
mediano(a)	*medium*	corto(a)	*short (in length)*
ancho(a)	*wide*	plano(a)	*flat*
estrecho(a)	*narrow*	redondo(a)	*round*
cuadrado(a)	*square*	triangular	*triangular*
circular	*circular*	rectangular	*rectangular*
alto(a)	*high, tall*		

Otras características   *Other characteristics*
(Lección 4)

duro(a)	*hard*	barato(a)	*inexpensive, cheap*
blando(a)	*soft*	• limpio(a)	*clean*
pesado(a)	*heavy*	• sucio(a)	*dirty*
ligero(a)	*light*	• moderno(a)	*modern*
nuevo(a)	*new*	• antiguo(a)	*ancient, old*
viejo(a)	*old*	• fácil	*easy*
caro(a)	*expensive*	• difícil	*difficult*

Los colores   *Colors*
(Lección 4)

rojo(a)	*red*	negro(a)	*black*
amarillo(a)	*yellow*	blanco(a)	*white*
azul	*blue*	gris	*gray*
anaranjado(a)	*orange*	pardo(a)	*brown*
verde	*green*	marrón	*brown*
morado(a)	*purple*	rosado(a)	*pink*
violeta	*violet*	plateado(a)	*silver*
color crema	*tan*	dorado(a)	*gold*
turquesa	*turquoise*		

(color) claro	*light (color)*
(color) oscuro	*dark (color)*

Las conjunciones   *Conjunctions [joining words]*
(Lección 4)

y [**e** before **i**, **hi**]	*and*
o [**u** before **o**, **ho**]	*or*
pero	*but*
porque	*because*
que	*that*
si	*if*
• sin embargo	*however, nevertheless*
• sino	*but rather [after a negative]*

Los animales   *Animals*
(Lección 5)

Los animales domésticos   *Domestic animals*

el burro	*donkey*	la oveja	*sheep*
el caballo	*horse*	el pato	*duck*
la cabra	*goat*	el pavo	*turkey*
el cerdo/el puerco	*pig*	el perro	*dog*
la gallina	*hen*	el toro	*bull*
el gallo	*rooster*	la vaca	*cow*
el gato	*cat*		

Los animales salvajes   *Wild animals*

la ardilla	*squirrel*	el mono	*monkey*
el búfalo	*buffalo*	el murciélago	*bat*
el camello	*camel*	el oso	*bear*
el canguro	*kangaroo*	el pájaro	*bird*
la cebra	*zebra*	el pez	*fish*
el ciervo	*deer*	el perico	*parrot*
el conejo	*rabbit*	el periquito	*parakeet*
el elefante	*elephant*	la rata	*rat*
el gorila	*gorilla*	el ratón	*mouse*
el hipopótamo	*hippopotamus*	el rinoceronte	*rhinoceros*
la jirafa	*giraffe*	la serpiente	*snake*
el león	*lion*	el tigre	*tiger*
el leopardo	*leopard*	el zorro	*fox*

Los animales acuáticos   *Aquatic animals*

la almeja	*clam*	la rana	*frog*
la ballena	*whale*	el sapo	*toad*
el cangrejo	*crab*	el tiburón	*shark*
el pulpo	*octopus*	la tortuga	*turtle*

Los insectos   *Insects*

la abeja	*bee*	la mariposa	*butterfly*
la araña	*spider*	la mosca	*fly*
la cucaracha	*cockroach*	el mosquito	*mosquito*
la hormiga	*ant*		

Los juguetes   *Toys*
(Lección 5)

el bate	*baseball bat*	el osito de peluche	*teddy bear*
la bicicleta	*bicycle*	los patines de rueda	*roller skates*
los bloques	*blocks*	los patines de hielo	*ice skates*
el caballo balancín	*rocking horse*	la pelota	*ball*
el cajón de arena	*sandbox*	el rompecabezas	*puzzle*
las canicas	*marbles*	el silbato	*whistle*
la carreta	*wagon*	el soldado de juguete	*toy soldier*
la casa de muñecas	*dollhouse*	el tambor	*drum*
el columpio	*swing*	el títere	*puppet*
la cometa	*kite*	el tren eléctrico	*electric train*
el globo	*balloon*	el triciclo	*tricycle*
el juego de damas	*checkers*	el yoyo	*yo-yo*
el monopatín	*skateboard*	• la pistola de agua	*water gun*
la muñeca	*doll*	• la cuerda	*jump rope*

Otras cosas   *Other things*
(Lección 5)

el coche	*car*	• el anillo	*ring*
el disco compacto	*CD, compact disc*	• el despertador	*alarm clock*
el estéreo	*stereo*	• la guitarra	*guitar*
el radio	*radio*	• la llave	*key*
el teléfono	*telephone*	• el llavero	*keyring*
el televisor	*television set*	• la maleta	*suitcase*
la carta	*letter*	• el periódico	*newspaper*
el juego	*game*	• el reloj pulsera	*wristwatch*

Expresiones de cantidad   *Quantity expressions*
(Lección 5)

nada	*not at all, nothing*
un poco	*a little bit, a few*
bastante	*enough*
• suficiente	*sufficient*
mucho(a)	*a lot, much, many*
muchísimo	*very much*
• tanto(a)	*so much*
• tantos(as)	*so many*
• demasiado	*too much*

Las clases   *Classes*
(Lección 5)

Las artes	***Arts***
el arte	*art*
el drama	*drama, acting*
la música	*music*
la orquesta	*orchestra, band*
Las ciencias	***Sciences***
la biología	*biology*
la física	*physics*
la química	*chemistry*
Las ciencias sociales	***Social Sciences***
la geografía	*geography*
la historia	*history*
la sicología	*psychology*
El comercio	***Business***
la informática/computación	*computer science*
la clase de tecleo	*keyboarding*
la taquigrafía	*shorthand*
• la economía	*economics*
Las lenguas extranjeras	***Foreign Languages***
el alemán	*German*
el chino	*Chinese*
el español	*Spanish*
el francés	*French*
el italiano	*Italian*
el japonés	*Japanese*
el latín	*Latin*
el ruso	*Russian*
Las matemáticas	***Math***
el álgebra	*algebra*
• la aritmética	*arithmetic*
el cálculo	*calculus*
la geometría	*geometry*
la trigonometría	*trigonometry*
Otras materias	***Other subjects***
la educación física	*physical education*
• la mecánica	*mechanics*

Las escuelas y los niveles   *Schools and levels*
(Lección 5)

la escuela primaria	*elementary school, grade school*
la escuela secundaria	*secondary school, high school*
el colegio	*private high school*
la universidad	*college, university*
el primer año de secundaria	*freshman*
segundo año	*sophomore*
tercer año	*junior*
cuarto año	*senior*
el primer año de primaria	*first grade*

Estructura

VERBS

Ser   *to be*
(Lección 2)

	IMPERFECT *was/were* *used to be*	PRETERITE *was/were*	PRESENT *am/is/are*	FUTURE *will be*
yo	**era**	**fui**	**soy**	seré
tú	**eras**	**fuiste**	**eres**	serás
Ud./él/ella	**era**	**fue**	**es**	será
nosotros(as)	**éramos**	**fuimos**	**somos**	seremos
vosotros(as)	**erais**	**fuisteis**	**sois**	seréis
Uds./ellos/ellas	**eran**	**fueron**	**son**	serán

Estar   *to be*
(Lección 3)

	IMPERFECT *was/were* *used to be*	PRETERITE *was/were*	PRESENT *am/is/are*	FUTURE *will be*
yo	estaba	**estuve**	**estoy**	estaré
tú	estabas	**estuviste**	estás	estarás
Ud./él/ella	estaba	**estuvo**	está	estará
nosotros(as)	estábamos	**estuvimos**	estamos	estaremos
vosotros(as)	estabais	**estuvisteis**	estáis	estaréis
Uds./ellos/ellas	estaban	**estuvieron**	están	estarán

Tener *to have*
(Lección 3)

	IMPERFECT	PRETERITE	PRESENT	FUTURE
	had	*had*	*have/has*	*will have*
	was/were having		*am/is/are having*	
	used to have	*did have*	*do/does have*	
yo	tenía	**tuve**	**tengo**	**tendré**
tú	tenías	**tuviste**	tienes	**tendrás**
Ud./él/ella	tenía	**tuvo**	tiene	**tendrá**
nosotros(as)	teníamos	**tuvimos**	tenemos	**tendremos**
vosotros(as)	teníais	**tuvisteis**	tenéis	**tendréis**
Uds./ellos/ellas	tenían	**tuvieron**	tienen	**tendrán**

Doler (ue) *to hurt*
(Lección 3)

IMPERFECT	PRETERITE	PRESENT	FUTURE
hurt	*hurt*	*hurt(s)*	*will hurt*
was/were hurting		*is/are hurting*	
used to hurt	*did hurt*	*do/does hurt*	
(me) dolía	dolió	duele	dolerá
(me) dolían	dolieron	duelen	dolerán

Gustar *to be pleasing, to like*
(Lección 5)

IMPERFECT	PRETERITE	PRESENT	FUTURE	CONDITIONAL
used to please	*pleased*	*please(s)*	*will please*	*would please*
used to like	*liked*	*like(s)*	*will like*	*would like*
(me) gustaba	gustó	gusta	gustará	gustaría
(me) gustaban	gustaron	gustan	gustarán	gustarían

The differences between ser *and* estar
(Lección 3)

SER	ESTAR
1. to identify a person or thing (noun or pronoun)	1. to tell location (adverb or preposition of place)
2. to tell basic characteristics/normal state (adjective)	2. to tell condition/not normal state (adjective)
3. to tell when (time, date, etc.)	
4. to tell origin, owner, or material (**de** + noun)	
5. to tell where an <u>event</u> takes place	

NOUNS

Gender of nouns
(Lección 2)

...o
...l } = masculine   ...a
...r   ...d } = feminine
                       ...ión

Plural of nouns
(Lección 2)

VOWEL + S
CONSONANT + ES
Z = C + ES

Two nouns together
(Lección 4)

noun + **de** + *noun*

ADJECTIVES

Articles
(Lección 2)

	INDEFINITE *a, an, some*		**DEFINITE** *the*	
	SINGULAR	PLURAL	SINGULAR	PLURAL
MASCULINE	un	unos	el	los
FEMININE	una	unas	la	las

Position of adjectives
(Lección 2)

NUMBER	noun	
QUANTITY	noun	
POSSESSION	noun	
ARTICLE	noun	
DEMONSTRATIVE	noun	
	noun	DESCRIPTION

Possessive adjectives
(Lección 2)

mi(s)	*my*	nuestro(a)(os)(as)	*our*
tu(s)	*your*	vuestro(a)(os)(as)	*your*
su(s)	*your, his, her, its*	su(s)	*your, their*

Clarification of su/sus
(Lección 4)

el/la/los/las + *noun* +
de Ud./de Uds.
de él/de ellos
de ella/de ellas

Comparisons
(Lección 2)

más… que	*more . . . than*
menos… que	*less . . . than*
tan… como	*as . . . as*

Superlatives
(Lección 2)

el/la/los/las + más *(most)* / menos *(least)* + *(adjective)* + de *(of/in)* + *noun*

Demonstrative adjectives and pronouns
(Lección 4)

THIS	THESE	THAT	THOSE	THAT . . .	THOSE . . . OVER THERE
este	estos	ese	esos	aquel	aquellos
esta	estas	esa	esas	aquella	aquellas

If no noun follows, put an accent mark on the first **e**.

Using adjectives without the noun
(Lección 5)

When a noun has not been used:

LO + *adjective [masculine form]* = *the + adjective + part/thing*

When the noun has already been used:

EL/LA/LOS/LAS
UN/UNA/UNOS/UNAS + *adjective = the, a/an, some + adjective + one(s)*

PRONOUNS

Subject pronouns
(Lección 2)

yo	*I*		nosotros(as)	*we*
tú	*you [informal]*		vosotros(as)	*you [informal—Spain]*
usted (Ud.)	*you [formal]*		ustedes (Uds.)	*you [plural]*
él	*he*		ellos	*they [masculine or mixed]*
ella	*she*		ellas	*they [feminine]*

Direct object pronouns (it, them)
(Lección 5)

	IT	THEM
MASCULINE	lo	los
FEMININE	la	las

Indirect object pronouns (to/for someone)
(Lección 5)

me	=	*to/for me*
te	=	*to/for you*
le	=	*to/for you [formal]/him/her/it*
nos	=	*to/for us*
os	=	*to/for all of you [for that group of friends in Spain]*
les	=	*to/for all of you/them*

Position of object pronouns
(Lección 5)

Before the verb with the person–time ending
Attached to the end of the **-ar/-er/-ir** form of the verb

Clarifying or emphasizing indirect object pronouns
(Lección 5)

a mí	+	me	a nosotros(as)	+	nos
a ti	+	te	a vosotros(as)	+	os
a Ud.			a Uds.		
a él	} +	le	a ellos	} +	les
a ella			a ellas		

Esqueletos

Affirmative sentences
(Lección 2)

> **(pro)noun + verb + (rest of sentence)**

Yo era pequeño.   *I was small.*
El hombre es alto.   *The man is tall.*

Negative sentences
(Lección 2)

> **(pro)noun + NO + verb + (rest of sentence)**

Yo no soy alta.   *I am not tall.*
Yo no era fuerte.   *I was not strong.*

"Yes/no" questions
(Lección 2)

> **¿(pro)noun + verb + (rest of sentence)?**

¿Uds. son norteamericanos?   *You are North Americans?*
¿El hombre es fuerte?   *The man is strong?*

> **(pro)noun + verb + (rest of sentence), + ¿NO?**
> **¿VERDAD?**

Uds. son norteamericanos, ¿no?   *You are North Americans, aren't you?*
El hombre es fuerte, ¿verdad?   *The man is strong, right?*

"Yes/no" questions *(continued)*
(Lección 2)

> *¿verb + (pro)noun + (rest of sentence)?*

OR

> *¿verb + (rest of sentence) + (pro)noun?*

¿Son Uds. norteamericanos?   *Are you North Americans?*
¿Es fuerte el hombre?   *Is the man strong?*

Questions using question words
(Lección 2)

> *¿(preposition) + question word + verb + (pro)noun + (rest of sentence)?*

¿Cómo es Ud.?   *What are you like?*
¿De dónde es Ud.?   *Where are you from?*
¿A quién le escribe tu hermano?   *Who is your brother writing to?*

Comparisons
(Lección 2)

> (pro)noun + verb + **MÁS / MENOS / TAN** + *adjective* + **QUE / QUE / COMO** + (pro)noun

Mi padre es más alto que mi madre.   *My father is taller than my mother.*
Luis es menos hablador que Beto.   *Luis is less talkative than Beto.*
Juanita es tan simpática como Alicia.   *Juanita is as nice as Alicia.*

Superlatives
(Lección 2)

$$(pro)noun + verb + \frac{\text{EL/LOS}}{\text{LA/LAS}} + \frac{\text{MÁS}}{\text{MENOS}} + adjective + \text{DE} + noun$$

La mochila de Miguel es la más cara de toda la clase.
Miguel's backpack is the most expensive in the whole class.

El libro de español es el menos aburrido de todos mis libros.
The Spanish book is the least boring of all my books.

Doler (ue) *to hurt*
(Lección 3)

$$(\text{A} + person) + \frac{\text{ME/TE/LE}}{\text{NOS/OS/LES}} + \text{DOLER} + body\ part$$

Me duele el diente.   *My tooth hurts.*
A Juan le duelen los pies.   *Juan's feet hurt.*

Había / Hubo / Hay / Habrá
(Lección 4)

$$¿\text{QUÉ} + \frac{\text{HABÍA/HUBO}}{\text{HAY/HABRÁ}} + (rest\ of\ sentence)?$$

¿Qué habrá en el aula?   *What will there be in the classroom?*

$$\frac{¿\text{CUÁNTO(A)}}{¿\text{CUÁNTOS(AS)}} + noun + \frac{\text{HABÍA/HUBO}}{\text{HAY/HABRÁ}} + (rest\ of\ sentence)?$$

¿Cuánto dinero hay en tu bolso?   *How much money is there in your purse?*
¿Cuántas sillas hay en una fila?   *How many chairs are there in a row?*

$$\frac{\text{HABÍA/HUBO}}{\text{HAY/HABRÁ}} + (number) + noun(s) + (rest\ of\ sentence)$$

Había dos libros en la mesa.   *There were two books on the table.*
Había libros en el estante.   *There were books on the bookshelf.*

Position of direct object pronouns
(Lección 5)

> ### (pro)noun + object pronoun + verb

Yo lo tengo.   *I have it.*
Juan los tiene.   *Juan has them.*

> ### (pro)noun + verb + infinitive + object pronoun

Ellos van a escribirla.   *They are going to write it.*
María puede hacerlo.   *María can do it.*

OR

> ### (pro)noun + object pronoun + verb + infinitive

Ellos la van a escribir.   *They are going to write it.*
María lo puede hacer.   *María can do it.*

Position of indirect object pronouns
(Lección 5)

> ### (A + person) + ME/TE/LE NOS/OS/LES + verb + (infinitive) + noun(s)

Le van a dar un regalo.   *They are going to give him a gift.*

> ### (A + person) + verb + infinitive + ME/TE/LE NOS/OS/LES + noun(s)

Van a darle un regalo.   *They are going to give him a gift.*

Gustar   *to be pleasing, to like*
(Lección 5)

> ### (A + person) + ME/TE/LE NOS/OS/LES + GUSTAR + (noun/infinitive)

Me gusta la escuela.   *I like school.*
A Juan le gustan los perros.   *Juan likes dogs.*
Nos gusta visitar a los amigos.   *We like to visit friends.*

Comencemos de nuevo

Welcome back! Did you have an enjoyable vacation? We hope so. Did you have an opportunity to speak Spanish? Since you probably forgot some of what you learned last year, let's begin again by reviewing. For those of you who did not use **Compañeros: Spanish for Communication** last year, this will be an opportunity to "fill in the missing pieces." We hope you enjoy communicating in Spanish. And now, **¡Manos a la obra!** *(Let's get busy!)*.

Vocabulario

Note: The vocabulary in this section of each lesson is for reference purposes. You are not expected to memorize every word. You may use these words and other words you know to do the activities in this lesson. Words preceded by a dot (•) indicate that they are new to **Compañeros, Book 2**.

Los saludos   *Greetings*

Buenos días.	*Good morning.*
Buenas tardes.	*Good afternoon.*
Buenas noches.	*Good evening, Good night. [after sundown]*
Hola.	*Hello, Hi.*

Las despedidas   *Farewells*

Adiós.	*Good-bye.*
Hasta la vista.	*See you later.*
Hasta mañana.	*See you tomorrow.*
¡Chau!	*Bye!*

Expresiones de cortesía   *Courtesy expressions*

¿Cómo estás?	*How are you? [informal]*
¿Cómo está usted (Ud.)?	*How are you? [formal]*
¿Y usted (Ud.)?	*And you? [formal]*
¿Qué tal?	*How's everything? [informal]*
¿Y tú?	*And you? [informal]*
Muy bien.	*Fine.*
Mal.	*Bad.*
Así, así.	*So-so, OK.*
Regular.	*Fair, OK.*
No muy bien.	*Not very well.*
Lo siento.	*I'm sorry.*
¡Qué lástima!	*That's too bad!*
Por favor.	*Please.*
• Favor de + *infinitive*.	*Please + verb.*
Gracias.	*Thank you.*
De nada.	*You're welcome.*
Con permiso.	*Excuse me. [before doing something]*
Perdón.	*Pardon me. [after doing something]*

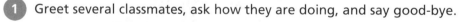

1 Greet several classmates, ask how they are doing, and say good-bye.

EJEMPLO: Hola, Miguel.

¿Qué tal, Anita?

¡Muy bien!

Adiós, hasta la vista.

2 Pretend to be twenty years older and greet each other as business acquaintances, using the **Ud.** forms and formal instead of informal expressions.

EJEMPLO: Buenos días, señor Jones. ¿Cómo está Ud.?

Muy bien, gracias. ¿Y Ud.?

Bien. Adiós, hasta mañana.

Vocabulario

Instrucciones del profesor   *Instructions from the teacher*

Note: Add **n** when commanding more than one person (**Uds**. command).

• Abra(n) el libro.	*Open the book.*
la puerta.	*the door.*
la ventana.	*the window.*
• Cierre(n)…	*Close . . .*
• Ponga(n) los libros aquí.	*Put the books here.*
allí.	*there.*
en el pupitre.	*on the desk.*
en el suelo.	*on the floor.*
• Saque(n) la tarea.	*Take out the homework.*
• Vaya(n) a la pizarra.	*Go to the chalkboard.*
• Escriba(n).	*Write.*
• Repita(n).	*Repeat.*
• Conteste(n).	*Answer.*
• Silencio, por favor.	*Quiet, please.*
• Siénte(n)se.	*Be seated.*

Los pedidos del estudiante   *Student requests*

Repita, por favor.	*Repeat, please.*
Más alto.	*Louder.*
Más despacio.	*Slower.*
• ¿Puedo ir al baño?	*May I go to the bathroom?*
usar un lápiz?	*use a pencil?*

Preguntando cómo se dice   *Asking how to say*

¿Cómo se dice… en español/en inglés?   *How do you say . . . in Spanish/in English?*

Otras expresiones   *Other expressions*

Yo (no) sé.   *I (don't) know.*
Yo (no) comprendo.   *I (don't) understand.*

3 ***Sit-Con (Situation-Conversation)***   Take turns pretending to be the teacher. The teacher will make requests and the student will respond or act them out.

EJEMPLO: Teacher: Miguel, ¡escriba su nombre!
               Teacher: Carlos, ¿Cómo se dice «house» en español?
               Carlos: Se dice «casa». / No sé.

4 ***Sit-Con***   Now take turns being the student and make requests of the teacher. The teacher will respond to the request.

EJEMPLO: Señora Chávez, ¿puedo ir al baño?

              Claro *(Of course)*, Juan.

Remember: Use these expressions whenever you can in the classroom.

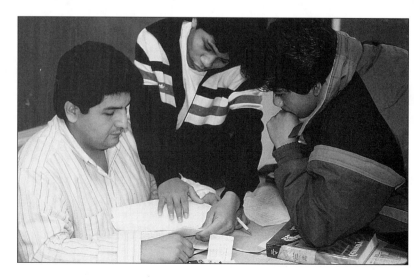

Vocabulario

Conociendo a alguien   *Meeting someone*

¿Cómo te llamas?   *What's your name? [informal]*
¿Cómo se llama Ud.?   *What's your name? [formal]*
Me llamo… *[first and last name]*   *My name is . . . , I'm called . . .*
¿Cuál es tu/su nombre/apellido?   *What's your first name/last name?*
Mi nombre/apellido es…   *My first name/last name is . . .*
¿Cómo se llama el muchacho/la muchacha?   *What's the boy's/the girl's name?*
Se llama…   *His/Her name is . . .*

Los títulos   *Titles*

señor/Sr.   *Mr.*
señora/Sra.   *Mrs., Ms.*
señorita/Srta.   *Miss, Ms.*
doctor(a)/Dr., Dra.   *Doctor*
don + *first name*   *[title of respect: male]*
doña + *first name*   *[title of respect: female]*

Note: When using a title in talking <u>about</u> a person, add **el** or **la**.

Es el señor Gómez.
Es la señora Gómez.

Titles are not capitalized in the middle of a sentence unless they are abbreviated.

El <u>s</u>eñor Gómez…
El <u>S</u>r. Gómez…

Presentando a alguien *Introducing someone*

Quiero presentarte a…	*I want to introduce you to . . . [informal]*
Quiero presentarle a…	*I want to introduce you to . . . [formal]*
Mucho gusto, señor/señora/señorita.	*I'm pleased to meet you, sir/ma'am/miss.*
El gusto es mío.	*The pleasure is mine.*
Igualmente.	*The same here, Likewise.*

5 Ask several students their names. They will ask yours. Say that you are pleased to meet them. Then introduce them to a friend.

EJEMPLO: ¿Cómo te llamas?

Me llamo Ricardo.

¿Cuál es tu apellido?

Mi apellido es Rivera.

Mucho gusto.

El gusto es mío.

Ricardo, quiero presentarte a mi amigo Miguel.

Mucho gusto, Miguel.

Igualmente, Ricardo.

6 Find out the names of several of your classmates' friends and family members.

EJEMPLO: ¿Cómo se llama tu hermano?

Se llama Julio.

Vocabulario

Las letras del alfabeto español *Letters of the Spanish alphabet*

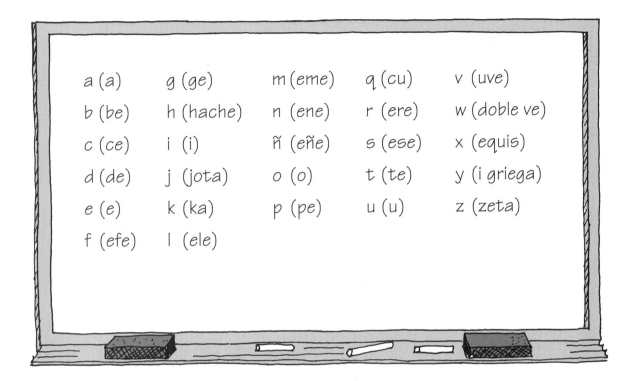

a (a)	g (ge)	m (eme)	q (cu)	v (uve)
b (be)	h (hache)	n (ene)	r (ere)	w (doble ve)
c (ce)	i (i)	ñ (eñe)	s (ese)	x (equis)
d (de)	j (jota)	o (o)	t (te)	y (i griega)
e (e)	k (ka)	p (pe)	u (u)	z (zeta)
f (efe)	l (ele)			

Until 1994 **ch** and **ll** were separate letters of the alphabet. Dictionaries printed before then will have **ch** listed after **cu** and **ll** listed after **lu**.

¿Cómo se escribe... ? *How do you spell . . . ?*

¿Qué letra es?	*What letter is it?*
¿Cómo se escribe… ?	*How do you spell . . . ?*
Se escribe…	*It's spelled . . .*

Pronunciación

El sistema fonológico del español   *The sound system of Spanish*

Vowels

Remember that the sounds of the Spanish letters are sometimes different from English. Here are the vowel sounds.

A has the sound of *ah* as in *father*.
E has the sound of *a* as in *late*.
I has the sound of *e* as in *beet*.
O has the sound of *o* as in *wrote*.
U has the sound of *oo* as in *boot*.

Consonants with sounds very different from English

GE, GI, and **J** are pronounced like the *h* in *house* but a little hoarser.
H has no sound. It is always silent.
Ñ is pronounced like the *ny* in *canyon* or *onion*.
QU has the sound of *k* as in *kite* (no *w* sound as in *quick*).
V is the same as **b**.
Z has the sound of *s*.
R has no equivalent in English. It sounds a little like the *tt* in *kitty*. (Your teacher will model it for you.)

In Spanish, each of these double consonants represents one sound.

CH has the sound of *ch* as in *chair*.
LL has the sound of *y* as in *yes*.
RR has no equivalent in English. It is like the single **r** in Spanish, but a long trilled sound.
(Your teacher will model it for you.)

7 Practice saying the following rhymes.

A E I O U
El burro sabe más que tú.

A E I O U
Manzanillo del Perú.
¿Cuántos años tienes tú?

Before doing the following activities, review the alphabet on page 33.

8 Practice saying the alphabet in Spanish.

9 Take turns pointing to different letters of the alphabet for your partner to identify.

10 Ask another student how to spell some words. Take turns.

11 Ask several classmates how to spell their first and last names.

EJEMPLO: ¿Cómo se escribe tu nombre y apellido?

   Se escribe R-O-B-E-R-T-O S-M-Y-T-H-E.

Vocabulario

Los números hasta cien *Numbers to a hundred*

0 cero		
1 uno	11 once	10 diez
2 dos	12 doce	20 veinte
3 tres	13 trece	30 treinta
4 cuatro	14 catorce	40 cuarenta
5 cinco	15 quince	50 cincuenta
6 seis	16 diez y seis	60 sesenta
7 siete	17 diez y siete	70 setenta
8 ocho	18 diez y ocho	80 ochenta
9 nueve	19 diez y nueve	90 noventa
10 diez	20 veinte	100 cien(to)
	21 veinte y uno	
	22 veinte y dos	
	etc.	

- los números pares   even numbers
- los números impares   odd numbers

Note: The numbers 16 through 19 and 21 through 29 may be written as one word:
dieciséis, diecisiete, *etc.*
veintiuno, veintidós, *etc.*

12 Practice counting forward and backward, by twos, by fives, and by tens.

13 Write a number between 0 and 100 for your partner to say in Spanish. Take turns until you have each done ten numbers.

14 Count various objects in the classroom.

EJEMPLO: ventanas: Hay ocho ventanas.
armarios: Hay cuatro armarios.

15 **Juego** *Take turns.*   Write a number but don't let your partner see it. Your partner will try to guess the number in fewer than ten tries. If the number guessed is too high, say **Menos**. If the number guessed is too low, say **Más**. Take turns and keep score.

Preguntando la edad   *Asking the age*

¿Cuántos años tienes?	*How old are you? [informal]*
¿Cuántos años tiene Ud.?	*How old are you? [formal]*
Tengo… años.	*I'm . . . years old.*
¿Cuántos años tiene tu padre?	*How old is your father?*
Tiene… años.	*He is . . . years old.*
¿Cuántos años tienen tus hermanos?	*How old are your brothers?*
Tienen… años.	*They are . . . years old.*

16 Find out the ages of several of your classmates.

EJEMPLO: ¿Cuántos años tienes?

 Tengo quince años.

17 Ask your partner to guess the ages of several people you know, for example, your teacher, the principal, a classmate, etc.

EJEMPLO: ¿Cuántos años tiene el profesor?

 Tiene cincuenta y cinco años.

Vocabulario

El calendario   *The calendar*

LOS DÍAS DE LA SEMANA	*THE DAYS OF THE WEEK*		LOS MESES DEL AÑO	*THE MONTHS OF THE YEAR*
lunes	*Monday*		enero	*January*
martes	*Tuesday*		febrero	*February*
miércoles	*Wednesday*		marzo	*March*
jueves	*Thursday*		abril	*April*
viernes	*Friday*		mayo	*May*
sábado	*Saturday*		junio	*June*
domingo	*Sunday*		julio	*July*
			agosto	*August*
			septiembre	*September*
			octubre	*October*
			noviembre	*November*
			diciembre	*December*

Note: To say *on* with a day, use the article **el** or **los**.
          el lunes   *on Monday*
          los lunes   *on Mondays*

Preguntando el día   *Asking the day*

¿Qué día es hoy?	*What day is today?*
mañana?	*tomorrow?*
pasado mañana?	*the day after tomorrow?*

Preguntando la fecha   *Asking the date*

¿Cuál es la fecha de hoy?	*What is the date today?*
Hoy es el (primero) de enero.	*Today is the (first) of January.*
(dos)	*(second)*
(tres)	*(third)*
¿Cuándo es tu cumpleaños?	*When is your birthday?*
Mi cumpleaños es el *[date]* de *[month]*.	*My birthday is the [date] of [month].*

Su cumpleaños es el primero de mayo. ¿Cuándo es tu cumpleaños?

La hora   *Time*

¿Qué hora es?	*What time is it?*
¿A qué hora es… ?	*At what time is . . . ?*
Es mediodía.	*It's noon.*
Es medianoche.	*It's midnight.*
Es la una.	*It's one o'clock.*
Son las dos.	*It's two o'clock.*
Son las dos y cuarto.	*It's a quarter after two, It's 2:15.*
Son las dos y media.	*It's half past two, It's 2:30.*
Son las dos menos cuarto.	*It's a quarter to two, It's 1:45.*
Son las dos y cinco.	*It's five minutes after two, It's 2:05.*
Son las dos menos cinco.	*It's five minutes to two, it's 1:55.*
Son las seis de la mañana.	*It's six o'clock in the morning, It's 6 A.M.*
Son las tres de la tarde.	*It's three o'clock in the afternoon, It's 3 P.M.*
Son las diez de la noche.	*It's ten o'clock at night, It's 10 P.M.*

18 Ask someone on which day certain events will take place.

EJEMPLO: ¿Cuándo es el partido de fútbol?

El partido de fútbol es el viernes.

19 Ask several classmates when their birthdays are.

EJEMPLO: ¿Cuándo es tu cumpleaños?

Mi cumpleaños es el 3 de febrero.

20 Tell what time it is on the following clocks.

a.   b.   c.

d.   e.   f.

21 Make your own clocks and practice telling time with your partner.

Ven a una fiesta

Voy a celebrar mi cumpleaños
y te invito a mi fiesta

Nombre: José Luis

Fecha: sábado, el
tres de octubre

Hora: 16:00

Dirección: Avenida
Insurgentes 3318

¿Vienes?

ENCUENTRO PERSONAL

It's the first day of school and everyone is getting to know each other. Who is the new person in the class? Why is this a special day?

SRTA. BLANCO:	Buenos días, estudiantes. Silencio, por favor. Siéntense todos. Rosita y Paulina, cállense y vayan a sus pupitres.
TODOS:	Buenos días, profesora. ¿Cómo está Ud.?
SRTA. BLANCO:	Estoy bien, gracias. Bueno, este año hay un estudiante nuevo en la clase. Estudiantes, quiero presentarles a Santiago Bermúdez. Él es de Miami, pero sus padres son de Cuba.
INÉS:	Hola, Santiago. Bienvenido a nuestra clase de español. ¿Cómo te va en tu nueva escuela hoy?
SANTIAGO:	No muy bien, Inés. El problema es que no tengo amigos aquí y no hablo inglés perfectamente bien.
INÉS:	Lo siento, Santiago. Nosotros seremos tus nuevos amigos.
ROSITA:	¿Cómo se llama el nuevo muchacho, Paulina?
PAULINA:	Se llama Santiago y su apellido es Bermúdez. Es un cubano de Miami. Santiago, ésta es Rosita.
ROSITA:	Mucho gusto, Santiago. ¿Cómo se escribe tu apellido?
SANTIAGO:	El gusto es mío, Rosita. Mi apellido se escribe B-e-r-m-u- acento -d-e-z. Es fácil, ¿no?

INÉS:	¿Cuántos años tienes, Santiago?
SANTIAGO:	Tengo diez y seis años. ¿Y tú, Inés?
INÉS:	¡Eso es perfecto! Yo tengo quince años. Mi cumpleaños es el 3 de febrero.
SRTA. BLANCO:	Perdón, estudiantes, pero, manos a la obra. ¿Cuál es la fecha de hoy?
PAULINA:	¡Yo sé! Hoy es jueves, el primero de septiembre.
SRTA. BLANCO:	¡Correcto!, Paulina. Y, ¿por qué es importante esta fecha?
ROSITA:	¿Porque es el cumpleaños de la profesora?
SRTA. BLANCO:	¡Tienes razón, Rosita!
PAULINA:	¿Cuántos años tiene Ud., profesora?
SRTA. BLANCO:	Yo soy muy vieja, Paulina; tengo setenta y nueve años.
PAULINA:	No comprendo. Más despacio, por favor. Y, ¿cómo se dice «*joker*» en español?
ROSITA:	Cállate, Paulina. Mañana es viernes, el dos de septiembre. Nosotros vamos a celebrar el cumpleaños de la «vieja» profesora con una fiesta grande a las tres de la tarde en el aula de español.
SRTA. BLANCO:	Bueno, adiós a todos. Y hasta mañana.

¿Comprendes?

1. ¿Qué les dice la señorita Blanco a los estudiantes al principio de la clase?
2. ¿Quién es el estudiante nuevo? ¿De dónde es?
3. ¿Qué nacionalidad es? ¿Cuántos años tiene?
4. ¿Cual es la fecha del primer día de clase? ¿Por qué es importante?
5. ¿Cuántos años tiene la señorita Blanco? ¿La cree Paulina?
6. ¿Qué van a hacer mañana los estudiantes? ¿A qué hora?

¡Te toca!

Make up a conversation between a teacher and students. Make the teacher seem really bossy. Have her give a lot of commands to the students.

Leemos y contamos

Paulina is writing to her cousin Eduardo, who has returned to Mexico after spending a year with Paulina's family in the United States. Read what she tells him and then answer the questions that follow.

Sábado, el 3 de septiembre

Querido primo Eduardo,

¡Hola! ¿Qué tal? Ya estoy otra vez en la escuela con todos mis amigos. Me gusta estar aquí pero es difícil pensar en la escuela ahora porque el verano fue muy divertido. En junio hubo una reunión del Club Hispano con nuestros amigos por correspondencia en México. En julio todo el mundo fue a la playa y celebramos mi cumpleaños con una fiesta el 12 de agosto. Salvador ya no es mi novio. En agosto fue a Santo Domingo para vivir con su abuela. Ella es muy vieja y necesita mucha ayuda. Hay un estudiante nuevo en mi clase de español. Se llama Santiago. Es de Miami.

¡Tengo quince años ahora! Ya estoy en mi segundo año de la escuela secundaria y después iré a la universidad. Pero ahora tengo unos planes interesantes para este año. Para ganar dinero voy a trabajar en una tienda de ropa de mujeres después de la escuela. También estudiaré mucho para sacar buenas notas porque no quiero vender ropa toda mi vida. Mis padres siempre me dicen que para tener un buen empleo con buen salario, es necesario tener una buena preparación en la escuela.

Quiero saber lo que tú haces en estos días. ¿Pasaste unas buenas vacaciones después de regresar a México? ¿Qué planes tienes para este año escolar? Escríbeme pronto, por favor.

Tu prima que te quiere,
Paulina

1. ¿A Paulina le gusta estar otra vez en la escuela? ¿Por qué?
2. ¿Qué eventos especiales había durante las vacaciones?
3. ¿Cuándo era el cumpleaños de Paulina y cuántos años tiene?
4. ¿Qué planes tiene Paulina para el futuro?
5. ¿Por qué va a estudiar mucho? ¿Estás de acuerdo? *(Do you agree?)*

¡Así es!

Las vacaciones

Como muchos estudiantes en los Estados Unidos, los estudiantes en muchos países de habla española generalmente tienen sus vacaciones en junio, julio y agosto, pero no todos. Los estudiantes que viven en el hemisferio sur, por ejemplo en Chile y Argentina, tienen sus vacaciones en diciembre, enero y febrero. ¿Por qué? Porque en el hemisferio sur las estaciones son al revés. ¡Para ellos el verano es del 21 de diciembre al 21 de marzo! Cuando ellos están en la escuela, nosotros tenemos vacaciones y cuando ellos están de vacaciones, nosotros estamos en la escuela.

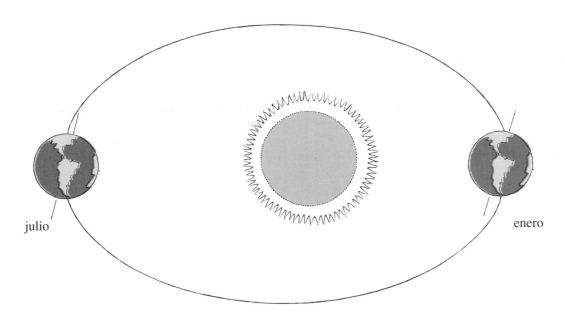

julio

enero

En el mes de enero, es el invierno en el hemisferio norte;
es el verano en el hemisferio sur.

¿Quién es? Las personas

Talking about people can be a lot of fun. Let's review the vocabulary and structures we need to identify, describe, and compare the people we know.

Vocabulario

Las personas   *People*

1. el hombre	*man*		13. el novio	*boyfriend*
2. la mujer	*woman*		14. la novia	*girlfriend*
3. el joven	*young person [m.]*	•	15. todo el mundo	*everyone*
4. la joven	*young person [f.]*	•	16. la gente	*people [in general]*
5. el muchacho	*boy*	•	17. el chico	*boy, teenager*
6. la muchacha	*girl*	•	18. la chica	*girl, teenager*
7. el niño	*small boy*	•	19. el compañero	*friend [m.]*
8. la niña	*small girl*	•	20. la compañera	*friend [f.]*
9. el bebé	*baby boy*	•	21. el vecino	*neighbor [m.]*
10. la bebé	*baby girl*	•	22. la vecina	*neighbor [f.]*
11. el amigo	*friend [m.]*	•	23. los habitantes	*inhabitants*
12. la amiga	*friend [f.]*			

Vocabulario

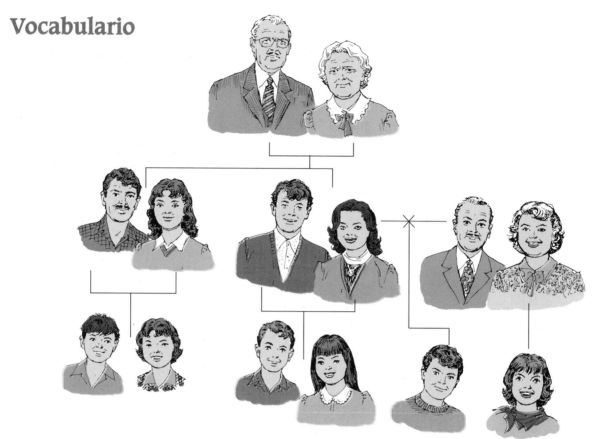

La familia   *The family*

el padre	*father*	el tío	*uncle*
la madre	*mother*	la tía	*aunt*
el padrino	*godfather*	el sobrino	*nephew*
la madrina	*godmother*	la sobrina	*niece*
el hijo	*son*	el primo	*cousin [m.]*
la hija	*daughter*	la prima	*cousin [f.]*
el ahijado	*godson*	el padrastro	*stepfather*
la ahijada	*goddaughter*	la madrastra	*stepmother*
el hermano	*brother*	el hermanastro	*stepbrother*
la hermana	*sister*	la hermanastra	*stepsister*
el hermano menor	*younger brother*	el esposo	*husband*
la hermana menor	*younger sister*	la esposa	*wife*
el hermano mayor	*older brother*	el suegro	*father-in-law*
la hermana mayor	*older sister*	la suegra	*mother-in-law*
el gemelo	*twin brother*	el yerno	*son-in-law*
la gemela	*twin sister*	la nuera	*daughter-in-law*
el abuelo	*grandfather*	el cuñado	*brother-in-law*
la abuela	*grandmother*	la cuñada	*sister-in-law*
el nieto	*grandson*	• el hijastro	*stepson*
la nieta	*granddaughter*	• la hijastra	*stepdaughter*

Vocabulario

Las carreras y los trabajos   *Careers and jobs*

1. el/la abogado(a)	*lawyer*	8. el/la artista	*artist*
2. el actor	*actor*	9. el/la banquero(a)	*banker*
3. la actriz	*actress*	10. el/la bombero(a)	*firefighter*
4. el/la agente	*agent*	11. el/la contador(a)	*accountant*
5. el/la agricultor(a)	*farmer*	12. el/la criado(a)	*servant, housekeeper*
6. el ama de casa	*homemaker*	13. el/la dentista	*dentist*
7. el/la arquitecto(a)	*architect*	14. el/la dependiente	*salesperson*

Las carreras y los trabajos   *Careers and jobs* (continued)

15. el/la enfermero(a)	*nurse*	22. el/la médico(a)	*doctor*
16. el/la estudiante/alumno(a)	*student, pupil*	23. el/la mesero(a)	*waiter, waitress*
17. el/la farmacista	*pharmacist*	24. la mujer de negocios	*businesswoman*
18. el/la gerente	*manager*	25. el/la músico(a)	*musician*
19. el hombre de negocios	*businessman*	26. el/la obrero(a)	*laborer, worker*
20. el/la ingeniero(a)	*engineer*	27. el/la periodista	*journalist*
21. el/la mecánico(a)	*mechanic*	28. el/la policía	*police officer*

29. el/la profesor(a)	teacher	• 36. el/la camarero(a)	waiter, waitress
30. el/la secretario(a)	secretary	• 37. el/la carpintero(a)	carpenter
• 31. el/la albañil	bricklayer, mason	• 38. el/la cartero(a)	mail carrier
• 32. el/la aeromozo(a)	flight attendant	• 39. el/la científico(a)	scientist
• 33. el/la ayudante	assistant, aide	• 40. el/la cocinero(a)	cook, chef
• 34. el/la barbero	barber	• 41. el/la conductor(a) de camión	truck driver
• 35. el/la cajero(a)	cashier	• 42. el/la electricista	electrician

Las carreras y los trabajos   *Careers and jobs* (continued)

- 43. el/la embajador(a)   *ambassador*
- 44. el/la jardinero(a)   *gardener*
- 45. el/la jugador(a)   *player*
- 46. el/la obrero(a)   *construction*
     de construcción   *worker*
- 47. el/la payaso(a)   *clown*

- 48. el/la peluquero(a)   *hairdresser*
- 49. el/la pescador(a)   *fisherperson*
- 50. el/la plomero(a)   *plumber*
- 51. el/la soldado(a)   *soldier*
- 52. el/la vaquero(a)   *cowboy, cowgirl*

Note: **El policía** can also mean *the police*.

   Un/una are not used with professions unless an adjective follows.

   El señor García es abogado. Es un abogado bueno.

Vocabulario

Las características físicas *Physical characteristics*

1. fuerte	*strong*		11. rubio(a)	*blond*
2. débil	*weak*		12. moreno(a)	*dark-haired, brunette*
3. grande	*large, big*		13. canoso(a)	*gray-haired*
4. pequeño(a)	*small, little*		14. pelirrojo(a)	*redhead*
5. alto(a)	*tall*		15. guapo(a)	*handsome, good-looking*
6. bajo(a)	*short*		16. bonito(a)	*pretty*
7. gordo(a)	*fat*		17. feo(a)	*ugly*
8. mediano(a)	*medium*		18. viejo(a)	*old*
9. delgado(a)	*thin*		19. joven	*young*
10. calvo(a)	*bald*			

Vocabulario

Las características de la personalidad *Personality characteristics*

1. interesante	*interesting*		8. sincero(a)	*sincere*
2. aburrido(a)	*boring*		9. fantástico(a)	*fantastic, great*
3. feliz	*happy*		10. inteligente	*intelligent*
4. alegre	*cheerful*		11. listo(a)	*clever*
5. triste	*sad*		12. tonto(a)	*foolish*
6. egoísta	*selfish*		13. tímido(a)	*shy, timid*
7. generoso(a)	*generous*		14. amistoso(a)	*friendly*

Las características de la personalidad   *Personality characteristics* (continued)

15. popular — *popular*
16. simpático(a) — *nice*
17. antipático(a) — *not nice*
18. atlético(a) — *athletic*
19. amable — *kind*
20. ambicioso(a) — *ambitious*
21. perezoso(a) — *lazy*

22. trabajador(a) — *hardworking*
23. hablador(a) — *talkative*
24. callado(a) — *quiet*
• 25. chistoso(a) — *funny*
• 26. cortés — *courteous*
• 27. curioso(a) — *curious*
• 28. descortés — *rude*

- 29. divertido(a)   *fun-loving*
- 30. estúpido(a)   *stupid*
- 31. famoso(a)   *famous*
- 32. hipócrita   *hypocrite*
- 33. intelectual   *intellectual*

- 34. loco(a)   *crazy*
- 35. paciente   *patient*
- 36. serio(a)   *serious*
- 37. sociable   *social*
- 38. tacaño(a)   *stingy*

Otras palabras   *Other words*

muy   *very*
bastante   *quite, enough*
un poco   *a little*

Following is the verb **ser**, a verb that we can use with the preceding words to make sentences. The forms in bold print do not follow the regular patterns. Remember that if the subject is obvious, the subject pronoun can be omitted.

Yo soy inteligente. Soy inteligente.   *I am intelligent.*
Nosotros somos altas. Somos altas.   *We are tall.*

SER *to be*

	IMPERFECT *was/were* *used to be*	PRETERITE *was/were*	PRESENT *am/is/are*	FUTURE *will be*
yo	**era**	**fui**	**soy**	seré
tú	**eras**	**fuiste**	**eres**	serás
Ud./él/ella	**era**	**fue**	**es**	será
nosotros(as)	**éramos**	**fuimos**	**somos**	seremos
vosotros(as)	**erais**	**fuisteis**	**sois**	seréis
Uds./ellos/ellas	**eran**	**fueron**	**son**	serán

Vosotros(as) *[you, plural]* is used in Spain when talking to a group that is addressed informally. It will be included in verb charts so that you become familiar with it, if you need to use it.

Ahora soy estudiante.

Antes yo era bebé.

En el futuro seré piloto.

NOUNS

GENDER OF NOUNS

Most nouns that end in **o, l, r** as well as nouns that refer to male people are masculine.

el libro, el papel, el profesor, el padre

Most nouns that end in **a, d, ión** as well as nouns that refer to female people are feminine.

la casa, la libertad, la nación, la madre

If a noun ends in another letter or is an exception, the gender must be learned individually.

Another letter: la clase *[feminine]*
el chocolate *[masculine]*
el lápiz *[masculine]*
la luz *[feminine]*

Exceptions: el día *[masculine]*
el avión *[masculine]*
la mano *[feminine]*
la flor *[feminine]*

MAKING NOUNS PLURAL

If the noun ends in a vowel, add **s**.

libro ⟶ libros
cinta ⟶ cintas

If the noun ends in a consonant, add **es**.

papel ⟶ papeles
televisor ⟶ televisores

If the noun ends in **z**, change **z** to **c** and add **es**.

pez ⟶ peces
lápiz ⟶ lápices

unas cintas,
unos papeles, unos lápices

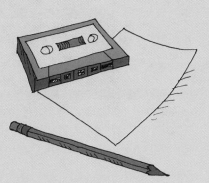

una cinta, un papel, un lápiz

ARTICLES

INDEFINITE ARTICLES *a, an, some*

UN	UNOS
UNA	UNAS

DEFINITE ARTICLES *the*

EL	LOS
LA	LAS

When talking about something in a general sense, use the article **el/la/los/las**.

Los bomberos son fuertes.   *Firefighters are strong.*
La contaminación es seria.   *Pollution is serious.*

ADJECTIVES

POSITION IN RELATION TO THE NOUN

Most adjectives precede the noun. Descriptive adjectives (color, size, characteristics) usually follow the noun.

NUMBER	noun		<u>tres</u> libros	*three books*
QUANTITY	noun		<u>muchos</u> libros	*many books*
POSSESSION	noun		<u>mis</u> libros	*my books*
ARTICLE	noun		<u>el</u> libro	*the book*
DEMONSTRATIVE	noun		<u>ese</u> libro	*that book*
	noun	DESCRIPTION	libro <u>rojo</u>	*red book*
			libro <u>grande</u>	*big book*
			libro <u>interesante</u>	*interesting book*

ADJECTIVE–NOUN AGREEMENT: NUMBER AND GENDER

If the noun is plural, the adjective has to be plural. Adjectives form the plural in the same way as nouns.

  If the adjective ends in a vowel, add **s**.
  If the adjective ends in a consonant, add **es**.
  If the adjective ends in **z**, change **z** to **c** and add **es**.

If the noun is feminine, the adjective has to be feminine.

  If the adjective ends in **o**, change **o** to **a**.
  If the adjective ends in **or**, add **a**.
  Most other adjectives are the same for masculine and feminine.
    El hombre es listo, trabajador y amable.   *The man is clever, hardworking, and kind.*
    La mujer es lista, trabajadora y amable.   *The woman is clever, hardworking, and kind.*

Possessive adjectives agree with the noun in number and gender.

mi(s)	*my*	nuestro(a)(os)(as)	*our*
tu(s)	*your*	vuestro(a)(os)(as)	*your*
su(s)	*your, his, her, its*	su(s)	*your, their*

AFFIRMATIVE SENTENCES

The basic sentence pattern in Spanish is the same as in English: The subject, which is either a noun or pronoun, is followed by the verb and then the rest of the sentence.

Esqueleto

(pro)noun + verb + (rest of sentence)

Yo era pequeño.　*I was small.*
El hombre es alto.　*The man is tall.*

1 Using words from the vocabulary list on pages 52 and 53, describe some people you know.

EJEMPLO:　Mi profesor es simpático, amable y generoso.

2 Identify and describe the people in the picture.

EJEMPLO:　Es un hombre. El hombre es alto.

3 Tell your partner several things about the following people. Tell about them in the past, present, and future.

EJEMPLO: Mi amigo era pequeño, pero ahora es bastante alto. Es muy listo y será abogado o médico. Es muy amable.

a. yourself
b. your family as a whole
c. a family member
d. your friend

e. your favorite singer or group
f. your favorite actor or actress
g. a teacher

4 Tell your partner three things about the members of your family. For the first sentence, use a noun subject. For the second sentence, replace the noun with a pronoun. For the third sentence, omit the subject.

EJEMPLO: Mi madre es bonita. Ella es inteligente. Es muy amable.
Mi hermano es alto. Él es atlético. Es muy fuerte.

NEGATIVE SENTENCES

To make a sentence negative *(not)*, put **no** before the verb.

Esqueleto

(pro)noun + NO + verb + (rest of sentence)

Yo no soy alta.   *I am not tall.*
Yo no era fuerte.   *I was not strong.*

5 Tell your partner several things about your family by using negative sentences.

EJEMPLO: Mi padre no es médico.
Mi hermana no es antipática.

6 Tell your partner what characteristics you think people of different occupations have and do not have.

EJEMPLO: Un bombero es fuerte. No es perezoso.

YES/NO QUESTIONS

There are three patterns for questions that are to be answered with **sí** or **no**.

1. Raise the pitch of your voice at the end (when speaking) or put question marks before and after the question (when writing).

2. Add **¿no?** or **¿verdad?** to the end of the question.

3. Put the subject after the verb.

Esqueletos

¿(pro)noun + verb + (rest of sentence)?

¿Uds. son norteamericanos?   *You are North Americans?*
¿El hombre es fuerte?   *The man is strong?*

(pro)noun + verb + (rest of sentence), + ¿NO?
¿VERDAD?

Uds. son norteamericanos, ¿no?   *You are North Americans, aren't you?*
El hombre es fuerte, ¿verdad?   *The man is strong, right?*

¿verb + (pro)noun + (rest of sentence)?

OR

¿verb + (rest of sentence) + (pro)noun?

¿Son Uds. norteamericanos?   *Are you North Americans?*
¿Es fuerte el hombre?   *Is the man strong?*

7 Ask your partner questions about herself or himself and the family that have to be answered with **sí** or **no**. Remember, the subject pronoun can be omitted if it is understood. Have your partner answer your questions.

EJEMPLO: ¿Eres (tú) ambicioso(a)?
¿Son tus hermanos gemelos?

Vocabulario

Las palabras interrogativas   *Question words*

¿Cómo?	*How?*
¿Dónde?	*Where (to)?*
¿Adonde?	*Where?*
¿Quién(es)?	*Who?*
¿Qué?	*What?, Which?*
¿Cuándo?	*When?*
¿Por qué?	*Why?*
¿Cuánto(a)?	*How much?*
¿Cuántos(as)?	*How many?*
¿Cuál(es) + *verb*?	*Which?, What?*

Note: **Lo que** *(What)* is used in statements.

Lo que quiero es un carro nuevo.   *What I want is a new car.*

Note: To ask *Which?*, use **¿Cuál?** except when a noun follows immediately. In that case, use **¿Qué?**

¿Cuál es tu libro?   *Which is your book?*

¿Qué libro es tu libro?   *Which book is your book?*

QUESTIONS USING QUESTION WORDS

When asking a question using a question word, put the question word first and put the subject after the verb. If there is a preposition (**a**, **de**, etc.), put it before the question word.

Esqueleto

 ¿(preposition) + question word *+ verb + (pro)noun + (rest of sentence)?*

¿<u>Cómo</u> es Ud.?   *What are you like?*
¿<u>De dónde</u> es Ud.?   *Where are you from?*
¿<u>A quién</u> le escribe tu hermano?   *Who is your brother writing to?*

8 Answer the following questions about yourself.

a. ¿De dónde eres?
b. ¿Cómo eres?
c. ¿Quién es tu mejor amigo o amiga?
d. ¿Qué serás en el futuro?
e. ¿Cuándo es tu clase de inglés?
f. ¿Por qué eres listo(a)?
g. ¿Cuánto es tu libro?
h. ¿Cuál es tu número de teléfono?

9 Find someone in your class whom you do not know well and take turns asking and answering the questions in Activity 8.

EJEMPLO: ¿De dónde eres?

   Soy de…

COMPARISONS

To compare two people or things in Spanish, use **más... que** to say that something is *more . . . than*, **menos... que** to say that something is *less . . . than,* and **tan... como** to say *as . . . as.*

Note that in English we use *-er* as an ending instead of *more* for comparisons with short adjectives. In Spanish we must still use the pattern **más... que** with these adjectives.

    más alto que   *taller than*
    más pequeño que   *smaller than*

These adjectives have irregular forms that are used instead of **más** + *adjective* + **que**.

    bueno(a) *good*   mejor que *better than*
    malo(a) *bad*   peor que *worse than*
    joven *young*   menor que *younger than*
    viejo(a) *old*   mayor que *older than*

    Este libro es mejor que el otro.   *This book is better than the other one.*
    Mi hermano es mayor que mi hermana.   *My brother is older than my sister.*

The irregular forms **mayor** and **menor** are usually used with people. To describe the age of things, use **más/menos viejo(a).**

    Mi carro es más viejo que tu carro.   *My car is older than your car.*

Esqueleto

	MÁS		QUE	
(pro)noun + *verb* +	**MENOS**	+ *adjective* +	**QUE** +	*(pro)noun*
	TAN		**COMO**	

Mi padre es más alto que mi madre.   *My father is taller than my mother.*
Luis es menos hablador que Beto.   *Luis is less talkative than Beto.*
Juanita es tan simpática como Alicia.   *Juanita is as nice as Alicia.*

10 Compare the people in the picture. Tell who is *more* . . . and who is *less* . . .

Julia   Teresa   Señora   Señorita   Manuel   Javier   Gregorio   Teodoro
                        Montoya   Lara

Federico

Eugenio

Carmen

Estela

Señor
Sandoval

Señor
Pelayo

11 With your partner, using the vocabulary list on pages 52 and 53, choose several physical and personality characteristics. Compare yourselves on those traits.

EJEMPLO: Yo soy más alto. Tú eres menos alta.

Yo soy más hablador. Tú eres menos habladora.

12 Compare people that you know.

EJEMPLO: Mi hermana es más alta que tu hermana.
Mi profesor de inglés es tan inteligente como mi profesor de matemáticas.

SUPERLATIVES

To say something is *the most . . .* or *the least . . .* with an adjective, add **el/la/los/las** before **más** or **menos**.

Este cuadro es más interesante.   *This picture is more interesting.*
Ese cuadro es el más interesante.   *That picture is the most interesting.*

In English we use *-est* as an ending with short adjectives instead of *the most . . .*
In Spanish we must still use the pattern **el/la/los/las + más** with these adjectives.

Este cuadro es más grande.   *This picture is bigger.*
Ese cuadro es el más grande.   *That picture is the biggest.*

With the adjectives that have irregular forms for the comparison, add **el/la/los/las** before the adjective.

el/la/los/las mejor(es)   *best*
el/la/los/las peor(es)   *worst*
el/la/los/las menor(es)   *youngest*
el/la/los/las mayor(es)   *oldest*

Este libro es el mejor.   *This book is the best.*
Mi hermano es el mayor.   *My brother is the oldest.*

If you want to say that something is *the most . . .* or *the least . . .* <u>of</u> or <u>in</u> a group, use **de**.

José es el más guapo <u>de</u> la clase.   *José is the most handsome <u>in</u> the class.*

Alicia está contenta.

Beatriz está más
contenta que Alicia.

Victoria está la más
contenta de todas.

Esqueleto

| (pro)noun + verb + | EL/LOS
LA/LAS | + | MÁS
MENOS | + adjective + DE + noun |

La mochila de Miguel es la más cara de toda la clase.
Miguel's backpack is the most expensive in the whole class.

El libro de español es el menos aburrido de todos mis libros.
The Spanish book is the least boring of all my books.

13 Tell about several people that are *the most . . .* or *the least . . .* in your school.

EJEMPLO: La señora González es la más amable de la escuela.

14 Ask your partner who is *the most . . .* or *the least . . .* of her or his friends.

EJEMPLO: ¿Quién es el más interesante de tus amigos?
¿Quién es la menos aburrida de tus amigas?

15 **Juego**   One person goes into the hallway while the class chooses an object. The person returns. By asking questions that can be answered with **sí** or **no**, he or she tries to guess what the object is in fewer than ten questions.

EJEMPLO: ¿Es más grande que un elefante?

 No, es menos grande que un elefante.

ENCUENTRO PERSONAL

Paulina and her social studies class are meeting with the career counselor, Señora Jiménez. They are talking about relatives in various professions and what they are like. Think of people you know in these professions. Do you agree or disagree with the characteristics necessary for these careers?

INÉS: Mi tío es un actor bastante famoso. Me gustan los actores y las actrices porque son muy chistosos y populares. ¿Qué piensas, Sean?

SEAN: Sí, es verdad, Inés, pero también son tontos a veces. Yo prefiero los policías porque son trabajadores y generosos. Por ejemplo, mi prima es policía en una gran ciudad y trabaja mucho con los jóvenes del barrio. Y tú, Santiago, ¿qué piensas?

SANTIAGO: Mi pariente favorito es mi abuelo porque es muy patriota. Él fue soldado en la Segunda Guerra Mundial *(World War II)*. Es un hombre interesante. Era fuerte y muy atlético en esos días, pero ahora es un poco débil porque tiene setenta y dos años.

PAULINA: Pues, mi pariente favorito es mi hermano mayor. Es enfermero en un hospital en el centro. Yo creo que los enfermeros son amables y también muy inteligentes porque estudian medicina por muchos años. Yo también seré enfermera o médica en el futuro. ¿Qué cree Ud., señora Jiménez?

SEÑORA JIMÉNEZ: Eres muy ambiciosa, Paulina. También eres inteligente y sincera. Pero también eres un poco perezosa y tú sabes que es necesario estudiar mucho para ser médica. Si *(If)* eres más trabajadora y seria en el futuro, creo que sí serás enfermera como tu hermano. Y si estudias muchísimo *(very much)*, estoy segura que serás médica.

¿Comprendes?

1. ¿Quién es el pariente favorito de Inés? ¿Por qué?
2. ¿Quiénes son los parientes favoritos de Sean, Santiago y Paulina? ¿Por qué?
3. ¿Qué cree Paulina que será en el futuro?
4. ¿Que piensa la señora Jiménez de los planes de Paulina?
5. ¿Qué consejos *(advice)* le da a Paulina? ¿Estás de acuerdo? *(Do you agree?)*

¡Te toca!

Take turns with your classmates talking about the relative you would most want to be like. Tell his or her good and bad qualities. Then tell which qualities you would like to have.

Leemos y contamos

A. After the discussion in class, the social studies teacher asked her students to write an essay about their favorite relative. She also asked them to describe the profession of that particular relative and what he or she is like. Here is what Sean wrote.

¿Quién es mi pariente favorito? Es mi padrastro, don Ramón. ¿Qué es? Es abogado. ¿Cómo es? Es mediano, delgado y muy fuerte y mi madre piensa que es muy guapo. Es un hombre muy sincero, sociable y generoso. Claro que es inteligente. No es egoísta ni hipócrita, como algunas personas creen que son los abogados. Mi padrastro trabaja con la gente pobre en la Oficina de Servicios Sociales. Es muy trabajador. Yo quiero ser un abogado importante como mi padrastro algún día.

Mi pariente favorita es mi madrina. Ella es mesera en un restaurante pequeño. Ella es alta, pelirroja, un poco gorda y muy bonita. No es muy vieja; sólo tiene treinta y dos años. Es muy simpática y contenta. No es una persona importante ni rica, pero tiene muchos amigos y es una excelente madre y esposa. Yo no deseo ser mesero, deseo ser abogado como dije antes (as I said before), pero sí deseo ser una persona amable y tener muchos amigos como mi madrina.

Una persona a quien no deseo imitar es mi primo Jerónimo. Jerónimo tiene veinte y seis años. Es muy amable, chistoso, fuerte y guapo; pero es muy perezoso. No era un buen estudiante y ahora no es un buen empleado. Muchas veces no tiene empleo (a job) y no tiene dinero para comprar nada. Yo deseo tener un coche bonito y otras cosas. Yo trabajaré mucho y seré como mi padrastro y mi madrina.

1. ¿Quiénes son los parientes favoritos de Sean?
2. ¿Cuáles son sus profesiones?
3. ¿Cómo son ellos?
4. ¿Por qué no desea Sean ser como su primo Jerónimo?
5. ¿Desea Sean ser como sus parientes favoritos? ¿Por qué?

B. It's your turn now to describe your favorite male and female. Tell what they are like and what their professions are.

¡Así es!

Los títulos

Señor, señora, señorita son títulos de cortesía. Cuando se usan sin el apellido significan *Sir, Ma'am* o *Miss*. También los hispanos usan los títulos con la profesión (pero sin el nombre) para mostrar cortesía cuando llaman o hablan a una persona: por ejemplo: **Sr. profesor** o **Sra. doctora**.

En español, no existe un equivalente exacto a la *Ms.* en inglés. Se usa **señorita** si la mujer no está casada. Si Ud. no sabe si una mujer está casada, debe usar **señora** o **señorita** según la edad de la mujer.

Otros títulos que se usan en los países de habla española son **don** y **doña** con el nombre de la persona, por ejemplo: **don Carlos, doña Elena**. No hay equivalente en inglés. Estos títulos muestran respeto a una persona mayor—un vecino, los amigos de los padres o el jefe *(boss)*.

Hay otros títulos comunes en español pero no en inglés como **gerente, ingeniero** y **licenciado** *(graduate)* para los que tienen este título de la universidad.

No se usan letras mayúsculas *(capital letters)* con los títulos si no están abreviados.

NATALICIOS

La señora de Uriarte Muerza (don Jaime), de soltera María Luisa Ayestarán Martínez, ha tenido una niña, primera de sus hijos, que en el Bautismo recibirá el nombre de María Isabel Eugenia y será apadrinada por su tía paterna, María Jiménez Muerza, y su tío materno, Ignacio José Ayestarán Martínez.

La señora de Barrigón Jiménez (don Antonio), de soltera Ana María Caro y Pilar, ha tenido un niño, segundo de sus hijos, que recibirá el nombre de Francisco de Borja y será apadrinado por sus tíos, doña Mercedes Barrigón Jiménez y don Pedro Miguel Pérez Velasco.

Gs PRIX DE MEXICO
ZONA SURESTE

ADITIVOS AUTOMOTRICES

Heriberto Arce Padilla

VENTAS

APARTADO POSTAL 68
ARRIAGA, CHIS.

TELEFO

Lic. José Mena Baca y Asociados

ABOGADOS

**Tels.: 15-01-91
15-17-83 15-02-51**

GALEANA 678 C.P. 32000

¿Cómo estás? ¿Qué tienes?

We all have our good and bad days. Sometimes it's our health that isn't normal; sometimes it's our emotional state, and other times it's our physical condition. In this lesson we will talk about the changes that can take place on a day-to-day basis. Let's start by reviewing the parts of the body.

Vocabulario

El cuerpo *The body*

1. el cuerpo	*body*	22. la pierna	*leg*
2. la cabeza	*head*	23. la rodilla	*knee*
3. la frente	*forehead*	24. el tobillo	*ankle*
4. el cerebro	*brain*	25. el talón	*heel*
5. el cuello	*neck*	26. el pie	*foot*
6. la garganta	*throat*	27. el dedo del pie	*toe*
7. el hombro	*shoulder*	28. la cara	*face*
8. el pecho	*chest*	29. el pelo	*hair*
9. los pulmones	*lungs*	30. el ojo	*eye*
10. el estómago	*stomach*	31. la nariz	*nose*
11. el hígado	*liver*	32. la oreja	*ear*
12. el corazón	*heart*	33. la mejilla	*cheek*
13. la espalda	*back*	34. el bigote	*mustache*
14. el brazo	*arm*	35. la boca	*mouth*
15. el codo	*elbow*	36. el diente	*tooth*
16. las nalgas	*buttocks*	37. el mentón	*chin*
17. la mano	*hand*	38. la barba	*beard*
18. el pulgar	*thumb*	• 39. la ceja	*eyebrow*
19. el dedo	*finger*	• 40. el oído	*inner ear*
20. la uña	*nail*	• 41. el labio	*lip*
21. la muñeca	*wrist*		

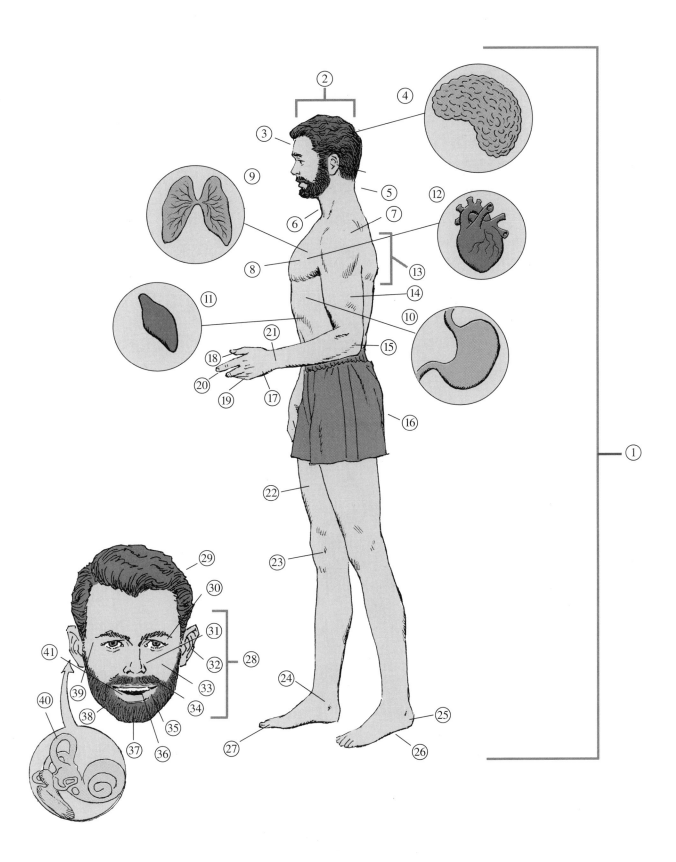

1 Point to the various parts of the body in the preceding picture and identify them in Spanish.

2 **Juego** *Stump your partner!*   With your partner, take turns pointing to and identifying different parts of the body, but do not always identify it correctly. If your partner corrects you, he or she scores the point. If he or she does not, tell what it is and you score the point.

EJEMPLO: *pointing to the head*   Es la cabeza.

Sí, tienes razón.

pointing to the hand   Es el pie.

No, no tienes razón. Es la mano. *[First person scores a point.]*

pointing to the eye   Es la boca.

Tienes razón.

No, no es la boca. Es el ojo. *[First person scores another point.]*

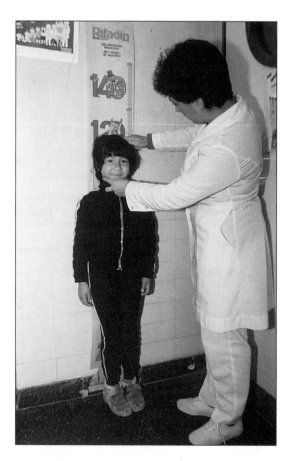

3 Draw a picture that shows the entire body (or find one in a magazine). Label it.

4 Draw a pictue of a face (or find one in a magazine) and label it.

The following two verbs are used when we are talking about our physical or emotional state.

ESTAR *to be*

	IMPERFECT *was/were* *used to be*	PRETERITE *was/were*	PRESENT *am/is/are*	FUTURE *will be*
yo	estaba	**estuve**	**estoy**	estaré
tú	estabas	**estuviste**	estás	estarás
Ud./él/ella	estaba	**estuvo**	está	estará
nosotros(as)	estábamos	**estuvimos**	estamos	estaremos
vosotros(as)	estabais	**estuvisteis**	estáis	estaréis
Uds./ellos/ellas	estaban	**estuvieron**	están	estarán

TENER *to have*

	IMPERFECT *had* *was/were having* *used to have*	PRETERITE *had* *did have*	PRESENT *have/has* *am/is/are having* *do/does have*	FUTURE *will have*
yo	tenía	**tuve**	**tengo**	**tendré**
tú	tenías	**tuviste**	tienes	**tendrás**
Ud./él/ella	tenía	**tuvo**	tiene	**tendrá**
nosotros(as)	teníamos	**tuvimos**	tenemos	**tendremos**
vosotros(as)	teníais	**tuvisteis**	tenéis	**tendréis**
Uds./ellos/ellas	tenían	**tuvieron**	tienen	**tendrán**

Estoy muy nerviosa.

Tengo mucha prisa.
Tengo mucho calor.

Estoy muy cansada.
Tengo mucha sed.

Vocabulario

Estados físicos y emocionales con «estar»   *Physical and emotional states* with estar

1. estar aburrido(a)	*to be bored*	7. estar enfermo(a)	*to be ill, sick*
2. estar agitado(a)	*to be upset*	8. estar enojado(a)	*to be angry*
3. estar cansado(a)	*to be tired*	9. estar loco(a)	*to be crazy*
4. estar celoso(a)	*to be jealous*	10. estar nervioso(a)	*to be nervous*
5. estar contento(a)	*to be happy, content*	11. estar ocupado(a)	*to be busy*
6. estar enamorado(a)	*to be in love*	12. estar preocupado(a)	*to be worried*

13. estar tranquilo(a)	*to be calm*	• 19. estar peor	*to be worse*
14. estar triste	*to be sad*	• 20. estar asustado(a)	*to be frightened*
15. estar bien	*to be well, fine*	• 21. estar casado(a)	*to be married*
16. estar mejor	*to be better*	• 22. estar entusiasmado(a)	*to be excited*
17. estar así, así	*to be so-so*	• 23. estar orgulloso(a)	*to be proud*
• 18. estar mal	*to not be well*	• 24. estar cómodo(a)	*to be comfortable*

Vocabulario

Estados físicos y emocionales con «tener»   *Physical and emotional states with* tener

	¿Qué tienes?	*What's the matter?*
1.	tener catarro	*to have a cold*
2.	tener tos	*to have a cough*
3.	tener fiebre	*to have a fever*
4.	tener la gripe	*to have the flu*
5.	tener dolor de…	*to have an ache/pain in . . . , . . . hurt(s)*
6.	tener infección de…	*to have an infection of . . .*
7.	tener (mucha/poca) hambre	*to be (very/not very) hungry*
8.	tener (mucha) sed	*to be (very) thirsty*
9.	tener (mucho) calor	*to be (very) warm/hot*
10.	tener (mucho) frío	*to be (very) cold*
11.	tener (mucha) prisa	*to be in a (big) hurry*
12.	tener (mucho) sueño	*to be (very) sleepy*
13.	tener (mucha) suerte	*to be (very) lucky*
14.	tener (mucho) miedo	*to be (very) afraid*
15.	tener razón	*to be right*
16.	no tener razón	*to be wrong*
• 17.	tener (mucho) cuidado	*to be (very) careful*
• 18.	tener celos	*to be jealous*

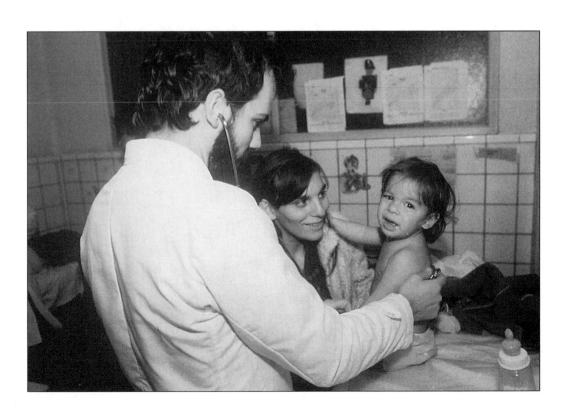

When we talk about our health, we need to be able to tell what hurts us. Following is the verb **doler** that will allow us to tell about our aches and pains.

DOLER (UE) *to hurt*

	IMPERFECT	PRETERITE	PRESENT	FUTURE
	hurt	*hurt*	*hurt(s)*	*will hurt*
	was/were hurting		*is/are hurting*	
	used to hurt	*did hurt*	*do/does hurt*	
SINGULAR	dolía	dolió	duele	dolerá
PLURAL	dolían	dolieron	duelen	dolerán

Doler is used in the singular or plural (*it* or *they*) forms with an indirect object pronoun.

Notice that **o** changes to **ue** in the present tense.

With this construction, the articles **el/la/los/las** are used instead of the possessive adjective with parts of the body.

Me duelen <u>los</u> pies.   *<u>My</u> feet hurt.*

¡Me duele todo!

Esqueleto

  (A + *person*) + ME/TE/LE NOS/OS/LES + DOLER + *body part*

Me duele el diente.   *My tooth hurts.*
A Juan le duelen los pies.   *Juan's feet hurt.*

5 Inquire about the health of several of your classmates. If they are not feeling well, find out why.

EJEMPLO: ¿Cómo estás?

No estoy bien.

¿Qué tienes?

Me duele la espalda.

¡Qué lástima!

6 *Sit-Con Hypochondriac's Convention*   Everyone thinks he or she is sick. Describe all your ills—real and imagined. Try to be "sicker" than the previous person.

EJEMPLO: Me duele el dedo.

Me duelen todos los dedos.

Me duelen todos los dedos de las manos y de los pies.

7 **Encuesta**   Survey several of your classmates to find out how they feel. Choose five of the emotional states below.

triste	agitado(a)	nervioso(a)	enamorado(a)
enojado(a)	aburrido(a)	cansado(a)	ocupado(a)
preocupado(a)	contento(a)	enfermo(a)	loco(a)
tranquilo(a)			

EJEMPLO: ¿Estás triste?

Sí, estoy triste. / No, no estoy triste.

Prepare a report of your findings.

EJEMPLO: De las seis personas a quienes pregunté «¿Estás triste?», cinco contestaron que no y una contestó que sí.

¡Ella está enojada, agitada, preocupada y celosa! ¡Ellos están contentos, tranquilos y enamorados!

8 **Encuesta**   Survey several of your classmates to find out how they feel. Choose three of the conditions below.

tienes (mucha/poca) hambre	tienes (mucha) sed
tienes (mucho) calor	tienes (mucho) frío
tienes (mucha) prisa	tienes (mucho) sueño
tienes (mucha) suerte	tienes (mucho) miedo

EJEMPLO: ¿Tienes mucha o poca hambre?

Tengo mucha hambre.

Prepare a report of your findings.

EJEMPLO: De las seis personas a quienes pregunté «¿Tienes mucha o poca hambre?», cinco tenían mucha hambre y una tenía poca hambre.

9 **Juego**   One person acts out an emotional or physical state. The others try to guess in fewer than ten questions how the person is feeling.

EJEMPLO: *Actor holds hand on stomach and makes a sad face.*
Guesses: ¿Tienes hambre? ¿Estás enfermo?

10 *Sit-Con*   You are visiting a friend and wake up feeling ill in the middle of the night. Tell your friend what the problem is. Describe your symptoms for each of the following situations.

• You have the flu.
• You have an upset stomach.
• You have a bad toothache.
• You have a bad cold.

Since there are two verbs in Spanish that mean *to be*, it is important to use them appropriately. Here are the differences between **ser** and **estar**.

THE DIFFERENCES BETWEEN SER AND ESTAR

SER	ESTAR
1. to identify a person or thing (noun or pronoun)	1. to tell location (adverb or preposition of place)
Es una mesa. *It's a table.*	La mesa está allí. *The table is there.*
Somos estudiantes. *We are students.*	Estamos en la escuela. *We are in school.*
¿Quién es? Soy yo. *Who is it? It's me.*	
2. to tell basic characteristics/normal state (adjective)	2. to tell condition/not normal state (adjective)
Juan es alto. *Juan is tall.*	Juan está enfermo. *Juan is ill.*
Juan es feliz. *Juan is a happy person.*	Hoy Juan está triste. *Today Juan is sad.*
¿Cómo eres? *What are you like?*	¿Cómo estás? *How are you feeling?*
3. to tell when (time, date, etc.)	
¿Qué hora es? *What time is it?*	
Es el dos de febrero. *It's February 2.*	
4. to tell origin, owner, or material (**de** + noun)	
Mi padre es de Chile. *My father is from Chile.*	
El libro es de Juanita. *The book is Juanita's.*	
La mesa es de plástico. *The table is plastic.*	
5. to tell where an <u>event</u> takes place	
El concierto es en el parque. *The concert is in the park.*	

Both **ser** and **estar** are used with adjectives, but each has its own function. Study the chart below for the different meanings of adjectives depending on whether they are used with **ser** or **estar**.

SER VS. ESTAR WITH ADJECTIVES

SER	ESTAR
Characteristics:	Condition:
What something is normally like	How something is physically or emotionally
How we expect to find it	changed from its characteristic state

La sopa de pollo <u>es</u> caliente.   *Chicken soup is hot.*
[characteristic/the way it was expected to be]

La sopa de pollo <u>está</u> fría. *The chicken soup is cold.*
[condition/not the way it was expected to be]

If we heat it again, then we've changed its condition:
Ahora la sopa de pollo <u>está</u> caliente.
Now the chicken soup is hot. [change of condition]

When does a condition become a characteristic?
Answer: When we expect the person or thing to be that way!

Use **ser** with these characteristics that can change.

| rico | *rich (money)* | nuevo | *new* | joven | *young* |
| pobre | *poor* | viejo | *old* | feliz | *happy* |

Use **estar** with these conditions:

| solo | *alone* | casado | *married* | roto | *broken* |
| juntos | *together* | muerto | *dead* | | |

The meaning of some adjectives changes when used with **ser** or **estar**.

Juan es aburrido. *Juan is <u>boring</u>.*	Juan está aburrido. *Juan is <u>bored</u>.*
Yo soy lista. *I am <u>clever</u>.*	Yo estoy lista. *I am <u>ready</u>.*
Somos seguros. *We are <u>safe</u>.*	Estamos seguros. *We are <u>sure/certain</u>.*

Vocabulario

Los adjetivos que cambian significado con «ser» y «estar» *Adjectives that change meaning with ser and estar*

Some adjectives have a different meaning when used with **ser** or **estar**. Can you explain why?

ser aburrido(a)	*to be boring*	estar aburrido(a)	*to be bored*
ser listo(a)	*to be clever*	estar listo(a)	*to be ready*
ser seguro(a)	*to be safe*	estar seguro(a)	*to be certain*
ser rico(a)	*to be rich*	estar rico(a)	*to be delicious*
ser malo(a)	*to be bad*	estar malo(a)	*to be ill*
ser nuevo(a)	*to be brand new*	estar nuevo(a)	*to be like new*
ser vivo(a)	*to be lively*	estar vivo(a)	*to be alive*
ser verde	*to be green*	estar verde	*to be unripe*

11 Tell the characteristics of some people and things you know. Then tell their condition. Be careful to choose the correct verb.

EJEMPLO: Juan es alegre.
Juan está de mal humor.

La nieve es blanca.
La nieve está sucia.

12 Use the questions in the structure box on page 84 to interview your partner. Be careful to use the correct verbs for your questions and answers. Then prepare a short report about your partner based on the information you received in your interview.

13 Prepare a report about a famous person of your choosing. Be sure to answer each of the preceding questions. Of course, you can tell more about the person if you like.

14 **¿Quién es... ?**   Tell some people you know who are or who are not characteristically each of the adjectives listed on page 86.

EJEMPLO: Mi profesor de historia no es aburrido.
Mi bisabuela *(great-grandmother)* es viva.

15 Tell when people or things feel a certain way. Use each of the adjectives listed on page 86.

EJEMPLO: Estoy aburrido cuando todos mis amigos están de vacación con sus familias.
La comida en este restaurante siempre está rica.

ENCUENTRO PERSONAL

Have you ever heard some old people (or not so old!) complaining about their health? Well, one day Paulina overheard her grandmother and her grandmother's friend, Luisa, discussing their ills. See if you can follow the conversation.

ABUELITA: Hola, Luisa. ¿Cómo estás hoy?

LUISA: Soy una mujer honesta y admito que no estoy muy bien hoy.

ABUELITA: Lo siento, Luisa. ¿Qué tienes?

LUISA: Estoy un poco enferma. Me duelen las piernas y tengo un gran dolor de cabeza.
También me duele el pecho cuando respiro. Pero soy una mujer optimista y mañana
estaré mucho mejor. Y tú, ¿cómo estás hoy?

ABUELITA: Como tú sabes, Luisa, soy débil y vieja y me duele todo el cuerpo todo el tiempo.
No puedo hacer nada. Pero no estoy aburrida porque para mí la vida no es aburrida;
siempre es interesante. Soy religiosa y tengo fé (faith) en que todo estará bien.

LUISA: Sí, eres una persona sincera y simpática, y por eso siempre serás mi amiga.

(Paulina entra en la sala.)

PAULINA: Buenas tardes, abuelita. Buenas tardes, señora. ¿Cómo están Uds. hoy?

ABUELITA: Estamos perfectamente bien, gracias. Luisa, ésta es mi nieta Paulina.

LUISA: Mucho gusto, Paulina.

PAULINA: El gusto es mío, doña Luisa.

ABUELITA: Paulina vive en la ciudad y es estudiante de segundo año en la escuela secundaria. Es una muchacha lista y buena.

LUISA: Y tú eres una abuela muy orgullosa y alegre, ¿no?

ABUELITA: Sí, soy una abuela muy afortunada *(fortunate, lucky)*, Luisa.

¿Comprendes?

1. ¿Cómo es Luisa?
2. ¿Qué tiene Luisa? ¿Cómo estará en el futuro?
3. ¿Cómo es la abuelita de Paulina? ¿Cómo está ella hoy?
4. ¿Cómo es Paulina?
5. ¿Cómo es la abuelita cuando habla de Paulina?

¡Te toca!

Pretend that you and a friend are hypochondriacs *(too concerned about your health)*. Create a conversation between the two of you.

Leemos ycontamos

A. **El choque del futuro**   Here is a story in a science fiction magazine about an astronaut who has just returned from a twenty-year trip in space. What changes does she notice in the people she knows?

Año 2020. En el año 2000, yo era una de los cinco astronautas que salieron de la Tierra *(Earth)* para explorar el espacio. Acabamos de regresar *(We have just returned)* de nuestro viaje y estoy muy contenta. Físicamente estoy bien, pero mentalmente no estoy segura. Tengo un dolor de cabeza muy grande. ¿Por qué? Pues, soy una persona optimista pero estoy confundida *(confused)* porque todas las personas son muy diferentes. En el año 2000 mi familia era pobre y trabajadora. Ahora mis padres son ricos y un poco perezosos. Mi padre era un hombre interesante pero en estos días está aburrido porque no trabaja. Mi madre es más vieja pero tan habladora como siempre. Antes mis abuelos eran viejos pero fuertes. Ahora son muy viejos y débiles, pero afortunadamente no están muertos. Mi hermana menor era joven (tenía diez años) y bonita. Ahora está casada y es madre de cinco hijos. Su esposo es policía y ella es abogada. ¿Y yo? Antes era joven y atlética, y ahora, en contraste, soy una persona de edad media *(middle-aged)* e intelectual. Pero estoy muy alegre de estar aquí con mis amigos y mis parientes.

1. ¿Cuándo y adónde salieron los cinco astronautas?
2. ¿Cómo está la astronauta físicamente? ¿Mentalmente?
3. ¿Por qué tiene ella un dolor de cabeza?
4. ¿Cómo cambiaron las personas mientras ella estaba en el espacio?
5. ¿Cómo son sus abuelos?
6. ¿Cómo es su hermana menor?
7. ¿Está triste o alegre de estar con su familia y sus amigos?

B. Suppose you could project yourself twenty years into the future using a time machine. How do you think the people in your family will change? Use your imagination, but try to be realistic.

¡Así es!

Los modales *Manners*

Cuando alguien te hace un cumplido *(pays a compliment)*, es cortés decirle **Ud. es amable** y que estás contento que le gusta algo. Si dices solamente **Gracias** o **Muchas gracias**, indica que piensas que mereces *(deserve)* el cumplido. En algunos países, si expresas que te gusta algo que tiene otra persona, él o ella insistirá en dártelo. ¡Ten cuidado de lo que dices! *(Be careful what you say!)*

Los hispanos frecuentemente hablan en voz alta y usan mucho las manos. También interrumpen cuando otra persona habla. En vez de ser descortés, es una indicación de su interés en lo que dice la otra persona. Cuando los hispanos hablan, se quedan *(they stand)* más cerca de la otra persona que los norteamericanos. Es descortés alejarse *(move away)* de una persona que te habla. También, es común tocar *(touch)* el brazo, la mano o el hombro de la otra persona mientras le hablas.

¡Ten cuidado también de los gestos *(gestures)* de la mano. No tienen la misma significación en todos los países y un gesto positivo en un país puede ser vulgar en otro. Por ejemplo, el gesto para *OK* (un círculo con el dedo índice y el pulgar) que usamos aquí es vulgar en algunas áreas.

Los hombres siempre dan la mano *(shake hands)* cuando se encuentran *(meet)* y generalmente cuando salen. Las mujeres generalmente se besan *(kiss each other)* en la mejilla. En algunos países las jóvenes besan tres veces—dos para saludar… ¡y una vez para suerte en hallar *(finding)* un esposo!

Las cosas en el aula

How well do you know your classroom? Let's review numbers and the names of the things that you might find in your classroom. We'll also talk about other things we have and learn the words to describe things.

Vocabulario

Los números hasta los millones   *Numbers to the millions*

First review the numbers which follow.

0 cero			
1 uno	11 once	10 diez	100 cien(to)
2 dos	12 doce	20 veinte	200 doscientos
3 tres	13 trece	30 treinta	300 trescientos
4 cuatro	14 catorce	40 cuarenta	400 cuatrocientos
5 cinco	15 quince	50 cincuenta	500 quinientos
6 seis	16 diez y seis	60 sesenta	600 seiscientos
7 siete	17 diez y siete	70 setenta	700 setecientos
8 ocho	18 diez y ocho	80 ochenta	800 ochocientos
9 nueve	19 diez y neuve	90 noventa	900 novecientos
10 diez	20 veinte	100 cien(to)	1.000 mil
	21 veinte y uno	101 ciento uno	2.000 dos mil
	22 veinte y dos	102 ciento dos	*etc.*
	etc.	*etc.*	1.000.000 un millón (de)
			2.000.000 dos millones (de)
			etc.

USING NUMBERS

Uno becomes **un** before a masculine noun and **una** before a feminine noun.

<u>un</u> hombre y <u>una</u> mujer   *one man and one woman*

Cien becomes **ciento** before numbers that are smaller than 100.

<u>ciento</u> veinte lápices   *one hundred twenty pencils*

Doscientos, etc. become feminine **(as)** with feminine nouns.

quinient<u>as</u> casas   *five hundred houses*

Mil never has **un** in front of it and does not use a plural form when preceded by another number.

Hay <u>mil</u> libros en la casa.   *There are a (one) thousand books in the house.*
Hay <u>dos mil</u> libros allí.   *There are two thousand books there.*

Millón adds **es** for plural and uses **de** before a noun.

Hay <u>un millón de</u> libros aquí.   *There are a (one) million books here.*
Hay <u>dos millones de</u> libros aquí.   *There are two million books here.*

In some areas of the Spanish-speaking world, periods are used to separate thousands and hundreds, and commas are used to indicate decimals.

1.000.000   un millón
1,5%   uno punto cinco por ciento

Years are expressed in the same way as the number in thousands.

1999   mil novecientos noventa y nueve
2025   dos mil veinticinco

TIPOS DE CAMBIO CRUZADOS

	Peseta	Dólar	Marco	Franco f.	Libra	100 liras	100 escudos	100 franc. b.	100 yens	ECU
Peseta		145,93	84,49	25,04	243,19	8,65	83,73	410,17	128,43	165,63
Dólar EE UU	0,0069		0,5788	0,1715	1,6654	0,0592	0,5726	2,8052	0,8797	1,1334
Marco	0,0118	1,7278		0,2964	2,8785	0,1023	0,9903	4,8513	1,5207	1,9593
Franco francés	0,0399	5,8307	3,3737		9,71	0,3452	3,3393	16,36	5,1335	6,6388
Libra esterlina	0,0041	0,6005	0,3474	0,1030		0,0355	0,3438	1,6844	0,5280	0,6834
Lira italiana	11,56	1689	977	289,68	2813		1034	4731	1489	1922
Escudo	1,1943	174,64	100,98	29,95	290,85	9,67		489,19	153,59	198,61
Franco belga	0,2438	35,65	20,61	6,1128	59,37	2,1137	20,44		31,35	40,59
Yen japonés	0,7787	113,67	65,76	19,48	189,39	6,7180	65,11	318,95		128,91
ECU	0,0060	0,8823	0,5104	0,1506	1,4632	0,0520	0,5035	2,4635	0,7757	

Fuente: InterMoney

Vocabulario

Las funciones aritméticas   *Arithmetic functions*

+	y, más	*and, plus*
−	menos	*minus*
×	por	*by, times*
÷	dividido por	*divided by*
=	es/son	*is, equals*

1 Write some important dates from history. Here are some to get you started. Take turns reading them in Spanish. Do you know why these dates are important?

a. 711   f. 1848
b. 1492   g. 1898
c. 1521   h. 1910
d. 1776   i. 1936
e. 1810   j. 1959

Now write your own.

2 Take turns creating arithmetic problems for your partner to solve.

EJEMPLO: 846
           + 629
           1.475

ochocientos cuarenta y seis
y seiscientos veinte y nueve
son mil cuatrocientos setenta y cinco

3 Write several numbers greater than 100. Have other people in the class read your number out loud.

EJEMPLO: 3.525.951 = tres millones, quinientos veinte y cinco mil, novecientos cincuenta y uno

Vocabulario

El cuarto   *The room*

1. el frente	*front*	7. la luz	*light*
2. el techo	*ceiling*	8. la parte de atrás	*back*
3. el lado	*side*	9. la fila	*row*
4. la puerta	*door*	10. el suelo	*floor*
5. la pared	*wall*	• 11. el rincón	*corner*
6. la ventana	*window*		

Vocabulario

Las cosas en el aula   *Things in the classroom*

1. la pizarra	*chalkboard*	
2. la tiza	*chalk*	
3. el borrador	*eraser*	
4. el estante	*bookshelf*	
5. el reloj	*clock*	
6. el armario	*cabinet, closet, locker*	
7. la bandera	*flag*	
8. el calendario	*calendar*	
9. el cuadro	*picture, painting*	
10. el tablero de anuncios	*bulletin board*	
11. el mapa	*map*	
12. el globo	*globe*	
13. el libro	*book*	
14. el retroproyector	*overhead projector*	
15. la videocasetera	*VCR, videocassette recorder*	
16. el casete	*cassette*	
17. el archivador	*file cabinet*	
18. el escritorio	*teacher's desk*	
19. el pupitre	*student's desk*	

20. el diccionario	*dictionary*
21. la cartera	*briefcase*
22. la mochila	*backpack, knapsack*
23. la papelera	*wastepaper basket*
24. el sacapuntas	*pencil sharpener*
25. las tijeras	*scissors*
26. la regla	*ruler*
27. la computadora	*computer*
28. la calculadora	*calculator*
29. la grabadora	*tape recorder*
30. la cinta	*tape*
31. el cuaderno	*notebook*
32. el papel	*paper*
33. el lápiz	*pencil*
34. el bolígrafo	*ballpoint pen*
35. la goma de borrar	*pencil eraser*
36. la silla	*chair*
37. la mesa	*table*

UNIVERSIDAD DE PUEBLOCHICO
CURSOS DE EDUCACIÓN CONTINUADA
PROGRAMACIÓN ABRIL - JUNIO de 19--
CURSOS COMIENZAN LA SEMANA DEL 14 DE ABRIL DE 19 .

• ADMINISTRACION DE EMPRESAS
Contabilidad básica
Gerencia de producción

• ADMINISTRACION Y SUPERVISIÓN
Técnicas y estrategias de
   supervisión
Técnicas y Estrategias de
   supervisión II

• CALIDAD AMBIENTAL
EPA Regulaciones

• COMPUTADORAS
Introducción a la computadora
MS Andes
Internet
Lotes 1,2,3 Básico
Wordperfect 6.1 flor Andes
Word/Power Point

• CURSOS ESPECIALES
Agente de viajes
Decoración de interiores
Diseño paisajista I
Jardines de interior
El retrato fotográfico
Facturación de planes médicos

• IDIOMAS
Inglés para principiantes
Inglés básico
Inglés conversacional- básico
Inglés conversacional - intermedio
Inglés conversacional - avanzado
Phonetics in English language
Basic English Grammar
Professional English Writing
   Techniques

• PARALEGAL
Introducción a la búsqueda legal
Derechos civiles: su impacto
   social e institucional

Derecho constitucional PR:
   Carta de derechos
Redacción de documentos legales

• SECRETARIA
Mecanografía básica
Escritura rápida en español

• SEGURIDAD E HIGIENE INDUSTRIAL
OSHA Regulations

Nota: Cualquier persona interesada
podrá matricularse en nuestros cursos.
La Universidad se reserva el derecho
de cancelar o hacer cambios de cursos
de no cubrir la matrícula mínima
establecido para su ofrecimiento

Para mayor información, llamar a los
teléfonos 764-0000 o 765-0000

Existencia   *Existence*

había	*there was, there were*
hubo	*there was, there were*
hay	*there is, there are*
habrá	*there will be*

Note: There is only one form for both singular and plural.

Había dos enamorados.

Hay una boda.

Habrá una familia grande.

HABÍA / HUBO / HAY / HABRÁ

Había, hubo, hay, and **habrá** are frequently used with quantities [un/una/unos/unas, mucho(s), poco(s)] and numbers to state <u>existence</u>, not location.

¿Qué hay en el estante?   *What is there in the bookcase?*
Hay unos libros en el estante.   *There are some books on the bookshelf.*
¿Cuántos libros hay?   *How many books are there?*
Hay muchos libros.   *There are a lot of books.*

Note: In most cases where the definite article **(el/la/los/las)** is used, the sentence tells location, not existence. Use the verb **estar.**

Allí está el carro nuevo.   *There is the new car.*
The new car is (over) there.

Esqueletos

¿QUÉ + **HABÍA/HUBO HAY/HABRÁ** + *(rest of sentence)*?

¿Qué habrá en el aula?   *What will there be in the classroom?*

¿CUÁNTO(A) ¿CUÁNTOS(AS) + *noun* + **HABÍA/HUBO HAY/HABRÁ** + *(rest of sentence)*?

¿Cuánto dinero hay en tu bolso?   *How much money is there in your purse?*
¿Cuántas sillas hay en una fila?   *How many chairs are there in a row?*

HABÍA/HUBO HAY/HABRÁ + *(number)* + *noun(s)* + *(rest of sentence)*

Había dos libros en la mesa.   *There were two books on the table.*
Había libros en el estante.   *There were books on the bookshelf.*

4 Ask your partner what there is in the classroom and how many.

EJEMPLO: ¿Qué hay en la clase?

Hay pupitres.

¿Cuántos pupitres hay?

Hay veinte y ocho pupitres.

¿Qué más hay?

5 Tell the things that will be found in your ideal classroom of the future.

EJEMPLO: Habrá veinte y cuatro estudiantes.

6 Tell some of the things that you have at home. How many were there last year?

EJEMPLO: Ahora hay tres radios en mi casa. Había cuatro radios el año pasado.

Now let's tell what the classroom objects look like.

Vocabulario

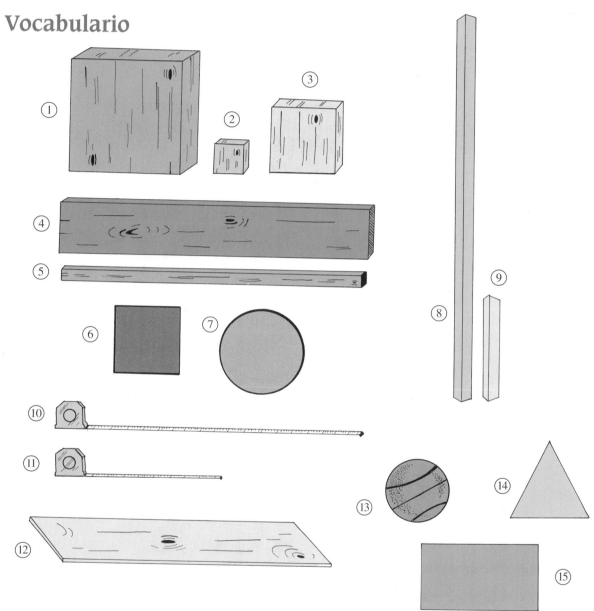

Las formas y los tamaños   *Shapes and sizes*

1. grande	*big*	9. bajo(a)	*low, short (in height)*
2. pequeño(a)	*small*	10. largo(a)	*long*
3. mediano(a)	*medium*	11. corto(a)	*short (in length)*
4. ancho(a)	*wide*	12. plano(a)	*flat*
5. estrecho(a)	*narrow*	13. redondo(a)	*round*
6. cuadrado(a)	*square*	14. triangular	*triangular*
7. circular	*circular*	15. rectangular	*rectangular*
8. alto(a)	*high, tall*		

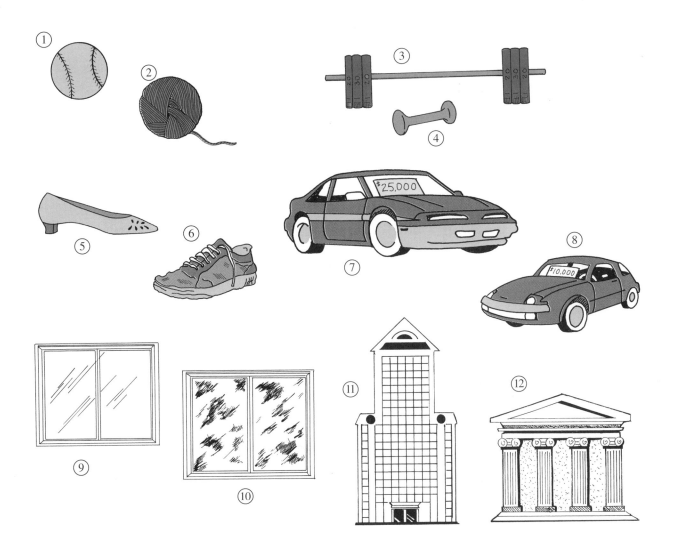

$$9 \times 6 = 54$$

$$2y = \frac{-1}{2} + \sqrt{\frac{3}{2x}}$$

Otras características   *Other characteristics*

1. duro(a)	*hard*	
2. blando(a)	*soft*	
3. pesado(a)	*heavy*	
4. ligero(a)	*light*	
5. nuevo(a)	*new*	
6. viejo(a)	*old*	
7. caro(a)	*expensive*	

8. barato(a)	*inexpensive, cheap*	
• 9. limpio(a)	*clean*	
• 10. sucio(a)	*dirty*	
• 11. moderno(a)	*modern*	
• 12. antiguo(a)	*ancient, old*	
• 13. fácil	*easy*	
• 14. difícil	*difficult*	

Los colores   *Colors*

rojo(a)	*red*	negro(a)	*black*
amarillo(a)	*yellow*	blanco(a)	*white*
azul	*blue*	gris	*gray*
anaranjado(a)	*orange*	pardo(a)	*brown*
verde	*green*	marrón	*brown*
morado(a)	*purple*	rosado(a)	*pink*
violeta	*violet*	plateado(a)	*silver*
color crema	*tan*	dorado(a)	*gold*
turquesa	*turquoise*		

(color) claro	*light (color)*
(color) oscuro	*dark (color)*

Las conjunciones   *Conjunctions [joining words]*

y [**e** before **i, hi**]	*and*
o [**u** before **o, ho**]	*or*
pero	*but*
porque	*because*
que	*that*
si	*if*
• sin embargo	*however, nevertheless*
• sino	*but rather [after a negative]*

Note: As you do the following activities, remember that all nouns in Spanish are either masculine or feminine so describing adjectives have to agree in gender and number with the noun.

7 Make a list of things in your classroom and describe them. Don't forget to make the describing word agree in number and gender.

EJEMPLO: Hay tres sillas azules y veinte y siete sillas rojas.
Hay un globo redondo y un reloj circular.

8 Tell the size, shape, color, or other qualities of some objects that you possess.

EJEMPLO: Mi cuaderno es rojo.
Mi computadora es cara.

9 Ask your partner if her or his possessions have various qualities.

EJEMPLO: ¿Es nueva tu cartera?
¿Es anaranjado tu lápiz?

10 **Juego**   Describe an object in the classroom but do not tell what it is. See if your partner can guess what it is from your description.

EJEMPLO: Es pequeño y circular. Es gris y también plateado. Está cerca de la puerta. ¿Qué es? [el sacapuntas]

DEMONSTRATIVE ADJECTIVES AND PRONOUNS

THIS	THESE	THAT	THOSE	THAT . . .	THOSE . . . (OVER THERE)
este	estos	ese	esos	aquel	aquellos
esta	estas	esa	esas	aquella	aquellas

Demonstrative adjectives go before the noun. If no noun follows, put an accent mark on the first **e** to make it a pronoun.

¿Es interesante <u>este libro</u>?   *Is this book interesting?*
Sí, <u>éste</u> es interesante.   *Yes, this one is interesting.*

When referring to something nonspecific or vague where no gender can be assigned, use the neutral forms **esto, eso**, and **aquello**. These forms never have an accent.

Esto es increíble.   *This is incredible!*
¡Eso es!   *That's it.*
¿Qué es aquello?   *What's that?*

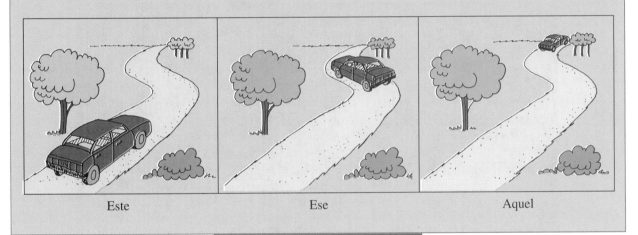

| Este | Ese | Aquel |

11   Describe various items in the class and use the demonstrative adjectives to point them out.

EJEMPLO: Esta pizarra es larga.
Aquel archivador es alto y gris.

12   Repeat the previous activity but leave out the noun.

EJEMPLO: Ésta es larga.
Aquél es alto y gris.

TWO NOUNS TOGETHER
NOUN + DE + NOUN

When one noun describes another noun, it follows and is separated by **de** *(of)*.

la tienda <u>de</u> ropa   *the clothing store*
el libro <u>de</u> español   *the Spanish book*

There is no apostrophe *s ('s)* to show possession in Spanish. Use the two nouns separated by **de** *(of)* instead.

la silla <u>del</u> profesor   *the teacher's chair*
la casa <u>de</u> María   *María's house*

13 Point out several items in the room and tell to whom each belongs.

EJEMPLO: Éste es el globo de Fernando.
Ésa es la calculadora de la estudiante nueva.

14 **Juego**   Each person puts an item on the table. The class tries to identify the owner.

EJEMPLO: Es la regla de Miguel.
Son las tijeras de Isabel.

15 Describe the possessions of several of your classmates.

EJEMPLO: El bolígrafo de Miguel es nuevo.
            La cartera de la profesora es cara.

16 Work with your partner in pointing out objects for which you do not know the Spanish word. Use a Spanish-English dictionary to look up the word.

EJEMPLO: ¿Qué es esto? *(pointing to the electrical outlet)*

            (After looking up the word in the dictionary) Es un enchufe.

REVIEW OF POSSESSIVE ADJECTIVES

mi(s)	*my*	nuestro(a)(os)(as)	*our*
tu(s)	*your*	vuestro(a)(os)(as)	*your*
su(s)	*your, his, her, its*	su(s)	*your, their*

Remember: Add **s** to the possessive adjective only if the noun it describes is plural.

17 Describe various objects that belong to you and to your classmates. Use the possessive adjective to tell who owns each thing.

EJEMPLO: Nuestro tablero de anuncios es interesante.
Mi mochila es nueva.
Su cuaderno es amarillo.

18 Ask your partner if her or his possessions are new or old.

EJEMPLO: ¿Es nuevo o viejo tu diccionario?

    Mi diccionario es nuevo.

CLARIFICATION OF SU

Because **su** or **sus** can mean *his, her, its, your,* or *their,* the clarifying phrase **de** + *person* may be used after the noun instead of **su** or **sus** to specify who the owner is.

EL/LA/LOS/LAS + *noun* + DE UD./UDS.
DE ÉL/ELLA
DE ELLOS/ELLAS

el libro de Ud.   *your book*   el libro de Uds.   *your book*
el libro de él   *his book*   el libro de ellos   *their book*
el libro de ella   *her book*   el libro de ellas   *their book*

El libro de ella es nueva.   El libro de él es vieja.

19 Use the following dialogue pattern, substituting the items below for **libros**. Be careful to use the correct form of the adjectives.

EJEMPLO: Éste es el libro de María y ése es el libro de Juan.

Su libro es nuevo; su libro es viejo.

No comprendo.

El libro de ella es nuevo; el libro de él es viejo.

a. cuadros   d. sillas
b. papeles   e. bolígrafos
c. cintas   f. mapas

20 Tell some things that your classmates have in common. Then tell how the things are different.

EJEMPLO: Juan y María tienen libros. El libro de ella es pesado. El libro de él es más pesado.

ENCUENTRO PERSONAL

Paulina and her friend Rosita are shopping for school supplies at a store owned by Sr. Arcel, who is from Colombia. He likes to speak Spanish with the students.

SR. ARCEL: Buenas tardes, estudiantes. ¿Qué necesitan Uds. hoy?

PAULINA: Hola, Sr. Arcel. Necesito un cuaderno grande, un paquete *(package)* de papel para mi clase de inglés y un cuaderno para mi clase de historia.

SR. ARCEL: Aquí hay estos cuadernos en verde, amarillo y anaranjado, y tengo aquel papel en paquetes de quinientas hojas en amarillo, azul claro y verde claro. Tengo éste en blanco con líneas.

PAULINA: Me gustarían uno de ésos en blanco, un cuaderno amarillo y uno anaranjado. ¿Cuánto cuestan?

SR. ARCEL: Este paquete de papel sólo cuesta $2.50 (dos dólares, cincuenta centavos) y los cuadernos son $2.15 cada uno. *(Turning to Rosita)* ¿Y qué necesita Ud., señorita?

ROSITA: Yo necesito diez lápices con gomas buenas y un sacapuntas eléctrico. Éstos son para mi clase de matemáticas.

SR. ARCEL: Aquí lo tiene. A ver *(Let me see)*, diez lápices a quince centavos cada uno es $1.50 (un dólar cincuenta) y $9.95 por el sacapuntas eléctrico, es $11.45 en total, menos un descuento *(discount)* de 10% (por ciento) para estudiantes es, a ver,… ¡Ay, necesito mi calculadora!

Y el impuesto *(tax)* de 5 por ciento. A ver, $10.31 por 5 por ciento es $.51, $10.82 en total.

ROSITA: Aquí los tiene, Sr. Arcel.

SR. ARCEL: Y para Ud., señorita, el total es $6.43.

PAULINA: Y aquí está la tarjeta de crédito *(credit card)* de mi madre.

SR. ARCEL: Gracias, señoritas. Hasta luego.

¿Comprendes?

1. ¿Por qué hablan español Rosita y Paulina con el Sr. Arcel?
2. ¿Qué tipo de papel tiene el Sr. Arcel?
3. ¿Qué necesita Paulina? ¿Por qué?
4. ¿Cuánto cuestan los artículos?
5. ¿Qué necesita Rosita? ¿Para qué clase?
6. ¿Cuánto cuesta en total?
7. ¿Cuánto es el descuento para estudiantes?

¡Te toca!

Create your own conversation with Sr. Arcel as you buy school supplies for your classes.

Leemos y contamos

A. A sight-impaired person is visiting Señorita Blanco's classroom and wants to know what it looks like. Raúl has volunteered to describe the classroom in detail. Can you picture it in your mind also?

Primero, hay treinta y cinco pupitres pardos y pequeños en siete filas de cinco sillas. Los pupitres son de metal con mesas y sillas de plástico. Hay un gran escritorio gris de metal para la profesora. La silla de la profesora es de plástico azul. En el escritorio de la profesora hay unos bolígrafos rojos, unos lápices amarillos con gomas, una cartera parda, unos cuadernos y unas tijeras. De un lado hay diez ventanas rectangulares y en la parte de atrás hay unos armarios largos y anchos. En el otro lado hay una puerta alta y un archivador pesado con un globo. En el frente de la clase hay un tablero de anuncios de color crema con decoraciones anaranjadas y una pizarra verde oscuro con dos borradores y cinco tizas blancas. En la pared hay un sacapuntas viejo, unos cuadros y un mapa grande del mundo. Hay una computadora cara en una mesa pequeña. En el suelo hay una papelera redonda y un retroproyector rectangular. Hay un estante estrecho con cientos de libros de español, un diccionario grande y un calendario. En otro estante hay una calculadora solar, una videocasetera y una grabadora con muchos casetes. Y finalmente, hay una bandera roja, blanca y azul y un reloj redondo, blanco y negro.

1. Describe los pupitres en el aula de la señorita Blanco. ¿Cuántos hay y cómo son?
2. Describe las cosas de la profesora.
3. Describe las partes del aula.
4. ¿Qué hay en la pared, en el suelo y en los estantes?
5. ¿Qué más hay?

B. Make a list of the things in your classroom. Make another list of things that you would like to have in your classroom but do not.

¡Así es!

La enseñanza

La enseñanza *(Schooling)* es muy importante en todos los países de habla española pero la verdad es que en muchos países hay niños que van a la escuela por muy poco tiempo. En algunos países, por ejemplo Bolivia y Guatemala, el analfabetismo *(illiteracy)* alcanza *(reaches)* 40 por ciento de la población. En otros países, como México, Argentina, Chile y Costa Rica, alcanza 10 por ciento o menos. ¿Por qué no pueden ni leer ni escribir tantas personas? Una razón es que viven muy lejos de las escuelas. En las ciudades hay escuelas cerca de las casas, pero en las regiones rurales no hay muchas escuelas. Los niños tienen que caminar *(walk)* largas distancias y por eso muchos no asisten *(attend)* regularmente. Otra razón es que la gente es pobre y los niños tienen que trabajar. Para ellos comer es más importante que leer.

Me gusta y no me gusta

In this lesson we'll talk about the animals we like and dislike. Then we'll tell about things we have and tell what we like and do not like about them. Next we will talk about our school and our classes.

Vocabulario

Los animales   *Animals*

Los animales domésticos   *Domestic animals*

1. el burro	*donkey*	8. la oveja	*sheep*
2. el caballo	*horse*	9. el pato	*duck*
3. la cabra	*goat*	10. el pavo	*turkey*
4. el cerdo/puerco	*pig*	11. el perro	*dog*
5. la gallina	*hen*	12. el toro	*bull*
6. el gallo	*rooster*	13. la vaca	*cow*
7. el gato	*cat*		

Los animales salvajes   *Wild animals*

1. la ardilla	*squirrel*		14. el mono	*monkey*
2. el búfalo	*buffalo*		15. el murciélago	*bat*
3. el camello	*camel*		16. el oso	*bear*
4. el canguro	*kangaroo*		17. el pájaro	*bird*
5. la cebra	*zebra*		18. el pez	*fish*
6. el ciervo	*deer*		19. el perico	*parrot*
7. el conejo	*rabbit*		20. el periquito	*parakeet*
8. el elefante	*elephant*		21. la rata	*rat*
9. el gorila	*gorilla*		22. el ratón	*mouse*
10. el hipopótamo	*hippopotamus*		23. el rinoceronte	*rhinoceros*
11. la jirafa	*giraffe*		24. la serpiente	*snake*
12. el león	*lion*		25. el tigre	*tiger*
13. el leopardo	*leopard*		26. el zorro	*fox*

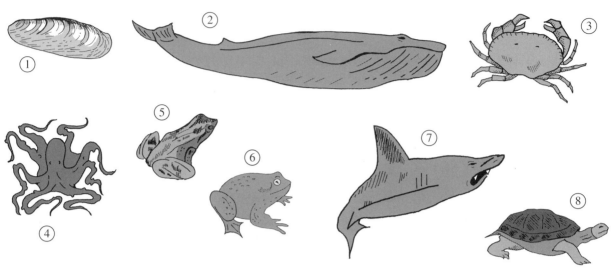

Los animales acuáticos   *Aquatic animals*

1. la almeja   *clam*
2. la ballena   *whale*
3. el cangrejo   *crab*
4. el pulpo   *octopus*
5. la rana   *frog*
6. el sapo   *toad*
7. el tiburón   *shark*
8. la tortuga   *turtle*

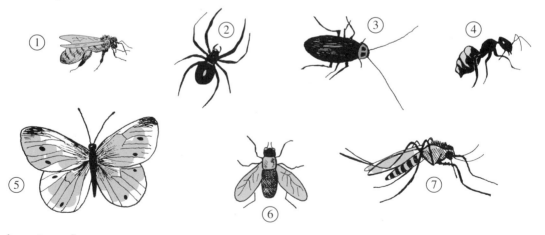

Los insectos   *Insects*

1. la abeja   *bee*
2. la araña   *spider*
3. la cucaracha   *cockroach*
4. la hormiga   *ant*
5. la mariposa   *butterfly*
6. la mosca   *fly*
7. el mosquito   *mosquito*

1 Make a list of animals that live in each of the following places.

   a. en casa con la familia
   b. en la granja *(farm)*
   c. en la selva *(jungle)*
   d. en el bosque *(forest)*
   e. en el agua *(water)*

Vocabulario

Los juguetes   *Toys*

1.	el bate	*baseball bat*	15. el osito de peluche	*teddy bear*
2.	la bicicleta	*bicycle*	16. los patines de rueda	*roller skates*
3.	los bloques	*blocks*	17. los patines de hielo	*ice skates*
4.	el caballo balancín	*rocking horse*	18. la pelota	*ball*
5.	el cajón de arena	*sandbox*	19. el rompecabezas	*puzzle*
6.	las canicas	*marbles*	20. el silbato	*whistle*
7.	la carreta	*wagon*	21. el soldado de juguete	*toy soldier*
8.	la casa de muñecas	*dollhouse*	22. el tambor	*drum*
9.	el columpio	*swing*	23. el títere	*puppet*
10.	la cometa	*kite*	24. el tren eléctrico	*electric train*
11.	el globo	*balloon*	25. el triciclo	*tricycle*
12.	el juego de damas	*checkers*	26. el yoyo	*yo-yo*
13.	el monopatín	*skateboard*	• 27. la pistola de agua	*water gun*
14.	la muñeca	*doll*	• 28. la cuerda	*jump rope*

Otras cosas   *Other things*

1. el coche	*car*	
2. el disco compacto	*CD, compact disc*	
3. el estéreo	*stereo*	
4. el radio	*radio*	
5. el teléfono	*telephone*	
6. el televisor	*television set*	
7. la carta	*letter*	
8. el juego	*game*	

• 9. el anillo	*ring*	
•10. el despertador	*alarm clock*	
•11. la guitarra	*guitar*	
•12. la llave	*key*	
•13. el llavero	*keyring*	
•14. la maleta	*suitcase*	
•15. el periódico	*newspaper*	
•16. el reloj pulsera	*wristwatch*	

Expresiones de cantidad   *Quantity expressions*

nada	*not at all, nothing*
un poco	*a little bit, a few*
bastante	*enough*
• suficiente	*sufficient*
mucho(a)	*a lot, much, many*
muchísimo	*very much*
• tanto(a)	*so much*
• tantos(as)	*so many*
• demasiado	*too much*

Tener   *to have [possession]*

In Lesson 3, we used the verb **tener** to tell about physical and emotional conditions. **Tener** is also used to tell what we possess.

Yo tenía una muñeca.

Yo tengo un estéreo.

Yo tendré una casa.

2 Make a list of things you possess. How many do you have of each thing? Use the vocabulary from this lesson as well as from previous ones.

EJEMPLO: Tengo un estéreo.
Tengo cincuenta discos compactos (más o menos).

3 Make a list of things you used to have as a child.

EJEMPLO: Tenía un tambor.
Tenía un silbato.

4 Using the vocabulary in this lesson, describe some of the things you have. Use describing words from pages 13 and 14.

EJEMPLO: Tengo un perro pequeño.

5 **Chismes**   Tell your partner about the things that people you know have and describe those things.

EJEMPLO: Mis hermanos tienen relojes viejos, demasiados juegos y muchos amigos.

6 Take turns asking your partner if he or she has various things.

EJEMPLO: 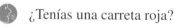 ¿Tienes un anillo?

   No, no tengo un anillo.

7 Take turns asking your partner if he or she used to have different toys.

EJEMPLO:  ¿Tenías una carreta roja?

   Sí, tenía una carreta roja.

8 Ask your partner what things he or she will have in twenty years.

EJEMPLO: En veinte años, ¿tendrás un coche grande?

   No, no tendré un coche grande.

9 **Encuesta**   Ask several people what they expect to have in ten years, twenty years, and fifty years. Make a brief report.

EJEMPLO: 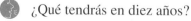 ¿Qué tendrás en diez años?

   Tendré un carro pequeño.

Vocabulario

Las clases   *Classes*

Las artes   ***Arts***
    el arte   *art*
    el drama   *drama, acting*
    la música   *music*
    la orquesta   *orchestra, band*

Las ciencias   ***Sciences***
    la biología   *biology*
    la física   *physics*
    la química   *chemistry*

Las ciencias sociales   ***Social Sciences***
    la geografía   *geography*
    la historia   *history*
    la sicología   *psychology*

El comercio   ***Business***
    la informática/computación   *computer science*
    la clase de tecleo   *keyboarding*
    la taquigrafía   *shorthand*
  • la economía   *economics*

Las lenguas extranjeras   ***Foreign Languages***
    el alemán   *German*
    el chino   *Chinese*
    el español   *Spanish*
    el francés   *French*
    el italiano   *Italian*
    el japonés   *Japanese*
    el latín   *Latin*
    el ruso   *Russian*

Las matemáticas   ***Math***
    el álgebra   *algebra*
  • la aritmética   *arithmetic*
    el cálculo   *calculus*
    la geometría   *geometry*
    la trigonometría   *trigonometry*

Otras materias   ***Other subjects***
    la educación física   *physical education*
  • la mecánica   *mechanics*

Las escuelas y los niveles   *Schools and levels*

la escuela primaria	*elementary school, grade school*
la escuela secundaria	*secondary school, high school*
el colegio	*private high school*
la universidad	*college, university*
el primer año de secundaria	*freshman*
segundo año	*sophomore*
tercer año	*junior*
cuarto año	*senior*
el primer año de primaria	*first grade*

10 Ask your partner which classes he or she has this year or had in other years.

EJEMPLO: ¿Tienes clase de historia?

Sí, tengo clase de historia.

¿Qué clases tenías en la escuela primaria?

Tenía clase de música.

COLEGIO KENNEDY		
Horario		
Año escolar: 20??– 20?? **Semestre:** Primero		
Nombre: Rodríguez, Paulina **Año:** segundo **Consejero(a):** Wojacowski		
Padres: Oscar y Dorotea Rodríguez **Teléfono:** (123) 543–7890		
HORA	CLASE	PROFESOR
1. 7:30 – 8:15	biología	Bugg
2. 8:20 – 9:05	geometría	Fletcher
3. 9:10 – 9:55	español	Blanco
4. 10:00 – 10:45	historia de los EE. UU.	Collins
5. 10:50 – 11:35	arte - escultura	Gilbert
6. 11:35 – 12:15	almuerzo	
7. 12:15 – 1:30	inglés	Rubin
8. 1:35 – 2:15	informática	Veiling

USING ADJECTIVES WITHOUT A NOUN—Part I

When referring to something that has already been mentioned in a previous sentence without repeating the noun, use the appropriate definite article (**el/la/los/las**) or indefinite article (**un/una/unos/unas**) with the adjective. The article and adjective agree in number and gender with the noun they refer to.

EL/LA/LOS/LAS
UNO/UNA/UNOS/UNAS   + *adjective = the, a/an, some + adjective + one(s)*

Tenía un cuaderno rojo y <u>uno azul</u>.   *I had a red notebook and <u>a blue one</u>.*
<u>El rojo</u> era para mi clase de matemáticas.   *<u>The red one</u> was for math class.*

11 Tell about and compare some of your possessions.

EJEMPLO: Tengo dos maletas, una grande y una pequeña. La grande era más cara que la pequeña.

USING ADJECTIVES WITHOUT A NOUN—Part II

When you want to use an adjective to describe something indefinite or vague, use **lo** instead of the article with the masculine form of the adjective.

LO + *adjective [masculine form]* = *the + adjective + thing/part*

Lo importante es estudiar.   *The important thing is studying.*
Lo difícil era la tarea.   *The hard part was the homework.*

Lo mejor de la fiesta son los amigos.   Lo peor es limpiar la casa.

12 Complete the following sentences as they refer to Spanish class or to one of your other classes.

    a. Lo bueno de la clase de español es [*noun/infinitive . . .*].
    b. Lo malo es…
    c. Lo mejor es…
    d. Lo peor es…
    e. Lo fácil es…
    f. Lo difícil es…
    g. Lo interesante es…
    h. Lo aburrido es…
    i. Lo importante es…
    j. Lo imposible es…

13 Using the same sentence beginnings as in Activity 12, complete them as they refer to vacations and other situations, such as going to parties, finding a job, shopping for clothes, etc.

    a. Lo bueno de las vacaciones es…

Buenas Notícias

más importante

■ Lo más probable es que usted va a vivir más. Aunque haya fumado por años, déjelo ahora y podrá agregar años a su vida. Mejores años.

■ Usted tendrá más dinero. Si deja de fumar, lo más probable es que no estará enfermo tan a menudo. ¿Qué puede perder?

Déjelo ahora
y vea como ganar

DIRECT OBJECT PRONOUNS

The direct object receives the action of the verb. In English the direct object pronouns follow the verb, but in Spanish they come before the verb when it has the person–time endings. Here are the direct object pronouns to say *it* or *them*.

IT	THEM
lo	los
la	las

¿Dónde están mis libros?

Yo los tengo.

Tengo <u>el libro</u>.   <u>Lo</u> tengo.   *I have it.*
Tengo <u>la chaqueta</u>.   <u>La</u> tengo.   *I have it.*
Tengo <u>los cuadernos</u>.   <u>Los</u> tengo.   *I have them.*
Tengo <u>las flores</u>.   <u>Las</u> tengo.   *I have them.*

Did you notice the similarity between the definite article *the* and the direct object pronouns?

Nouns that use **la** are replaced with the pronoun **la**.
Nouns that use **los** are replaced with the pronoun **los**.
Nouns that use **las** are replaced with the pronoun **las**.
But nouns that use **el** are replaced with the pronoun **lo**.

Note: When replacing part or all of a sentence, use **lo**.

Ejemplo: Juan:—Elvira tiene un perro grande.   *Elvira has a big dog.*
          José:—No lo creo.   *I don't believe it.* [**lo** = Elvira tiene un perro grande.]

POSITION OF OBJECT PRONOUNS

The object pronouns are placed before the verb when the verb has a person–time ending.

When the verb with a person–time ending is followed by an infinitive form of the verb (**-ar, -er, -ir**), the object pronouns can be attached to the end of the infinitive form.

Esqueletos

(pro)noun + object pronoun + verb

Yo lo tengo.   *I have it.*
Juan los tiene.   *Juan has them.*

(pro)noun + verb + infinitive + object pronoun

Ellos van a escribir<u>la</u>.   *They are going to write it.*
María puede hacer<u>lo</u>.   *María can do it.*

OR

(pro)noun + object pronoun + verb + infinitive

Ellos <u>la</u> van a escribir.   *They are going to write it.*
María <u>lo</u> puede hacer.   *María can do it.*

14 Tell some things that you have and then tell if you have them at home **(en casa)** or if you have them with you **(conmigo)**.

EJEMPLO: Tengo una cartera. La tengo conmigo.
*(Why do you use **La** to replace cartera? Because **cartera** is feminine.)*

15 Ask your partner if he or she has different classroom objects. Then find out if he or she has them here in school **(aquí en la escuela)** or at home **(en casa)**.

EJEMPLO: ¿Tienes un sacapuntas?

Sí, tengo un sacapuntas.

¿Lo tienes aquí en la escuela o en casa?

Lo tengo aquí.
*(Why is **sacapuntas** replaced by **lo**? Because **sacapuntas** is masculine.)*

16 **Encuesta**   Make a list of three toys. Find out if several different people had these toys when they were children. Find out if they still have them.

EJEMPLO:

De niño(a), ¿tenías un bate?

Sí, yo tenía un bate.

¿Lo tienes todavía?

Sí, lo tengo todavía.

INDIRECT OBJECT PRONOUNS

The indirect object tells *to* or *for whom* something is done.

me = *to/for me*
te = *to/for you*
le = *to/for you/him/her/it*
nos = *to/for us*
os = *to/for all of you [for a group of friends in Spain]*
les = *to/for all of you/them*

direct object

subject   indirect object

Mi amiga <u>me</u> dio un libro.   *My friend gave a book <u>to me</u>.*
Miguel <u>nos</u> habla en español.   *Miguel talks to us <u>in Spanish</u>.*
Arturo <u>te</u> compró un regalo.   *Arturo bought a book <u>for you</u>.*

Elvira le da el libro
al muchacho.

A + *the person* can be used with the indirect object pronoun in order to clarify or emphasize to whom it refers. It can go at the beginning or end of the sentence.

a mí	+ me	a nosotros(as)	+ nos
a ti	+ te	a vosotros(as)	+ os
a Ud.		a Uds.	
a él	} + le	a ellos	} + les
a ella		a ellas	

Susana le dio un regalo a él.   *Susana gave a gift to him.*
Eva le dio las flores a ella.   *Eva gave the flowers to her.*

If the sentence has an indirect object noun, the indirect object pronoun **le** or **les** must be added also.

A los niños les leí un cuento.   *I read a story to the children.*
Le enseñaron la canción a Timoteo.   *They taught the song to Timoteo.*

Indirect object pronouns, like direct object pronouns, come before a verb with the person–time ending or can be attached to an infinitive.

Esqueletos

| (A + *person*) + | ME/TE/LE NOS/OS/LES | + *verb* + (*infinitive*) + *noun(s)* |

Le van a dar un regalo.   *They are going to give him a gift.*

| (A + *person*) + *verb* + *infinitive* + | ME/TE/LE NOS/OS/LES | + *noun(s)* |

Van a darle un regalo.   *They are going to give him a gift.*

17 Make a list of things that people have given to you lately. Tell who gave it to you.

EJEMPLO: Mi amiga me dio un suéter.
Mi hermana me dio una barra de chocolate.

18 Make a list of things that your family has received. Tell who gave them to you *[plural]*.

EJEMPLO: Mis primos nos dieron una invitación a una fiesta.
Mis tíos nos dieron un regalo.

19 *Sit-Con*   You are baby-sitting and the child won't stop crying. Try to bribe him into being quiet. Tell him what you will give him if he stops crying.

EJEMPLO: Te daré un dulce.
Te daré un osito.

20 Make a list of things you will give your friends and family for their birthdays. Tell to whom you will give them.

EJEMPLO: A Jorge le daré una camisa roja.
Le daré una muñeca de China a Amelia.

GUSTAR *to be pleasing, to like*

When we talk about what things or activities we like in Spanish, we tell what pleases us.

Notice that like **doler** on page 82, **gustar** is used in the *it* or *they* forms with an indirect object pronoun. **Gustar** is generally used in the singular form with singular nouns and infinitives and in the plural form with plural nouns. Notice that the subject is usually at the end of the sentence.

Me gusta mi clase de arte.   *I like my art class.*
Me gusta cantar y bailar.   *I like to sing and dance.*
Me gustan tus juguetes.   *I like your toys.*

Use **el/la/los/las** when talking about something in a general sense.

Me gusta el chocolate.   *I like chocolate.*
Me gustan los animales.   *I like animals.*

Here are the forms of **gustar**.

IMPERFECT	PRETERITE	PRESENT	FUTURE	CONDITIONAL*
used to please	*pleased*	*please(s)*	*will please*	*would please*
used to like	*liked*	*like(s)*	*will like*	*would like*
gustaba	gustó	gusta	gustará	gustaría
gustaban	gustaron	gustan	gustarán	gustarían

*Note: The conditional is a tense you will be learning in Unit III. It means *would* and is often used with **gustar** to make a request for something more polite.

Me gustaría una hamburguesa, por favor.   *I would like a hamburger, please.*

"Me gusta jugar cartas,
correr bicicleta, quiero ser pediatra,
me graduo de 6to. grado
(Escuela Carmen Barroso Morales),
tengo Distrofia Muscular,
mi color favorito es el azul claro
y mi comida favorita es
el arroz con corned beef."

I v e t t e   B á e z

ASOCIACION CONTRA LA DISTROFIA MUSCULAR MDA
La Herramienta para su Calidad de Vida.

Esqueleto

 (A + *person*) + **ME/TE/LE NOS/OS/LES** + **GUSTAR** + (*noun/infinitive*)

Me gusta la escuela.   *I like school.*
A Juan le gustan los perros.   *Juan likes dogs.*
Nos gusta visitar a los amigos.   *We like to visit friends.*

21 Write a report telling about your classes. Which classes do you have this year? Do you like them? Why or why not?

EJEMPLO: Tengo una clase de español. Me gusta mucho porque me gusta hablar español.
Tengo una clase de química. No me gusta nada porque no me gusta hacer experimentos.

22 **Encuesta**   Find out from several classmates which animals they like most and least, and why. Write a report summarizing what you found out.

EJEMPLO: ¿Qué animal te gusta mas?

Me gustan más los gatos.

¿Por qué?

Porque son muy inteligentes.

¿Qué animal te gusta menos?

No me gustan los leopardos porque me dan miedo.

23 As a child, which toys did you like most? Which toys did your classmates like most? Compare your preferences with those of your classmates.

EJEMPLO: De niño(a), ¿qué juguete te gustaba más y por qué?

Me gustaban las pelotas porque hay muchos juegos con pelotas.

24 Make a list of things you would like to have when you are thirty years old.

EJEMPLO: Me gustaría tener un carro deportivo y una casa en las montañas.

ENCUENTRO PERSONAL

I. Paulina and her friends are discussing their classes. Are your classes anything like theirs?

PAULINA: No me gusta mi clase de matemáticas este año. Tengo un profesor que nos da mucha tarea.

RAÚL: Sí, Paulina, y lo difícil es hacer los cálculos. Me gustaría tener una calculadora buena para hacerlas.

ROSITA: Raúl, tengo una muy buena. Y la tengo aquí. ¿Te gustaría usarla?

PAULINA: Rosita, ¿le das tu calculadora a él? ¿No la necesitas tú?

ROSITA: No, mi profesora nos da mucha tarea, pero siempre la hago con Inés. Lo importante es tener amigos generosos.

RAÚL: Y tú lo eres, Rosita. Te daré la calculadora mañana.

ROSITA: Está bien, Raúl, no la necesito ahora. Adiós.

TODOS: Hasta mañana.

¿Comprendes?

1. ¿Qué no le gusta a Paulina este año? ¿Por qué no le gusta?
2. ¿Qué es lo difícil para Raúl?
3. ¿A Raúl, qué le gustaría tener?
4. ¿Qué le da Rosita a él? ¿Por qué no la necesita ella?
5. ¿Cuándo le dará Raúl la calculadora a ella?

ENCUENTRO PERSONAL

II. Paulina, Santiago, and Inés are discussing the animals that they like best at the zoo. Do you share any of their likes and dislikes?

PAULINA: Me gusta visitar el parque zoológico porque hay muchos animales interesantes. Mis favoritos son los elefantes. Son tan grandes y grises—¡y también son inteligentes!

SANTIAGO: Lo interesante para mí son los tigres. Son muy fuertes y bonitos. Y me gustan mucho los monos porque son tan (*so*) chistosos. Siempre corren (*run*) y juegan. Y a ti, Inés, ¿cuáles te gustan?

INÉS: Yo prefiero los animales domésticos como los perros y los gatos, las tortugas y los peces.

SANTIAGO: Ah, entonces, ¿te gustan los ratones y las arañas, y también los mosquitos, las moscas y las cucarachas? Puedo llevarte a la cafetería para verlos.

PAULINA: ¡Ay, Santiago! Generalmente me gusta comer en la cafetería del parque zoológico, pero hoy no puedo. Sólo pienso en los insectos y no tengo ganas de comer con ellos.

SANTIAGO: Lo siento, Paulina, sólo estaba bromeando (*joking*).

¿Comprendes?

1. ¿Por qué le gusta a Paulina visitar el parque zoológico?
2. ¿Qué es lo interesante para Santiago? ¿Por qué?
3. ¿Qué animales le gustan a Inés?
4. ¿Qué animales e insectos menciona Santiago?
5. ¿Por qué no desea Paulina comer en la cafetería del parque zoológico hoy?

¡Te toca!

Talk to other students in your class about what animals you like or do not like and why.

Conociendo...

el zoológico y sus alrededores

ciudad de MEXICO

ZOOLOGICO Y LAGO DE CHAPULTEPEC: (2)

El parque Zoológico tiene antecedentes autóctonos; ya el emperador Moctezuma contaba con "casas de recreación" dentro de la ciudad en donde había todo género de aves, desde el águila hasta el más pequeño pajarillo; Hernán Cortés en sus Cartas de Relación menciona además de los asombrosos acuarios y aviarios del reino de Iztapalapa, 'gran casa de las fieras' un museo zoológico en la gran Tenochtitlán que fundado a mediados del siglo XVI por Moctezuma II se convirtió en el primer zoológico de América. El emperador Netzahualcoyotl también poseía grandes zoológicos en su reino de Texcoco.

En nuestros días el zoológico exhibe un gran número de animales de muy variadas especies, muchos traídos de lejanos lugares y algunos que se han reproducido en cautiverio, como el pequeño Oso Panda.

Aquí el visitante podrá además encontrar otras diversiones como el ferrocarril escénico, alquiler de caballos o paseos por el viejo lago de Chapultepec en una de sus tradicionales lanchas de remos.

Ubicación: Terrenos adyacentes al jardín de la Casa del Lago.
Días de visita: Martes a Sábado
Horario: 9:00 a 19:00 Hrs.
            Domingo de 10:00 a 17:00 Hrs.
Entrada: Libre
Servicios: Sanitarios

Leemos y contamos

A. Here is part of a letter from Marisol, our pen pal in Mexico.

Hola, amigos,

    El otro día vi a unas niñas que jugaban con una muñeca de trapo (rag) y recordé mi muñeca favorita cuando yo era niña. Me gustaría tener ahora esa muñeca de trapo que me dio mi abuelita cuando yo tenía cuatro años. La muñeca era pequeña y tenía botones (buttons) *negros para los ojos y una boca en forma de un corazón. Siempre jugaba con mi muñeca. Cuando se puso* (became) *muy vieja y sucia, quería una nueva. Mi madre me compró una de plástico con pelo rubio y ojos que cerraban* (closed). *Me gustaba la nueva y no jugaba más con la vieja. Ya no tengo las muñecas. No sé dónde están, pero ahora pienso mucho en la vieja porque mi abuela la hizo* (made). *No era bonita, pero lo importante es que la hizo mi abuela. Algún día, le daré una muñeca de trapo a mi hija porque la querré* (I will love her) *mucho.*

1. ¿Qué juguete tenía Marisol de niña?
2. ¿Por qué quería una nueva?
3. ¿Cuál le gustaría tener ahora? ¿Por qué?
4. ¿Qué le dará ella a su hija algún día?
5. ¿Tenías o tienes tú un juguete que te dio tu abuela o abuelo? ¿Te gusta o no? ¿Estás de acuerdo *(Do you agree)* que lo importante de un regalo es el amor con que lo da una persona?

B. Write at least ten sentences telling about your favorite toys that you had when you were a child. Describe them and tell who gave them to you.

C. Your friend wants to buy a pet animal. Make some suggestions and compare the advantages and disadvantages of each. (Use some **lo + *adjective* + es…** sentences.)

¡Así es!

Los animales

Claro que hay muchos animales comunes en los países de habla española—perros, gatos, caballos y vacas, por ejemplo: jaguares, pumas, ocelotes, monos, perezosos *(sloths)*, guanacos, tapires, armadillos y murciélagos vampiros existen en muchos países hispanos. También hay pericos y araraunas *(macaws)* y otros pájaros exóticos. Hay serpientes venenosas *(poisonous)* y constrictoras *(constricting)*, caimanes *(caymans)*, lagartos *(lizards)* y tortugas. La anaconda, una de las serpientes más grandes del mundo, es de las regiones Amazonas. Hay llamas, alpacas y vicuñas en las montañas de Bolivia y Perú. Muchos pájaros llegan a los Estados Unidos en el verano y regresan a la América del Sur durante nuestro invierno.

A unos 600 millas al oeste de Ecuador se hallan *(are found)* las Islas Galápagos. En estas islas viven animales muy distintos de los de otras partes del mundo. En 1835, el famoso Charles Darwin visitó las Islas Galápagos y allí formuló su teoría de la evolución.

Unidad II

⇒Unidad II⇐
Tools

Vocabulario

La casa y el apartamento *The house and the apartment*
(Lección 1)

el cuarto	*room*	el comedor	*dining room*
el desván/•la azotea	*attic*	la cocina	*kitchen*
el primer piso	*second floor, one floor up*	• el ascensor	*elevator*
la planta baja	*ground floor*	la sala	*living room*
el sótano	*basement*	la sala de estar	*family room, den*
la alcoba	*bedroom*	• la lavandería	*laundry room*
el cuarto de baño	*bathroom*	• el garaje	*garage*
el pasillo	*hallway*	• el jardín	*garden, yard*
la escalera	*stairs*	el patio	*inner courtyard, yard*
• el balcón	*balcony*		

Preposiciones de ubicación *Prepositions of location*
(Lección 1)

a	*to, at*	alrededor de	*around, surrounding*
de	*of, from, about*	delante de	*in front of*
encima de	*on top of, above*	detrás de	*behind*
en	*in, on, at*	al lado de	*next to, beside*
con	*with*	• en el medio de	*in the middle of*
sin	*without*	al otro lado de	*on the other side of*
fuera de	*outside of*	cerca de	*near*
dentro de	*inside of*	lejos de	*far from*
sobre	*over, on*	• junto a	*next to*
debajo de	*under*	• enfrente de	*opposite*
a la derecha de	*to the right of*	• a través de	*across*
a la izquierda de	*to the left of*	• por aquí	*over here*
entre	*between, among*		

Lugares en la ciudad *Places in the city*
(Lección 1)

el edificio	building	el templo	temple
la casa	house	la librería	bookstore
la tienda	store	la florería	flower shop
el rascacielos	skyscraper	la papelería	stationery store
el correo	post office	la pastelería	pastry shop
el banco	bank	la zapatería	shoe store
el parque	park	la ropería	clothing store
la playa	beach	la lechería	dairy
la escuela	school	la heladería	ice cream parlor
la biblioteca	library	la panadería	bakery
el museo	museum	la carnicería	butcher shop
el hotel	hotel	la joyería	jewelry store
la estación de gasolina	gas station	la relojería	clock store
el teatro	theater	la dulcería	candy store
el restaurante	restaurant	la juguetería	toy store
el cine	movie theater	• la fábrica	factory
el supermercado	supermarket	• la oficina	office
el almacén	department store	• la cárcel	jail
el consultorio	office	• el monumento	monument
...del dentista	dentist's ...	• la plaza	town square
...del médico	doctor's ...	• el centro comercial	mall
la farmacia	pharmacy	• la peluquería	beauty shop
el hospital	hospital	• la tintorería	dry cleaners
la iglesia	church	• la pescadería	fish store
la sinagoga	synagogue	• la pizzería	pizzeria
la mezquita	mosque	• el aeropuerto	airport

La geografía *Geography*
(Lección 1)

el país	country	• la colina	hill
la capital	capital	el río	river
el estado	state	el lago	lake
la ciudad	city	la costa	coast
el centro	center, downtown	la isla	island
el pueblo	town	el océano	ocean
las afueras	suburbs	el mar	sea
el campo	countryside	el norte	north
el habitante	inhabitant	el sur	south
la frontera	border	el este	east
la montaña	mountain	el oeste	west
• la sierra	mountain range	• el mundo	world
la selva	forest, jungle	• el hemisferio	hemisphere
los llanos	plains	• el ecuador	equator
el desierto	desert	• el continente	continent
• el valle	valley		

Las estaciones *Seasons*
(Lección 1)

el invierno	*winter*
la primavera	*spring*
el verano	*summer*
el otoño	*fall, autumn*

El tiempo *Weather*
(Lección 1)

¿Qué tiempo hace?	*What's the weather like?*
Hace buen tiempo.	*It's nice weather.*
Hace mal tiempo.	*It's bad weather.*
Hace sol.	*It's sunny.*
Hace mucho sol.	*It's very sunny.*
Hace (mucho) viento.	*It's (very) windy.*
Hace (mucho) frío.	*It's (very) cold.*
Hace (mucho) calor.	*It's (very) warm/hot.*
Hace fresco.	*It's cool.*
Nieva.	*It's snowing, It snows.*
Llueve.	*It's raining, It rains.*
Está (muy) húmedo.	*It's (very) humid.*
Está (muy) nublado.	*It's (very) cloudy.*
Está claro.	*It's clear.*
• Hay un arco iris.	*There is a rainbow.*

Otras preposiciones *Other prepositions*
(Lección 1)

antes de	*before*	desde	*from, since*
después de	*after*	hasta	*until*
por	*for, by, through*	• contra	*against*
para	*for, by, in order to*	• al + *infinitive*	*while, on, upon*
en vez de	*instead of*		

Los medios de transporte *Means of transportation*
(Lección 1)

en coche/auto/carro	*by car*	por tren	*by train*
por avión	*by plane*	en bicicleta	*by bike*
en taxi	*by taxi*	por moto(cicleta)	*by motorcycle*
por barco	*by boat*	a pie	*on foot*
en autobús	*by bus*		

La ropa *Clothing, clothes*
(Lección 2)

el abrigo	*coat*	• el suéter de cuello en V	*V-neck sweater*
el impermeable	*raincoat*	• el suéter de cuello redondo	*round-neck sweater*
la chaqueta	*jacket*	el traje de baño	*swimsuit*
el sombrero	*hat*	el vestido	*dress*
el gorro	*cap, knit hat*	• el chaleco	*vest*
el traje	*suit*	la blusa	*blouse*
el saco	*sport coat*	la falda	*skirt*
la camisa de manga larga	*long-sleeved shirt*	los pantalones	*pants*
de manga corta	*short-sleeved shirt*	los pantalones cortos	*shorts*
deportiva	*sport shirt*	los pantalones vaqueros	*jeans*
la camiseta	*T-shirt*	• el pantalón de sudadera	*sweatpants*
• de cuello alto	*turtle neck*	• la sudadera	*sweatshirt*
• sin mangas	*tank top*		

La ropa interior *Underwear*

• la bata	*robe*	• los calzoncillos	*undershorts*
la pijama	*pajamas*	la camiseta	*undershirt*
las medias	*stockings*	• el camisón	*nightgown*
• la pantimedia	*pantyhose*	las zapatillas	*slippers*
• la combinación	*slip*	los calcetines	*socks*

Los zapatos *Shoes*

• los mocasines	*moccasins, loafers*
los tacones altos	*high-heeled shoes*
los zapatos tenis	*tennis shoes*
las sandalias	*sandals*
las botas	*boots*

Los artículos personales *Personal articles*

los lentes/•los anteojos	*eyeglasses*	la corbata	*tie*
los lentes de contacto	*contact lenses*	• la cinta	*ribbon*
el cinturón	*belt*	el paraguas	*umbrella*
la bolsa	*purse*	la mochila	*backpack, knapsack*
• la cartera	*wallet*	• los mitones	*mittens*
• el portabilletes	*money clip*	• el llavero	*keyring*
• el pañuelo	*handkerchief*	• la bufanda	*scarf*
• los guantes	*gloves*	• las gafas de sol	*sunglasses*
• el bolsillo	*pocket*	• el botón	*button*

Las joyas *Jewelry*
(Lección 2)

el reloj (de) pulsera	*wristwatch*	• la cadena	*chain*
• el brazalete	*bracelet*	• el anillo	*ring*
• el pasador	*barrette*	• el pendiente	*earring*
• el collar	*necklace*	• el gemelo	*cufflink*
• las perlas	*pearls*	• el pisacorbatas	*tie bar*
• el broche	*pin*	• el alfiler de corbata	*tie tack*

•Los diseños   *Patterns*
(Lección 2)

• a cuadros	*checkered*	• cachemira	*paisley*
• sólido(a)	*solid*	• escocés(esa)	*plaid*
• estampado(a)	*print*	• a rayas	*striped*
• estampado(a) de flores	*flowered*	• de bolitas	*polka dot*
• bordado(a)	*embroidered*		

•Las telas   *Fabrics*
(Lección 2)

• lana	*wool*	• seda	*silk*
• algodón	*cotton*	• cuero	*leather*
• nilón	*nylon*	• poliéster	*polyester*
• alpaca	*alpaca*	• lino	*linen*
• casimir	*cashmere*	• fieltro	*felt*
• franela	*flannel*	• piel	*fur*
• encaje	*lace*	• charol	*patent leather*
• raso	*satin*	• gamuza	*suede*
• tafetán	*taffeta*	• terciopelo	*velvet*
• pana	*corduroy*	• dril	*denim*
• tejido	*knit*		

Lo que hacemos con la ropa   *What we do with clothing*
(Lección 2)

llevar	*to wear, to carry*	• limpiar en seco	*to dry clean*
comprar	*to buy*	• admirar	*to admire*
mirar	*to look at*	• ensuciar	*to soil*
dar de regalo	*to give as a gift*	• desgarrar	*to rip, to tear*
• lavar a mano	*to hand wash*	• reparar	*to repair*
• a máquina	*to machine wash*	coser	*to sew*

Las comidas   *Meals*
(Lección 3)

el desayuno	*breakfast*
el almuerzo	*lunch*
la comida	*dinner, midday main meal*
la cena	*supper, evening meal, dinner*
la merienda	*snack*
el entremés	*appetizer*
el plato principal	*main dish*
el postre	*dessert*
la bebida	*beverage*

Las legumbres   *Vegetables*
(Lección 3)

el ajo	*garlic*	los frijoles	*beans*
la cebolla	*onion*	los guisantes	*peas*
la ensalada	*salad*	las judías	*string beans*
la lechuga	*lettuce*	la remolacha	*beet*
el apio	*celery*	la papa	*potato*
el pepino	*cucumber*	las papas fritas	*French fries*
el rábano	*radish*	la batata	*sweet potato*
el tomate	*tomato*	• el brócoli	*broccoli*
la zanahoria	*carrot*	• la col	*cabbage*
la coliflor	*cauliflower*	• las espinacas	*spinach*
el maíz	*corn*	• el nabo	*turnip*
el pimiento	*pepper*	• la mazorca	*corn on the cob*

La carne   *Meat*
(Lección 3)

la carne de res	*beef*	el tocino	*bacon*
la ternera	*veal*	la salchicha	*sausage*
el rosbif	*roast beef*	el perro caliente	*hot dog*
la carne molida	*ground meat*	el pavo	*turkey*
la hamburguesa	*hamburger*	el pollo	*chicken*
la carne de cordero	*lamb*	• la albóndiga	*meatball*
la chuleta de…	*. . . chop*	• el bistec	*steak*
la carne de cerdo	*pork*	• el guisado	*stew*
el jamón	*ham*	• el filete	*filet*

Los mariscos y el pescado   *Shellfish and fish*
(Lección 3)

la langosta	*lobster*	el pescado	*fish*
los camarones	*shrimp*	• el atún	*tuna*
las almejas	*clams*	• el salmón	*salmon*
las ostras	*oysters*		

Los productos lácteos   *Dairy products*
(Lección 3)

el huevo	*egg*	la crema	*cream*
el queso	*cheese*	el yogur	*yogurt*
la leche	*milk*	• la margarina	*margarine*
la mantequilla	*butter*		

Las frutas   *Fruits*
(Lección 3)

los arándanos	*blueberries*	la sandía	*watermelon*
las cerezas	*cherries*	la toronja	*grapefruit*
las frambuesas	*raspberries*	las uvas	*grapes*
las fresas	*strawberries*	• el aguacate	*avocado*
el limón	*lemon*	• el durazno	*peach*
la manzana	*apple*	• el mango	*mango*
la naranja	*orange*	• el melón	*melon*
la pera	*pear*	• la papaya	*papaya*
la piña	*pineapple*	• la pasa	*raisin*
el plátano	*banana*		

El pan y las pastas   *Bread and pastas*
(Lección 3)

el pan tostado	*toast*	• el barquillo	*waffle*
el panecillo	*roll*	la galleta	*cracker*
• la rebanada	*slice*	• los espaguetis	*spaghetti*
• la tortilla	*Mexican flat bread*	• los macarrones	*macaroni*
• el panqueque	*pancake*	• los tallarines	*noodles*

Los cereales   *Cereals*
(Lección 3)

el arroz	*rice*
la avena	*oats*
el trigo	*wheat*
• la cebada	*barley*
• el maíz	*corn*

El postre y los bocaditos   *Dessert and snacks*
(Lección 3)

el flan	*custard*	• la gelatina	*gelatin dessert*
el helado...	*. . . ice cream*	los dulces	*candy*
de vainilla	*vanilla*	la tableta de chocolate	*chocolate bar*
de chocolate	*chocolate*	el cacahuete/•el maní	*peanut*
de fresas	*strawberry*	la nuez	*nut*
la torta	*cake*	las palomitas de maíz	*popcorn*
el pastel	*pastry, pie*	las papitas fritas	*potato chips*
la rosquilla	*doughnut*	• el chicle	*gum*
la galletita dulce	*cookie*		

Las bebidas *Beverages*
(Lección 3)

el agua *(f.)*	*water*	la leche	*milk*
el café	*coffee*	el refresco/la soda	*soft drink*
con crema	*with cream*	el jugo de…	*. . . juice*
sin azúcar	*without sugar*	• el chocolate	*hot chocolate*
el té	*tea*		

Los condimentos y otras comidas *Seasonings and other foods*
(Lección 3)

la sal	*salt*	• la crema de maní	*peanut butter*
la pimienta	*pepper*	la jalea de…	*. . . jelly*
la salsa picante	*hot sauce*	el sándwich de…	*. . . sandwich*
• el catsup	*ketchup*	la sopa de…	*. . . soup*
• la mostaza	*mustard*	la pizza	*pizza*
• la mayonesa	*mayonnaise*		
• la miel	*honey*		

La preparación de la comida *Preparation of food*
(Lección 3)

• al vapor	*steamed*	• encurtido(a)	*pickled*
• asado(a)	*broiled*	• frito(a)	*fried*
• cocido(a)	*cooked*	• horneado(a)	*baked, roasted*
• congelado(a)	*frozen*	• hervido(a)	*boiled*
• crudo(a)	*raw*	• quemado(a)	*burned*
• la masa	*dough*		

Lo que hacemos con la comida *What we do with food*
(Lección 3)

desayunar	*to eat/have breakfast*	cocinar	*to cook*
almorzar (ue)	*to eat/have lunch*	• freír (i, i)	*to fry*
cenar	*to eat/have dinner*	• asar	*to broil*
• merendar (ie)	*to snack*	• ahumar	*to smoke*
vender	*to sell*	• hervir (ie, i)	*to boil*
• escoger	*to choose*	• hornear	*to bake*
comprar	*to buy*	• quemar	*to burn*
pagar por	*to pay for*	• congelar	*to freeze*
preparar	*to prepare*	comer	*to eat*
• cortar	*to cut*	beber	*to drink*
• mezclar	*to mix*	tomar	*to drink, to take*
añadir	*to add*	• gozar de	*to enjoy*

Lo que necesitamos para poner la mesa   *What we need to set the table*
(Lección 3)

• el mantel	*tablecloth*	• la cucharita	*teaspoon*
• la servilleta	*napkin*	• el tenedor	*fork*
• el centro de mesa	*centerpiece*	• el cuchillo	*knife*
• el candelero	*candlestick*	• el salero	*salt shaker*
• el cubierto	*place setting*	• el pimentero	*pepper shaker*
el plato	*plate, dish*	• la jarra	*pitcher*
• el platillo	*saucer*	• la ensaladera	*salad bowl*
• la cuenca	*bowl*	• la cremera	*creamer*
• la taza	*cup*	• la azucarera	*sugar bowl*
• el vaso	*glass*	• la cafetera	*coffeepot*
• la copa	*goblet*	• la tetera	*teapot*
• la cuchara	*spoon*		

Los verbos como «gustar»   *Verbs like* gustar
(Lección 3)

gustar	*to be pleasing, to like*	faltar	*to need, to be lacking*
quedar	*to have left*	doler (ue)	*to hurt*
• disgustar	*to annoy, to displease*	• importar	*to matter*
• encantar	*to love, to adore*	• interesar	*to interest*
• fascinar	*to fascinate*	• molestar	*to bother*

¿Dónde vives?   *Where do you live?*
(Lección 4)

¿Cuál es tu dirección?	*What is your address?*
la dirección	*address*
el número	*number*
la calle	*street*
el paseo	*drive*
el camino	*road*
la avenida	*avenue*
la ciudad	*city*
las afueras	*suburbs*
el campo	*country*
el centro	*downtown*
el barrio	*neighborhood*
la granja	*farm*
la casa	*house*
el apartamento	*apartment*
el condominio	*condominium*
de un piso	*one story*
de dos pisos	*two stories*

Dando direcciones   *Giving directions*
(Lección 4)

Ve (tú)/Vaya (Ud.)…	*Go . . .*
Toma (tú)/Tome (Ud)…	*Take . . .*
la calle	*street*
• la carretera	*highway, expressway*
• la autopista	*expressway, turnpike*
• la salida	*expressway/exit*
Sigue (tú)/Siga (Ud.)…	*Continue, Follow . . .*
hasta llegar a	*until you get to*
• todo derecho	*straight ahead*
al norte	*to the north*
sur	*south*
este	*east*
oeste	*west*
noreste	*northeast*
suroeste	*southwest*
• Dobla (tú)/Doble (Ud.)…	*Turn . . .*
a la derecha	*to the right*
a la izquierda	*to the left*
• en el semáforo	*at the traffic light*
Está a dos cuadras de	*It's two blocks from*
a dos millas de	*two miles from*
en la esquina de	*on/at the corner of*
enfrente de	*in front of, across from*
cerca de	*near*
lejos de	*far from*
al lado de	*at the side of, next to*

Verbos para dar las direcciones   *Verbs for giving directions*
(Lección 4)

vivir	*to live*
ir a casa	*to go home*
dar instrucciones	*to give instructions*
escribir direcciones	*to write addresses*
seguir (i, i) adelante	*to continue ahead*
seguir (i, i) las instrucciones	*to follow the instructions*
• describir la casa	*to describe the house*
subir a	*to go up, to get on*
bajar	*to go down, to get off*
salir de	*to leave, to go out of*
ver	*to see*
oír	*to hear*

Los números ordinales   *Ordinal numbers*
(Lección 4)

primero(a)	*first*	sexto(a)	*sixth*
segundo(a)	*second*	séptimo(a)	*seventh*
tercero(a)	*third*	octavo(a)	*eighth*
cuarto(a)	*fourth*	noveno(a)	*ninth*
quinto(a)	*fifth*	décimo(a)	*tenth*

Un edificio   *A building*
(Lección 4)

el sótano	*basement*
la planta baja	*ground floor*
el primer piso	*first floor (up)*
el segundo piso	*second floor*
el tercer piso	*third floor*
el cuarto piso	*fourth floor*
el quinto piso	*fifth floor*
el sexto piso	*sixth floor*
el séptimo piso	*seventh floor*
el octavo piso	*eighth floor*
el noveno piso	*ninth floor*
el décimo piso	*tenth floor*
el piso once	*eleventh floor*

Lo que hacemos en la escuela   *What we do in school*
(Lección 5)

asistir a las clases	*to attend classes*
comer en la cafetería	*to eat in the cafeteria*
• consultar con el consejero	*to consult with the counselor*
• hacer cola	*to stand in line*
• conseguir (i, i) algo en el armario	*to get something from the locker*
• enseñar	*to teach, to show*
tomar apuntes	*to take notes*
practicar	*to practice*
trabajar mucho	*to work a lot*
estudiar	*to study*
aprender	*to learn*
hablar en voz alta/baja	*to talk in a loud/soft voice*
comprender la lección	*to understand the lesson*
hacer la tarea	*to do homework*
prepararse para los exámenes	*to prepare for tests*

Lo que hacemos en la escuela   *What we do in school* (continued)
(Lección 5)

tomar una prueba	*to take a quiz/test*
un examen	*an exam*
recibir una A	*to receive an A*
sacar buenas/malas notas	*to get good/bad grades*
aprobar (ue) un examen	*to pass an exam*
suspender un examen	*to fail an exam*
salir bien	*to do well*
cerrar (ie) la puerta	*to close the door*
abrir el libro	*to open the book*
hacer una pregunta	*to ask a question*
contestar	*to answer*
leer una novela	*to read a novel*
una lectura	*a reading selection*
un cuento	*a story*
• un poema	*a poem*
la poesía	*poetry*
escribir la tarea	*to write the homework*
un tema	*a paper*
una carta	*a letter*
teclear	*to input*
• hacer un proyecto	*to do a project*
escuchar conferencias	*to listen to lectures*
discos compactos	*CDs*
discutir	*to discuss*
memorizar fechas	*to memorize dates*
hechos	*facts*
calcular	*to do arithmetic*
sumar	*to add*
restar	*to subtract*
multiplicar	*to multiply*
dividir	*to divide*
hacer investigaciones	*to do research*
esperar el autobús	*to wait for the bus*
regresar a casa	*to return home*

Expresiones de tiempo   *Time expressions*
(Lección 5)

anteayer	*day before yesterday*	antes	*before*
ayer	*yesterday*	ahora	*now*
hoy	*today*	después	*after*
mañana	*tomorrow*	entonces	*then*
pasado mañana	*day after tomorrow*	luego	*then, later*
un día	*one day*	• pronto	*soon*
en el pasado	*in the past*	por la mañana	*in the morning*
en el presente	*in the present*	por la tarde	*in the afternoon*
en el futuro	*in the future*	por la noche	*in the evening, at night*
siempre	*always*	una vez	*once*
frecuentemente	*frequently, often*	otra vez	*again*
mucho	*a lot, much*	(dos) veces	*(two) times*
poco	*a little, few*	de una vez	*all at once*
raramente	*rarely, seldom*	de vez en cuando	*from time to time*
nunca	*never*	alguna vez	*sometime*
mientras	*while*	a veces	*sometimes*
de repente	*suddenly*	muchas veces	*many times, often*
inmediatamente	*immediately*	• a menudo	*often*
de niño(a)	*as a child*	todavía	*still, yet*
de viejo(a)	*as an old person*	todavía no	*not yet*
a los… años	*at the age of . . .*	de nuevo	*again*
hace (seis meses)	*(six months) ago*	ya	*already*
en (seis meses)	*in (six months)*	ya no	*no longer*
el año pasado	*last year*	el próximo año	*next year*
el mes pasado	*last month*	el próximo mes	*next month*
la semana pasada	*last week*	la próxima semana	*next week*
el (lunes)	*on (Monday)*	tarde	*late*
todos los (lunes)	*every (Monday)*	más tarde	*later*
todos los días	*every day*	temprano	*early*
todas las semanas	*every week*	más temprano	*earlier*
todos los meses	*every month*		
todos los años	*every year*		

Verbos que se combinan con el infinitivo   *Verbs that combine with the infinitive*
(Lección 5)

deber	*ought to, should*	•	enseñar a	*to teach to*
desear	*to want to, to desire*		invitar a	*to invite to*
esperar	*to hope to*		ir a	*to be going to*
gustar	*to like to*	•	hay que	*one must/has to*
necesitar	*to need to*		tener que	*to have to*
odiar	*to hate (to)*		acabar de	*to have just*
preferir (ie, i)	*to prefer to*	•	gozar de	*to enjoy*
poder (ue)	*can, to be able to*		pensar de	*to think of/about [opinion]*
pensar (ie)	*to intend to, to plan to*		tener ganas de	*to feel like*
querer (ie)	*to want to*		tratar de	*to try to*
aprender a	*to learn to*		pensar en	*to think of/about [daydream]*
ayudar a	*to help (to)*		insistir en	*to insist on*

Cómo se hacen las cosas   *How things are done*
(Lección 5)

ambiciosamente	*ambitiously*	necesariamente	*necessarily*
cuidadosamente	*carefully*	nerviosamente	*nervously*
cómodamente	*comfortably*	nuevamente	*newly*
correctamente	*correctly*	solamente	*only*
fácilmente	*easily*	perfectamente	*perfectly*
especialmente	*especially*	posiblemente	*possibly*
rápidamente	*fast, quickly*	públicamente	*publicly*
finalmente	*finally*	raramente	*rarely*
frecuentemente	*frequently*	regularmente	*regularly*
generosamente	*generously*	tristemente	*sadly*
felizmente	*happily*	sinceramente	*sincerely*
inmediatamente	*immediately*	lentamente	*slowly*
incorrectamente	*incorrectly*	despacio	*slowly*
inteligentemente	*intelligently*	mal	*badly, not well, poorly*
perezosamente	*lazily*	bien	*well*

Estructura

VERBS

Person–time endings: -ar *verbs*
(Lección 2)

For the past and present, remove **-ar**.
Do not remove **-ar** for the future!

	IMPERFECT *-ed* *was/were -ing* *used to*	PRETERITE *-ed* *did*	PRESENT *-(s)* *am/is/are -ing* *do/does*	FUTURE *will*
yo	-aba	-é	-o	-é
tú	-abas	-aste	-as	-ás
Ud./él/ella	-aba	-ó	-a	-á
nosotros(as)	-ábamos	-amos	-amos	-emos
vosotros(as)	-abais	-asteis	-áis	-éis
Uds./ellos/ellas	-aban	-aron	-an	-án

Person–time endings: -er *verbs*
(Lección 3)

For the past and present, remove **-er**.
Do not remove **-er** for the future!

	IMPERFECT *-ed* *was/were -ing* *used to*	PRETERITE *-ed* *did*	PRESENT *-(s)* *am/is/are -ing* *do/does*	FUTURE *will*
yo	-ía	-í	-o	-é
tú	-ías	-iste	-es	-ás
Ud./él/ella	-ía	-ió	-e	-á
nosotros(as)	-íamos	-imos	-emos	-emos
vosotros(as)	-íais	-isteis	-éis	-éis
Uds./ellos/ellas	-ían	-ieron	-en	-án

Person–time endings: -ir *verbs*
(Lección 4)

For the past and present, remove **-ir**.
Do not remove **-ir** for the future!

	IMPERFECT	PRETERITE	PRESENT	FUTURE
	-ed	*-ed*	*-(s)*	*will*
	was/were -ing		*am/is/are -ing*	
	used to	*did*	*do/does*	
yo	-ía	-í	-o	-é
tú	-ías	-iste	-es	-ás
Ud./él/ella	-ía	-ió	-e	-á
nosotros(as)	-íamos	-imos	-imos	-emos
vosotros(as)	-íais	-isteis	-ís	-éis
Uds./ellos/ellas	-ían	-ieron	-en	-án

Preterite and imperfect
(Lección 1)

PRETERITE	IMPERFECT
Countable times	Uncountable times
(once or a stated number)	(indefinite number or unfinished)

reports:
   action completed at
      one point in time

describes:
   a. repeated (habitual) action
   b. ongoing (background) action

Double-verb construction
(Lección 5)

first verb: conjugated   +   second verb: infinitive
(person–time endings)   (**-ar, -er, -ir** ending)

Spelling variations to maintain the sound
(Lecciones 2, 3)

Before <u>A O U</u>   <u>E I</u>

c	⟷	qu
g	⟷	gu
z	⟷	c
j	⟵	g

Unaccented **i** between vowels becomes **y**.

IRREGULAR VERB CHARTS
(irregularities indicated in bold)

IR *to go*
(Lección 1)

	IMPERFECT	PRETERITE	PRESENT	FUTURE
	went	*went*	*go/goes*	*will go*
	was/were going		*am/is/are going*	
	used to go	*did go*	*do/does go*	
yo	**iba**	**fui**	**voy**	iré
tú	**ibas**	**fuiste**	**vas**	irás
Ud./él/ella	**iba**	**fue**	**va**	irá
nosotros(as)	**íbamos**	**fuimos**	**vamos**	iremos
vosotros(as)	**ibais**	**fuisteis**	**vais**	iréis
Uds./ellos/ellas	**iban**	**fueron**	**van**	irán

VENIR *to come*
(Lección 1)

	IMPERFECT	PRETERITE	PRESENT	FUTURE
	came	*came*	*come(s)*	*will come*
	was/were coming		*am/is/are coming*	
	used to come	*did come*	*do/does come*	
yo	venía	**vine**	**vengo**	**vendré**
tú	venías	**viniste**	vienes	**vendrás**
Ud./él/ella	venía	**vino**	viene	**vendrá**
nosotros(as)	veníamos	**vinimos**	venimos	**vendremos**
vosotros(as)	veníais	**vinisteis**	venís	**vendréis**
Uds./ellos/ellas	venían	**vinieron**	vienen	**vendrán**

DAR *to give*
(Lección 2)

	IMPERFECT	PRETERITE	PRESENT	FUTURE
	gave	*gave*	*give(s)*	*will give*
	was/were giving		*am/is/are giving*	
	used to give	*did give*	*do/does give*	
yo	daba	**di**	**doy**	daré
tú	dabas	**diste**	das	darás
Ud./él/ella	daba	**dio**	da	dará
nosotros(as)	dábamos	**dimos**	damos	daremos
vosotros(as)	dabais	**disteis**	dais	daréis
Uds./ellos/ellas	daban	**dieron**	dan	darán

PONER *to put, to place*
(Lección 3)

	IMPERFECT	PRETERITE	PRESENT	FUTURE
	put	*put*	*put(s)*	*will put*
	was/were putting		*am/is/are putting*	
	used to put	*did put*	*do/does put*	
yo	ponía	**puse**	**pongo**	**pondré**
tú	ponías	**pusiste**	pones	**pondrás**
Ud./él/ella	ponía	**puso**	pone	**pondrá**
nosotros(as)	poníamos	**pusimos**	ponemos	**pondremos**
vosotros(as)	poníais	**pusisteis**	ponéis	**pondréis**
Uds./ellos/ellas	ponían	**pusieron**	ponen	**pondrán**

SALIR (DE) *to go out, to leave*
(Lección 4)

	IMPERFECT	PRETERITE	PRESENT	FUTURE
	left	*left*	*leave(s)*	*will leave*
	was/were leaving		*am/is/are leaving*	
	used to leave	*did leave*	*do/does leave*	
yo	salía	salí	**salgo**	**saldré**
tú	salías	saliste	sales	**saldrás**
Ud./él/ella	salía	salió	sale	**saldrá**
nosotros(as)	salíamos	salimos	salimos	**saldremos**
vosotros(as)	salíais	salisteis	salís	**saldréis**
Uds./ellos/ellas	salían	salieron	salen	**saldrán**

OÍR *to hear*
(Lección 4)

	IMPERFECT	PRETERITE	PRESENT	FUTURE
	heard	*heard*	*hear(s)*	*will hear*
	was/were hearing		*am/is/are hearing*	
	used to hear	*did hear*	*do/does hear*	
yo	oía	oí	**oigo**	oiré
tú	oías	oíste	**oyes**	oirás
Ud./él/ella	oía	**oyó**	**oye**	oirá
nosotros(as)	oíamos	oímos	oímos	oiremos
vosotros(as)	oíais	oísteis	oís	oiréis
Uds./ellos/ellas	oían	**oyeron**	**oyen**	oirán

VER *to see*
(Lección 4)

	IMPERFECT *saw* *was/were seeing* *used to see*	PRETERITE *saw* *did see*	PRESENT *see(s)* *am/is/are seeing* *do/does see*	FUTURE *will see*
yo	**veía**	vi	**veo**	veré
tú	**veías**	viste	ves	verás
Ud./él/ella	**veía**	vio	ve	verá
nosotros(as)	**veíamos**	vimos	vemos	veremos
vosotros(as)	**veíais**	visteis	veis	veréis
Uds./ellos/ellas	**veían**	vieron	ven	verán

HACER *to do, to make*
(Lección 5)

	IMPERFECT
	did/made
	was/were
	  doing/making
	used to do/make
		PRETERITE
		did/made
		
		did do/make
			PRESENT
			do/does/make(s)
			am/is/are
			  doing/making
			do/does do/make
				FUTURE
				will do/make

yo	hacía	**hice**	**hago**	**haré**
tú	hacías	**hiciste**	haces	**harás**
Ud./él/ella	hacía	**hizo**	hace	**hará**
nosotros(as)	hacíamos	**hicimos**	hacemos	**haremos**
vosotros(as)	hacíais	**hicisteis**	hacéis	**haréis**
Uds./ellos/ellas	hacían	**hicieron**	hacen	**harán**

PRONOUNS

Pronouns following prepositions
(Lección 1)

mí	*me*	nosotros(as)	*us*
ti	*you*	vosotros(as)	*you*
Ud.	*you*	Uds.	*you*
él/ella	*him/her*	ellos/ellas	*them*

Note: con + mí = conmigo
       con + ti = contigo
       entre tú y yo

Personal a
(Lección 4)

When a person is the direct object, add the personal **a** before the noun.
   Exception: **tener**

Object pronouns
(Lección 2)

INDIRECT OBJECT PRONOUNS		DIRECT OBJECT PRONOUNS	
me	*to/for me*	me	*me*
te	*to/for you*	te	*you*
le	*to/for you/him/her/it*	lo	*you/him/it*
		la	*you/her/it*
nos	*to/for us*	nos	*us*
os	*to/for you*	os	*you*
les	*to/for you/them*	los	*you/them*
		las	*you/them*

Position of object pronouns
(Lección 2)

Object pronouns are placed before the verb with the person–time ending, or attached to the end of the **-ar, -er, -ir** form of the verb.

Double object pronouns
(Lección 2)

INDIRECT OBJECT PRONOUN + DIRECT OBJECT PRONOUN

le/les become **se** before **lo/la/los/las**

me lo	te lo	nos lo	se lo
me la	te la	nos la	se la
me los	te los	nos los	se los
me las	te las	nos las	se las

ADVERBS

Forming adverbs from adjectives
(Lección 5)

feminine singular form of the adjective + **mente**

Comparison of adverbs
(Lección 5)

más + *adverb* + **que**
menos + *adverb* + **que**
tan + *adverb* + **como**

Contraction of a + el
(Lección 1)

a + el = al
Do not contract: **a la/a los/a las**.

Contraction of de + el
(Lección 1)

de + el = del
Do not contract: **de la/de los/de las**.

Esqueletos

Duration of time
(Lección 5)

HACE + *time* + **QUE** + *present verb* + *(rest of sentence)*

Hace tres meses que trabajo aquí.   *I have been working here for three months.*

HACÍA + *time* + **QUE** + *imperfect verb* + *(rest of sentence)*

Hacía dos años que yo trabajaba allí.   *I had been working there for two years.*

Ago
(Lección 5)

HACE + *time* + **QUE** + *preterite verb*

Hace dos semanas que lo compré.   *I bought it two weeks ago.*

OR

preterite verb + **HACE** + *time*

Lo compré hace dos semanas.   *I bought it two weeks ago.*

⇜ Unidad II Lección 1 ⇝
¿Dónde está? ¿Cómo se va?

In this lesson we start moving! Let's talk about where various places are located beginning with our house, our city, and finally—the world! Then let's talk about going to all these interesting places!

Vocabulario

La casa y el apartamento   *The house and the apartment*

1.	el cuarto	*room*
2.	el desván/•la azotea	*attic*
3.	el primer piso	*second floor, one floor up*
4.	la planta baja	*ground floor*
5.	el sótano	*basement*
6.	la alcoba	*bedroom*
7.	el cuarto de baño	*bathroom*
8.	el pasillo	*hallway*
9.	la escalera	*stairs*
• 10.	el balcón	*balcony*
11.	el comedor	*dining room*
12.	la cocina	*kitchen*
• 13.	el ascensor	*elevator*
14.	la sala	*living room*
15.	la sala de estar	*family room, den*
• 16.	la lavandería	*laundry room*
• 17.	el garaje	*garage*
• 18.	el jardín	*garden, yard*
19.	el patio	*inner courtyard, yard*

Vocabulario

Preposiciones de ubicación   *Prepositions of location*

1. a	*to, at*		14. alrededor de	*around, surrounding*
2. de	*of, from, about*		15. delante de	*in front of*
3. encima de	*on top of, above*		16. detrás de	*behind*
4. en	*in, on, at*		17. al lado de	*next to, beside*
5. con	*with*		• 18. en el medio de	*in the middle of*
6. sin	*without*		19. al otro lado de	*on the other side of*
7. fuera de	*outside of*		20. cerca de	*near*
8. dentro de	*inside of*		21. lejos de	*far from*
9. sobre	*over, on*		• 22. junto a	*next to*
10. debajo de	*under*		• 23. enfrente de	*opposite*
11. a la derecha de	*to the right of*		• 24. a través de	*across*
12. a la izquierda de	*to the left of*		• 25. por aquí	*over here*
13. entre	*between, among*			

Estar   *to be*

In Unit I, Lesson 3, we used the verb **estar** to tell about physical and emotional conditions. **Estar** is also used to tell the location of people, things, and places.

ESTAR: How? = condition   El piloto esta ocupado.
The pilot is busy.

Where? = location   La cafetería está en la planta baja.
The cafeteria is on the ground floor.

Review the forms of **estar** in Unit I on page 18.

1 Review the vocabulary on page 164 relating to a house or apartment. Then tell where various things are in your home.

EJEMPLO: El televisor está en la sala.

2 Tell where people and things are in your classroom.

EJEMPLO: Los libros están en el estante.

3 Describe the location of several people and things in your class.

EJEMPLO: María está cerca de la puerta.
Mi cuaderno está debajo de mi pupitre.

Vocabulario

Lugares en la ciudad   *Places in the city*

1. el edificio	*building*	25. el templo	*temple*
2. la casa	*house*	26. la librería	*bookstore*
3. la tienda	*store*	27. la florería	*flower shop*
4. el rascacielos	*skyscraper*	28. la papelería	*stationery store*
5. el correo	*post office*	29. la pastelería	*pastry shop*
6. el banco	*bank*	30. la zapatería	*shoe store*
7. el parque	*park*	31. la ropería	*clothing store*
8. la playa	*beach*	32. la lechería	*dairy*
9. la escuela	*school*	33. la heladería	*ice cream parlor*
10. la biblioteca	*library*	34. la panadería	*bakery*
11. el museo	*museum*	35. la carnicería	*butcher shop*
12. el hotel	*hotel*	36. la joyería	*jewelry store*
13. la estación de gasolina	*gas station*	37. la relojería	*clock store*
14. el teatro	*theater*	38. la dulcería	*candy store*
15. el restaurante	*restaurant*	39. la juguetería	*toy store*
16. el cine	*movie theater*	• 40. la fábrica	*factory*
17. el supermercado	*supermarket*	• 41. la oficina	*office*
18. el almacén	*department store*	• 42. la cárcel	*jail*
19. el consultorio	*office*	• 43. el monumento	*monument*
...del dentista	*dentist's . . .*	• 44. la plaza	*town square*
...del médico	*doctor's . . .*	• 45. el centro comercial	*mall*
20. la farmacia	*pharmacy*	• 46. la peluquería	*beauty shop*
21. el hospital	*hospital*	• 47. la tintorería	*dry cleaners*
22. la iglesia	*church*	• 48. la pescadería	*fish store*
23. la sinagoga	*synagogue*	• 49. la pizzería	*pizzeria*
24. la mezquita	*mosque*	• 50. el aeropuerto	*airport*

4 Tell where different places in your city are located in relation to your house.

EJEMPLO: El hospital está lejos de mi casa.
La iglesia está delante de mi casa.

5 Tell where different places are located in relation to your school.

EJEMPLO: La papelería está enfrente de la escuela.

6 Draw a map of a business intersection in your town. Label the streets and identify the various stores.

Vocabulario

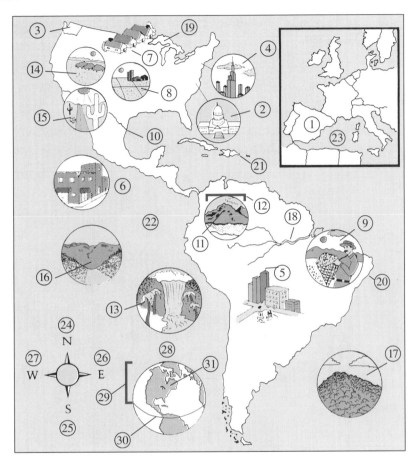

La geografía   *Geography*

1. el país — *country*
2. la capital — *capital*
3. el estado — *state*
4. la ciudad — *city*
5. el centro — *center, downtown*
6. el pueblo — *town*
7. las afueras — *suburbs*
8. el campo — *countryside*
9. el habitante — *inhabitant*
10. la frontera — *border*
11. la montaña — *mountain*
• 12. la sierra — *mountain range*
13. la selva — *forest, jungle*
14. los llanos — *plains*
15. el desierto — *desert*
• 16. el valle — *valley*

• 17. la colina — *hill*
18. el río — *river*
19. el lago — *lake*
20. la costa — *coast*
21. la isla — *island*
22. el océano — *ocean*
23. el mar — *sea*
24. el norte — *north*
25. el sur — *south*
26. el este — *east*
27. el oeste — *west*
• 28. el mundo — *world*
• 29. el hemisferio — *hemisphere*
• 30. el ecuador — *equator*
• 31. el continente — *continent*

7 **Un informe**   Choose a city anywhere in the world. Tell about its geographical location.

EJEMPLO: Chicago es una ciudad en Illinois. Está al norte del estado. Está al suroeste del Lago Michigan.

8 Using a map, tell where various countries of Latin America are located.

EJEMPLO: El Perú está en la América del Sur. Está en el oeste del continente, cerca de la costa del Océano Pacífico. La cordillera de los Andes es la frontera entre el Perú y Brasil en el este del país. Chile está al sur, Bolivia está al sureste y Ecuador y Colombia están al norte.

Vocabulario

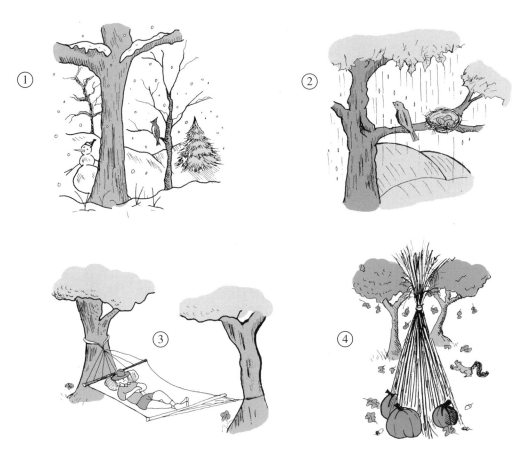

Las estaciones   *Seasons*

1. el invierno   *winter*
2. la primavera   *spring*
3. el verano   *summer*
4. el otoño   *fall, autumn*

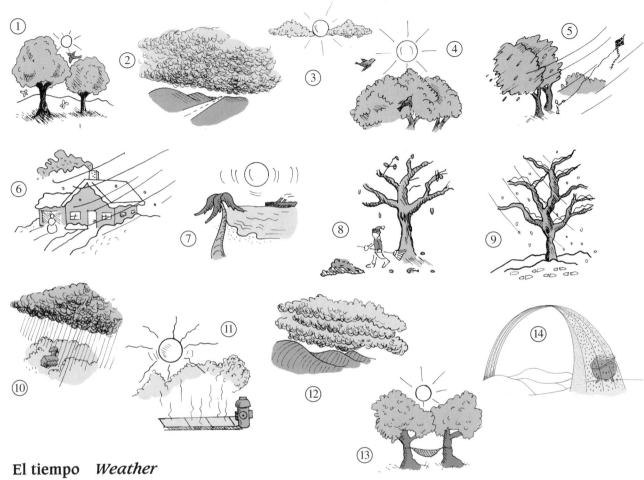

El tiempo   *Weather*

¿Qué tiempo hace?   *What's the weather like?*

1. Hace buen tiempo.	*It's nice weather.*	8. Hace fresco.	*It's cool.*
2. Hace mal tiempo.	*It's bad weather.*	9. Nieva.	*It's snowing, It snows.*
3. Hace sol.	*It's sunny.*	10. Llueve.	*It's raining, It rains.*
4. Hace mucho sol.	*It's very sunny.*	11. Está (muy) húmedo.	*It's (very) humid.*
5. Hace (mucho) viento.	*It's (very) windy.*	12. Está (muy) nublado.	*It's (very) cloudy.*
6. Hace (mucho) frío.	*It's (very) cold.*	13. Está claro.	*It's clear.*
7. Hace (mucho) calor.	*It's (very) warm/hot.*	• 14. Hay un arco iris.	*There is a rainbow.*

9 Describe the weather in your city or town now.

EJEMPLO: Hoy hace fresco. Está nublado y hace viento.

10 Tell what the weather is like where you live. Describe the different seasons.

EJEMPLO: En el invierno, hace fresco y llueve mucho.

11 *Sit-Con*   Pretend that you are the weather reporter on television. Using a weather map, tell what the weather is like today in different places.

Vocabulario

Otras preposiciones   *Other prepositions*

antes de	*before*		desde	*from, since*
después de	*after*		hasta	*until*
por	*for, by, through*		• contra	*against*
para	*for, by, in order to*		• al + *infinitive*	*while, on, upon*
en vez de	*instead of*			

PRONOUNS AFTER A PREPOSITION

Prepositions are words that describe a relationship (often of time or location) between two nouns or pronouns.

estudiantes <u>con</u> libros   *students <u>with</u> books*
el hombre <u>sin</u> guantes   *the man <u>without</u> gloves*
un libro <u>para</u> mi amiga   *a book <u>for</u> my friend*

¿Para mí?

Sí, para ti.

A noun following a preposition can be replaced with the following pronouns.

mí	*me*	nosotros(as)	*us*
ti	*you*	vosotros(as)	*you*
Ud.	*you*	Uds.	*you*
él/ella	*him/her*	ellos/ellas	*them*

Did you notice that the prepositional pronouns are the same as the subject pronouns except **mí** and **ti**?

Note the following exceptions:

• When **con** immediately precedes **mí** and **ti**, the forms become **conmigo** and **contigo**.

Ellos van conmigo, no contigo.   *They are going with me, not with you.*

• Use **tú** and **yo** with the preposition **entre**.

El pupitre de Miguel está entre tú y yo.   *Miguel's desk is between you and me.*

---

12   Tell where several of your classmates sit in relation to you.

EJEMPLO: Manuel está detrás de mí.
Carlota está cerca de mí.

13 **Encuesta**   Choose several people in the class below. Tell where other classmates sit in relation to them.

EJEMPLO: Escojí a Eugenio.
Sara está a la derecha de él.

Escojí a Adolfo y a Esperanza.
Felicia está detrás de ellos.

Vocabulario

Los medios de transporte   *Means of transportation*

1. en coche/auto/carro	*by car*	6. por tren	*by train*
2. por avión	*by plane*	7. en bicicleta	*by bike*
3. en taxi	*by taxi*	8. por moto(cicleta)	*by motorcycle*
4. por barco	*by boat*	9. a pie	*on foot*
5. en autobús	*by bus*		

Now that we have the means of transportation, we just need the verb *to go* and we're on our way!

IR *to go*

	IMPERFECT	PRETERITE	PRESENT	FUTURE
	went	*went*	*go/goes*	*will go*
	was/were going		*am/is/are going*	
	used to go	*did go*	*do/does go*	
yo	**iba**	**fui**	**voy**	iré
tú	**ibas**	**fuiste**	**vas**	irás
Ud./él/ella	**iba**	**fue**	**va**	irá
nosotros(as)	**íbamos**	**fuimos**	**vamos**	iremos
vosotros(as)	**ibais**	**fuisteis**	**vais**	iréis
Uds./ellos/ellas	**iban**	**fueron**	**van**	irán

The verb **ir** is followed by **a** before a place or an action.

Voy a la playa. *I am going to the beach.*
Voy a nadar. *I am going to swim.*

De niño iba en
bicicleta.

Ahora voy en auto.

En el futuro iré por
avión.

CONTRACTION OF A + EL

A *(to/at)* before **el** *(the)* becomes **al: a + el = al**.

Voy <u>al</u> parque. *I'm going <u>to the</u> park.*

Do not contract: **a la/a los/a las**.

Voy <u>a la</u> playa. *I'm going <u>to the</u> beach.*
Ayer fui <u>a los</u> museos. *Yesterday I went <u>to the</u> museums.*

14 Find out from several classmates where they went during their summer vacation and how they went there.

EJEMPLO: ¿Adónde fuiste durante tus vacaciones del verano?

Fui a California.

¿Cómo fuiste?

Fui por avión.

15 **Encuesta**   Find out where several classmates go on the weekend and with whom they go.

EJEMPLO: ¿Adónde vas durante el fin de semana?

Voy al cine.

¿Con quién vas?

Voy con mi amiga.

16 Make a list of the places you go to frequently. Tell where these places are. Then tell when you go there, with whom you go, and how you get there.

EJEMPLO: El cine: El cine está lejos de mi casa. Está en la Calle Chestnut, al otro lado de la biblioteca. Voy al cine con mis amigos los sábados. Vamos en autobús.

LA RIOJA

3 días

ITINERARIO: (T-049)

Mayo 13 (Sáb.).   MADRID - SORIA - LOGROÑO

Salida de nuestra TERMINAL, Plaza de Oriente, 8, a las 8.00 horas, hacia Medinaceli, Almazán y Soria. Recorrido panorámico y almuerzo. Salida hacia el Puerto de Piqueras, para llegar a Logroño. **Cena y alojamiento.**

Mayo 14 (Dom.).   LOGROÑO - LAGUARDIA - LA BASTIDA - BRIÑAS - HARO - LOGROÑO

Desayuno y salida para recorrer La Rioja alavesa, visitando las típicas poblaciones de Laguardia, rodeada de murallas y con interesantes iglesias y casonas; Samaniego y Labastida, elegante y señorial, para llegar a Briñas. **Almuerzo** y salida hacia la orilla derecha del Ebro y, por Haro y Cenicero, llegar de nuevo a Logroño. **Cena y alojamiento.**

Mayo 15 (Lun.).   LOGROÑO - SAN MILLAN DE LA COGOLLA - SANTO DOMINGO DE LA CALZADA - MADRID

Desayuno. Salida hacia Nájera y Berceo, para llegar a San Millán de la Cogolla, donde se encuentra el antiguo y grandioso monasterio llamado «El Escorial de la Rioja» y el Monasterio de Suso, el más antiguo de los cenobios de España. **Visita.** Continuación hasta Santo Domingo de la Calzada, lleno de aromas monásticos y tradiciones, mezcla de superstición y religión. **Visita** de su Catedral. **Almuerzo.** Por la tarde, salida hacia Belorado y Aranda de Duero para llegar de nuevo a Madrid, a nuestra TERMINAL.

We've gone to a lot of places. Now let's tell the place we are coming from.

VENIR *to come*

	IMPERFECT	PRETERITE	PRESENT	FUTURE
	came	*came*	*come(s)*	*will come*
	was/were coming		*am/is/are coming*	
	used to come	*did come*	*do/does come*	
yo	venía	**vine**	**vengo**	**vendré**
tú	venías	**viniste**	vienes	**vendrás**
Ud./él/ella	venía	**vino**	viene	**vendrá**
nosotros(as)	veníamos	**vinimos**	venimos	**vendremos**
vosotros(as)	veníais	**vinisteis**	venís	**vendréis**
Uds./ellos/ellas	venían	**vinieron**	vienen	**vendrán**

Note: **Venir** is used to tell the place where one was before his or her present location. **Ser de** is used to tell one's origin.

CONTRACTION OF DE + EL

De *(of/from)* before **el** *(the)* becomes **del: de + el = del.**

Vengo <u>del</u> parque.   *I'm coming <u>from the</u> park.*

Do not contract: **de la/de los/de las.**

Vengo <u>de la</u> playa.   *I'm coming <u>from the</u> beach.*

17 Ask several classmates which class they came from and which class they will go to next.

EJEMPLO: ¿De qué clase viniste?

Vine de la clase de álgebra.

¿A qué clase irás?

Iré a la clase de historia.

18 *Sit-Con*   Your friend has come to your family's reunion with you. Tell where several of your relatives came from to attend the reunion.

EJEMPLO: Mi prima Cecilia vino del Canadá.

19 **Juego: ¿Cómo iremos a**… ?   The first person names a place. The second person tells how you will get there, and the third person tells a different way to come back. (Refer to **Medios de transporte** on page 175.)

EJEMPLO: ¿Cómo iremos a la biblioteca?

Iremos a la biblioteca en coche.

Vendremos de la biblioteca a pie.

20 Find out and report where several people you know are from.

EJEMPLO: ¿De dónde eres, Anita?

Soy de Chile.

Reportaje: Anita es de Chile.

PRETERITE AND IMPERFECT
TWO WAYS OF TALKING ABOUT THE PAST

There are two forms of the past tense in Spanish: the preterite and the imperfect.

PRETERITE	IMPERFECT
Countable times	Uncountable times
(once or a stated number)	(indefinite number or unfinished)
reports:	describes:
action completed at	a. repeated (habitual) action
one point in time	b. ongoing (background) action

The *preterite* tells what was done once or a certain number of times at a specific point in time.

- El año pasado, fui <u>tres veces</u> al cine.
  Last year, I went to the movies <u>three times</u>. [specified number]
  (I tell the number of times I went.)

- Fui al cine ayer.
  I went to the movies <u>yesterday</u>.
  (The action was completed at a specific time. Once is implied.)

The *imperfect* is used for repeated habitual or ongoing background action.

- Cuando yo era niña, <u>iba</u> al cine.
  When I was a child, I <u>used to go (went)</u> to the movies. [repeated action]
  (I went more than once but the number of times is not important.)

- Ayer, yo <u>iba</u> al cine cuando vi a mi amigo.
  Yesterday, <u>I was going</u> to the movies when I saw my friend. [ongoing action]
  (I was on my way to the movies but hadn't arrived yet when something else happened.)

Compare the following sentences.

PRETERITE	IMPERFECT
Ayer fui a la tienda.	Siempre iba a la tienda.
Yesterday I went to the store.	*I always went to the store.*
(I went once: countable)	(I went an indefinite number of times.)
Anoche llovió mucho.	Llovía mientras dormía anoche.
It rained a lot last night.	*It was raining while I was sleeping last night.*
(At some point it stopped.)	(Neither action had stopped yet.)
Estudié para el examen.	Estudiaba cuando me telefoneó.
I studied for the test.	*I was studying when he telephoned me.*
(I finished studying.)	(My studying was interrupted.)

21 Tell where you used to go as a child. Use the imperfect tense.

EJEMPLO: De niño, iba a las tiendas con mi mamá.
De niña, iba al parque para jugar.

22 Tell where you went as a child and tell how many times you went there. Use the preterite tense.

EJEMPLO: Fui a Nueva York dos veces.

23 *Sit-Con* You are a detective investigating a burglary that took place yesterday at 5:00 P.M. Ask several people where they were at the time of the crime. Use the imperfect tense.

EJEMPLO: ¿Dónde estaba Ud. ayer a las cinco?

  Estaba en la biblioteca.

24 **La niñez de Paulina**   Complete the following story with the correct preterite or imperfect form of the verb **ir**. Watch for clues that tell you how many times the action took place.

Cuando yo era niña _____ a México todos los veranos para visitar a mis abuelos. Todos los
<u>1</u>

días la cocinera *(cook)* _____ al mercado para comprar la comida y yo _____ con ella.
<u>2</u>   <u>3</u>

Nosotras _____ directamente a la carnicería *(butcher shop)* para comprar carne y después
<u>4</u>

_____ a la panadería para el pan y los postres. Finalmente _____ a la frutería para comprar las
<u>5</u>   <u>6</u>

frutas y las legumbres. Después _____ a la casa con toda la comida.
<u>7</u>

Un día mi prima Amalia _____ con nosotras. Amalia y yo _____ al parque para jugar
<u>8</u>   <u>9</u>

mientras *(while)* la cocinera _____ a las tiendas. Yo _____ a jugar en los columpios y Amalia
<u>10</u>   <u>11</u>

_____ a jugar en el tobogán *(slide)*. Después nosotras _____ a jugar en el cajón de arena. La
<u>12</u>   <u>13</u>

cocinera compró la comida y nosotras _____ a casa. El próximo día yo _____ con la cocinera a
<u>14</u>   <u>15</u>

las tiendas, pero Amalia no _____ con nosotras.
<u>16</u>

25 **Más de la niñez de Paulina**   Complete the following story with the correct form of the indicated verb. Watch for clues.

Cuando yo (tener) _____ doce años, siempre (ir) _____ al cine con mi hermano Pablo y sus
                     1   2
amigos. Ellos (ir) _____ todos los sábados. Nosotros (ir) _____ en el coche de mi madre.
               3   4

Un día los amigos no (ir) _____ al cine con nosotros. Mi hermano y yo (ir) _____ solos. Mi
                         5   6
hermano (ir) _____ a comprar los billetes.
             7

—¿Por qué no (venir) _____ tus amigos al cine?—le pregunté a mi hermano. —¿Por qué no
                     8
(ir) _____ nosotros con ellos?
   9

—Mis amigos (ir) _____ a la playa esta semana. No (tener) _____ ganas de ir al cine. Pero
               10   11
la próxima semana ellos (ir) _____ al cine con nosotros.
                      12

Después de la película, mi hermano y yo (ir) _____ a casa. Mi hermano (tener) _____ que
                                   13   14
estacionar el coche en el garaje. Cuando yo (ir) _____ a la sala todo (estar) _____ preparado.
                                   15   16
(Ser) _____ el cumpleaños de mi hermano y todos sus amigos (venir) _____ a sorprenderlo
     17   18
(surprise him) con una fiesta.

ENCUENTRO PERSONAL

Paulina and her friends are telling about places they used to go to visit on vacation. Notice their use of the preterite and imperfect tenses.

PAULINA: De niña, mi familia y yo íbamos frecuentemente durante el verano a un lago cerca de nuestra casa. A veces mis abuelos iban con nosotros. Generalmente hacía buen tiempo y me gustaba mucho jugar en la playa. Cuando llovía, íbamos a la ciudad para visitar un museo o ir de compras. ¿Y tú, Santiago?

SANTIAGO: Nosotros íbamos casi siempre a la casa de campo de mis tíos. Vivían en un rancho en las montañas lejos de la ciudad. Era una casa pequeña de tres cuartos: una alcoba, un baño y una sala pequeña. Hacía frío por la noche, pero durante el día hacía mucho sol y viento. Íbamos en carro o a caballo a un río donde nadábamos y comíamos. ¿Qué hacías tú, Rosita?

ROSITA: Pues, el invierno pasado mi familia y yo fuimos a un hotel en Nueva York por cinco días. El hotel era muy grande y tenía un restaurante y muchas tiendas también. Cada día íbamos a pie a visitar varias partes de la ciudad. El último día fuimos a ver la famosa Estatua de la Libertad. Me gustó mucho. ¿Y tú, Raúl?

RAÚL: Yo también fui de vacaciones. En el otoño yo fui a Europa con mis padres. Mis hermanos fueron también. Visitamos España y hablé español con los españoles. Ellos hablaban con un acento diferente, pero generalmente podía comprenderlos. Algún día quiero volver a vivir allí para estudiar en la universidad.

¿Comprendes?

1. ¿Adónde iba Paulina de vacaciones?
2. ¿Qué tiempo hacía allí?
3. ¿Qué hacía ella?
4. Y Santiago, ¿adónde iba y qué hacía él?
5. ¿Adónde fue Rosita el invierno pasado?
6. ¿Con quién habló español Raúl?
7. ¿Qué desea Raúl hacer en el futuro? ¿Deseas tú hacer lo mismo *(the same)*?

¡Te toca!

Tell your friends where you went for your last vacation. What was the weather like? Who went with you?

Gijón, descanso de calidad

★★★★ PARADOR NACIONAL MOLINO VIEJO
Parque Isabel la Católica, s/n
33203 Gijón
Tel. 98.537 05 11 • Fax 98.537 02 33

Un antiguo molino, situado en uno de los rincones más apacibles de la ciudad. A cinco minutos del Palacio de Congresos. Capacidad: 40 habitaciones.

★★★★ HOTEL BEGOÑA PARK
Ctra. de la Providencia, s/n
33203 Gijón
Tel. 98.513 39 09 • Fax 98.513 16 02

En el apacible entorno de El Rinconín, próximo al Paseo Marítimo. Capacidad: 92 habitaciones. Habitaciones para familias con niños.

Hotel Albores

PROPIETARIA: CONSUELO ALBORES

4A. ORIENTE NUM. 15   TEL. 56

ARRIAGA. CHIS.

EL MEJOR HOTEL DEL SURESTE, CON 36 CUARTOS, TODOS CON BAÑO Y VENTILADORES.

GARAJE EXCLUSIVO PARA NUESTROS CLIENTES

Leemos y contamos

A. Here is a description of where Anita, a classmate of Paulina, lives. Can you picture it in your mind? After you read the description, answer the questions that follow.

Mi casa no es muy grande pero tiene muchos cuartos. En la planta baja hay una cocina y al lado está el comedor. Al otro lado del comedor está la sala. En frente de la sala está la oficina de mi papá y una sala de estar. En el medio hay un baño pequeño y la escalera. En el primer piso hay tres alcobas. Mi alcoba está a la derecha de la escalera, la de mis hermanos está a la izquierda y la de mis padres está entre los dos. Junto a mi cuarto hay un baño completo. Hay varios armarios y estantes dentro de la casa. Fuera de la casa hay un garaje y alrededor del patio hay una cerca (fence). No es una casa grande para cinco personas, pero para nosotros es casi perfecta.

Mi casa está al oeste de la ciudad, en una parte vieja pero muy bonita. Hay un parque pequeño en el otro lado de la calle y la escuela y la biblioteca no están muy lejos de mi casa. Cuando era niña iba al parque para jugar con mis amigos. Ahora voy al centro comercial que está muy cerca también.

En el centro comercial hay muchas roperías y zapaterías y en el medio hay un almacén grande. Paulina y yo vamos a las tiendas los sábados. Mi tienda favorita es la librería. Frecuentemente vamos al cine y después a la heladería o a la pizzería.

Mis padres van al centro comercial para ir al banco, al correo, al consultorio de su médico y al supermercado allí. Prefieren ir al supermercado, donde hay de todo, en vez de ir a la carnicería, la panadería, la lechería y la farmacia. Estoy muy contenta porque vivo en una casa buena en una ciudad buena. ¡Tengo mucha suerte!

1. ¿Cuántos cuartos hay en la casa de Anita?
2. ¿Cuáles son y dónde está cada uno?
3. ¿Qué más hay en la casa?
4. ¿Qué hay fuera de la casa?
5. ¿Cómo es la parte de la ciudad donde ella vive?
6. ¿Qué hay en el centro comercial cerca de su casa?
7. ¿Adónde va Anita en el centro comercial?
8. ¿Adónde va su madre? ¿Por qué?

B. Describe your house. Tell where things are in the house.

C. Describe your city. Tell where the places that are important to you are located.

¡Así es!

El regatear   *Bargaining*

Cuando vas de compras al mercado o le compras algo a un vendedor *(seller)* que no tiene una tienda, es costumbre «regatear» *(bargain)*. Cuando preguntas el precio del artículo, el vendedor te da un precio más alto de lo que *(what)* aceptará. Tú debes ofrecerle un precio menor de lo que pagarás. El vendedor te dice las ventajas *(advantages)* del artículo para recibir el precio más alto y tú le dices las razones por las que no deseas pagar tanto. Él baja su precio y tú aumentas *(raise)* tu precio hasta que lleguen *(you arrive)* a un precio que les satisfaga *(satisfies)* a los dos.

No debes comenzar a regatear si no deseas comprar el artículo cuando lleguen a un buen precio. El regatear es un juego y no debes enojarte *(get angry)*. En algunos países, cuando llegas a un precio que les satisface, Uds. se dan la mano. Es una buena idea observar a otras personas para aprender a regatear.

La ropa

In this lesson we are going to talk about something everybody needs—clothes!

Vocabulario

La ropa   *Clothing, clothes*

1. el abrigo	*coat*	
2. el impermeable	*raincoat*	
3. la chaqueta	*jacket*	
4. el sombrero	*hat*	
5. el gorro	*cap, knit hat*	
6. el traje	*suit*	
7. el saco	*sport coat*	
8. la camisa de manga larga	*long-sleeved shirt*	
9. de manga corta	*short-sleeved shirt*	
10. deportiva	*sport shirt*	
11. la camiseta…	*T-shirt*	
• 12. de cuello alto	*turtle neck*	
• 13. sin mangas	*tank top*	

- 14. el suéter de cuello en V — *V-neck sweater*
- 15. el suéter de cuello redondo — *round-neck*
- 16. el traje de baño — *swimsuit*
- 17. el vestido — *dress*
- 18. el chaleco — *vest*
- 19. la blusa — *blouse*
- 20. la falda — *skirt*
- 21. los pantalones — *pants*
- 22. los pantalones cortos — *shorts*
- 23. los pantalones vaqueros — *jeans*
- 24. el pantalón de sudadera — *sweatpants*
- 25. la sudadera — *sweatshirt*

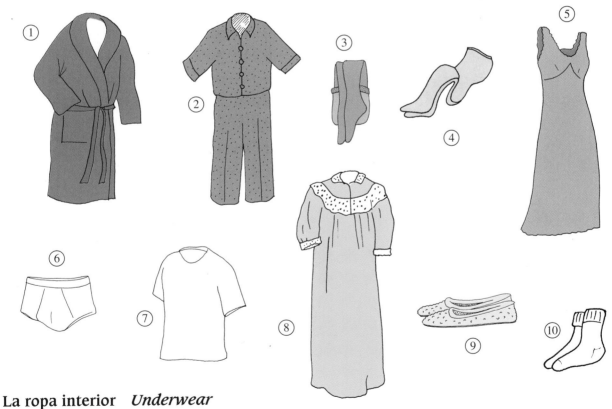

La ropa interior   *Underwear*

- 1. la bata — *robe*
- 2. la pijama — *pajamas*
- 3. las medias — *stockings*
- 4. la pantimedia — *pantyhose*
- 5. la combinación — *slip*

- 6. los calzoncillos — *undershorts*
- 7. la camiseta — *undershirt*
- 8. el camisón — *nightgown*
- 9. las zapatillas — *slippers*
- 10. los calcetines — *socks*

Vocabulario

Los zapatos   *Shoes*

- 1. los mocasines
  2. los tacones altos
  3. los zapatos tenis

moccasins, loafers
high-heeled shoes
tennis shoes

4. las sandalias
5. las botas

sandals
boots

Los artículos personales   *Personal articles*

1. los lentes/•los anteojos   *eyeglasses*
2. los lentes de contacto   *contact lenses*
3. el cinturón   *belt*
4. la bolsa   *purse*
- 5. la cartera   *wallet*
- 6. el portabilletes   *money clip*
- 7. el pañuelo   *handkerchief*
- 8. los guantes   *gloves*
- 9. el bosillo   *pocket*

10. la corbata   *tie*
- 11. la cinta   *ribbon*
12. el paraguas   *umbrella*
13. la mochila   *backpack, knapsack*
- 14. los mitones   *mittens*
- 15. el llavero   *keyring*
- 16. la bufanda   *scarf*
- 17. las gafas de sol   *sunglasses*
- 18. el botón   *button*

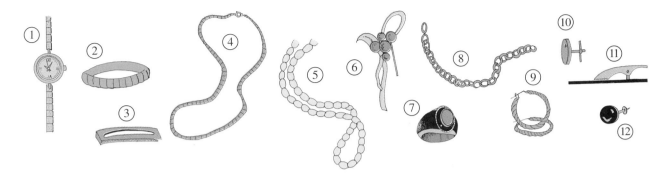

• Las joyas   *Jewelry*

- 1. el reloj (de) pulsera   *wristwatch*
- 2. el brazalete   *bracelet*
- 3. el pasador   *barrette*
- 4. el collar   *necklace*
- 5. las perlas   *pearls*
- 6. el broche   *pin*
- 7. la cadena   *chain*
- 8. el anillo   *ring*
- 9. el pendiente   *earring*
- 10. el gemelo   *cufflink*
- 11. el pisacorbatas   *tie bar*
- 12. el alfiler de corbata   *tie tack*

Los diseños   *Patterns*

- 1. a cuadros   *checkered*
- 2. sólido(a)   *solid*
- 3. estampado(a)   *print*
- 4. estampado(a) de flores   *flowered*
- 5. bordado(a)   *embroidered*
- 6. cachemira   *paisley*
- 7. escocés(esa)   *plaid*
- 8. a rayas   *striped*
- 9. de bolitas   *polka dot*

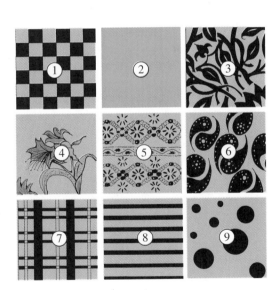

• Las telas   *Fabrics*

- lana   *wool*
- algodón   *cotton*
- nilón   *nylon*
- alpaca   *alpaca*
- casimir   *cashmere*
- franela   *flannel*
- encaje   *lace*
- raso   *satin*
- tafetán   *taffeta*
- pana   *corduroy*
- tejido   *knit*
- seda   *silk*
- cuero   *leather*
- poliéster   *polyester*
- lino   *linen*
- fieltro   *felt*
- piel   *fur*
- charol   *patent leather*
- gamuza   *suede*
- terciopelo   *velvet*
- dril   *denim*

Let's begin by telling what we wear, using the regular **-ar** verb **llevar** (*to wear, to carry, to take along*).

LLEVAR *to wear, to carry*

	IMPERFECT *wore* *was/were wearing* *used to wear*	PRETERITE *wore* *did wear*	PRESENT *wear (s)* *am/is/are wearing* *do/does wear*	FUTURE *will wear*
yo	llev**aba**	llev**é**	llev**o**	llevar**é**
tú	llev**abas**	llev**aste**	llev**as**	llevar**ás**
Ud./él/ella	llev**aba**	llev**ó**	llev**a**	llevar**á**
nosotros(as)	llev**ábamos**	llev**amos**	llev**amos**	llevar**emos**
vosotros(as)	llev**abais**	llev**asteis**	llev**áis**	llevar**éis**
Uds./ellos/ellas	llev**aban**	llev**aron**	llev**an**	llevar**án**

If you want to say *I will wear*, start at the line with **yo** and follow across to the column labeled *will wear*. The word where the column and the line meet is **llevaré**, which means *I will wear*.

Llevar is a regular **-ar** verb, so you can use the same endings (in bold print on the chart above) on any regular **-ar** verb.

¿Qué llevas tú hoy?

1. Take turns with your classmates and describe what you wore yesterday. Be sure to mention the color, pattern, and fabric whenever possible.

    EJEMPLO: Yo llevé un suéter azul claro de lana.
    Yo llevé una camisa amarilla y parda de manga larga.

2. Ask your partner what several other people are wearing today. Answer telling the style, color, and fabric.

    EJEMPLO: ¿Qué lleva Diego hoy?

      Diego lleva pantalones negros, una camisa roja, calcetines blancos y zapatos tenis.

3 Tell what the following people are wearing and why. Then ask your partner what he or she wears in the same situations.

EJEMPLO: 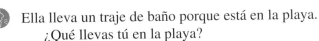 Ella lleva un traje de baño porque está en la playa.
¿Qué llevas tú en la playa?

Yo llevo un traje de baño también.

a.

b.

c.

d.

4 Using a magazine or newspaper, look at what the people are wearing. Tell whether you like or don't like the clothing. If necessary, review the verb **gustar** on page 132.

EJEMPLO: Me gusta este vestido azul, pero no me gustan estos zapatos negros.

5 Find out what your partner wore to school when he or she was a child. Did the school have a uniform **(un uniforme)**?

EJEMPLO: De niño(a), ¿qué llevabas a la escuela?

Llevaba un uniforme—pantalones grises, (etc.).

6 **Un desfile de moda**   Write a detailed description of what your partner is wearing to school today. Then use this description to describe your partner's performance in the fashion show.

7 *Sit-Con*   Invite a friend to go somewhere (to a movie, a party, shopping, etc.) with you. Decide what will you wear.

EJEMPLO: Vamos al cine.

¡Buena idea! ¿Qué llevarás?

Voy a llevar…

8 **Juego: Diez preguntas**   One person thinks of an article of clothing. The other person tries to guess what it is by asking questions.

EJEMPLO: ¿De qué color es?
¿Cuándo lo llevas?
¿Es para hombres o para mujeres?

9 **Juego**   Have a member of the class go into the hallway. See who can describe the clothing that person is wearing.

Vocabulario

Lo que hacemos con la ropa   *What we do with clothing*

1. llevar   *to wear, to carry*
2. comprar   *to buy*
3. mirar   *to look at*
4. dar* de regalo   *to give as a gift*
• 5. lavar a mano   *to hand wash*
• 6.   a máquina   *to machine wash*

• 7. limpiar en seco   *to dry clean*
• 8. admirar   *to admire*
• 9. ensuciar   *to soil*
• 10. desgarrar   *to rip, to tear*
• 11. reparar   *to repair*
• 12. coser   *to sew*

*Note: **Dar** is irregular in the preterite. The forms for **dar** are given later in this lesson on page 198.

Most verbs in Spanish are "regular," meaning that once we learn one set of endings, we can use these for many other verbs that follow the same pattern. Let's see how it works with the verb **invitar** *(to invite)*.

THE INFINITIVE AND PERSON–TIME ENDINGS FOR -AR VERBS

The infinitive form of a verb (action word) in Spanish is made of two parts: a <u>stem,</u> which tells what the action is, and an <u>ending,</u> which is the equivalent of *to*.

INVITAR	*to invite*
STEM	ENDING
invit	**ar**

The infinitive ending of the verb (**-ar, -er,** or **-ir**) does not tell us <u>who</u> is doing the action or <u>when</u>. To tell <u>who</u> and <u>when</u> in the past or present, remove **-ar**, then add a <u>person–time ending</u> to the stem of the verb. In the future, add the <u>person–time ending</u> to the infinitive. This is called "conjugating" the verb.

	IMPERFECT	PRETERITE	PRESENT	FUTURE
	-ed	*-ed*	*-(s)*	*will*
	was/were -ing		*am/is/are -ing*	
	used to	*did*	*do/does*	
yo	**-aba**	**-é**	**-o**	**-é**
tú	**-abas**	**-aste**	**-as**	**-ás**
Ud./él/ella	**-aba**	**-ó**	**-a**	**-á**
nosotros(as)	**-ábamos**	**-amos**	**-amos**	**-emos**
vosotros(as)	**-abais**	**-asteis**	**-áis**	**-éis**
Uds./ellos/ellas	**-aban**	**-aron**	**-an**	**-án**

Some consonants are pronounced differently depending on the vowel that follows. As a result, in some tenses some verbs will have spelling changes in the last letter of the stem in order to preserve its sound when different endings are added.

C
G } before { A O U } changes to { QU J C } before { E I }
Z

In the preterite, verbs ending in **-car, -gar,** and **-zar** will have a spelling change before the **é** in the **yo** form.

c → qu	buscar	yo bus<u>qué</u>	tú buscaste, *etc.*
g → gu	pagar	yo pa<u>gué</u>	tú pagaste, *etc.*
z → c	comenzar	yo comen<u>cé</u>	tú comenzaste, *etc.*

10 Tell what you do with your clothing. Remember that possessive adjectives are not usually used with clothing.

EJEMPLO: Compro la ropa en el almacén.
Lavo la ropa con detergente.

11 Tell what else the person who washes your clothes does with them.

EJEMPLO: Ana lava mucha ropa a máquina.
Ana repara la ropa.

OBJECT PRONOUNS

An indirect object answers the question <u>to</u> or <u>for whom</u> the action was done.
   (In English, <u>to</u> or <u>for</u> may be implied but not stated.)
A direct object answers the question <u>who</u> or <u>what</u> receives the action of the verb.

Indirect and direct object pronouns share the forms **me, te, nos,** and **os.** They differ only in the forms starting with l.

INDIRECT OBJECT PRONOUNS		DIRECT OBJECT PRONOUNS	
me	*to/for me*	me	*me*
te	*to/for you*	te	*you*
le	*to/for you/him/her/it*	lo	*you/him/it*
		la	*you/her/it*
nos	*to/for us*	nos	*us*
os	*to/for you*	os	*you*
les	*to/for you/them*	los	*you/them*
		las	*you/them*

In Spanish, the indirect object pronoun must be used whenever there is an indirect object, even if the indirect object noun is mentioned in the sentence.

   Yo <u>le</u> di un regalo <u>a mi hermano</u>.   *I gave a gift to my brother.*

POSITION OF OBJECT PRONOUNS

Object pronouns are placed before the verb with the person–time ending.

   Yo <u>le</u> escribí una carta.   *I wrote <u>her</u> a letter.*
   Mi madre <u>los</u> va a comprar.   *My mother is going to buy <u>them</u>.*

Object pronouns may be attached to the end of the **-ar, -er, -ir** form of the verb.

   Mi madre va a comprar<u>los</u>.   *My mother is going to buy <u>them</u>.*

12 Make a list of several items of clothing. Then tell when you wear each item, using a direct object pronoun.

EJEMPLO: los guantes   Los llevo cuando hace frío.
           la corbata   Nunca la llevo.

13 Use the same list of clothing and tell when you are going to wear each item of clothing next.

EJEMPLO: los guantes   Voy a llevarlos en el invierno.
           la corbata   Nunca voy a llevarla.

14 **Encuesta**   Either use the list from Activity 12 or create a new one. Find out from several other people when they wear each of the items you listed.

EJEMPLO: ¿Cuándo llevas los guantes?

           Los llevo en el invierno.

15 Find out what your classmates do when they tear their favorite clothing.

EJEMPLO: ¿Qué haces cuando desgarras la ropa?

           Yo la reparo o mi madre la repara.

16 *Sit-Con*   You are buying a gift of clothing for your best friend. Your partner is the clerk in the store. Discuss with the clerk what to buy and the cost of each item. Choose one item to purchase and then pay for it.

17 Ask your partner if he or she remembers where the clothing that he or she is wearing today was purchased.

EJEMPLO: ¿Recuerdas dónde compraste los calcetines?

           Los compré en… / No, no recuerdo. / No los compré. Mi hermano me los regaló.

18 Ask your partner how he or she cleans various items of clothing.

EJEMPLO: ¿Cómo limpias la chaqueta?

           La lavo a mano.

Do you give clothing as gifts? Do other people give you clothing? Let's review the verb **dar** (*to give*) so we can talk about giving things to others and tell what they gave us.

DAR *to give*

	IMPERFECT *gave* *was/were giving* *used to give*	PRETERITE *gave* *did give*	PRESENT *gives(s)* *am/is/are giving* *do/does give*	FUTURE *will give*
yo	daba	**di**	**doy**	daré
tú	dabas	**diste**	das	darás
Ud./él/ella	daba	**dio**	da	dará
nosotros(as)	dábamos	**dimos**	damos	daremos
vosotros(as)	dabais	**disteis**	dais	daréis
Uds./ellos/ellas	daban	**dieron**	dan	darán

Irregularities:
preterite: **Dar** uses the regular **-er** and **-ir** endings (without accents).
present: **doy**

---

19 Tell what you give to different people you know for their birthdays. Be sure to include the indirect object pronoun even if the indirect object noun is also in the sentence.

EJEMPLO: Le doy cintas a mi amigo.
Le doy tarjetas a mi abuela.

20 Tell what different people give you for your birthday.

EJEMPLO: Mis padres me dan ropa.
Mi novio me da dulces *(candy)*.

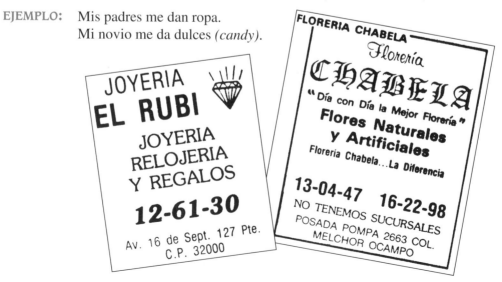

JOYERIA
EL RUBI
JOYERIA
RELOJERIA
Y REGALOS
12-61-30
Av. 16 de Sept. 127 Pte.
C.P. 32000

FLORERIA CHABELA
Florería
CHABELA
" Día con Día la Mejor Florería "
**Flores Naturales
y Artificiales**
Florería Chabela...La Diferencia
13-04-47   16-22-98
NO TENEMOS SUCURSALES
POSADA POMPA 2663 COL.
MELCHOR OCAMPO

DOUBLE OBJECT PRONOUNS

When there are two object pronouns in the same sentence, the <u>indirect object</u> pronoun comes first, and the <u>direct object</u> pronoun follows. **Se** replaces either **le** or **les** before **lo, la, los,** or **las**.

Mi abuela me dio el libro.   *My grandmother gave me a book.*
Mi abuela <u>me lo</u> dio.   *My grandmother gave <u>it to me</u>.*

El profesor nos dio el examen.   *The teacher gave us the test.*
El profesor <u>nos lo</u> dio.   *He gave <u>it to us</u>.*

Juan le dio la mochila.   *Juan gave her the backpack.*
Juan <u>se la</u> dio.   *Juan gave <u>it to her</u>.*

When attaching two pronouns to the end of the verb, add an accent mark on the vowel before the pronouns.

Mi primo desea compr<u>ár</u>melo.   *My cousin wants to buy <u>it for me</u>.*
Mi primo va a d<u>ár</u>melo.   *My cousin is going to give <u>it to me</u>.*

Practice saying these common patterns so that the word order will become more familiar to you.

me lo	te lo	nos lo	se lo
me la	te la	nos la	se la
me los	te los	nos los	se los
me las	te las	nos las	se las

21 Make a list of clothing items you no longer wear but are too good to throw away. Tell who you will give them to.

EJEMPLO: la camisa de seda blanca   Se la daré a mi mamá.
las botas para la nieve   Se las daré a la criada.
tres pares de zapatos   Se los daré a los pobres.

22 Make a list of things that your friends would like for their birthdays. Then tell that you will buy those things for them.

EJEMPLO: María desea un reloj pulsera. Yo se lo compraré.

ENCUENTRO PERSONAL

Paulina's class is going to another city for a student conference to learn more about the environment. She needs some casual and dress clothes so her mother is taking her shopping.

PAULINA: Mamá, primero necesito ropa informal. Por ejemplo, necesito una nueva sudadera azul claro, unos pantalones vaqueros azul oscuro, una camiseta, unos zapatos tenis y…

MAMÁ: Un momento, Paulina. Voy a comprarte ropa pero no voy a comprarte toda la tienda. ¿Por qué necesitas toda esta ropa nueva? Ya tienes una sudadera y pantalones vaqueros.

PAULINA: Sí, mamá, pero están viejos y sucios. Y mi camiseta favorita está desgarrada. ¿Me comprarás la ropa nueva si te doy un poco de dinero de mi cuenta de banco?

MAMÁ: Claro, hija, te la compraré si ayudas a pagar algo. Pero prefiero darles dinero a mis hijos para comprarse ropa formal. Por ejemplo, ¿por qué no te compramos este vestido de raso o esta falda de lana, esta blusa elegante de mangas largas estampada de flores, unos zapatos de tacones altos y un collar con brazalete y pendientes… ?

PAULINA: Mamá, cálmate. No tenemos todo el dinero del mundo. Tengo una idea. ¿Por qué no me compras un vestido formal para el baile y yo me compro unos nuevos zapatos tenis?

MAMÁ: Sí, y yo puedo repararte la camiseta desgarrada y tú puedes lavar la sudadera y los pantalones vaqueros. Y para tu cumpleaños te daré un collar y pendientes.

PAULINA: Perfecto, mamá. Te quiero mucho.

¿Comprendes?

1. ¿Qué ropa desea comprar Paulina?
2. ¿Por qué no se la desea comprar su mamá?
3. ¿Por qué necesita Paulina ropa nueva?
4. ¿Qué ropa desea comprarle su madre?
5. ¿Qué solución ofrece Paulina?
6. ¿Qué sugiere su mamá?

¡Te toca!

Describe the type of clothing that you want to buy and the type of clothing that your parents prefer to buy for you. Explain why you need so much new clothing. Do you have enough money to buy it? If not, what solutions are there?

Leemos y contamos

A. After Paulina returned from her class trip, she wrote a letter to her aunt describing what she wore. Read what she wrote and answer the questions that follow.

Querida tía,

¿Cómo están tú y toda la familia? Mi familia y yo estamos muy bien. ¿Sabías que yo fui de viaje con mi clase para aprender más acerca de la contaminación del ambiente? Pues, mi viaje fue magnífico. Primero visitamos la granja donde yo llevé mis pantalones vaqueros azul oscuro y una camiseta a rayas con mis zapatos tenis. Por la tarde fuimos a la ciudad donde nos registramos en el hotel. Entonces visitamos unos museos y el instituto de arte donde yo llevé una falda pardo oscuro y una blusa casual de color crema.

Pero lo que me gustó más fue el baile de bienvenida (welcome) que nos dieron nuestros amigos por correspondencia que viven allí. Fue un baile formal y por eso llevé el nuevo vestido de seda rosada que me compró mi mamá. También llevé unos pendientes y un collar de perlas que me prestó (lent) mamá. Llevé mis zapatos de gamuza negra de tacones altos y una pantimedia. Todos se vistieron (got dressed up) muy elegantemente y todo fue muy bonito. Cuando visitamos una escuela el próximo día, llevé mis pantalones gris claro de pana con un cinturón blanco y un suéter negro de cuello en V sobre una blusa escocesa con unos zapatos negros casuales y los calcetines grises que me diste tú. Todos comentaron que yo estaba muy bonita en la nueva ropa que me compraron mamá y tú.

Besos a toda la familia,
Paulina

1. ¿Qué llevó Paulina a la granja?
2. ¿Qué llevó para visitar los museos?
3. ¿Qué llevó para el baile?
4. ¿Qué llevó a la escuela?
5. ¿Quién le prestó las joyas?
6. ¿Quién le compró los calcetines a Paulina?
7. ¿Qué le comentaron todos a Paulina?
8. Para Paulina, ¿qué era más importante, aprender de la contaminación del ambiente o la ropa que ella llevó durante el viaje?

B. Write a detailed description of what you wore recently to a special occasion. (Use the preterite tense.)

C. Write a description of what you used to wear (use the imperfect tense) to parties as a child and what you will wear (use the future tense) to parties as an adult.

D. Write a dialogue between two people shopping for a suit to wear to a job interview.

¡Así es!

¿Qué llevan los hispanos?

Las camisetas y los pantalones vaqueros—es el uniforme internacional de los jóvenes, pero en la mayoría de los países de habla española, la gente lleva vestido más formal y conservador que aquí en los EE. UU. Los hombres llevan corbatas y sombreros más que en los EE. UU. Las mujeres generalmente llevan faldas y blusas o vestidos en la calle. Los pantalones cortos son para los deportes o la playa y no para llevar en la calle.

En muchos países tropicales para estar más cómodos cuando no es necesario llevar traje y corbata, los hombres llevan una camisa que se llama «guayabera» o «panabrisa». Tiene bolsillos en frente y se lleva *(one wears)* esta camisa sobre los pantalones. Generalmente son bordadas o tienen encaje.

En las montañas, donde hace fresco, muchos hombres llevan un poncho (en Colombia se llaman «ruana») sobre el traje y las mujeres llevan un rebozo *(shawl)*.

En el campo de los países donde hay muchos indios, se ve *(one sees)* un distinto estilo de ropa entre ellos. En Bolivia las campesinas llevan sombreros que se llaman hongos *(bowler hats)*. También, muchas mujeres llevan gorros de béisbol porque son más baratos. Si visitas un área de indios, no debes llevar la ropa típica de los indios porque muchos creen que los turistas se burlan de ellos *(make fun of them)*.

La comida

The word **comida** comes from the verb **comer**. **Comida** can mean *food, meals*, or *dinner*. Of course, food is an important part of everyone's life, so let's talk about food and meals in Spanish. Hopefully all this talk about food will not make you too hungry!

Vocabulario

Las comidas *Meals*

1. el desayuno	*breakfast*	6. el entremés	*appetizer*
2. el almuerzo	*lunch*	7. el plato principal	*main dish*
3. la comida	*dinner, midday main meal*	8. el postre	*dessert*
4. la cena	*supper, evening meal, dinner*	9. la bebida	*beverage*
5. la merienda	*snack*		

Vocabulario

Las legumbres   *Vegetables*

1.	el ajo	*garlic*	13.	los frijoles	*beans*
2.	la cebolla	*onion*	14.	los guisantes	*peas*
3.	la ensalada	*salad*	15.	las judías	*string beans*
4.	la lechuga	*lettuce*	16.	la remolacha	*beet*
5.	el apio	*celery*	17.	la papa	*potato*
6.	el pepino	*cucumber*	18.	las papas fritas	*French fries*
7.	el rábano	*radish*	19.	la batata	*sweet potato*
8.	el tomate	*tomato*	• 20.	el brócoli	*broccoli*
9.	la zanahoria	*carrot*	• 21.	la col	*cabbage*
10.	la coliflor	*cauliflower*	• 22.	las espinacas	*spinach*
11.	el maíz	*corn*	• 23.	el nabo	*turnip*
12.	el pimiento	*pepper*	• 24.	la mazorca	*corn on the cob*

Vocabulario

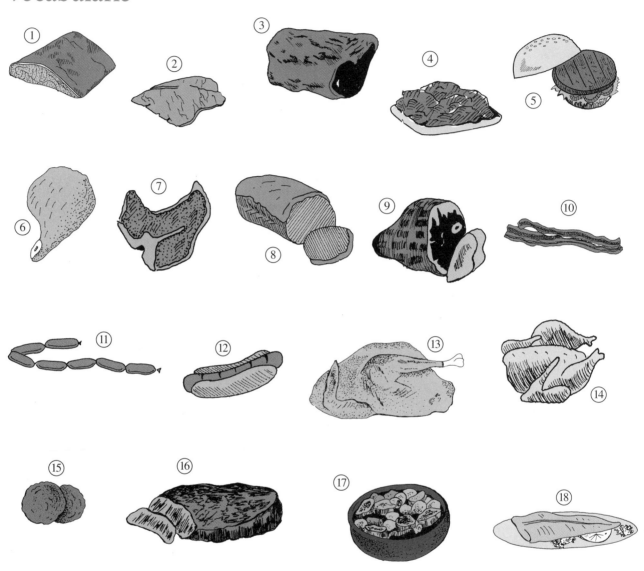

La carne   *Meat*

1. la carne de res	*beef*	10. el tocino	*bacon*
2. la ternera	*veal*	11. la salchicha	*sausage*
3. el rosbif	*roast beef*	12. el perro caliente	*hot dog*
4. la carne molida	*ground meat*	13. el pavo	*turkey*
5. la hamburguesa	*hamburger*	14. el pollo	*chicken*
6. la carne de cordero	*lamb*	• 15. la albóndiga	*meatball*
7. la chuleta de…	*. . . chop*	• 16. el bistec	*steak*
8. la carne de cerdo	*pork*	• 17. el guisado	*stew*
9. el jamón	*ham*	• 18. el filete	*filet*

Vocabulario

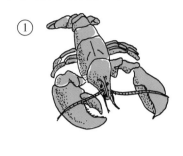

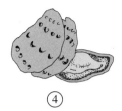

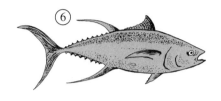

Los mariscos y el pescado   *Shellfish and fish*

1. la langosta   *lobster*
2. los camarones   *shrimp*
3. las almejas   *clams*
4. las ostras   *oysters*

5. el pescado   *fish*
- 6. el atún   *tuna*
- 7. el salmón   *salmon*

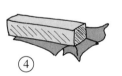

Los productos lácteos   *Dairy products*

1. el huevo   *egg*
2. el queso   *cheese*
3. la leche   *milk*
4. la mantequilla   *butter*

5. la crema   *cream*
6. el yogur   *yogurt*
- 7. la margarina   *margarine*

Vocabulario

Las frutas *Fruits*

1. los arándanos — *blueberries*
2. las cerezas — *cherries*
3. las frambuesas — *raspberries*
4. las fresas — *strawberries*
5. el limón — *lemon*
6. la manzana — *apple*
7. la naranja — *orange*
8. la pera — *pear*
9. la piña — *pineapple*
10. el plátano — *banana*
11. la sandía — *watermelon*
12. la toronja — *grapefruit*
13. las uvas — *grapes*
• 14. el aguacate — *avocado*
• 15. el durazno — *peach*
• 16. el mango — *mango*
• 17. el melón — *melon*
• 18. la papaya — *papaya*
• 19. la pasa — *raisin*

Vocabulario

El pan y las pastas   *Bread and pastas*

1. el pan tostado — *toast*
2. el panecillo — *roll*
• 3. la rebanada — *slice*
• 4. la tortilla — *Mexican flat bread*
• 5. el panqueque — *pancake*

• 6. el barquillo — *waffle*
7. la galleta — *cracker*
• 8. los espaguetis — *spaghetti*
• 9. los macarrones — *macaroni*
• 10. los tallarines — *noodles*

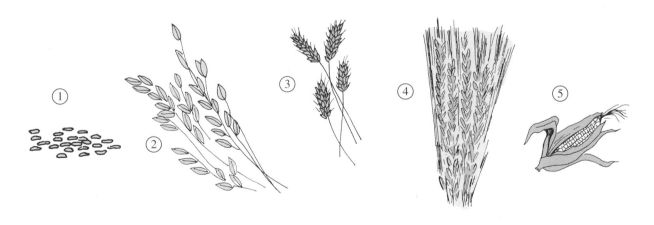

Los cereales   *Cereals*

1. el arroz — *rice*
2. la avena — *oats*
3. el trigo — *wheat*

• 4. la cebada — *barley*
• 5. el maíz — *corn*

Vocabulario

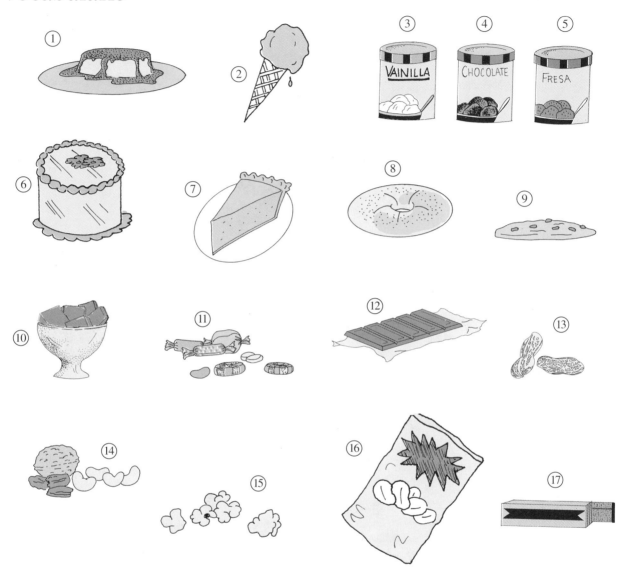

El postre y los bocaditos   *Dessert and snacks*

1. el flan	*custard*	• 10. la gelatina	*gelatin dessert*
2. el helado…	*…ice cream*	11. los dulces	*candy*
3. de vainilla	*vanilla*	12. la tableta de chocolate	*chocolate bar*
4. de chocolate	*chocolate*	13. el cacahuete/•el maní	*peanut*
5. de fresas	*strawberry*	14. la nuez	*nut*
6. la torta	*cake*	15. las palomitas de maíz	*popcorn*
7. el pastel	*pastry, pie*	16. las papitas fritas	*potato chips*
8. la rosquilla	*doughnut*	• 17. el chicle	*gum*
9. la galletita dulce	*cookie*		

Vocabulario

  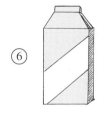   

Las bebidas   *Beverages*

1. el agua *(f.)* — *water*
2. el café — *coffee*
3.   con crema — *with cream*
4.   sin azúcar — *without sugar*
5. el té — *tea*

6. la leche — *milk*
7. el refresco/la soda — *soft drink*
8. el jugo de… — *… juice*
• 9. el chocolate — *hot chocolate*

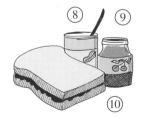  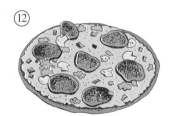

Los condimentos y otras comidas   *Seasonings and other foods*

1. la sal — *salt*
2. la pimienta — *pepper*
3. la salsa picante — *hot sauce*
• 4. el catsup — *ketchup*
• 5. la mostaza — *mustard*
• 6. la mayonesa — *mayonnaise*

• 7. la miel — *honey*
• 8. la crema de maní — *peanut butter*
9. la jalea de… — *… jelly*
10. el sándwich de… — *… sandwich*
11. la sopa de… — *… soup*
12. la pizza — *pizza*

La preparación de la comida   *Preparation of food*

- al vapor   *steamed*
- asado(a)   *broiled*
- cocido(a)   *cooked*
- congelado(a)   *frozen*
- crudo(a)   *raw*
- la masa   *dough*

- encurtido(a)   *pickled*
- frito(a)   *fried*
- horneado(a)   *baked, roasted*
- hervido(a)   *boiled*
- quemado(a)   *burned*

Lo que hacemos con la comida   *What we do with food*

desayunar	*to eat/have breakfast*
almorzar (ue)	*to eat/have lunch*
cenar	*to eat/have dinner*
• merendar (ie)	*to snack*
vender	*to sell*
• escoger	*to choose*
comprar	*to buy*
pagar	*to pay for*
preparar	*to prepare*
• cortar	*to cut*
• mezclar	*to mix*
añadir	*to add*
cocinar	*to cook*
• freír (i, i)	*to fry*
• asar	*to broil*
• ahumar	*to smoke*
• hervir (ie, i)	*to boil*
• hornear	*to bake*
• quemar	*to burn*
• congelar	*to freeze*
comer	*to eat*
beber	*to drink*
tomar	*to drink, to take*
• gozar de	*to enjoy*

Sopa de carne con vegetales

Ingredientes

1½ lb. de carne de res molida	½ cebolla mediana, picadita
½ lb. de carne de cerdo molida	1 tomate mediano, picadito
1 taza de zanahoria picada en cuadritos	2 dientes de ajo, triturados
1 taza de papa picada en cuadritos	1 lata de 8 oz. de puré de tomate
1 taza de chícharos	2 tazas de caldo de res
1 taza de calabacitas tiernas, picadas	1 taza de agua
1 taza de apio, picadita	1 cda. de aceite
	1 ramito de cilantro
	sal, pimienta y cominos al gusto

Preparación:

En una olla grande, sofría la cebolla y el ajo en el aceite bien caliente. Unale la carne y cocínela hasta que esté medio cocida. Agréguele después el resto de los ingredientes y cocine todo por unos 30 minutos o hasta que los vegetales estén blandos. Sírvala caliente y acompáñela con rebanadas de pan calientito o galleticas saltinas. Ofrézcale a su familia este rico y nutritivo plato en el almuerzo o en la cena antes del platillo principal. Buen provecho!

---

1 Tell what foods you like and those you don't like.

Now that we know how to say lots of foods, let's review the verb **comer**.

COMER *to eat*

	IMPERFECT *ate* *was/were eating* *used to eat*	PRETERITE *ate* *did eat*	PRESENT *eat(s)* *am/is/are eating* *do/does eat*	FUTURE *will eat*
yo	comía	comí	como	comeré
tú	comías	comiste	comes	comerás
Ud./él/ella	comía	comió	come	comerá
nosotros(as)	comíamos	comimos	comemos	comeremos
vosotros(as)	comíais	comisteis	coméis	comeréis
Uds./ellos/ellas	comían	comieron	comen	comerán

De niño no comía las legumbres. Ayer comí
zanahorias. Mañana comeré espinacas.

2 Tell what you would like for each of the meals on your birthday.

EJEMPLO: El día de mi cumpleaños, me gustaría comer:
Para el desayuno: panqueques, tocino, leche y…

3 *Sit-Con*   You and your friends are going on a picnic. Make a shopping list.

EJEMPLO: papitas fritas
perros calientes

4 Tell what you used to eat, ate yesterday, usually eat, and will eat in the future.

EJEMPLO: Ayer comí cereal para el desayuno.

Comer ends in **-er** and belongs to the **-er** group of verbs. Review the endings for **-er** verbs.

PERSON–TIME ENDINGS FOR -ER VERBS

For the past and present tenses, remove **-er**, then add the person–time ending. Do not remove **-er** for the future!

	IMPERFECT *-ed* *was/were -ing* *used to*	PRETERITE *-ed* *did*	PRESENT *-(s)* *am/is/are -ing* *do/does*	FUTURE *will*
yo	-ía	-í	-o	-é
tú	-ías	-iste	-es	-ás
Ud./él/ella	-ía	-ió	-e	-á
nosotros(as)	-íamos	-imos	-emos	-emos
vosotros(as)	-íais	-isteis	-éis	-éis
Uds./ellos/ellas	-ían	-ieron	-en	-án

Note spelling variations:

• If an unaccented **i** is between vowels, change **i** to **y**.

   caer ⟶ cayó, cayeron
   leer ⟶ leyó, leyeron

• If a verb ends in **-ger**, change **g** to **j** before **o** or **a**.

   escoger ⟶ yo escojo

---

5 Tell what you eat and drink with your meals and during other activities.

EJEMPLO: Como pan tostado con mi desayuno.
               Bebo refrescos cuando voy a la playa.

6 Tell where they sell various food products in your city.

EJEMPLO: Venden leche en el supermercado S & W.
               Venden fruta en la tienda de Farmer Pete.

7 Using the verbs in the list on page 214, tell some things you and others do with food.

EJEMPLO: Cuando mi padre cocina, siempre quema las papas.

"To conjugate" means "to change" the infinitive into person-time forms. The verb **poner** *(to put)* is conjugated much the same as the verb **tener** *(to have)*. Notice that the preterite endings of these verbs and a few others are a combination of **-ar** and **-er** endings without accents. We refer to this group as "combo" verbs.

PONER   *to put, to place*

	IMPERFECT	PRETERITE	PRESENT	FUTURE
	put	*put*	*put(s)*	*will put*
	was/were putting		*am/is/are putting*	
	used to put	*did put*	*do/does put*	
yo	ponía	**puse**	**pongo**	**pondré**
tú	ponías	**pusiste**	pones	**pondrás**
Ud./él/ella	ponía	**puso**	pone	**pondrá**
nosotros(as)	poníamos	**pusimos**	ponemos	**pondremos**
vosotros(as)	poníais	**pusisteis**	ponéis	**pondréis**
Uds./ellos/ellas	ponían	**pusieron**	ponen	**pondrán**

Irregularities:
preterite: **pus-** + "combo" endings
present: **-go** verb: **yo pongo**
future: irregular future stem = **pondr-**

Vocabulario

Lo que necesitamos para poner la mesa   *What we need to set the table*

- 1. el mantel — *tablecloth*
- 2. la servilleta — *napkin*
- 3. el centro de mesa — *centerpiece*
- 4. el candelero — *candlestick*
- 5. el cubierto — *place setting*
- 6. el plato — *plate, dish*
- 7. el platillo — *saucer*
- 8. la cuenca — *bowl*
- 9. la taza — *cup*
- 10. el vaso — *glass*
- 11. la copa — *goblet*
- 12. la cuchara — *spoon*

- 13. la cucharita — *teaspoon*
- 14. el tenedor — *fork*
- 15. el cuchillo — *knife*
- 16. el salero — *salt shaker*
- 17. el pimentero — *pepper shaker*
- 18. la jarra — *pitcher*
- 19. la ensaladera — *salad bowl*
- 20. la cremera — *creamer*
- 21. la azucarera — *sugar bowl*
- 22. la cafetera — *coffeepot*
- 23. la tetera — *teapot*

8 Tell where you put different items of food when you eat them.

EJEMPLO: Pongo carne en un plato.
Pongo café en una taza.

9 Tell how you set the table for different meals.

EJEMPLO: Para el desayuno, pongo las cuencas para el cereal, la cremera de leche, los vasos para el jugo de naranja, la azucarera y cucharas grandes.

10 **¡Vamos a poner la mesa!**   Use a sheet of plain paper for your "table" and draw the place settings and other things for a romantic dinner for two. Label them. Then tell what you did to set the table.

EJEMPLO: Puse platos, la ensaladera…

Now let's talk about the foods we like and don't like. Since we'll be using the verb **gustar**, review its pattern on page 132 first.

A Luisa no le gustaban las langostas.

Pero ahora le encanta comerlas.

11 Make a list of ten foods you like, ten you don't like and won't eat, and ten foods that you eat but don't particularly like. Compare your list with others.

Categories: Me gusta(n)...
No me gusta(n) nada y no como nunca...
No me gusta(n) pero como...

12 **Encuesta**   Make a list of five foods. Survey several people and find out how many like these foods. Also find out if they eat them.

EJEMPLO:  ¿Te gustan los camarones?

No, no me gustan los camarones.

¿Los comes?

No, no los como.

Reportaje: A Javier no le gustan los camarones. No los come.

13 How do you like different foods prepared? Make a list of foods you eat frequently and tell how you like them.

EJEMPLO: los huevos   Me gustan los huevos fritos.
el pan   Me gusta el pan tostado.

Vocabulario

Los verbos como «gustar»   *Verbs like* gustar

gustar	*to be pleasing, to like*	faltar	*to need, to be lacking*
quedar	*to have left*	doler (ue)	*to hurt*
• disgustar	*to annoy, to displease*	• importar	*to matter*
• encantar	*to love, to adore*	• interesar	*to interest*
• fascinar	*to fascinate*	• molestar	*to bother*

These verbs use the indirect object pronoun with either the *it* or *they* form of the verb based on whether the noun following is singular or plural.

disgustar   *to annoy, to displease*
   Me disgustan las moscas.   *Flies annoy me.*

encantar   *to love, to adore*
   ¡Me encantaba el chocolate!   *I used to love chocolate.*

faltar   *to need, to be lacking*
   Nos faltaron tenedores.   *We needed forks.*

fascinar   *to fascinate*
   Les fascinan las recetas.   *Recipes fascinate them.*

importar   *to matter*

¿Te importan los modales?

Do manners matter to you?

interesar   *to interest*

A Eva le interesaba cocinar.

Eva used to be interested in cooking.

molestar   *to bother*

No nos molestará preparar el picnic.

It will not bother us to prepare the picnic.

quedar   *to have left*

A Uds. les quedan cinco minutos.

You have five minutes left.

14 Write two sentences for each of the verbs that are like **gustar**. Make one singular and one plural.

EJEMPLO: Me interesa la ciencia ficción.

Me interesan los libros de ciencia ficción.

15 **¿Qué te falta?**   Tell what's missing from the following place settings.

EJEMPLO: Me falta un cuchillo.
Me faltan un tenedor y un vaso.

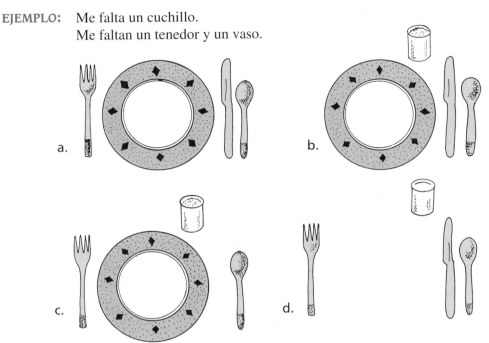

a.

b.

c.

d.

16 *Sit-Con*   You want to invite a friend out. Find out what she or he is interested in doing.

EJEMPLO: ¿Te interesa ir al parque?
No, no me interesa ir al parque. Me interesa ver una película.

17 Make a list of things that interest you and another list of things that don't.

EJEMPLO: Me interesa la historia.
No me interesa la política.

18 Do an inventory of your school supplies from the beginning of the year. How much is left from what you had at the beginning of the school year?

EJEMPLO: Tenía diez lápices. Me quedan tres.
Tenía tres cuadernos. Me queda uno.

19 Tell some things that bother you.

EJEMPLO: Me molesta mi hermanito.
Me molesta no tener las gafas cuando las necesito.

20 *Sit-Con*   It is dinnertime. Pretend to go to a restaurant and order a meal. Your partner will be the waiter or waitress **(el/la mesero[a])**. Ask for the check **(la cuenta)** when you are finished and don't forget to leave a tip **(una propina)**. Switch roles and replay the scene.

EJEMPLO: Mesero: ¿Qué le gustaría comer esta noche?
Cliente: Me gustaría comer el pollo frito y…

ENCUENTRO PERSONAL

It's Paulina's first date with Santiago. They are in a restaurant where nothing seems to be going right.

MESERO: Buenas noches. ¿En qué puedo servirles?

PAULINA: Pues primero nos faltan los cubiertos.

MESERO: Hay cucharas y cuchillos pero no hay tenedores. El lavaplatos no funciona hoy.

PAULINA: Bueno, queremos los menúes, por favor.

MESERO: Lo siento, aquí los tienen, pero son de ayer.

PAULINA: En este caso, yo quiero pollo con arroz.

SANTIAGO: Y yo quiero bistec con papas.

MESERO: Lo siento, señores, pero no podemos cocinar; no hay gas para la estufa *(stove)*.
             ¿Puedo sugerirles una ensalada y un sándwich de jamón?

PAULINA: Sí, tengo mucha hambre. Una ensalada y un sándwich están bien.

SANTIAGO: Pero no podemos comer ensalada sin tenedores y no me gusta el jamón.

MESERO: ¿Les gustan el cereal con leche y pan tostado? El tostador funciona perfectamente
             bien sin gas. Y pueden comerlos con una cuchara y cuchillo.

PAULINA: Sí, sí, señor, cereal y pan están bien. Pero pronto, por favor.
             [Unos minutos después]

MESERO: Lo siento, señores, pero la leche está en la tienda todavía. ¿Puedo sugerirles
             palomitas de maíz con gelatina? Se puede comerlo todo con una cuchara y no
             necesitamos leche para servirlo.

PAULINA: Sí, está bien. Ahora tengo muchísima hambre.

[Unos minutos después]

MESERO: Aquí están las palomitas de maíz. Están un poco quemadas. No podía hacer la gelatina porque no podía hervir el agua.

PAULINA: Deme las palomitas; no me importa que estén quemadas. ¿Dónde está la sal? Y necesito mantequilla también.

MESERO: Lo siento, no tenemos saleros en las mesas, pero aquí está el pimentero. No recibimos ni mantequilla ni leche hoy.

SANTIAGO: Esto es ridículo. Quiero hablar con el gerente (*manager*).

MESERO: Lo siento, pero el gerente no está porque el restaurante está cerrado (*closed*) los lunes.

PAULINA: Entonces, ¿por qué está Ud. aquí?

MESERO: Porque yo soy nuevo aquí y necesito practicar para mi primer día de trabajo mañana. Pero no se preocupen, ¡la comida es gratis (*free*) hoy!

¿Comprendes?

1. ¿Qué les falta a Paulina y a Santiago?
2. ¿Qué desean comer?
3. ¿Por qué no es posible servirlos?
4. ¿Qué sugiere el mesero?
5. ¿Por qué no lo quiere Santiago?
6. ¿Qué otras sugerencias hace el mesero?
7. ¿Qué otros problemas hay?
8. ¿Qué les dice el mesero de su trabajo?

¡Te toca!

Pretend you are in a restaurant and one person is the waiter or waitress and the others are customers. The customers order meals and the waiter or waitress writes the order down on the board.

Leemos y contamos

A. What are healthy foods? Should they be eaten cooked or raw? Do you agree with the following suggestions?

Un menú saludable *(healthy)*

D E S A Y U N O

Frutas frescas: manzana, naranja, plátano, uvas, toronja
Taza de yogur con germen de trigo
Nueces crudas como almendras *(almonds)*, maní,
    o semillas de girasol *(sunflower seeds)*
Media taza de queso cottage
Ensalada de frutas
Taza de avena integral cocida, con pasas u otra fruta

C O M I D A   P R I N C I P A L

Ensalada de legumbres crudas incluyendo lechuga, tomate, aguacate, zanahoria, pepino,
    espinacas, brócoli, col, rábano, coliflor, cebolla y todo tipo de brotes *(sprouts)*
Papas cocidas con cáscara *(skin)* (hervidas u horneadas, pero no fritas)
Legumbres cocidas al vapor o preparadas al horno. Por ejemplo:
    nopales *(cactus)*, espinacas, apio, batatas, calabazas *(squash)*,
    pimientos, col, brócoli, etc.
Rebanadas de pan o bollos de trigo, cebada u otros cereales 100
    por ciento integrales
Pollo (sin pellejo) *(skin),* pescado o carne magra *(lean)*

M E R I E N D A

Vaso de jugo de fruta o legumbre cruda
Taza grande de té de hierbas con miel
Fruta fresca

C E N A

Una taza grande de cereal integral, como trigo, avena,
    cebada o arroz con pasas, o fruta y leche
Plato grande de fruta
Plato de legumbres preparadas
Cuenca grande de yogur con fruta
Una o dos rebanadas de pan integral y queso

1. ¿Qué grupos de comida son buenos para la salud?
2. ¿Qué tipos de comida no están en la lista? ¿Por qué no?
3. ¿Es mejor cocinar legumbres o no? ¿Qué tipos de comida se deben cocinar?
4. ¿Qué maneras de cocinar son recomendables y no recomendables?
5. ¿Por qué hay más cosas para la comida principal que para la cena?
6. ¿Estás de acuerdo (*Do you agree*) con las recomendaciones? ¿Por qué?

B. You are opening a restaurant. Decide on a name for your restaurant and then write out your menu. Briefly describe the main dishes. Don't forget to add prices.

PIRÁMIDE DE GUÍA DE ALIMENTOS
UNA GUÍA PARA ELEGIR LOS ALIMENTOS DIARIOS

Grasas, aceites
e ingredientes dulces
ÚSELOS ESCASAMENTE

CLAVE
● Grasa (la que se presenta en forma natural y la que se añade)
▼ Azúcares (que se añaden)

Grupo de leche,
yogur y queso
DE 2-3 PORCIONES

Grupo de carne, aves,
pescado, frijoles secos,
huevos y nueces
DE 2-3 PORCIONES

Grupo de Vegetales
DE 3-5 PORCIONES

Grupo de frutas
DE 2-4 PORCIONES

Grupo de pan,
cereal, arroz y
pasta
DE 6-11
PORCIONES

¡Así es!

Los modales en la mesa *Table manners*

Algunos de los modales en la mesa en los países de habla española son distintos a los de los Estados Unidos. Aún *(Even)* entre los países hispanos hay distinciones y es una buena idea observar a la gente para aprender como comen y no ser maleducado *(rude)*. Éstos son algunos de los modales de la mesa hispana:

Los hispanos ponen las muñecas *(wrists)* o los brazos en el borde de la mesa. Nunca ponen las manos en el regazo *(lap)* ni los codos en la mesa.

Toman el tenedor en la mano izquierda para cortar la comida y también para llevarla a la boca. Cuando no usan el tenedor o el cuchillo, los ponen en el plato con el mango *(handle)* en la mesa. Cuando terminan de comer, ponen el tenedor y el cuchillo en el medio del plato. También en muchos países, comen la fruta con un tenedor y la cortan con un cuchillo.

En muchas casas, la criada sirve la comida. No es necesario siempre esperar a comer hasta que todos tengan su comida. Puedes mirar e imitar a las otras personas en la mesa. Debes comer un poco de todo lo que hay en tu plato. En algunos países es costumbre dejar *(to leave)* un poco en tu plato; en otros países debes comer todo, si puedes. Imita a las otras personas.

¿Dónde vives?

Vocabulario

¿Dónde vives?   *Where do you live?*

¿Cuál es tu dirección?	*What is your address?*	el campo	*country*
la dirección	*address*	el centro	*downtown*
el número	*number*	el barrio	*neighborhood*
la calle	*street*	la granja	*farm*
el paseo	*drive*	la casa	*house*
el camino	*road*	el apartamento	*apartment*
la avenida	*avenue*	el condominio	*condominium*
la ciudad	*city*	de un piso	*one story*
las afueras	*suburbs*	de dos pisos	*two stories*

Dando direcciones   *Giving directions*

Ve (tú)/Vaya (Ud.)…	*Go . . .*
Toma (tú)/Tome (Ud.)…	*Take . . .*
la calle	*street*
• la carretera	*highway, expressway*
• la autopista	*expressway, turnpike*
• la salida	*expressway exit*
Sigue (tú)/Siga (Ud.)…	*Continue, Follow . . .*
hasta llegar a	*until you get to*
• todo derecho	*straight ahead*
al norte	*to the north*
sur	*south*
este	*east*
oeste	*west*
noreste	*northeast*
suroeste	*southwest*
• Dobla (tú)/Doble (Ud.)…	*Turn . . .*
a la derecha	*to the right*
a la izquierda	*to the left*
• en el semáforo	*at the traffic light*
Está a dos cuadras de	*It's two blocks from*
a dos millas de	*two miles from*
en la esquina de	*on/at the corner of*
enfrente de	*in front of, across from*
cerca de	*near*
lejos de	*far from*
al lado de	*at the side of, next to*

Verbos para dar las direcciones   *Verbs for giving directions*

vivir	*to live*
ir a casa	*to go home*
dar instrucciones	*to give instructions*
escribir direcciones	*to write addresses*
seguir (i, i) adelante	*to continue ahead*
seguir (i, i) las instrucciones	*to follow the instructions*
• describir la casa	*to describe the house*
subir a	*to go up, to get on*
bajar	*to go down, to get off*
salir* de	*to leave, to go out of*
ver*	*to see*
oír*	*to hear*

Note: Verbs with an asterisk (*) have some irregularities. They appear later in this lesson.

Writing addresses

An address in Spanish is written so that the word *Street*, *Avenue*, etc., is first, then the street name, then the house number.

Mi dirección es Paseo Elm número 2465.   *My address is 2465 Elm Drive.*

RMT:
Celia Luisa González
José Martí 23
San José, Costa Rica

María Gómez Romero
Avenida Simón Bolívar 732
Caracas, Venezuela S.A.

1 How would your address be written in Spanish style? Address an envelope to yourself, using the preceding format.

2 Ask several of your classmates for their addresses. After they respond to you, address envelopes to them.

EJEMPLO: ¿Cuál es tu dirección?

Mi dirección es Avenida Woodward número 2465.

3 Draw a floor plan of your house or apartment. Label the rooms, then describe your house.

4 **¿Dónde está tu casa?**   Describe the location of your house in relation to other places in your city. (Review the vocabulary relating to places in the city and location on pages 143 and 144 before doing this activity.)

EJEMPLO: Mi casa está al norte de la ciudad, en la Avenida Sawyer. Está cerca de la estación de bomberos y a cuatro cuadras de la biblioteca.

5 Tell the location of your house and the houses of some of your friends in relation to your school.

EJEMPLO: Mi casa está tres millas al oeste de la escuela.
La casa de Juliana está cinco cuadras al este.

Following are the endings for **-ir** verbs. If you look carefully, you will see that they are identical to the **-er** verbs except for the **nosotros** and **vosotros** forms of the present.

PERSON–TIME ENDINGS FOR -IR VERBS

For the past and present tenses, remove **-ir**, then add the person–time ending. Do not remove **-ir** for the future!

	IMPERFECT *-ed* *was/were -ing* *used to*	PRETERITE *-ed* *did*	PRESENT *-(s)* *am/is/are -ing* *do/does*	FUTURE *will*
yo	**-ía**	**-í**	**-o**	**-é**
tú	**-ías**	**-iste**	**-es**	**-ás**
Ud./él/ella	**-ía**	**-ió**	**-e**	**-á**
nosotros(as)	**-íamos**	**-imos**	**-imos**	**-emos**
vosotros(as)	**-íais**	**-isteis**	**-ís**	**-éis**
Uds./ellos/ellas	**-ían**	**-ieron**	**-en**	**-án**

Note spelling variations:

•If an unaccented **i** is between two vowels, change **i** to **y**.

oír ⟶ oyó, oyeron
huir ⟶ huyó, huyeron

•If a verb ends in **gir**, change **g** to **j** before **o** or **a**.

eligir ⟶ yo elijo

De niño vivía en un apartamento en la ciudad.

Ahora vivimos en una casa en las afueras.

En el futuro viviré en un condominio en el campo.

6 **Encuesta**   Find out where several people lived when they were children. Then write a short report about it.

EJEMPLO: ¿Dónde vivías de niño(a)?

Yo vivía en…

Reportaje: Solamente tres personas vivían en esta ciudad cuando eran niños. Uno vivía en…

7 **Encuesta**   Where will you live in five years? In ten years? In twenty years? Find out from several of your classmates where they will live also. Then write a report about it.

EJEMPLO: ¿Dónde vivirás en cinco (diez, veinte) años?

En cinco años, viviré en Nueva York; en diez años viviré en…

Reportaje: Mis compañeros de clase tienen muchos planes para el futuro. Olivia desea vivir en Nueva York en cinco años pero después de eso, desea vivir en…

8 Give your partner directions for getting to your house from school.

EJEMPLO: Para ir a mi casa, tú sales de la escuela y vas a la derecha una milla hasta la Calle Franklin. Doblas a la derecha y vas tres cuadras…

9 Give your partner directions for getting to several places in your city.

10 Juego: ¿Adónde voy?   Use the map of Pueblochico or, if possible, a map of your city. Do not tell your destination. Tell the others where to begin, then give directions for getting to your destination. The person who arrives is the winner and gives directions to his or her destination.

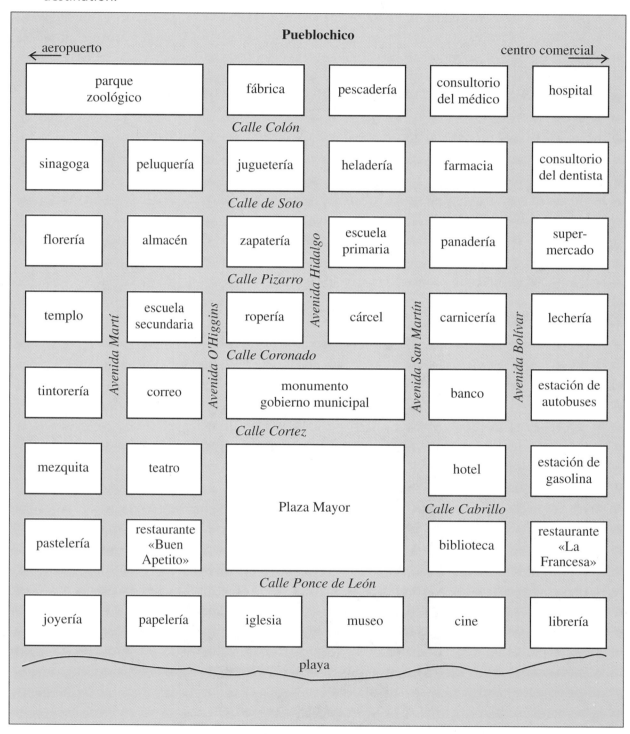

Many verbs that use the **-er** and **-ir** endings have irregular **yo** forms in the present tense and a different stem in one or more of the other tenses. The verbs **salir, oír,** and **ver** that follow are in this group of irregular verbs.

SALIR   *to go out, to leave*

	IMPERFECT *left* *was/were leaving* *used to leave*	PRETERITE *left* *did leave*	PRESENT *leave(s)* *am/is/are leaving* *do/does leave*	FUTURE *will leave*
yo	salía	salí	**salgo**	**saldré**
tú	salías	saliste	sales	**saldrás**
Ud./él/ella	salía	salió	sale	**saldrá**
nosotros(as)	salíamos	salimos	salimos	**saldremos**
vosotros(as)	salíais	salisteis	salís	**saldréis**
Uds./ellos/ellas	salían	salieron	salen	**saldrán**

Irregularities:
present: **-go** verb: **yo salgo**
future: irregular future stem = **saldr-**

When you leave from a place, the preposition **de** is used.
   Salgo <u>de</u> mi casa a las siete de la mañana.
   I leave my house at seven A.M.

¿A qué hora saliste para la escuela?

---

11 **Encuesta**   Find out the time several of your classmates leave for school every day. Then find out if they left at that time today.

EJEMPLO: ¿A qué hora sales para la escuela?

Salgo de mi casa a las siete menos diez.

¿A qué hora saliste de la casa esta mañana?

Yo salí a las siete en punto.

12 **Encuesta**   Find out what time several of your classmates will leave school today.

EJEMPLO: ¿A qué hora saldrás de la escuela?

Saldré a las cuatro y media.

Now let's look at the forms of the verb **oír**. Notice that the endings are the regular **-ir** endings—only the stem has irregular changes.

OÍR *to hear*

	IMPERFECT *heard* *was/were hearing* *used to hear*	PRETERITE *heard* *did hear*	PRESENT *hear(s)* *am/is/are hearing* *do/does hear*	FUTURE *will hear*
yo	oía	oí	**oigo**	oiré
tú	oías	oíste	**oyes**	oirás
Ud./él/ella	oía	**oyó**	**oye**	oirá
nosotros(as)	oíamos	oímos	oímos	oiremos
vosotros(as)	oíais	oísteis	oís	oiréis
Uds./ellos/ellas	oían	**oyeron**	**oyen**	oirán

Irregularities:

preterite: regular but with addition of accent on **i**, **i** changed to **y** between vowels

present: **-go** verb: **yo oigo**, accent on **í** in **oímos**, **y** added between vowels

¿Oíste eso?

No, no oigo nada.

PERSONAL A

When a person is the direct object, add the personal **a**.

Marisol visita <u>a</u> su amiga.   *Marisol visits her friend.*
Marisol visita <u>a</u> Elena.   *Marisol visits Elena.*

Exception: **tener**
        Tengo muchos amigos.   *I have a lot of friends.*

13 Listen carefully. What are some of the things you hear?

EJEMPLO: Oigo los carros en la calle.
Oigo a un muchacho que habla en el pasillo.
Oigo la tiza contra la pizarra.

14 Find out what your friends heard and report about it.

EJEMPLO: ¿Qué oíste?

Yo oí los carros en la calle.

Yo oí a un muchacho que habló en el pasillo.

Reportaje: Anita oyó los carros y Frederico oyó a un muchacho.

15 Make a list of things you and your friends hear on your way to school.

EJEMPLO: Oímos a los obreros que reparan la calle.
Oímos los carros, los autobuses y los trenes que pasan.

There are only three verbs that are irregular in the imperfect. You already know **ser** and **ir**. **Ver** is the third. Why do you think there are no accents in the **yo** and **él** forms of the preterite?

VER   *to see*

	IMPERFECT *saw* *was/were seeing* *used to see*	PRETERITE *saw* *did see*	PRESENT *see(s)* *am/is/are seeing* *do/does see*	FUTURE *will see*
yo	**veía**	vi	**veo**	veré
tú	**veías**	viste	ves	verás
Ud./él/ella	**veía**	vio	ve	verá
nosotros(as)	**veíamos**	vimos	vemos	veremos
vosotros(as)	**veíais**	visteis	veis	veréis
Uds./ellos/ellas	**veían**	vieron	ven	verán

Irregularities:
imperfect: stem = **ve-**
preterite: regular but without accents
present: **yo veo**

¿Viste ese monstruo?

No, no veo nada.

16 Find out where your classmates went last week and what they saw.

EJEMPLO:  ¿Adónde fuiste la semana pasada?

Fui a la biblioteca.

¿Qué viste allí?

Vi a muchos de mis amigos.

17 Find out from your classmates if there is anything they used to see that they don't see anymore.

EJEMPLO: ¿Hay algo que veías que no ves ahora?

Veía muchas ardillas pero no las veo mucho ahora.

18 Tell some things you see on your way to school every day.

EJEMPLO: Veo la estación de gasolina en la esquina de mi calle.

Vocabulario

Los números ordinales   *Ordinal numbers*

primero(a)	*first*	sexto(a)	*sixth*
segundo(a)	*second*	séptimo(a)	*seventh*
tercero(a)	*third*	octavo(a)	*eighth*
cuarto(a)	*fourth*	noveno(a)	*ninth*
quinto(a)	*fifth*	décimo(a)	*tenth*

USING ORDINAL NUMBERS

In Spanish, the ordinal numbers *first* through *tenth* (**primero, segundo**, etc.) are placed before the noun as in English. Beyond *tenth*, the regular counting numbers (**once, doce,** etc.) are used for *eleventh*, *twelfth*, etc., and are placed after the noun and often preceded by the word **número**.

Luis XIV (catorce)   *Louis the fourteenth*
el chico número doce   *the twelfth boy*

As adjectives, ordinal numbers agree in gender with noun.

la quint<u>a</u> clase   *the fifth class*
los primer<u>os</u> estudiantes   *the first students*

Primero and **tercero** drop the **o** before masculine singular nouns.

el primer hombre   *the first man*
el tercer libro   *the third book*
but: los primeros pisos   *the first floors*
       la tercera esquina   *the third corner*

19 Tell what classes you have and their order.

EJEMPLO: Mi primera clase es historia.
                    Mi segunda clase es geometría.

20 Tell where you sit in each of your classes.

EJEMPLO: En la clase de biología, estoy en la segunda silla de la tercera fila.

21 Tell in which row and seat your classmates are seated.

EJEMPLO: Miguel se sienta en el primer pupitre de la primera fila.
                    Carmen se sienta en el segundo pupitre de la quinta fila.

22 Tell the dates of some important events in your life. Remember, counting nouns are used with dates after **el primero**.

EJEMPLO: Mi cumpleaños es el primero de agosto.
El primer día de clases era el seis de septiembre.

23 Find out the birth date of several people in your class. Then make a list of the people in order of their age. Tell who is first, second, etc.

Vocabulario

Un edificio *A building*

1. el sótano	*basement*	8. el sexto piso	*sixth floor*
2. la planta baja	*ground floor*	9. el séptimo piso	*seventh floor*
3. el primer piso	*first floor (up)*	10. el octavo piso	*eighth floor*
4. el segundo piso	*second floor*	11. el noveno piso	*ninth floor*
5. el tercer piso	*third floor*	12. el décimo piso	*tenth floor*
6. el cuarto piso	*fourth floor*	13. el piso once	*eleventh floor*
7. el quinto piso	*fifth floor*		

24 Do you know anyone who lives in an apartment building? Tell what floor they live on.

EJEMPLO: Mis abuelos viven en el cuarto piso.
Mi amigo Miguel vive en la planta baja.

ENCUENTRO PERSONAL

Some of Paulina's friends are describing where they live to the rest of the class. Do any of the living situations resemble your own?

PROFESORA BLANCO:	¿Dónde viven Uds. y cómo es su casa o apartamento?
ROSITA:	Yo vivo en un apartamento grande, en el piso quince de un rascacielos en el centro de la ciudad, al lado del Banco Nacional. El balcón da *(faces)* al este, y por la mañana vemos salir el sol sobre el lago. Me gusta vivir en la ciudad porque estamos cerca de muchas tiendas, cines y museos.
PROFESORA BLANCO:	Debe ser muy bonito estar en el centro de la ciudad. Y tú, Santiago, ¿dónde vives tú?
SANTIAGO:	Yo vivo en las afueras de la ciudad en una casa pequeña pero cómoda. Tenemos un patio, pero no está dentro de la casa al estilo hispano. El patio está detrás de la casa. Allí tenemos una mesa y unas sillas. En el verano comemos allí frecuentemente porque hace más fresco que dentro de la casa.

PROFESORA BLANCO: Inés, ¿cómo es la casa donde viven tú y tu familia?

INÉS: Pues, ahora vivimos en un apartamento en el centro como Rosita, pero antes vivíamos en el campo, en un rancho con caballos, ovejas, gallinas y todo tipo de animales domésticos. Me gustaba mucho vivir en el campo pero nunca teníamos mucho dinero. Ahora mi padre tiene un buen empleo aquí en la ciudad y vamos al campo en las vacaciones para visitar a mis tíos, que todavía tienen una granja.

PROFESORA BLANCO: ¡Qué interesante, Inés! Gracias, estudiantes. Sus descripciones fueron muy buenas, ¡e interesantes también!

¿Comprendes?

1. ¿Dónde vive Rosita y cómo es su vivienda? ¿Le gusta a ella? ¿Por qué?
2. ¿Dónde vive Santiago? ¿Cómo es el patio de la casa?
3. ¿Dónde vivía Inés antes, y dónde vive ahora? ¿Qué vivienda le gusta más? ¿Por qué?

¡Te toca!

Describe the place where you live to your classmates.

Leemos y contamos

A. Paulina is going to visit her friend Sara near Detroit. Here are the directions Sara wrote in a letter. Do you think you could find Sara's house?

> Yo vivo en las afueras de Detroit, Michigan. Para llegar a mi casa desde tu casa, debes ir al norte por la Autopista I 75 hasta cruzar la frontera de Michigan. Cuando llegues al sur de la ciudad en la Autopista I 75, toma la salida de la derecha para la Carretera Southfield al norte. Debes seguir adelante más o menos cinco millas hasta cruzar la Autopista I 94. Busca la salida para la Calle Ford oeste y dobla a la izquierda. Sigue todo derecho por dos millas hasta llegar a la Calle Evergreen. Dobla otra vez a la izquierda y pasa por dos semáforos. Continúa todo derecho dos cuadras más y mi casa es la primera después de la esquina al lado oeste de la calle. Es una casa gris y blanca de dos pisos. Mi dirección es Calle Evergreen 5101.

B. Santiago wrote a description of where he lives. Can you picture it in your mind?

Nosotros vivimos en un condominio de dos pisos en las afueras de la ciudad. En la planta baja están el pasillo, el comedor, la sala de estar y la cocina. En el primer piso están las alcobas y el baño principal. En el desván no hay mucho excepto cajas y bolsas de ropa y juguetes viejos. Pero en el sótano están mis cosas favoritas: una mesa de Ping Pong, una mesa de billar y una máquina de juegos de vídeo. A mis amigos y a mí nos gusta pasar mucho tiempo en el sótano; esto le gusta a mi mamá también porque no oye la música y el ruido.

Now draw Santiago's house and the things he mentions.

C. Write detailed directions to your house from school. Then see if a classmate can locate where you live on a map by following your directions.

¡Así es!

Las viviendas hispanas   *Hispanic housing*

«Aquí Ud. está en su casa.» «Mi casa es su casa.» Así es como los hispanos les dan la bienvenida a las personas que los visitan.

¿Cómo son las casas donde viven los hispanos? No hay solamente un estilo. En las ciudades, muchas personas viven en apartamentos. Frecuentemente hay tiendas en la planta baja y apartamentos arriba. A veces una casa grande está dividida en apartamentos. También hay apartamentos modernos en rascacielos. Los distritos residenciales no se parecen *(look)* a los distritos residenciales norteamericanos. Generalmente la entrada de la casa está directamente al lado de la acera. Las ventanas que dan a *(face)* la calle tienen rejas *(grillwork)*. En el centro de la casa hay un patio privado para la familia.

En las afueras y en el campo, muchas casas tienen muros *(walls)* altos alrededor del jardín. En algunas ciudades, adonde mucha gente pobre se han mudado *(have moved)* recientemente, no es extraño *(strange)* ver chozas *(huts)* cerca de una casa lujosa *(luxurious)*. En muchos países el gobierno ayuda en la construcción de grandes edificios de apartamentos para los pobres.

En la escuela

Is your school day busy? Let's talk about the things we do and when and how we do them.

Vocabulario

Lo que hacemos en la escuela *What we do in school*

asistir a las clases	*to attend classes*
comer en la cafetería	*to eat in the cafeteria*
• consultar con el consejero	*to consult with the counselor*
• hacer cola	*to stand in line*
• conseguir (i, i) algo en el armario	*to get something from the locker*
• enseñar	*to teach, to show*
tomar apuntes	*to take notes*
practicar	*to practice*
trabajar mucho	*to work a lot*
estudiar	*to study*
aprender	*to learn*
hablar en voz alta/baja	*to talk in a loud/soft voice*
comprender la lección	*to understand the lesson*
hacer la tarea	*to do homework*
prepararse para los exámenes	*to prepare for tests*
tomar una prueba	*to take a quiz/test*
un examen	*an exam*
recibir una A	*to receive an A*
sacar buenas/malas notas	*to get good/bad grades*
aprobar (ue) un examen	*to pass an exam*
suspender un examen	*to fail an exam*
salir bien	*to do well*

cerrar (ie) la puerta	*to close the door*
abrir el libro	*to open the book*
hacer una pregunta	*to ask a question*
contestar	*to answer*
leer una novela	*to read a novel*
una lectura	*a reading selection*
un cuento	*a story*
• una poema	*a poem*
la poesía	*poetry*
escribir la tarea	*to write the homework*
un tema	*a paper*
una carta	*a letter*
teclear	*to input*
• hacer un proyecto	*to do a project*
escuchar conferencias	*to listen to lectures*
discos compactos	*CDs*
discutir	*to discuss*
memorizar fechas	*to memorize dates*
hechos	*facts*
calcular	*to do arithmetic*
sumar	*to add*
restar	*to subtract*
multiplicar	*to multiply*
dividir	*to divide*
hacer investigaciones	*to do research*
esperar el autobús	*to wait for the bus*
regresar a casa	*to return home*

Expresiones de tiempo   *Time expressions*

anteayer	*day before yesterday*	antes	*before*
ayer	*yesterday*	ahora	*now*
hoy	*today*	después	*after*
mañana	*tomorrow*	entonces	*then*
pasado mañana	*day after tomorrow*	luego	*then, later*
un día	*one day*	• pronto	*soon*
en el pasado	*in the past*	por la mañana	*in the morning*
en el presente	*in the present*	por la tarde	*in the afternoon*
en el futuro	*in the future*	por la noche	*in the evening, at night*
siempre	*always*	una vez	*once*
frecuentemente	*frequently, often*	otra vez	*again*
mucho	*a lot, much*	(dos) veces	*(two) times*
poco	*a little, few*	de una vez	*all at once*
raramente	*rarely, seldom*	de vez en cuando	*from time to time*
nunca	*never*	alguna vez	*sometime*
mientras	*while*	a veces	*sometimes*
de repente	*suddenly*	muchas veces	*many times, often*
inmediatamente	*immediately*	• a menudo	*often*
de niño(a)	*as a child*	todavía	*still, yet*
de viejo(a)	*as an old person*	todavía no	*not yet*
a los… años	*at the age of . . .*	de nuevo	*again*
hace (seis meses)	*(six months) ago*	ya	*already*
en (seis meses)	*in (six months)*	ya no	*no longer*
el año pasado	*last year*	el próximo año	*next year*
el mes pasado	*last month*	el próximo mes	*next month*
la semana pasada	*last week*	la próxima semana	*next week*
el (lunes)	*on (Monday)*	tarde	*late*
todos los (lunes)	*every (Monday)*	más tarde	*later*
todos los días	*every day*	temprano	*early*
todas las semanas	*every week*	más temprano	*earlier*
todos los meses	*every month*		
todos los años	*every year*		

1 Tell what you do in school every day. Use the present tense.

EJEMPLO: Asisto a todas mis clases.
Aprendo mucho en mi clase de historia.

2 What did you do in school yesterday? Use the preterite tense.

EJEMPLO: Ayer escuché una conferencia.
Leí un poema en mi clase de inglés.

3 What did you used to do when you were in kindergarten? Use the imperfect tense.

EJEMPLO: En el jardín de niños, yo jugaba con los bloques alfabéticos y el cajón de arena.

4 What will you do next year in school? Use the future tense.

EJEMPLO: El próximo año, estudiaré química y trabajaré
                    en el laboratorio.

Now let's review the verb for asking what someone is doing.

HACER   *to do, to make*

	IMPERFECT *did/made* *was/were* *doing/making* *used to do/make*	PRETERITE *did/made* *did do/make*	PRESENT *do/does/make(s)* *am/is/are* *doing/making* *do/does do/make*	FUTURE *will do/make*
yo	hacía	**hice**	**hago**	**haré**
tú	hacías	**hiciste**	haces	**harás**
Ud./él/ella	hacía	**hizo**	hace	**hará**
nosotros(as)	hacíamos	**hicimos**	hacemos	**haremos**
vosotros(as)	hacíais	**hicisteis**	hacéis	**haréis**
Uds./ellos/ellas	hacían	**hicieron**	hacen	**harán**

Irregularities:
preterite: irregular stem, "combo" endings, **hizo**
present: **yo hago**
future: irregular stem: **har-**

Note: English *do/does/did* as used in questions or in negative sentences is not expressed in Spanish.

<u>Do</u> you sing?   ¿Cantas?
I <u>do</u> not sing.   No canto.

¿Hiciste mucho ejercicio el año pasado?

No, pero de niña hacía mucho ejercicio y en el futuro haré más.

5 **Encuesta**   Find out from several of your classmates what each does in English class.

EJEMPLO: ¿Qué haces en tu clase de inglés?

   Leo cuentos y escribo temas.

6 Find out from your partner what is done in all of his or her classes. Since you want to know what the whole class does, use the plural *you:* **Uds**. Your partner should answer with **nosotros**, since he or she is speaking for the entire class.

EJEMPLO: ¿Qué hacen Uds. en la clase de matemáticas?

Nosotros sumamos, restamos, multiplicamos y dividimos.

7 **Encuesta** Find out what several people did last weekend.

EJEMPLO: ¿Qué hiciste durante el pasado fin de semana?

Visité a mis abuelos. / Mis abuelos y yo fuimos al cine.

8 Find out from your partner what she or he used to do in elementary school.

EJEMPLO: ¿Qué hacías en la escuela primaria?

Leía, calculaba, escribía y jugaba.

9 What do you think college life will be like? Find out from your partner what his or her expectations are.

EJEMPLO: ¿Qué harás en la universidad?

Leeré, calcularé y escribiré.

DURATION OF TIME

The verb **hacer** is used with a time expression to tell how long something has been happening. The present tense of **hacer** and the verb are used if the action is still happening. The imperfect tense of **hacer** and the verb are used if the action took place for a period of time in the past. (Note that in English a form of *have been + ing* is often used.)

Esqueletos

HACE + *time* + **QUE** + *present verb* + *(rest of sentence)*

Hace tres meses que trabajo aquí.   *I have been working here for three months.*

HACÍA + *time* + **QUE** + *imperfect verb* + *(rest of sentence)*

Hacía dos años que trabajaba allí.   *I had been working there for two years.*

10 Tell for how long you have done various things at school.

EJEMPLO: Hace dos años que asisto a la clase de álgebra.
Hace quince minutos que estoy en la clase de español.

11 Tell some things you like to do. Then tell for how long you have been doing them.

EJEMPLO: Me gusta patinar. Hace tres años que patino los sábados.
Me gusta cantar. Hace seis meses que canto con el coro.

12 What were some activities you participated in when you were younger? Tell for how long you did them.

EJEMPLO: Hacía cuatro años que estudiaba baile.
Hacía dos años que nadaba con un equipo.

AGO

To tell how long ago something happened, use **hace** with a time expression and the preterite of the verb.

Esqueletos

HACE + *time* + QUE + *preterite verb*

Hace dos semanas que lo compré. *I bought it two weeks ago.*

OR

preterite verb* + HACE + *time

Lo compré hace dos semanas. *I bought it two weeks ago.*

13 Encuesta Choose an activity. Find out how long ago several classmates did that activity.

EJEMPLO: ¿Cuánto tiempo hace que suspendiste un examen?

Hace tres años que suspendí un examen.

14 Tell several things you did and how long ago you did them.

EJEMPLO: Bailé con mi novio hace tres semanas.
Hace una hora que recibí una carta de Bolivia.

DOUBLE-VERB CONSTRUCTION

In Spanish, as well as in English, when there are two verbs next to each other the first verb has the person–time endings (conjugated) and the second verb has the **-ar, -er, -ir** (infinitive) endings.

first verb: conjugated   +   second verb: infinitive
(person–time ending)   (**-ar, -er, -ir** ending)

Yo dese<u>o</u> dorm<u>ir</u>. *I want to sleep.*
Nosotros deb<u>emos</u> estudi<u>ar</u>. *We ought to study.*

Vocabulario

Verbos que se combinan con el infinitivo   *Verbs that combine with the infinitive*

Here are some verbs that are often used with an infinitive following.

deber	*ought to, should*
desear	*to want to, to desire*
esperar	*to hope to*
gustar	*to like to*
necesitar	*to need to*
odiar	*to hate (to)*
preferir (ie, i)	*to prefer to*
poder (ue)	*can, to be able to*
pensar (ie)	*to intend to, to plan to*
querer (ie)	*to want to*

Some verbs have a word separating the verb from the infinitive.

aprender a	*to learn to*
ayudar a	*to help (to)*
• enseñar a	*to teach to*
invitar a	*to invite to*
ir a	*to be going to*
• hay que	*one must/has to*
tener que	*to have to*
acabar de	*to have just*
• gozar de	*to enjoy*
pensar de	*to think of/about [opinion]*
tener ganas de	*to feel like*
tratar de	*to try to*
pensar en	*to think of/about [daydream]*
insistir en	*to insist on*

> Tengo ganas de invitar a mis amigos a una fiesta pero tengo que estudiar.

Note: **Pensar** *(to think, to intend)*, **preferir** *(to prefer)*, **querer** *(to want to)* and **poder** *(can, to be able to)* are stem-changing verbs in the present tense. Look at the forms that follow and notice that the letter **i** is added to some forms and the **o** is changed to **ue** in **poder**.

pienso	prefiero	quiero	puedo
piensas	prefieres	quieres	puedes
piensa	prefiere	quiere	puede
pensamos	preferimos	queremos	podemos
piensan	prefieren	quieren	pueden

(**Querer** and **poder** have additional irregularities in other tenses. These will be taught in Unit III, Lesson 3.)

15 Use each of the preceding verbs to tell something about yourself.

EJEMPLO: Yo deseo ir a casa.
            Yo necesito estudiar mucho.

16 Use each of the preceding verbs to tell something about your family.

EJEMPLO: Nosotros deseamos viajar a Hawaii.
            Vamos a comprar una casa nueva.

17 *Sit-Con*   You will be late for dinner tonight. Call home to explain that you will be late and why. Give several different explanations using double verbs.

EJEMPLO: Yo estaré tarde para la cena porque…
            tengo que ir a la tienda.
            necesito estudiar en la biblioteca.

18 Give your parents several reasons why they should buy you a car.

EJEMPLO: Uds. deben comprarme un coche porque…
            acabo de recibir mi permiso.
            odio caminar.

19 *Sit-Con*   You are the attendance counselor at your school. Several people were late to school today. Find out why.

EJEMPLO: ¿Por qué llegas tarde?

            Tenía que hallar mi tarea.

            Tuve que ayudar un perro perdido.

THE MEANINGS OF PENSAR

The verb **pensar (ie)** usually means *to think*, but it also has other possible meanings depending on how it is used. Here are some of them.

Pensar de + infinitive/noun   *to think of/about [asking for an opinion or conclusion]*

   ¿Qué piensas del nuevo profesor?   *What do you think of the new teacher?*

Pensar que   *to think that [expressing an opinion or conclusion]*

   Pienso que él es simpático.   *I think that he is nice.*

Pensar en + infinitive/noun   *to think of/about to oneself, to daydream*

   Pienso en mi novia todas las noches.   *I think about my girlfriend every night.*
   Pienso en estar en la playa.   *I'm thinking about being at the beach.*

Pensar + infinitive   *to plan to, intend to, to think of (doing)*

   Pienso estudiar esta noche.   *I plan to study tonight.*

¿Qué piensas de la Antártida?

Prefiero no pensar en el frío. Pienso volver a Florida.

20 Tell your partner some things you used to think.

EJEMPLO: Pensaba que las vacas marrones daban leche con chocolate.
Pensaba que mi hermano era muy fuerte.

21 Ask your partner what his or her opinion is of the following things.

EJEMPLO: ¿Qué piensas de…
Pienso que es muy…

a. la moda de hoy *(the styles)*
b. la música clásica
c. la cafetería de tu escuela
d. el equipo de básquetbol
e. el arte moderno

22 **Encuesta**   Find out what people think about when they are alone.

EJEMPLO: ¿En que piensas cuando estás solo(a)?

 Pienso en mi familia.

23 What are some things you plan to do?

EJEMPLO: Pienso ir al cine mañana por la noche.
Pienso ser ingeniero.

FORMING ADVERBS FROM ADJECTIVES

If the adjective ends in **o**, change to **a** and add **mente**. Otherwise, add **mente** to the invariable form.

correcto ⟶ correcta ⟶ correctamente
feliz ⟶ felizmente
inteligente ⟶ inteligentemente

When using a series of adverbs, only the last will end in **mente**.

Vivimos cómoda y felizmente.   *We live comfortably and happily.*

Vocabulario

Cómo se hacen las cosas   *How things are done*

ambiciosamente	*ambitiously*	necesariamente	*necessarily*
cuidadosamente	*carefully*	nerviosamente	*nervously*
cómodamente	*comfortably*	nuevamente	*newly*
correctamente	*correctly*	solamente	*only*
fácilmente	*easily*	perfectamente	*perfectly*
especialmente	*especially*	posiblemente	*possibly*
rápidamente	*fast, quickly*	públicamente	*publicly*
finalmente	*finally*	raramente	*rarely*
frecuentemente	*frequently*	regularmente	*regularly*
generosamente	*generously*	tristemente	*sadly*
felizmente	*happily*	sinceramente	*sincerely*
inmediatamente	*immediately*	lentamente	*slowly*
incorrectamente	*incorrectly*	despacio	*slowly*
inteligentemente	*intelligently*	mal	*badly, not well, poorly*
perezosamente	*lazily*	bien	*well*

24 What are some things you do? How do you do them?

EJEMPLO: Escribo mi tarea cuidadosamente.
Hablo español frecuentemente.

25 How do your friends do their homework?

EJEMPLO: Paco lo hace inmediatamente.
Pedro lo hace rápidamente.

COMPARISON OF ADVERBS

Adverbs are compared using the same pattern as comparing adjectives.

más + *adverb* + que
menos + *adverb* + que
tan + *adverb* + como

Luis escribe menos frecuentemente que yo.   *Luis writes less frequently than I.*

Mi tía va de compras tan regularmente como mi madre.   *My aunt goes shopping as regularly as my mother.*

26 How does the worst student do his work compared to the best student?

EJEMPLO: El peor estudiante estudia menos cuidadosamente que el mejor.

27 Compare the way you do things with the way one of your friends does it.

EJEMPLO: Yo manejo más lentamente que mi amigo.

ENCUENTRO PERSONAL

Paulina and her friends are talking about what they used to do in grade school compared to what they do now and what they will do in the future in college. Does any of this sound familiar to you?

PAULINA: Cuando yo era estudiante en la escuela primaria, siempre quería jugar felizmente en el patio de recreo *(playground)* con mis amigas durante la hora de la siesta. Ahora prefiero comer rápidamente y hablar contentamente con mis amigos en la cafetería.

SANTIAGO: Y, ¿qué querrás hacer en el futuro en la universidad, Paulina?

PAULINA: Creo que tendré que estudiar seriamente porque deseo sacar buenas notas y salir bien en mis clases. Y tú, Santiago, ¿cómo era para ti en la escuela primaria?

SANTIAGO: Bueno, en la escuela primaria me gustaba asistir a mis clases porque nos enseñaban a aprender a leer y me gusta leer. Pero ahora no me gusta asistir tanto a las clases, porque tengo que tomar unas clases de cálculo, y es muy difícil. En la universidad trataré de tomar clases más fáciles, como el español. ¿Y tú, Rosita?

ROSITA: Yo estoy de acuerdo. No me gusta calcular, pero acabo de tomar una prueba de geometría. Espero poder aprobarla; escuchaba bien las conferencias, tomaba buenos apuntes y le hacía muchas preguntas a la profesora, pero todavía me era difícil comprender la materia.

PAULINA: ¡Buena suerte en la prueba, Rosita! Para mí la clase más difícil es la clase de historia. Odio memorizar fechas y hay que escribir muchos temas. También necesitas hacer muchas investigaciones en la biblioteca. Prefiero leer novelas o lecturas en español y escribirle poemas de amor a mi novio.

SANTIAGO: Hablas muy románticamente hoy, Paulina. ¿Qué piensas de ir a estudiar juntos? Yo puedo ayudarte a escribir la tarea para la clase de historia y tú puedes responder a todas mis preguntas sobre el cálculo.

PAULINA: ¿Y qué más piensas hacer, Santiago?

SANTIAGO: Solamente pienso mirarte los ojos, escuchar tu voz y pensar en salir contigo.

PAULINA: ¡Yo no soy la única romántica hoy!

¿Comprendes?

1. ¿Cuáles son las actividades de Paulina en la escuela en el pasado, ahora y en el futuro?
2. ¿Y para Santiago?
3. ¿Qué prueba acaba de tomar Rosita? ¿Cómo salió?
4. ¿Qué clase es más difícil para Paulina y por qué?
5. ¿Qué prefiere hacer Paulina?
6. ¿Qué solución tiene Santiago?
7. ¿Cuál es la reacción de Paulina?

¡Te toca!

Ask your classmates about their school activities in the past, present, and future.

Leemos y contamos

A. Paulina wrote a letter to her pen pal Marisol, who lives in Mexico, asking her to describe what she does in school. Here is Marisol's response.

> Querida Paulina,
>
> En tu carta tú me hiciste muchas preguntas sobre cómo es asistir a clases aquí en México. Generalmente es semejante (similar) a la escuela en los Estados Unidos: los estudiantes en todo el mundo prefieren jugar y charlar en vez de trabajar y estudiar. Y, como a Uds., no nos gusta hacer la tarea, escribir temas ni asistir a clases todos los días. Pero a veces hay una clase especialmente interesante a causa de la materia, el profesor, los amigos o un novio. En estos casos tenemos muchas ganas de asistir y no podemos esperar a ir a la clase. A mí la clase de inglés es la que más me gusta. El profesor es muy simpático y todos mis amigos están en la clase, pero para mí lo más importante es que me fascina el idioma.
>
> Para nosotros los mexicanos el inglés es más que una lengua extranjera: es el boleto (ticket) para entrar en un maravilloso mundo de sueños. Muchos de nosotros tenemos la impresión de que todos los norteamericanos son ricos, que viven cómodamente (comfortably) en mansiones grandes, que manejan carros rápidos y que pasan el tiempo felizmente. La mayoría de nosotros sabemos que no es la realidad, pero preferimos perseguir (pursue) el sueño (dream) de viajar a, conocer o aún vivir en «el Norte». También queremos comprender la música, las películas y los programas de la televisión de los Estados Unidos e Inglaterra que tenemos por todas partes. Hace dos años, tuve la oportunidad magnífica de visitar los EE. UU. y algún día me gustaría vivir allí.

1. ¿Qué prefieren hacer los estudiantes?
2. ¿Qué no les gusta hacer?
3. ¿Cómo es la clase de inglés de Marisol?
4. ¿Por qué es importante el inglés para los mexicanos?
5. ¿Qué quiere hacer Marisol algún día?

B. Do you have a favorite class? Describe what you do in the class and why you like it.

C. What did you and your friends do during the last weekend?

D. What are your career plans for the future?

¡Así es!

La enseñanza

Cuando el hispano dice «educación», generalmente habla de *upbringing* en vez de lo que pasa en la escuela. Una persona «bien educada» es una persona cortés y que se porta *(behaves)* bien. Cuando nos referimos a la instrucción en las escuelas, la palabra es «enseñanza». Sin embargo, muchos países tienen un Ministerio de Educación.

Las escuelas en el mundo hispano no son como las escuelas en los Estados Unidos. Las escuelas secundarias generalmente se concentran más en lo académico y no hay ni deportes ni otras actividades.

En la mayoría de los países, los estudiantes van a la escuela primaria por seis años y luego a la escuela secundaria por seis años más. La escuela secundaria se llama «colegio, instituto, academia o liceo» según *(according to)* el país y el tipo de escuela.

Generalmente las clases son grandes y los estudiantes no participan ni hacen preguntas en la clase. El profesor habla y ellos toman apuntes. Al fin del año hay exámenes escritos y, a veces, orales.

Cuando terminan su enseñanza secundaria, los estudiantes reciben su título que se llama un «bachillerato». Una persona que tiene su título se llama un «bachiller». En algunos países, tienen que tomar un examen para recibir este título.

Hay muchas escuelas privadas *(private)*, y la mayoría de éstas son católicas. A veces los muchachos y muchachas están separados en distintas escuelas y frecuentemente llevan uniformes. También hay muchas escuelas donde se enseña en otro idioma como, por ejemplo, inglés, francés o alemán.

⊱ Unidad III ⊰

⇒ Unidad III ⇐
Tools

Vocabulario

Los pasatiempos   *Pastimes*
(Lección 1)

Los deportes   *Sports*

el fútbol	*soccer*	• el béisbol	*baseball*
el fútbol norteamericano	*football*	• el vólibol	*volleyball*
• los bolos	*bowling*	• el hockey sobre hielo	*ice hockey*
• el tenis	*tennis*	• el baloncesto	*basketball*
• la arquería	*archery*	• el badminton	*badminton*
• el golf	*golf*	• la lucha	*wrestling*

• Los juegos   *Games*

las damas	*checkers*
los naipes	*cards*
• el escondite	*hide and seek*
• los videojuegos	*video games*
• el ajedrez	*chess*
• los dominós	*dominos*
• la lotería	*game similar to "Bingo"*

Los instrumentos musicales   *Musical instruments*

el piano	*piano*
la guitarra	*guitar*
el tambor	*drum*
el violín	*violin*
• la flauta	*flute*
• el saxofón	*saxophone*
• el trombón	*trombone*
• el acordeón	*accordion*
• la tuba	*tuba*
• la trompeta	*trumpet*
• el clarinete	*clarinet*
• la trompa francesa	*French horn*

Lo que hacemos durante el tiempo •libre   *What we do during free time*

divertirse (ie, i)	*to enjoy oneself, to have a good time, to have fun*
jugar (ue) a un deporte	*to play a sport*
ir a una •práctica de…	*to go to . . . practice*
mirar •un partido de…	*to watch a . . . game/event*
jugar (ue) a un juego	*to play a game*
tocar un instrumento musical	*to play a musical instrument*
ir de compras	*to go shopping*
asistir a un concierto	*to attend a concert*
mirar la televisión	*to watch television*
• coleccionar estampillas	*to collect stamps*
escuchar discos compactos	*to listen to CDs*
dibujar y pintar	*to draw and paint*
correr	*to run*
hacer •ejercicio	*to exercise*
hacer •jogging	*to jog*
hablar por teléfono	*to talk on the telephone*
broncearse	*to sunbathe*
dar un paseo a pie	*to go for a walk*
dar un paseo en coche	*to go for a drive*
visitar a los abuelos	*to visit grandparents*
escuchar la radio	*to listen to the radio*
• montar en bicicleta	*to ride a bike*
• pasar el tiempo	*to spend time*
• perder (ie) tiempo	*to waste time*
patinar	*to skate*
nadar	*to swim*
pescar	*to fish*
encontrarse (ue) con los amigos	*to meet friends*
hacer la tarea	*do homework*
descansar	*to rest*
dormir (ue, u) una siesta	*to take a nap*
ayudar en la casa	*to help around the house*
ganar dinero	*to earn money*
cuidar de los niños	*to babysit*
ir a un trabajo	*to go to a job (work)*
trabajar en…	*to work in/at . . .*
discutir con los hermanos	*to argue with siblings*
levantar pesas	*to lift weights*

Verbos de cambio radical   *Stem-changing verbs*
(Lección 1)

E ⟶ IE

• atravesar	*to cross*
cerrar	*to close*
comenzar a	*to begin/start to*
• confesar	*to confess*
• empezar a	*to begin/start to*
• nevar	*to snow*
pensar en/de	*to think of/about*
pensar + *infinitive*	*to plan to*
• recomendar	*to recommend*
• encender	*to light, to turn on*
perder	*to lose, to waste*
querer	*to want*
querer a + *person*	*to love*
• mentir	*to tell a lie*
preferir	*to prefer*
sentir	*to be sorry, to regret*
• sugerir	*to suggest*

E ⟶ I

• conseguir	*to get, to obtain*
• impedir	*to prevent*
pedir	*to ask for, to order*
repetir	*to repeat*
seguir	*to continue, to follow*
servir	*to serve*
vestir	*to dress*

O ⟶ UE

almorzar	*to eat lunch*
contar	*to count, to tell a story*
costar	*to cost*
• encontrar	*to find, to meet*
• mostrar	*to show*
• probar	*to taste, to try (out)*
recordar	*to remember*
sonar	*to sound*
soñar con	*to dream about*
• volar	*to fly*
doler	*to ache, to hurt*
• devolver	*to give back, to return*
llover	*to rain*
• mover	*to move*
poder	*to be able, can*
• resolver	*to solve*
• soler	*to be accustomed to*
volver	*to return, to go back*
dormir	*to sleep*
morir	*to die*

U ⟶ UE

jugar	*to play*

La rutina diaria   *Daily routine*
(Lección 2)

despertarse (ie)	*to wake up*
levantarse	*to get up*
sentarse (ie)	*to sit down*
• prepararse	*to get ready*
• arreglarse	*to get fixed up*
bañarse	*to take a bath*
ducharse	*to take a shower*
lavarse	*to wash*
• secarse	*to dry (off)*
afeitarse	*to shave*
cepillarse	*to brush*

vestirse (i, i)	*to get dressed*
ponerse	*to put on (clothing)*
peinarse	*to comb one's hair*
maquillarse	*to put on makeup*
despedirse (i, i)	*to say good-bye*
irse	*to go away*
quedarse	*to stay, to remain*
• cansarse	*to get tired*
quitarse	*to take off (clothing)*
acostarse (ue)	*to go to bed, to lie down*
dormirse (ue, u)	*to go to sleep, to fall asleep*

En la escuela   *In school*
(Lección 2)

• portarse bien/mal	*to behave well/badly*
• callarse	*to be quiet*
• ocuparse	*to be busy*
• equivocarse	*to make a mistake*
• preocuparse	*to worry*
divertirse (ie, i)	*to have a good time, to enjoy oneself, to have fun*
• aburrirse	*to be bored*
• hacerse buen estudiante	*to become a good student*
• graduarse	*to graduate*

Un cuento de amor   *A love story*
(Lección 2)

conocerse	*to meet each other*
• llevarse bien/mal	*to get along well/badly*
• sentirse (ie, i) contento(a)	*to feel happy*
• besarse	*to kiss each other*
• abrazarse	*to hug each other*
darse un regalo	*to give each other a gift*
un abrazo	*a hug*
un beso	*a kiss*
un ramillete	*a bouquet of flowers*
• enamorarse (de)	*to fall in love (with)*
decirse «Te quiero»	*to tell each other "I love you"*
• alegrarse (de)	*to be happy (about)*
• comprometerse (con)	*to become engaged (to)*
• casarse (con)	*to get married (to)*
vivir •felizmente	*to live happily*
• burlarse (de)	*to make fun (of)*
• enojarse (con)	*to become angry (with)*
• ponerse celoso(a)	*to become jealous*
• quejarse (de)	*to complain (about)*
• darse cuenta (de)	*to realize*
• separarse	*to separate*
• divorciarse	*to get divorced*
• llorar	*to cry*

Los días •festivos   *Holidays*
(Lección 3)

la Nochevieja	*New Year's Eve*
el Año Nuevo	*New Year's Day*
el Día de los Reyes •Magos	*Day of the Magi (Three Kings)*
• el Carnaval	*Mardi Gras*
el Día de la •Pascua Florida	*Easter*
los huevos de colores	*colored eggs*
• la canasta	*basket*
los dulces de goma	*gumdrops*
el conejo	*rabbit*
• el Desfile de Pascua	*Easter Parade*
el Día de •la Raza	*Day of the Hispanic Race (Columbus Day)*
el Día de Todos •los Santos	*All Saints' Day*
el Día de •los Muertos	*Day of the Dead*
• la calavera	*skull*
el esqueleto	*skeleton*
• el cementerio	*cemetery*
• el sepulcro	*grave*
• la Nochebuena	*Christmas Eve*
• la Misa del Gallo	*Midnight Mass*
• la Navidad	*Christmas*
• los villancicos	*carols*
el árbol de Navidad	*Christmas tree*
• la piñata	*papier mâché figure*
• llena de dulces	*filled with candy*
la Januca	*Hanukah*
el Ramadán	*Ramadan*

Fiestas de España   *Holidays of Spain*

La Semana •Santa	*Holy Week*
• la estatua	*statue*
• el paso	*platform for carrying statues*
• la vela	*candle*
• La Feria de Sevilla	*Seville Fair*
• el baile flamenco	*flamenco dance*
• el desfile	*parade*
el circo	*circus*
• las diversiones	*amusements*
• Las Fallas de Valencia	*Festival of Valencia*
• la falla	*figurine, statue*
• el carro alegórico	*float*
poner •fuego a	*to set fire to*

Fiestas de España   *Holidays of Spain (continued)*

Las Fiestas de San Fermín	*Festival of San Fermín*
• el encierro de los toros	*roundup of the bulls*
• los fuegos artificiales	*fireworks*
• la plaza de toros	*bullfighting arena*

Fiestas de los Estados Unidos   *Holidays of the United States*

El Día de San Valentín	*Valentine's Day*
mandar tarjetas (con un corazón)	*to send greeting cards (with a heart)*
• Cupido	*Cupid*
• verso romántico	*romantic verse*
• regalar una caja en forma de corazón	*to give as a gift a heart-shaped box*
El Día de las Brujas	*Halloween*
el fantasma	*ghost*
• la bruja en escoba	*witch on a broom*
• el duende	*goblin*
• la máscara	*mask*
• el disfraz	*costume*
el murciélago	*bat*
• la linterna de calabaza	*jack-o-lantern*
El Día de Acción de Gracias	*Thanksgiving*
• la calabaza	*pumpkin*
• el peregrino	*pilgrim*
el barco	*ship*
• el indio	*Native American*
la cena de pavo	*turkey dinner*
dar gracias	*to give thanks*

Los quehaceres   *Chores*
(Lección 4)

limpiar la casa	*to clean the house*	pasar •la aspiradora	*to vacuum*
• barrer el suelo	*to sweep the floor*	comprar la comida	*to buy food*
• fregar el suelo	*to mop the floor*	cocinar la cena	*to cook dinner*
hacer •la cama	*to make the bed*	poner la mesa	*to set the table*
• cambiar las sábanas	*to change the sheets*	quitar la mesa	*to clear the table*
lavar la ropa	*to wash the clothes*	lavar los platos	*to wash the dishes*
• secar las toallas	*to dry the towels*	• fregar las ollas	*to scrub the pots*
• doblar las toallas	*to fold the towels*	lavar las ventanas	*to wash windows*
• planchar las camisas	*to iron the shirts*	reparar el coche	*to repair the car*
• colgar (ue) la ropa	*to hang up the clothes*	cortar •el césped	*to cut the lawn*
• pulir los muebles	*to polish the furniture*	recoger •las hojas	*to rake the leaves*
quitar •el polvo	*to dust*	sacar •la basura	*to take out the garbage*
• sacudir los tapetes	*to shake (out) the rugs*	sacar la nieve	*to shovel the snow*

•Los muebles y otros objetos en los cuartos   *Furniture and other objects in the rooms*
(Lección 4)

En la sala   *In the living room*

el televisor	*television set*
el estéreo	*stereo*
el estante	*bookcase*
• las cortinas	*drapes, curtains*
• el sofá	*sofa*
• el sillón	*large chair*
• la mesita	*small table*
• la lámpara	*lamp*
• el tapete	*throw rug*
• la alfombra	*carpet*

En la cocina   *In the kitchen*

• el refrigerador	*refrigerator*
• la estufa	*stove*
• el fregadero	*sink*
• el horno de microondas	*microwave oven*
• el lavaplatos	*dishwasher*
• el abrelatas	*can opener*
• la lavadora	*washer*
• la secadora	*dryer*
• la tostadora	*toaster*
• la olla	*pot*
la sartén	*frying pan*

En el comedor   *In the dining room*

la mesa	*table*
• el chinero	*china cabinet*
la silla	*chair*
• el aparador	*buffet*
• el candelabro	*chandelier*

En la alcoba   *In the bedroom*

• la cama	*bed*
• el colchón	*mattress*
• la almohada	*pillow*
• la mesita de noche	*night table*
el despertador	*alarm clock*
el armario	*cupboard, closet*
• la cómoda	*chest of drawers*
• el tocador	*dresser, bureau*

En el baño   *In the bathroom*

el espejo	*mirror*
• el inodoro	*toilet*
• la bañera	*bathtub*
• el lavabo	*sink*
• la balanza	*scale*

Las cosas para limpiar   *Things for cleaning*
(Lección 4)

• el cubo	*pail, bucket*
• el jabón líquido	*liquid soap*
• el detergente	*detergent*
• el líquido limpiaventanas	*window cleaner*
• el recogedor de polvo	*dust pan*
• el limpiador en polvo	*cleanser*
• el guardapolvo	*feather duster*

• el papel absorbente	*paper towel*
• el trapo	*rag*
• la escoba	*broom*
• la esponja	*sponge*
• la aspiradora	*vacuum cleaner*
• el fregasuelos	*mop*

Las expresiones neutrales y negativas   *Neutral and negative expressions*
(Lección 4)

alguien	*someone, anyone*	nadie	*no one, nobody, not anyone*
algo	*something, anything*	nada	*nothing, not anything*
alguno(a, os, as)	*some*	ninguno(a, os, as)	*none, not any, no*
siempre	*always*	nunca	*never, not ever*
también	*also*	tampoco	*neither, not either*
o... o	*either . . . or*	ni... ni	*neither . . . nor . . .*
• de alguna manera	*some way, somehow*	• de ninguna manera	*no way*
• a/en alguna parte	*somewhere*	• a/en ninguna parte	*nowhere*

Una fiesta   *A party*
(Lección 5)

Dar una fiesta   *To give a party*

una fiesta de cumpleaños	*a birthday party*
• de aniversario	*anniversary*
• de graduación	*graduation*
• de sorpresa	*surprise*

Antes de la fiesta   *Before the party*

invitar a los amigos	*to invite friends*
• telefonear	*to telephone*
escribir las invitaciones	*to write the invitations*
aceptar la invitación	*to accept the invitation*
ayudar con las preparaciones	*to help with preparations*
comprar los refrescos	*to buy refreshments*
hacer la comida	*to make the food*
• cubrir la mesa	*to cover the table*
poner la mesa	*to set the table*

En la fiesta   *At the party*

llegar a las siete	*to arrive at seven o'clock*
traer discos compactos	*to bring CDs*
llevar a los amigos	*to take friends*
llevar la ropa buena	*to wear good clothing*
saludar a los invitados	*to greet the guests*
• al anfitrión	*the host*
• a la anfitriona	*the hostess*
divertirse (ie, i)	*to have a good time, to have fun, to enjoy oneself*
• aburrirse	*to be bored*
bailar	*to dance*
buscar a los amigos	*to look for friends*

ver a un viejo amigo	*to see an old friend*
conocer a una persona nueva	*to meet a new person [first time]*
• encontrarse (ue) con los amigos	*to meet friends [not first time]*
cantar canciones	*to sing songs*
celebrar un cumpleaños	*to celebrate a birthday*
dar un regalo	*to give a present*
abrir los regalos	*to open the presents*
romper •una piñata	*to break a piñata*
contar (ue) •chistes	*to tell jokes*
charlar con los amigos	*to chat with friends*
escuchar la música	*to listen to music*
mirar la televisión	*to watch television*
tocar la guitarra	*to play the guitar*
tocar música	*to play music*
tomar refrescos	*to drink/have refreshments*
sacar fotos	*to take pictures*

Despues de la fiesta   *After the party*

despedirse (i, i)	*to say good-bye*
dar las gracias	*to thank*
volver (ue) a casa	*to return home*

Los participios pasados irregulares   *Irregular past participles* (Lección 5)

abrir	**abierto**	*opened*
• cubrir	**cubierto**	*covered*
• descubrir	**descubierto**	*discovered*
decir	**dicho**	*said*
escribir	**escrito**	*written*
• describir	**descrito**	*described*
hacer	**hecho**	*made, done*
• deshacer	**deshecho**	*undone*
morir	**muerto**	*died, dead*
poner	**puesto**	*put*
• imponer	**impuesto**	*imposed*
• componer	**compuesto**	*composed*
• resolver	**resuelto**	*resolved*
romper	**roto**	*broken*
ver	**visto**	*seen*
volver	**vuelto**	*returned*
• devolver	**devuelto**	*returned*
• envolver	**envuelto**	*wrapped*

Estructura

STEM-CHANGING VERBS

Stem-changing -ar, -er, -ir verbs   Present tense, "boot" forms
(Lección 1)

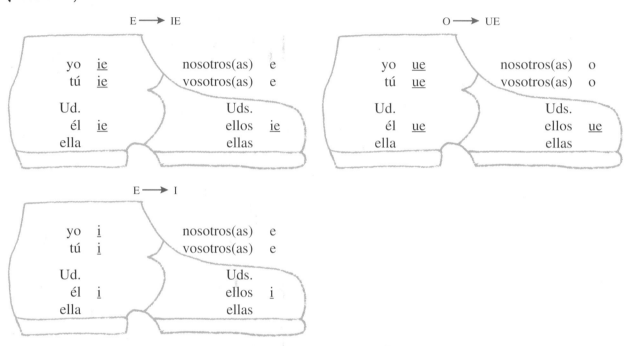

E ⟶ IE

yo	ie	nosotros(as)	e
tú	ie	vosotros(as)	e
Ud.		Uds.	
él	ie	ellos	ie
ella		ellas	

O ⟶ UE

yo	ue	nosotros(as)	o
tú	ue	vosotros(as)	o
Ud.		Uds.	
él	ue	ellos	ue
ella		ellas	

E ⟶ I

yo	i	nosotros(as)	e
tú	i	vosotros(as)	e
Ud.		Uds.	
él	i	ellos	i
ella		ellas	

Stem-changing -ir verbs   Preterite tense, "slipper" forms
(Lección 1)

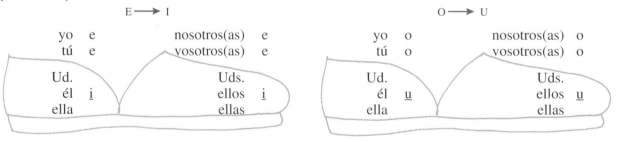

E ⟶ I

yo	e	nosotros(as)	e
tú	e	vosotros(as)	e
Ud.		Uds.	
él	i	ellos	i
ella		ellas	

O ⟶ U

yo	o	nosotros(as)	o
tú	o	vosotros(as)	o
Ud.		Uds.	
él	u	ellos	u
ella		ellas	

Summary of stem-changing verbs
(Lección 1)

IMPERFECT	PRETERITE **-ir** only	PRESENT **-ar, -er, -ir**	FUTURE
no changes	e ⟶ i	e ⟶ ie	no changes
	o ⟶ u	e ⟶ i	
		o ⟶ ue	

IRREGULAR VERBS

Poder (ue)   *to be able, can*
(Lección 3)

	IMPERFECT *could* *was/were able* *used to be able*	PRETERITE *could* *succeeded* *[neg.] failed* *did succeed*	PRESENT *can* *am/is/are able*	FUTURE *will be able*
yo	podía	**pude**	puedo	**podré**
tú	podías	**pudiste**	puedes	**podrás**
Ud./él/ella	podía	**pudo**	puede	**podrá**
nosotros(as)	podíamos	**pudimos**	podemos	**podremos**
vosotros(as)	podíais	**pudisteis**	podéis	**podréis**
Uds./ellos/ellas	podían	**pudieron**	pueden	**podrán**

Querer (ie)   *to want, to love*
(Lección 3)

	IMPERFECT
	wanted/loved
	was/were
	  wanting/loving
	used to want/love
		PRETERITE
		wanted/loved
		 tried
		[neg.]refused
		did want/love
			PRESENT
			want(s)/love(s)
			am/is/are
			  wanting/loving
			do/does want/love
				FUTURE
				will want/love

yo	quería	**quise**	quiero	**querré**
tú	querías	**quisiste**	quieres	**querrás**
Ud./él/ella	quería	**quiso**	quiere	**querrá**
nosotros(as)	queríamos	**quisimos**	queremos	**querremos**
vosotros(as)	queríais	**quisisteis**	queréis	**querréis**
Uds./ellos/ellas	querían	**quisieron**	quieren	**querrán**

Decir   *to say, to tell*
(Lección 3)

	IMPERFECT
	said/told
	was/were
	  saying/telling
	used to say/tell
		PRETERITE
		said/told
		
		did say/tell
			PRESENT
			say(s)/tell(s)
			am/is/are
			  saying/telling
			do/does say/tell
				FUTURE
				will say/tell

yo	decía	**dije**	**digo**	**diré**
tú	decías	**dijiste**	dices	**dirás**
Ud./él/ella	decía	**dijo**	dice	**dirá**
nosotros(as)	decíamos	**dijimos**	decimos	**diremos**
vosotros(as)	decíais	**dijisteis**	decís	**diréis**
Uds./ellos/ellas	decían	**dijeron**	dicen	**dirán**

Traer   *to bring*
(Lección 3)

	IMPERFECT *brought* *was/were bringing* *used to bring*	PRETERITE *brought* *did bring*	PRESENT *bring(s)* *am/is/are bringing* *do/does bring*	FUTURE *will bring*
yo	traía	**traje**	**traigo**	traeré
tú	traías	**trajiste**	traes	traerás
Ud./él/ella	traía	**trajo**	trae	traerá
nosotros(as)	traíamos	**trajimos**	traemos	traeremos
vosotros(as)	traíais	**trajisteis**	traéis	traeréis
Uds./ellos/ellas	traían	**trajeron**	traen	traerán

Saber *or* conocer   *to know*
(Lección 3)

Saber   facts, information, or skills
Conocer   acquainted with—usually a person or a place
   Note: **yo** form of **conocer** in present tense is **conozco**.

Saber   *to know (how)*
(Lección 3)

	IMPERFECT *knew* *used to know*	PRETERITE *found out* *did find out*	PRESENT *know(s)* *do/does know*	FUTURE *will know*
yo	sabía	**supe**	**sé**	**sabré**
tú	sabías	**supiste**	sabes	**sabrás**
Ud./él/ella	sabía	**supo**	sabe	**sabrá**
nosotros(as)	sabíamos	**supimos**	sabemos	**sabremos**
vosotros(as)	sabíais	**supisteis**	sabéis	**sabréis**
Uds./ellos/ellas	sabían	**supieron**	saben	**sabrán**

Haber   *to have (done something) [used with past participles]*
(Lección 5)

	IMPERFECT *had*	PRETERITE *had*	PRESENT *has/have*	FUTURE *will have*
yo	había	**hube**	**he**	**habré**
tú	habías	**hubiste**	**has**	**habrás**
Ud./él/ella	había	**hubo**	**ha**	**habrá**
nosotros(as)	habíamos	**hubimos**	**hemos**	**habremos**
vosotros(as)	habíais	**hubisteis**	**habéis**	**habréis**
Uds./ellos/ellas	habían	**hubieron**	**han**	**habrán**

Summary of irregular verbs

(Lección 3)

IMPERFECT [add the person endings]

ir —→ IBA   ser —→ ERA   ver —→ VEÍA

PRETERITE: "COMBO" VERBS

		IRREGULAR STEM	"COMBO" ENDINGS
tener	—→	TUV-	-E
estar	—→	ESTUV-	-ISTE
poder	—→	PUD-	-O
poner	—→	PUS-	-IMOS
saber	—→	SUP-	-ISTEIS
haber	—→	HUB-	-IERON*
venir	—→	VIN-	
hacer	—→	HIC-	*Note: no **i** after **j**
querer	—→	QUIS-	
decir	—→	DIJ-	
traer	—→	TRAJ-	

OTHER IRREGULAR PRETERITE VERBS:

ser and ir: fui, fuiste, fue, fuimos, fuisteis, fueron
dar: regular **-er/-ir** endings: di, diste, dio, dimos, disteis, dieron

PRESENT: Irregular YO forms

-GO		**-OY**		**OTHER**	
tener —→ TENGO*	ser —→ SOY		ver —→ VEO		
venir —→ VENGO*	estar —→ ESTOY		saber —→ SÉ		
hacer —→ HAGO	dar —→ DOY		conocer —→ CONOZCO**		
poner —→ PONGO	ir —→ VOY		haber —→ HE		
decir —→ DIGO*					
traer —→ TRAIGO					
salir —→ SALGO					
oír —→ OIGO					
caer —→ CAIGO					

*Stem-changing verbs in remaining forms
Most verbs ending in **-cer or **-cir** add **z** before **co** (**-zco**).

Other irregular present verb forms

ser: soy, eres, es, somos, sois, son
ir: voy, vas, va, vamos, vais, van

haber: he, has, ha, hemos, habéis, han
oír: oigo, oyes, oye, oímos, oís, oyeron

FUTURE: Irregular stems

•drop some letters	•change the last vowel to **d**
hacer —→ HAR-	tener —→ TENDR-
poder —→ PODR-	venir —→ VENDR-
decir —→ DIR-	poner —→ PONDR-
querer —→ QUERR-	salir —→ SALDR-
haber —→ HABR-	

Verbs with additional meanings in preterite
(Lección 3)

conocer	*met for the first time*	no poder	*failed*
saber	*found out*	querer	*tried*
poder	*succeeded*	no querer	*refused*

PARTICIPLES

Present participles
(Lección 4)

-ar verbs: add **-ando** to the stem
-er and **-ir** verbs: add **-iendo** to the stem
-ir stem-changing verbs: same change as the preterite—**e** to **i** and **o** to **u**
   verbs that have a vowel before **iendo**: change the **i** to **y**

Progressive form of verbs
(Lección 4)

estar + present participle
Ir *(to go)* and **venir** *(to come)* are not used in the progressive form.

Object pronouns with progressive verbs
(Lección 4)

Attached to the end of the present participle with an accent over **a** or **e** or placed before **estar**

Past participles
(Lección 5)

-ar verbs: add **-ado** to the stem
-er and **-ir** verbs: add **-ido** to the stem
Some verbs have irregular past participles that must be learned individually (see page 275).

Summary of past participle usage
(Lección 5)

- as an adjective (showing condition)

   (pro)noun + ESTAR + *verb stem* $\begin{array}{l} \text{-ADO(A)(OS)(AS)} \\ \text{-IDO(A)(OS)(AS)} \end{array}$

- as a passive (indicating the subject was acted upon)

   (pro)noun + SER + *verb stem* $\begin{array}{l} \text{-ADO(A)(OS)(AS)} \\ \text{-IDO(A)(OS)(AS)} \end{array}$ + POR + *person/thing*

- as a perfect tense (relating a previous action to a specific time)

   (pro)noun + HABER + *verb stem* $\begin{array}{l} \text{-ADO} \\ \text{-IDO} \end{array}$

OTHER STRUCTURES

Reflexive pronouns
(Lección 2)

REFLEXIVE VERBS	RECIPROCAL ACTION	IMPERSONAL SUBJECT
me		
te		
se		
nos	nos	
os	os	
se	se	se

Position of reflexive pronouns
(Lección 2)

Before the verb with the person–time ending [conjugated form] or
Attached to the end of the infinitive if there is one

Possessive adjectives   Short and long forms
(Lección 4)

SHORT FORM [BEFORE THE NOUN]		LONG FORM [AFTER THE NOUN]	
mi	*my*	mío	*(of) mine*
tu	*your*	tuyo	*(of) yours*
su	*your/his/her/its/their*	suyo	*(of) yours/his/hers/theirs*
nuestro	*our*	nuestro	*(of) ours*
vuestro	*yours*	vuestro	*(of) yours*

The possessive adjectives agree with the noun in number and gender.

Possessive pronouns
(Lección 4)

el mío	la mía	los míos	las mías	*mine*
el tuyo	la tuya	los tuyos	las tuyas	*yours*
el suyo	la suya	los suyos	las suyas	*yours/his/hers/theirs*
el nuestro	la nuestra	los nuestros	las nuestras	*ours*
el vuestro	la vuestra	los vuestros	las vuestras	*yours*

Neutral and negative expressions
(Lección 4)

No or another negative word before the verb; any number of negative words after the verb

Esqueletos

Reflexive pronouns
(Lección 2)

> **subject + reflexive pronoun + conjugated verb**

Yo me comprendo bien.   *I understand myself well.*

> **subject + reflexive pronoun + conjugated verb + infinitive**

Yo me quiero lavar.   *I want to wash myself.*

> **subject + conjugated verb + infinitive + reflexive pronoun**

Yo quiero lavarme.   *I want to wash myself.*

Progressive form of verbs
(Lección 4)

> **ESTAR + *verb stem*   -ANDO [*for* -ar]**
> **-IENDO [*for* -er/-ir]**

Estábamos estudiando.   *We were studying.*
Estoy comiendo.   *I am eating.*
Estarán escribiendo.   *They will be writing.*

Pronouns with progressive verbs
(Lección 4)

> **(pro)noun + ESTAR + *verb* -ÁNDO/-IÉNDO + *object pronoun***
> **(pro)noun + *object pronoun* + ESTAR + *verb* -ANDO/-IENDO**

¿La cocina? Estoy limpiándola ahora. OR La estoy limpiando ahora.
The kitchen? I'm cleaning it now.

¿Mi madre? Estaba hablándole hace diez minutos. OR Le estaba hablando.
My mother? I was talking to her ten minutes ago.

¿Mis amigos? Están divirtiéndose en la fiesta. OR Se están divirtiendo.
My friends? They are enjoying themselves at the party.

Negative expressions
(Lección 4)

> **negative word + verb**
> **NO + verb + negative word**

Juan nunca va al cine.
Juan no va nunca al cine.   *Juan never goes to the movies.*

Using past participles as adjectives
(Lección 5)

> **noun + ESTAR + verb stem +   -ADO(A)(OS)(AS)**
> **-IDO(A)(OS)(AS)**

La torta está decorada.   *The cake is decorated.*
Las decoraciones están rotas.   *The decorations are broken.*

Using past participles in passive sentences
(Lección 5)

> **(pro)noun + SER + past participle + POR + person/thing**

La mesa es puesta por la criada.   *The table is set by the maid.*
Los libros fueron leídos por los estudiantes.   *The books were read by the students.*
La casa será pintada por mi padre.   *The house will be painted by my father.*

Perfect tenses
(Lección 5)

> **(pro)noun + HABER + past participle + (rest of sentence)**

Nosotros habíamos visto el avión.   *We had seen the airplane.*
Ellos han comprado los regalos.   *They have bought gifts.*
Tú habrás hecho la tarea.   *You will have done the homework.*

Después de la escuela

What do you do when you are not in school?

Vocabulario

Los pasatiempos *Pastimes*

Los deportes *Sports*

1. el fútbol	soccer	• 7. el béisbol	baseball
2. el fútbol norteamericano	football	• 8. el vólibol	volleyball
• 3. los bolos	bowling	• 9. el hockey sobre hielo	ice *hockey*
• 4. el tenis	tennis	• 10. el baloncesto	basketball
• 5. la arquería	archery	• 11. el badminton	badminton
• 6. el golf	golf	• 12. la lucha	wrestling

Los juegos   *Games*

- 1. las damas   *checkers*
- 2. los naipes   *cards*
- • 3. el escondite   *hide and seek*
- • 4. los videojuegos   *video games*

- • 5. el ajedrez   *chess*
- • 6. los dominós   *dominos*
- • 7. la lotería   *game similar to "Bingo"*

Los instrumentos musicales   *Musical instruments*

- 1. el piano   *piano*
- 2. la guitarra   *guitar*
- 3. el tambor   *drum*
- 4. el violín   *violin*
- • 5. la flauta   *flute*
- • 6. el saxofón   *saxophone*

- • 7. el trombón   *trombone*
- • 8. el acordeón   *accordion*
- • 9. la tuba   *tuba*
- • 10. la trompeta   *trumpet*
- • 11. el clarinete   *clarinet*
- • 12. la trompa francesa   *French horn*

Lo que hacemos durante el tiempo •libre   *What we do during free time*

divertirse (ie, i)	*to enjoy oneself, to have a good time, to have fun*
jugar (ue) a un deporte	*to play a sport*
ir a una •práctica de…	*to go to . . . practice*
mirar •un partido de…	*to watch a . . . game/event*
jugar (ue) a un juego	*to play a game*
tocar un instrumento musical	*to play a musical instrument*
ir de compras	*to go shopping*
asistir a un concierto	*to attend a concert*
mirar la televisión	*to watch television*
• coleccionar estampillas	*to collect stamps*
escuchar discos compactos	*to listen to CDs*
dibujar y pintar	*to draw and paint*
correr	*to run*
hacer •ejercicio	*to exercise*
hacer •jogging	*to jog*
hablar por teléfono	*to talk on the telephone*
broncearse	*to sunbathe*
dar un paseo a pie	*to go for a walk*
dar un paseo en coche	*to go for a drive*
visitar a los abuelos	*to visit grandparents*
escuchar la radio	*to listen to the radio*
• montar en bicicleta	*to ride a bike*
• pasar el tiempo	*to spend time*
• perder (ie) tiempo	*to waste time*
patinar	*to skate*
nadar	*to swim*
pescar	*to fish*
encontrarse (ue) con los amigos	*to meet friends*
hacer la tarea	*to do homework*
descansar	*to rest*
dormir (ue, u) una siesta	*to take a nap*
ayudar en la casa	*to help around the house*
ganar dinero	*to earn money*
cuidar de los niños	*to babysit*
ir a un trabajo	*to go to a job (work)*
trabajar en…	*to work in/at . . .*
discutir con los hermanos	*to argue with siblings*
levantar pesas	*to lift weights*

Note: The verb **jugar** is used for games and sports. The **a** before the game or sport is often left out. The verb **tocar** is used for playing music (on an instrument, stereo, etc.)

1 Make a list of things you like to do after school and another list of things you do not like to do.

EJEMPLO: Me gusta mirar la televisión.
Â No me gusta cuidar de los niños.

2 Find out from several of your classmates what they like to do and what they do not like to do after school.

EJEMPLO: 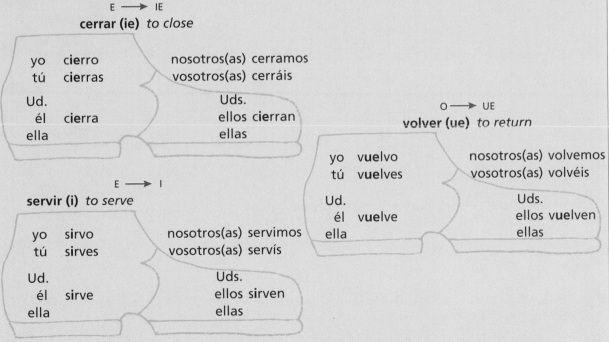 ¿Qué te gusta hacer después de la escuela?

Me gusta patinar en ruedas.

3 What do you do with your friends? Tell with whom you spend your time after school and what you do. Use the **nosotros** form.

EJEMPLO: Mi amigo Juan y yo hacemos la tarea juntos.

STEM-CHANGING VERBS: PRESENT TENSE

In some Spanish verbs, the vowel preceding the person–time endings changes in the present tense in all the forms except **nosotros(as)** and **vosotros(as)**. If we draw a line around the forms that have the change, (all except **nosotros** and **vosotros**), the line forms a "boot." We can refer to these verbs as "stem-changing verbs" or "boot verbs."

There are three groups: those that change **e** to **ie**, **e** to **i**, and **o** to **ue**. In dictionaries or vocabulary lists, the change is often indicated after the infinitive. Here are sample verbs from each group.

E ⟶ IE

cerrar (ie) *to close*

| yo | cierro | nosotros(as) cerramos |
| tú | cierras | vosotros(as) cerráis |

Ud.		Uds.
él	cierra	ellos cierran
ella		ellas

O ⟶ UE

volver (ue) *to return*

| yo | vuelvo | nosotros(as) volvemos |
| tú | vuelves | vosotros(as) volvéis |

Ud.		Uds.
él	vuelve	ellos vuelven
ella		ellas

E ⟶ I

servir (i) *to serve*

| yo | sirvo | nosotros(as) servimos |
| tú | sirves | vosotros(as) servís |

Ud.		Uds.
él	sirve	ellos sirven
ella		ellas

Note: Stem-changing verbs that change to **ie** and **ue** may belong to any of the three infinitive groups: **-ar**, **-er**, or **-ir**. Verbs that change to **i** all belong to the **-ir** infinitive group.

Vocabulario

Verbos de cambio radical   *Stem-changing verbs*

Following are some verbs that follow the "boot" pattern. Note that there are verbs of the **-ar, -er,** and **-ir** categories. Be careful to put the corresponding **-ar, -er,** and **-ir** endings on the verbs.

E ⟶ IE

• atravesar	*to cross*
cerrar	*to close*
comenzar a	*to begin/start to*
• confesar	*to confess*
• empezar a	*to begin/to start*
• nevar	*to snow*
pensar en/de	*to think of/about*
pensar + *infinitive*	*to plan to*
• recomendar	*to recommend*
• encender	*to light, to turn on*
perder	*to lose, to waste*
querer*	*to want*
querer* a + *person*	*to love*
• mentir	*to tell a lie*
preferir	*to prefer*
sentir	*to be sorry, to regret*
• sugerir	*to suggest*

E ⟶ I

• conseguir	*to get, to obtain*
• impedir	*to prevent*
pedir	*to ask for, to order*
repetir	*to repeat*
seguir	*to continue, to follow*
servir	*to serve*
vestir	*to dress*

O ⟶ UE

almorzar	*to eat lunch*
contar	*to count, to tell a story*
costar	*to cost*
• encontrar	*to find, to meet*
• mostrar	*to show*
• probar	*to taste, to try (out)*
recordar	*to remember*
sonar	*to sound*
soñar con	*to dream about*
• volar	*to fly*
doler	*to ache, to hurt*
• devolver	*to give back, to return*
llover	*to rain*
• mover	*to move*
poder*	*to be able, can*
• resolver	*to solve*
• soler	*to be accustomed to*
volver	*to return, to go back*
dormir	*to sleep*
morir	*to die*

U ⟶ UE

jugar	*to play*

*****Querer** and **poder** have irregular preterite forms and will be explained in Lesson 3.
Note: **Jugar** (*to play a game*) is the only verb that has a **u ⟶ ue** change.

4 Review the vocabulary pertaining to clothing on pages 146–147. Then tell what some of your preferences are.

EJEMPLO: Prefiero los cuellos redondos.
Prefiero las camisas de algodón.

5 **Encuesta** Choose two afterschool activities that *you* prefer to do. Ask several people which one they prefer.

EJEMPLO: 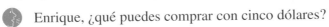 ¿Qué prefieres, jugar o dar un paseo?

Prefiero jugar.

6 Report on other people's preferences.

EJEMPLO: Esteban prefiere el ajedrez pero Marta prefiere la lotería.
Nosotros preferimos dibujar y ellos prefieren pintar.

In the following activities, ask at least five people for the information indicated and report on what you have found out.

7 Find out what people want to do after school today.

EJEMPLO: Federico, ¿qué quieres hacer después de la escuela hoy?

Quiero visitar a mi amigo.

Reportaje: Federico quiere visitar a su amigo.

8 Find out what sports your friends play.

EJEMPLO: José, ¿a qué deportes juegas?

Juego al béisbol.

Reportaje: José juega al béisbol.

9 Find out how long people sleep each night.

EJEMPLO: Ana María, ¿cuántas horas duermes por la noche?

Duermo siete u ocho horas.

Reportaje: Ana María duerme siete u ocho horas.

10 Find out what people are able to buy with five dollars.

EJEMPLO: Enrique, ¿qué puedes comprar con cinco dólares?

Puedo comprar calcetines.

Reportaje: Enrique puede comprar calcetines con cinco dólares.

11 Find out if people open or close the door when they study.

EJEMPLO: Timoteo, ¿abres o cierras la puerta cuando estudias?

Cierro la puerta cuando estudio.

Reportaje: Timoteo cierra la puerta cuando estudia.

12 Find out what your classmates order at their favorite fast food restaurant. (Refer to the list of foods on pages 147–150.)

EJEMPLO: Linda, ¿qué pides en el restaurante?

Pido pollo y papas fritas.

Reportaje: Linda pide pollo y papas fritas en el restaurante.

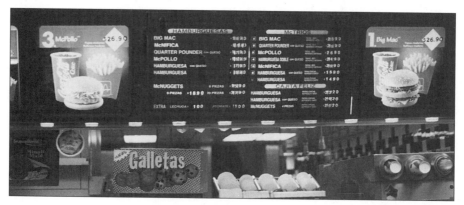

¿Qué piden Uds. para comer?

Pedimos hamburguesas y papas fritas.

13 Find out at what time people and the families eat lunch. (If you need to review telling time, refer to page 38.)

EJEMPLO: Ramón, ¿a qué hora almuerzan tú y tu familia?

Generalmente almorzamos a las doce.

Reportaje: Ramón y su familia almuerzan a las doce.

14 Find out if people remember an event that took place recently at your school.

EJEMPLO: ¿Recuerdas la visita del alcalde *(mayor)*?

Sí, la recuerdo.

15 **Juego** *(Play with groups of up to five people)* **Guess the cost of . . .**   One person in the group chooses an item and puts a "price" on it. The others try to guess its cost. The person helps them by saying **más** or **menos**. The group tries to guess the price in fewer than eight tries. Then the next person offers an item for sale.

EJEMPLO: ¿Cuánto cuesta un cuaderno? *(one dollar)*

Cuesta setenta y nueve centavos.

Más.

Cuesta un dólar, veinte y cinco centavos.

Menos.

Continue until someone guesses or until eight guesses have been made. Then the next person has a turn, etc.

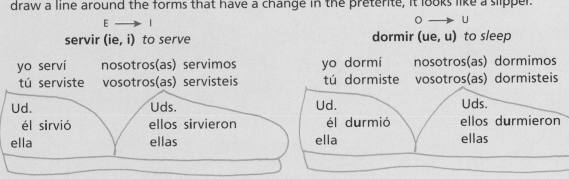

STEM-CHANGING VERBS: PRETERITE TENSE

-Ar and **-er** "boot verbs" have no stem changes in the preterite.

-Ir "boot verbs" change the **e** to **i** and **o** to **u** in the **él** and **ellos** forms of the preterite. If we draw a line around the forms that have a change in the preterite, it looks like a slipper.

E ⟶ I
servir (ie, i) *to serve*

yo serví	nosotros(as) servimos
tú serviste	vosotros(as) servisteis
Ud.	Uds.
él sirvió	ellos sirvieron
ella	ellas

O ⟶ U
dormir (ue, u) *to sleep*

yo dormí	nosotros(as) dormimos
tú dormiste	vosotros(as) dormisteis
Ud.	Uds.
él durmió	ellos durmieron
ella	ellas

Following are the **-ir** stem-changing verbs from the list on page 288 with both stem changes indicated: The first change indicated is for present tense (boot forms). The second change indicated is for the preterite tense (slipper forms).

E ⟶ IE

preferir (ie, i)	*to prefer*
sugerir (ie, i)	*to suggest*
sentir (ie, i)	*to be sorry, to regret*
mentir (ie, i)	*to tell a lie*

E ⟶ I

pedir (i, i)	*to ask for, to order*
repetir (i, i)	*to repeat*
impedir (i, i)	*to prevent*
vestir (i, i)	*to dress*
servir (i, i)	*to serve*
seguir (i, i)	*to continue, to follow*
conseguir (i, i)	*to get, to obtain*

O ⟶ UE

| morir (ue, u) | *to die* |
| dormir (ue, u) | *to sleep* |

16 Find out from several people which television programs they watched recently and which they preferred. Report about what you find out.

EJEMPLO:

 ¿Qué programas viste recientemente?

 Vi… y…

¿Cuál preferiste?

Preferí…

¿Cuál prefirió tu amigo(a)?

 Mi amigo(a) prefirió…

■ **Canal Sur**	■ **Telemadrid**
6.45 Carta de presentación.	**7.30 Cine matinal.** *Bésame, Kate.* Estados Unidos, 1953 (106 minutos).
7.00 Tele Expo. Programa de servicios.	**9.20 El nuevo mundo de Cousteau.**
9.30 Testigos hoy. Programa religioso.	**10.10 La banda.**
10.00 La pequeña Lulú. Dibujos animados inspirados en el clásico del tebeo.	— 10.10 *La banda de…* 'Bananas'.
10.30 Teletrasto. Programa infantil.	— 11.35 *La banda de…* 'Kidd Video'
12.00 Festival de Tom y Jerry. Un clásico de los dibujos animados popular en todo el mundo.	— 11.00 'El planeta perdido de Gilligan'.
13.20 ¿Y tú de quién eres? (Repetición).	— 12.25 'Las tortugas ninja'.
14.05 Dinosaucers. Dibujos animados.	— 12.50 'Los dinosaucers'.
14.30 El diario fin de semana.	— 12.15 *La banda de…* 'Los droids'
15.00 El tiempo.	— 12.40 *La banda de…* película. *Chitty Chitty Bang Bang.*
15.05 Las tortugas ninja II. Dibujos.	**14.30 Telenoticias.**
15.30 Las grandes aventuras del cine. *Escrito bajo el sol (The Wings of Eagles).* Estados Unidos, 1957. Color. (105 minutos). Director: John Ford.	**14.55 El tiempo.**
	15.00 Las tortugas ninja.
	15.25 La telemanía.
17.25 La vuelta al mundo en 80 días.	— 15.25 'Teddy Z'.
17.55 Pulaski. Nueva miniserie de siete capítulos de una hora.	— 15.50 'El picapleitos'
	— 16.15 'Benson'
18.45 Los estrenos de Canal Sur. *El vengador (The Avenging).* Estados Unidos, 1984 (96 minutos). Color.	**16.40 Cine: pantalla del domingo.** *Capítulo dos.* Estados Unidos, 1980 (123 minutos). Director: Robert Moore.
	18.45 Chan-tatachán (repetición).

17 Find out from several people how many hours they slept last night. Then be prepared to report on the information you learned.

EJEMPLO: ¿Cuántas horas dormiste ayer, Isabel?

Dormí ocho horas.

Reportaje: Isabel durmió ocho horas.

18 Find out what birthday gifts several of your classmates asked for.

EJEMPLO: Antonio, ¿qué pediste para tu cumpleaños?

Pedí una chaqueta de cuero (*leather jacket*).

Reportaje: Antonio pidió una chaqueta de cuero.

19 Find out who served the meal at your classmates' houses last night.

EJEMPLO: ¿Quién sirvió la comida?

Mi madre y mi hermano la sirvieron.

20 **¡Qué triste!**   Make a list of people and animals you knew who died and tell when.

EJEMPLO: El presidente John F. Kennedy murió en 1963.
Hace una semana mi vecino murió.
Mi perro murió cuando yo tenía diez años.

SUMMARY OF STEM-CHANGING VERBS

IMPERFECT	PRETERITE -ir only	PRESENT -ar, -er, -ir	FUTURE
no changes	slipper forms	boot forms	no changes
	e ⟶ i o ⟶ u	e ⟶ ie e ⟶ i o ⟶ ue	

PEDIR VS. PREGUNTAR

In Spanish there are two verbs that mean *to ask:*

pedir (i, i)   *to ask for something, to request, to order*
preguntar   *to ask about (in a question), to inquire*

Le pregunté si el centro comercial está lejos de aquí.   *I asked him if the shopping center is far from here.*

Pedí direcciones para ir allí.   *I asked for directions to go there.*

21 **¿Qué pides?**   Make a list of several things that you frequently request from your parents.

EJEMPLO: Pido dinero.
Pido el coche.

22 Find out what your friends will ask for for their next birthday. Then report about it.

EJEMPLO: Tomás, ¿qué pedirás para tu cumpleaños?

Pediré un estéreo nuevo.

Reportaje: Tomás pedirá un estéreo nuevo.

23 **¿Qué preguntas?**   Make a list of five things that you ask your friends about.

EJEMPLO: Les pregunto cómo están.
Les pregunto adónde van.

24 **Encuesta**   In Activity 12 on page 290, you found out what your friends usually order at their favorite restaurant. Now find out what they actually ordered the last time they were at their favorite restaurant. Then report to the class.

EJEMPLO: Diana, ¿qué pediste la última vez que fuiste a un restaurante?

Pedí bistec y papas fritas.

Reportaje: Diana pidió bistec y papas fritas.

ENCUENTRO PERSONAL

Paulina and her friends are talking about what they used to do after school and what they do now. How do their activities compare to yours?

PAULINA: Cuando yo estaba en la escuela primaria, mis amigos y yo jugábamos a las canicas en el parque. Pero ahora prefiero jugar al tenis o tocar el piano. Ahora no juego al golf, pero en el futuro creo que lo jugaré con mis colegas después del trabajo.

RAÚL: Mi padre juega mucho al golf, y a veces jugamos juntos. Pero yo prefiero ir al parque con mis amigos para charlar y pasar el tiempo.

ROSITA: De niña yo también pasaba tiempo charlando con mis amigas después de la escuela, pero ahora no pierdo mucho tiempo hablando con mis amigas por teléfono porque tengo tanta tarea que hacer y también trabajo en la ropería. Pero en mis ratos libres durante los fines de semana me gusta mirar la televisión o simplemente dormir tarde.

SANTIAGO: ¡Me gustaría tener tiempo para dormir tarde! Yo nunca duermo tarde porque tengo que ir a trabajar en el restaurante a las seis de la mañana los sábados, y el domingo nos levantamos temprano para ir a la iglesia. Después de graduarme, quiero obtener un buen trabajo donde ganaré mucho dinero y no tendré que levantarme temprano.

INÉS: En mi quinto año de escuela primaria, me encantaba encontrarme con mis amigas en frente de la heladería para charlar y mirar a los muchachos que pasaban. Pero ahora tengo que cuidar de mis hermanos todos los días porque mi madre trabaja y no vuelve del trabajo hasta las cinco y media de la tarde.

PAULINA: Pues, tengo una pregunta para todos Uds: ¿por qué estamos aquí perdiendo tiempo charlando cuando todos tenemos tanto que hacer? Tengo una idea. ¿Por qué no vienen todos a mi casa el sábado por la noche para una fiesta informal? Podemos pedir una pizza y mirar unos vídeos de música y bailar y cantar.

TODOS: ¡Buena idea, Paulina! Hasta el sábado por la noche.

¿Comprendes?

1. ¿Qué hacían Paulina y sus amigos después de la escuela?
2. ¿Qué prefiere ella hacer ahora y qué hará en el futuro?
3. ¿Cómo pasaba Rosita tiempo antes y qué hace ahora?
4. ¿Por qué no duerme tarde Santiago? ¿Qué quiere hacer en el futuro?
5. ¿Qué prefiere hacer Inés y qué hace? ¿Por qué?
6. ¿Qué pregunta y qué sugiere Paulina?

¡Te toca!

Take a survey of your classmates to find out what they used to like to do after class in grade school and what they do now. Report your findings to the class.

Leemos y contamos

A. Here is a letter from Paulina's pen pal Marisol, describing her friends and her own afterschool activities.

Querida Paulina,

En tú última carta me preguntaste cómo mis amigos y yo pasamos nuestro tiempo libre. Es una buena pregunta pero difícil de contestar en pocas palabras porque hacemos de todo. En mi caso, prefiero pasar mi tiempo libre en las actividades mentales: leer libros, jugar al ajedrez, hacer rompecabezas, etc. Pero mi amiga Alicia no quiere hacer estas actividades. Prefiere las actividades al aire libre: hacer jogging, dar un paseo en el parque o montar en bicicleta. Y a mi amigo Pedro le gustan los pasatiempos más físicos como hacer gimnasia, jugar al fútbol o escalar (climb) montañas. Y claro, nos gusta mirar la televisión o hablar con nuestros amigos por teléfono.

Creo que todos nosotros ayudamos a la familia en casa. Por ejemplo, mis hermanos y yo siempre ayudamos a lavar y secar los platos y limpiar la casa. Mis hermanos y yo tenemos que ayudar a mantener el jardín: cortar el césped, reparar las cercas (fences) y cuidar de los animales.

Algunos de nosotros también trabajamos fuera de la casa para ganar dinero. A veces yo cuido de los niños de mi tía, y mi amiga Alicia trabaja de noche en una tienda de ropa. Pedro sirve de guía en un parque durante los fines de semana y en el verano. Y por supuesto, todos tenemos que hacer la tarea. Y cuando tenemos tiempo nos gusta dar fiestas donde escuchamos música, bailamos, comemos y tomamos refrescos.

Con todas estas actividades no dormimos mucho, pero nos divertimos mucho y hacemos lo necesario.

Hasta la próxima,
Tu fiel amiga de siempre, Marisol

1. ¿Qué tipos de actividades prefiere hacer Marisol? ¿Por ejemplo?
2. ¿Y su amiga Alicia?
3. ¿Y su amigo Pedro?
4. ¿Qué otras actividades hacen ellos en la casa y fuera de la casa?
5. ¿Qué actividad tienen que hacer todos ellos?
6. ¿Qué hacen en las fiestas?

B. Write a report about the things you prefer to do every day. Use as many stem-changing "boot verbs" as possible. Underline each "boot verb" that you use. Indicate how many you use at the end of your report.

C. Write a report describing a day from the past. Use as many "slipper verbs" as you can. Underline each "slipper verb." Keep score and record how many you use at the end of your report.

Así es

Los pasatiempos de los jóvenes

La vida de los jóvenes de los países de habla española es más o menos como la vida de los jóvenes estadounidenses. Claro, durante la semana, pasan su tiempo en la escuela. Después tienen que hacer su tarea. Pero cuando no tienen que estudiar, les gusta pasar el tiempo con sus amigos.

¿Adónde van? Van al cine, a las fiestas, al parque, a un café o restaurante, al centro comercial o a la playa. A muchos les gusta asistir a un partido de fútbol o a un espectáculo de música.

Pero hay algunas diferencias. Por ejemplo, los jóvenes hispanos pasan generalmente más tiempo con sus familias. Van frecuentemente a fiestas familiares para celebrar un cumpleaños o aniversario. Los domingos, muchos van al parque o a otro lugar con sus padres, hermanos y abuelos.

También hay más restricciones para las muchachas. Los padres son generalmente más conservadores con sus hijas y no les permiten la libertad que gozan (*enjoy*) la mayoría de las muchachas en los EE. UU. Generalmente pueden ir adonde quieren con un grupo de amigas y amigos; pero en muchas familias, las muchachas no pueden salir a solas con un muchacho. Si quieren salir con su novio, ¡tienen que ir acompañadas de otra persona de la familia, por ejemplo un hermano o una tía!

La rutina diaria

What is a typical day like for you? There are many things that you do routinely, aren't there? In this lesson we'll be talking about some things that most people do every day. How many of the following activities do you do regularly? Later in this lesson we'll talk about a romance.

Vocabulario

A note on reflexive verbs (verb + -*self* pronoun):
There are many verbs in Spanish that use reflexive (-self) pronouns when the subject is doing something to itself even though we may not use a -self pronoun in English. These verbs are identified by **-se** (-self) attached to the end of the infinitive. Following are some common verbs that use reflexive pronouns in Spanish.

La rutina diaria   *Daily routine*

1. despertarse (ie)	*to wake up*		12. vestirse (i, i)	*to get dressed*
2. levantarse	*to get up*		13. ponerse	*to put on (clothing)*
3. sentarse (ie)	*to sit down*		14. peinarse	*to comb one's hair*
• 4. prepararse	*to get ready*		15. maquillarse	*to put on makeup*
5. arreglarse	*to get fixed up*		16. despedirse (i, i)	*to say good-bye*
6. bañarse	*to take a bath*		17. irse	*to go away*
7. ducharse	*to take a shower*		18. quedarse	*to stay, to remain*
8. lavarse	*to wash*		• 19. cansarse	*to get tired*
• 9. secarse	*to dry (off)*		20. quitarse	*to take off (clothing)*
10. afeitarse	*to shave*		21. acostarse (ue)	*to go to bed, to lie down*
11. cepillarse	*to brush*		22. dormirse (ue, u)	*to go to sleep, to fall asleep*

En la escuela   *In school*

- portarse bien/mal — *to behave well/badly*
- callarse — *to be quiet*
- ocuparse — *to be busy*
- equivocarse — *to make a mistake*
- preocuparse — *to worry*
  divertirse (ie, i) — *to have a good time, to enjoy oneself to have fun*
- aburrirse — *to be bored*
- hacerse buen estudiante — *to become a good student*
- graduarse — *to graduate*

1 Tell the things that everyone has to do every day and things that people should do every day.

EJEMPLO: Todo el mundo tiene que despertarse todos los días.
Todo el mundo debe cepillarse los dientes.

REFLEXIVE (-SELF) PRONOUNS

me	*myself*		nos	*ourselves*
te	*yourself* [informal]		os	*yourselves* [informal in Spain]
se	*yourself* [formal]		se	*yourselves*
	himself/herself/itself/oneself			*themselves*

- Reflexive pronouns are used with <u>reflexive verbs</u> to show that the subject is doing something to itself. The action "reflects" back on the subject. The subject and the object are the same. Notice that the reflexive pronouns are similar to object pronouns and that they function as the direct or indirect object of the sentence.

  Yo me miro en el espejo.   *I look at myself in the mirror.*
  Elena se compró un libro.   *Elena bought a book for herself.*

Yo me miro en el espejo.   Nosotros nos miramos en el espejo.

- Reflexive pronouns **nos** and **se** are also used to show that an action is <u>reciprocal</u>, that is, that the people are doing something to each other.

  Nos hablamos a menudo.   *We talk to each other often.*
  Se escriben en español.   *They write to each other in Spanish.*

- The reflexive pronoun **se** is used as an <u>indefinite subject</u> much like "one" or an unspecified "you." Use a plural verb with a plural noun.

  ¿Cómo se dice *"house"* en español?   *How do you say "house" in Spanish?*
  Se venden botas.   *They sell boots.*

POSITION OF REFLEXIVE PRONOUNS

Ellos se saludan.

Reflexive pronouns follow the same pattern as object pronouns.

Before the verb with the person–time ending [conjugated form]
Attached to the end of the infinitive if there is one

Esqueletos

subject + reflexive pronoun + conjugated verb

Yo me comprendo bien.   *I understand myself well.*

subject + reflexive pronoun + conjugated verb + infinitive

Yo me quiero lavar.   *I want to wash myself.*

subject + conjugated verb + infinitive + reflexive pronoun

Yo quiero lavarme.   *I want to wash myself.*

REFLEXIVE VERBS

Reflexive verbs express that the subject is doing an action to itself. These verbs are identified by the **se** attached to the end of the infinitive. Many reflexive verbs have a nonreflexive form to indicate that the action is being done to someone or something other than the subject.

Yo <u>me</u> despierto a las seis.   *I wake (myself) up at six o'clock.*
Yo despierto a mi hermano después.   *I wake my brother up afterward.*

When the person–time ending is added, the appropriate reflexive pronoun precedes the verb. Following is the pattern, using **lavarse** *(to wash oneself).*

yo	me lavo	nosotros(as)	nos lavamos
tú	te lavas	vosotros (as)	os laváis
Ud./él/ella	se lava	Uds./ellos/ellas	se lavan

Some reflexive verbs do not have a "-self" meaning. The reflexive pronoun changes the meaning of the verb.

dormir: *to sleep*
Duermo nueve horas por noche.   *I sleep nine hours a night.*

dormirse: *to fall asleep*
Me duermo a las diez.   *I fall asleep at ten o'clock.*

Note: When using a reflexive verb, use an article and not the possessive adjective with parts of the body and clothing.

Me lavo <u>las</u> manos antes de salir.   *I wash my hands before leaving.*

---

2 Make a list of things that you do to or for yourself and another list of things that you do to or for others.

EJEMPLO: Me despierto temprano.
Luego, despierto a mi hermano.

3 Tell some things that you have to do every day.

EJEMPLO: Tengo que despertarme temprano.
Tengo que lavarme el pelo.

4 Ask your partner what time he or she does various activities.

EJEMPLO: ¿A qué hora te acuestas?

Generalmente me acuesto a las diez.

5 Tell when you and your friends have fun together.

EJEMPLO: Nos divertimos cuando jugamos al fútbol.

6 Tell when you and your friends say good-bye.

EJEMPLO: Nos despedimos después de las clases.

7 Describe your routine for a school day. Use as many of the verbs from the list on page 299 as you can and expand your sentences to give more information. Watch for stem-changing verbs. (Refer to page 269.)

EJEMPLO: Me despierto a las siete.
Me levanto inmediatamente.

Me ducho y me seco.

Me levanto inmediatamente.

Me despierto a las siete.

Me visto.

Me acuesto tarde.

8 Describe the routine of someone you know.

EJEMPLO: Mi amiga se despierta muy temprano.

9 **Cuando voy a una fiesta...**   Describe what you do to get ready to go to a party.

EJEMPLO: Me ducho y me seco. Entonces me visto.

10 Describe your day today. Tell what you did already (preterite), tell what you are doing now (present) and tell what you will do (future). Not all your actions will require reflexive verbs—just those where you do something to yourself.

EJEMPLO: Me desperté a las seis.
Cuando llego a la clase de español, me siento y hablo con mi amigo.
Esta tarde, haré mi tarea y esta noche, miraré la televisión y me acostaré tarde.

11 Describe a typical day on the weekend.

EJEMPLO: No salgo. Me quedo en casa. Descanso y hago mi tarea.

12 **Un día en la vida de...**   Choose a famous person and describe what you think her or his day is like.

EJEMPLO: El presidente de los Estados Unidos se despierta temprano y se levanta inmediatamente. Se viste y se desayuna. No tiene que salir a trabajar porque vive en la Casa Blanca y su oficina está allí.

13 *Sit-Con*   You have been granted the wish of doing whatever you want on your birthday. Describe your day.

EJEMPLO: El día de mi cumpleaños me gustaría dormir hasta tarde. Me despertaré a las once de la mañana. No me levantaré inmediatamente. Me levantaré media hora después…

14 *Sit-Con   A day in the life of a pet*   Choose an animal that is a pampered pet and describe its life. Since the owner does many things for the pet, not all verbs will be reflexive. Be careful.

EJEMPLO: Soy el perro de Rosita. Rosita me despierta cuando ella se despierta…

Remember: Most verbs are not reflexive!
Estudio español.   *I study Spanish.*
Miramos la televisión.   *We watch television.*

Before doing Activities 15, 16, and 17, review the use of "each other" on page 300.

15 Tell some things that you and your friends do to and for each other.

EJEMPLO: Mi amiga y yo nos escuchamos.
Mi amiga y su novio se hablan todos los días.

Vocabulario

Following are additional verbs we can use with reflexive pronouns to talk about the course of a romance. Notice that some are reflexive verbs, others have the meaning of *each other* (reciprocal).

Un cuento de amor   *A love story*

conocerse	*to meet each other*
• llevarse bien/mal	*to get along well/badly*
• sentirse (ie, i) contento(a)	*to feel happy*
• besarse	*to kiss each other*
• abrazarse	*to hug each other*
darse un regalo	*to give each other a gift*
un abrazo	*a hug*
un beso	*a kiss*
un ramillete	*a bouquet of flowers*
• enamorarse (de)	*to fall in love (with)*
decirse «Te quiero»	*to tell each other "I love you"*
• alegrarse (de)	*to be happy (about)*
• comprometerse (con)	*to become engaged (to)*
• casarse (con)	*to get married (to)*
vivir •felizmente	*to live happily*
• burlarse (de)	*to make fun (of)*
• enojarse (con)	*to become angry (with)*
• ponerse celoso(a)	*to become jealous*
• quejarse (de)	*to complain (about)*
• darse cuenta (de)	*to realize*
• separarse	*to separate*
• divorciarse	*to get divorced*
• llorar	*to cry*

16 Describe the progress of the relationship between two of your friends.

    EJEMPLO: Se conocieron el año pasado.
                     Se hablaron por teléfono de sus intereses.
                     Se vieron de vez en cuando.

17 Tell about how you would like your courtship to be.

    EJEMPLO: Mi novio(a) y yo nos conoceremos en una fiesta…

TO BECOME

Following are two ways to say *become* in Spanish.

Ponerse is used with emotions. **Hacerse** is the result of one's efforts or conscious actions.

Me puse muy furioso.   *I became very angry.*
Me hice abogado.   *I became a lawyer.*

18 Tell some things that have happened to you and tell how you reacted emotionally to them.

EJEMPLO: Mi mejor amiga se fue a vivir a otra ciudad. Me puse muy triste.

19 **Encuesta**   Find out from classmates what various family members became as an occupation.

EJEMPLO: ¿Qué se hizo tu padre?

    Mi padre se hizo mecánico.

Before doing Activities 20 and 21, review the use of **se** as an impersonal subject on page 300.

20 Tell several things that people generally do and do not do in your school.

EJEMPLO: Se habla inglés.
Se come en la cafetería.
No se llevan sombreros en la clase.

21 *Sit-Con*   A new person has moved to your city and wants to know where to go shopping. Tell her or him where they go for various things.

EJEMPLO: Se vende comida en el supermercado B & C.
Se compra gasolina en el GASOL.
Se prestan libros en la biblioteca.

Se solicita
ARQUITECTO (A)
- Licencia
- Bilingüe
- Experiencia en Diseño y Supervisión
- Experiencia en AutoCAD

Favor de enviar resume al FAX 725-9180 y/o llamar al Tel. 725-9030 para entrevista.

SE HABLA ESPAÑOL

SUMMARY OF REFLEXIVE PRONOUNS

-SELF		EACH OTHER		UNKNOWN SUBJECT	
me	myself				
te	yourself				
se	yourself				
	himself				
	herself				
nos	ourselves	nos	each other		
se	yourselves	se	each other	se	one, you, they
	themselves				

ENCUENTRO PERSONAL

Señorita Blanco is the sponsor of the Hispanic Club at Paulina's school. She has invited the members of the club to her wedding. Inés telephoned Paulina while she was getting ready to go to the ceremony.

INÉS: Hola, Paulina, ¿cómo estás? ¿Qué haces ahora?

PAULINA: ¡Oh, Inés, eres tú! Estoy bien. Me visto para ir a la boda de la señorita Blanco.

INÉS: Yo también. Ya me duché y me lavé el pelo. Me sequé y me peiné. Entonces, me puse un vestido nuevo de seda rosada… ¿tú lo recuerdas?… y ahora me maquillo.

PAULINA: Me alegré mucho de haber recibido *(having received)* la invitación a la boda. Todos nuestros amigos recibieron una invitación, ¿verdad? Creo que la manera en que la señorita Blanco y su novio se conocieron es muy romántica.

INÉS: Sí, se conocieron en la playa en Acapulco durante las vacaciones de primavera. Se llevaron bien y se dieron cuenta que tenían mucho en común. Se enamoraron casi inmediatamente y ahora se casan. Sí, es muy romántico. Quizás *(Maybe)* algún día yo también encuentre a un hombre guapo y romántico y…

PAULINA: Sí, me siento feliz de que hayan decidido *(they have decided)* invitar a los miembros del Club Hispánico a la ceremonia en la iglesia y también a la fiesta.

INÉS: Los muchachos quieren saber si habrá una piñata para nosotros. Les dije que las piñatas son para las fiestas de cumpleaños y no para las bodas.

PAULINA: De vez en cuando me enojo mucho con ellos. Se portan como tontos. Probablemente se quejan ahora porque tienen que llevar trajes y corbatas.

INÉS: Sí… ¡Ay! Acabo de darme cuenta de la hora. Tengo que darme prisa o no estaré lista para ir a la ceremonia. Tengo que despedirme de ti.

PAULINA: Bueno, nos vemos en la iglesia.

¿Comprendes?

1. ¿Qué hace Paulina?
2. ¿Qué acaba de hacer Inés?
3. ¿Cuándo se conocieron los novios?
4. ¿Cómo se siente Paulina? ¿Por qué?
5. ¿Qué hacían los muchachos del Club Hispánico?
6. ¿Qué tiene que hacer Inés ahora?

¡Te toca!

Have you had a special day in your family recently (wedding, birthday, graduation, etc.)? Take turns with your partner describing the sequence of events for getting ready that morning. What did each person in the family do? (You may want to read the letter on page 310 before you decide what to say.)

Leemos y contamos

A. Read the following letter Marisol wrote to Paulina about her sister's wedding.

Querida Paulina,

Hola, ¿cómo estás? Yo estoy muy cansada pero también muy contenta porque ayer se casó mi hermana mayor. El día comenzó muy temprano. Mi hermana y yo nos levantamos a las cinco y media. Yo no me bañé inmediatamente porque tenía tanto trabajo que hacer antes de la boda. Pero sí me arreglé un poco y le ayudé a mi hermana a prepararse para su día especial. Primero ella se duchó y se lavó el pelo. Luego se lo secó, y se peinó y yo le ayudé a maquillarse y ponerse su vestido de boda. Ella se puso muy emocionada. Después de ayudar a mi mamá y a mis tías a preparar la comida para la recepción, yo me bañé y me arreglé también.

Antes de ir a la iglesia, los novios y sus padres se fueron al Palacio de Justicia (courthouse) para la ceremonia civil. Todos nosotros fuimos directamente a la iglesia para la ceremonia religiosa. Cuando llegaron los novios, todos nos pusimos muy entusiasmados de verlos. Fue un maravilloso matrimonio tradicional. Hubo una misa, y después el sacerdote (priest) leyó las palabras oficiales de casamiento (marriage). El novio le dio a la novia una bolsa pequeña de monedas (coins) para simbolizar que le estaba dando todo lo que poseía. Y había un lazo (tie) también. Un lazo es una cinta (ribbon) en forma de círculo que se pone sobre los hombros de los novios y simboliza su unión eterna. Por supuesto algunas personas lloraron de alegría.

En la recepción todos nos divertimos mucho. Bailamos, hablamos y, por supuesto, comimos hasta las altas horas de la noche. Yo no me acosté hasta las cuatro de la mañana y no me dormí hasta las cinco por estar tan entusiasmada. Fue un día magnífico que siempre recordaré.

Recibe el cariño de tu amiga,
Marisol

1. ¿Cómo ayudó Marisol a su hermana a prepararse para la boda?
2. ¿Y cómo se preparó Marisol?
3. ¿Qué hicieron antes de irse a la iglesia?
4. Describe la ceremonia religiosa.
5. ¿Qué pasó en la fiesta?
6. ¿A qué hora se acostó Marisol? ¿Se durmió inmediatamente? ¿Por qué?

B. Write a letter describing what you did to get ready to go to a wedding or a party.

C. Create a "soap opera" relationship between two characters. Describe the course of their romance.

Así es

El matrimonio

En el pasado, los padres escogían las parejas para su hijos, pero hoy la mayoría de los jóvenes escogen su propia pareja. Cuando deciden casarse, todavía es costumbre que el hombre le pida permiso al padre de su novia. A veces los padres anuncian su compromiso, generalmente en el periódico.

Como leímos en la carta de Marisol, los novios generalmente tienen dos ceremonias de matrimonio: una ceremonia civil para hacer legal su unión y también una ceremonia religiosa. Después de la ceremonia religiosa hay una fiesta de recepción.

En una familia tradicional, la esposa depende de su marido para ganar la vida para la familia y hacer las decisiones importantes. Pero dentro de la casa es la mujer que se encarga de la vida de la familia. Generalmente es la mujer que cuida de los niños, cocina, lava la ropa, va de compras y frecuentemente arregla los asuntos financieros de la familia. Pero ahora en el mundo moderno los papeles *(roles)* están cambiando. Si la mujer trabaja fuera de la casa, es normal que los esposos compartan los quehaceres de la casa, incluso el cuidado de los niños. Pero todavía hay muchas personas que prefieren la vida tradicional y desean que la mujer se quede en casa y que no trabaje. La Iglesia Católica raramente permite el divorcio, entonces todavía es menos común en los países hispanos que en los EE. UU.

Los días festivos

In general, holidays in the Hispanic world have a religious or historical origin. But the origin is not as important as the opportunity to change the daily routine and to get together with family and friends. Following are some holidays celebrated in the Hispanic world, as well as some celebrated in the United States. Included also are some things associated with celebrating these holidays.

Vocabulario

Los días •festivos *Holidays*

la Nochevieja	*New Year's Eve*
el Año Nuevo	*New Year's Day*
el Día de los Reyes •Magos	*Day of the Magi (Three Kings)*
• el Carnaval	*Mardi Gras*
el Día de la •Pascua Florida	*Easter*
1. los huevos de colores	*colored eggs*
• 2. la canasta	*basket*
3. los dulces de goma	*gumdrops*
4. el conejo	*rabbit*
• 5. el Desfile de Pascua	*Easter Parade*
el Día de •la Raza	*Day of the Hispanic Race (Columbus Day)*
el Día de Todos •los Santos	*All Saints' Day*

6.

7.

8.

9.

10.

11.

12.

13.

el Día de •los Muertos   *Day of the Dead*
- 6. la calavera   *skull*
  7. el esqueleto   *skeleton*
- 8. el cementerio   *cemetery*
- 9. el sepulcro   *grave*
- la Nochebuena   *Christmas Eve*
- la Misa del Gallo   *Midnight Mass*

• la Navidad   *Christmas*
- 10. los villancicos   *carols*
  11. el árbol de Navidad   *Christmas tree*
- 12. la piñata   *papier mâché figure*
  - 13. llena de dulces   *filled with candy*

la Januca   *Hanukah*
el Ramadán   *Ramadan*

Fiestas de España   *Holidays of Spain*

La Semana •Santa   *Holy Week*
- la estatua   *statue*
- el paso   *platform for carrying statues*
- la vela   *candle*

• La Feria de Sevilla   *Seville Fair*
- el baile flamenco   *flamenco dance*
- el desfile   *parade*
  el circo   *circus*
- las diversiones   *amusements*

• Las Fallas de Valencia   *Festival of Valencia*
- la falla   *figurine, statue*
- el carro alegórico   *float*
  poner •fuego a   *to set fire to*

Las Fiestas de San Fermín   *Festival of San Fermín*
- el encierro de los toros   *roundup of the bulls*
- los fuegos artificiales   *fireworks*
- la plaza de toros   *bullfighting arena*

Vocabulario

Fiestas de los Estados Unidos   *Holidays of the United States*

El Día de San Valentín	*Valentine's Day*
14. mandar tarjetas (con un corazón)	*to send greeting cards (with a heart)*
• 15. Cupido	*Cupid*
• 16. verso romántico	*romantic verse*
• 17. regalar una caja en forma de corazón	*to give as a gift a heart-shaped box*

El Día de las Brujas	*Halloween*
18. el fantasma	*ghost*
• 19. la bruja en escoba	*witch on a broom*
• 20. el duende	*goblin*
• 21. la máscara	*mask*
• 22. el disfraz	*costume*
23. el murciélago	*bat*
• 24. la linterna de calabaza	*jack-o-lantern*

El Día de Acción de Gracias	*Thanksgiving*
• 25. la calabaza	*pumpkin*
• 26. el peregrino	*pilgrim*
27. el barco	*ship*
• 28. el indio	*Native American*
29. la cena de pavo	*turkey dinner*
30. dar gracias	*to give thanks*

---

1   Tu día festivo favorito   Tell your partner about your favorite holiday and how you celebrate it.

EJEMPLO: Mi día favorito es el Día de San Valentín. Mi novia y yo nos damos tarjetas, y yo le doy una caja de chocolates.

2   La próxima fiesta que celebraremos   Tell how you will celebrate the next holiday. How will your partner celebrate it?

EJEMPLO: Vamos a celebrar el Día de las Madres.
Yo prepararé el desayuno para mi mamá.

Mi hermano y mi cuñada vendrán a visitarnos
y todos cenaremos juntos en un restaurante.

IRREGULAR VERBS: REVIEW

Most verbs in Spanish are regular verbs; that is, they show the person and time by adding person–time endings either to the verb or to the stem after removing the **-ar**, **-er**, or **-ir** ending. As we saw on page 287, some verbs have a change in the stem, but they follow a pattern of how and where the stem changes.

A small number of verbs have irregularities in the stem and/or endings. We have already worked with the following verbs that are irregular. Refer to the verb chart in the Tools.

ser	*to be*	(page 18)	**poner**	*to put, to place*	(page 160)
estar	*to be*	(page 18)	**salir**	*to leave, to go out*	(page 160)
tener	*to have*	(page 19)	**oír**	*to hear*	(page 160)
ir	*to go*	(page 159)	**ver**	*to see*	(page 161)
venir	*to come*	(page 159)	**hacer**	*to do, to make*	(page 161)

Did you notice that the irregular verbs **estar, tener, venir, poner,** and **hacer** have some patterns in common? We are going to learn some more irregular verbs in this lesson that follow a similar pattern. Watch for the following patterns that these new verbs share with the preceding verbs.

- PRESENT TENSE: "**GO**" VERBS: "**-GO**" ending in the **yo** form of the present tense
  yo TEN**GO**, yo VEN**GO**, yo PON**GO**, yo SAL**GO**, yo HA**GO**

- FUTURE TENSE: Irregular future stems (instead of the infinitive)
  yo **TENDRÉ**, yo **VENDRÉ**, yo **PONDRÉ**, yo **SALDRÉ**, yo **HARÉ**

- PRETERITE TENSE: "COMBO" verbs have irregular stems and endings in the preterite. The endings are a combination (combo) of the regular **-ar** and **-er/-ir** endings.

Irregular stem	"COMBO" endings
TUV-	-E
VIN-	-ISTE
ESTUV-	-O
PUS-	-IMOS
HIC-	-ISTEIS
	-IERON

Tuve una fiesta el sábado. ¿Dónde estuviste?

Tuve un accidente y me pusieron en el hospital.

The following are some other common verbs that have irregularities in one or more forms that we will learn in this lesson:

poder   *to be able, can*   **traer**   *to bring*
decir   *to say, to tell*   **saber**   *to know (facts, skills)*
querer   *to want, to wish*   **conocer**   *to know (people, places)*

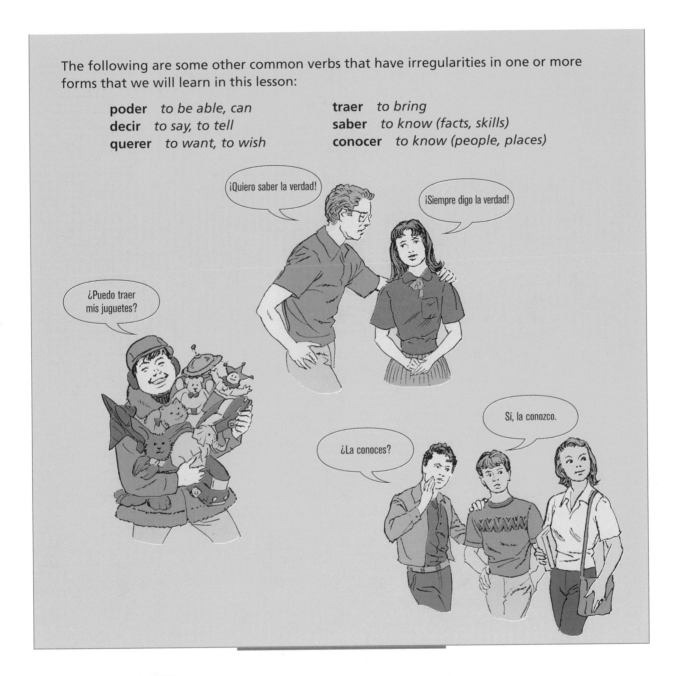

VINE, VI Y VENCÍ

VER ES CREER

SER ES MEJOR QUE TENER

QUERER ES PODER

PODER (UE)   *to be able, can*

	IMPERFECT *could* *was/were able* *used to be able*	PRETERITE *could* *succeeded* *[neg.] failed* *did succeed*	PRESENT *can* *am/is/are able*	FUTURE *will be able*
yo	podía	**pude**	puedo	**podré**
tú	podías	**pudiste**	puedes	**podrás**
Ud./él/ella	podía	**pudo**	puede	**podrá**
nosotros(as)	podíamos	**pudimos**	podemos	**podremos**
vosotros(as)	podíais	**pudisteis**	podéis	**podréis**
Uds./ellos/ellas	podían	**pudieron**	pueden	**podrán**

Irregularities:

preterite: irregular stem: **pud-** + "combo" endings
present: stem change **o ⟶ ue**
future: irregular future stem: **podr-**

Note: When **poder** is used in the preterite tense it may mean *succeeded* or when used as a negative preterite it may mean *failed*. **Poder** is used more often in the imperfect tense to say *could, was/were able* or *used to be able*.

---

3 What are some things you can do on a holiday that you cannot do every day? Use the present tense.

EJEMPLO: Puedo dormir hasta más tarde.
Puedo visitar a mis abuelos.

4 Say if you succeeded or failed at something you tried to do. Use the preterite tense.

EJEMPLO: De niño(a), traté de subir un árbol, pero no pude.
Anoche traté de hacer una linterna de calabaza, y pude.

5 Tell some things you were able to do and were not able to do when you were on vacation. Use the imperfect tense.

EJEMPLO: Podía pasar mucho tiempo con mis compañeros.
Podíamos comer en el patio.

6 Tell some things you will be able to do when you are older.

EJEMPLO: Podré manejar un coche.
Podré ir a la universidad.

QUERER (IE) *to want, to love*

	IMPERFECT	PRETERITE	PRESENT	FUTURE
	wanted/loved	*wanted/loved*	*want(s)/love(s)*	*will want/*
	was/were	*tried*	*am/is/are*	*love*
	wanting/loving	*[neg.] refused*	*wanting/loving*	
	used to want/love	*did want/love*	*do/does want/love*	
yo	quería	**quise**	quiero	**querré**
tú	querías	**quisiste**	quieres	**querrás**
Ud./él/ella	quería	**quiso**	quiere	**querrá**
nosotros(as)	queríamos	**quisimos**	queremos	**querremos**
vosotros(as)	queríais	**quisisteis**	queréis	**querréis**
Uds./ellos/ellas	querían	**quisieron**	quieren	**querrán**

Irregularities:
preterite: irregular stem: **quis-** + "combo" endings
present: regular but stem change **e ⟶ ie** in boot forms
future: irregular future stem: **querr-**

Note: When **querer** is used in the preterite, it may mean *tried*. When used in the negative and in the preterite it may mean *refused*. It is used more often in the imperfect to say *wanted/loved* or *used to want/love*.

---

7 When you were a child, what did you want to be for Halloween? Use the imperfect tense. Tell what you want to be now.

EJEMPLO: De niño(a), quería ser astronauta.
            Ahora quiero ser un extraterrestre.

8 Tell some things you will want to do after you graduate.

EJEMPLO: Querré conseguir un buen empleo.

9 Tell several things you tried to do and several more that you refused to do. Use the preterite tense.

EJEMPLO: El año pasado quise estudiar música pero no quise estudiar física.
            El sábado quise telefonear a mi tío pero no quise telefonear a mi primo.

DECIR   *to say, to tell*

	IMPERFECT *said/told* *was/were* *saying/telling* *used to say/tell*	PRETERITE *said/told* *did say/tell*	PRESENT *say(s)/tell(s)* *am/is/are* *saying/telling* *do/does say/tell*	FUTURE *will say/tell*
yo	decía	**dije**	**digo**	**diré**
tú	decías	**dijiste**	dices	**dirás**
Ud./él/ella	decía	**dijo**	dice	**dirá**
nosotros(as)	decíamos	**dijimos**	decimos	**diremos**
vosotros(as)	decíais	**dijisteis**	decís	**diréis**
Uds./ellos/ellas	decían	**dijeron**	dicen	**dirán**

Irregularities:
preterite: irregular stem: **dij-** + "combo" endings,
    Uds./ellos/ellas = **dijeron** (no **i** in ending)
present: **-go** verb: **digo**, e ⟶ **i** stem change in boot forms
future: irregular future stem: **dir-**

¿Qué dijiste?

¡Dije que no sé nadar!

---

10 Tell what various members of your family used to say on certain holidays.

EJEMPLO: En el Día de Acción de Gracias mi mamá siempre decía, «Estoy cansada de cocinar».
Mi padre decía, «¿Cuándo vamos a comer?»

11 Tell what your friends said they did for **El Día de la Independencia**. Use the preterite tense.

EJEMPLO: Miguel dijo que fue a la playa.
Juan y Juanita dijeron que fueron a un desfile.

12 Mario and his girlfriend Alicia just broke up. Tell what his friends say to console him. Use the present tense.

EJEMPLO: Carlos dice que hay más peces en el mar.
Yo le digo que Alicia no era muy simpática.

13 Santa Claus is making an early visit. Tell what you and your friends will tell him you want as a gift. Use the future tense.

EJEMPLO: Le diré que quiero un carro.
Anita le dirá que quiere un televisor.

TRAER *to bring*

	IMPERFECT *brought* *was/were* *bringing* *used to bring*	PRETERITE *brought* *did bring*	PRESENT *bring(s)* *am/is/are* *bringing* *do/does bring*	FUTURE *will bring*
yo	traía	**traje**	**traigo**	traeré
tú	traías	**trajiste**	traes	traerás
Ud./él/ella	traía	**trajo**	trae	traerá
nosotros(as)	traíamos	**trajimos**	traemos	traeremos
vosotros(as)	traíais	**trajisteis**	traéis	traeréis
Uds./ellos/ellas	traían	**trajeron**	traen	traerán

Irregularities:

preterite: irregular stem: **traj-** + "combo" endings,
  Uds./ellos/ellas = **trajeron** (no **i** in ending)

present: **-go** verb: **traigo**

¿Trajiste tu traje de baño?

¡Claro, yo traje mi traje!

---

14 Tell what you think Santa Claus will or will not bring you and your friends. Will he bring what you asked for in Activity 13? Use the future tense.

EJEMPLO: Santa le traerá un televisor a Anita.
Santa no me traerá un carro.

15 What do you usually bring on vacation? Mention ten things. What do other people you know bring? Use the present tense.

EJEMPLO: Traigo mi paraguas. También traigo mucho dinero.
Mi padre trae una maleta grande y sus tarjetas de crédito.

16 **Encuesta ¿Qué trajiste?**   Ask five classmates to name several things they brought to school this morning, then report to the class. Use the preterite tense.

EJEMPLO: Victoria, ¿qué trajiste a la escuela esta mañana?

Yo traje una mochila, una bolsa y mi suéter.

Reportaje: Victoria trajo una mochila…

17 Take turns with your partner and tell what you always brought to a picnic when you were little. Use the imperfect tense.

EJEMPLO: Yo siempre traía mi pelota de vólibol.
Nosotros siempre llevábamos mucho que comer.

SABER OR CONOCER *to know*

Saber tells what you have learned: facts, information, or skills. It is often followed by **que** *(that)*, **si** *(if)*, or a question word. When used with an infinitive it has the meaning of *know how to*. In the preterite, **saber** means *found out*.

Sé cuando vendrán los Reyes Magos.
I know when the Three Wise Men will come.

Sé cortar una calabaza para hacer una linterna.
I know how to cut a pumpkin to make a jack-o-lantern.

Supe la fecha de su cumpleaños.
I found out the date of his birthday.

Conocer tells what you are acquainted with—usually a person or a place. It is also used with things you have heard of but not yet learned. In the preterite, **conocer** can mean *met for the first time*.

Conozco a Juan Morales.
I know Juan Morales. (I'm acquainted with him.)

Conozco Madrid.
I know Madrid. (I've been there.)

Conozco la canción.
I know (of) the song; (But I haven't learned it.)

Conocí a mi novio en una fiesta.
I met my boyfriend at a party. (I met him for the first time.)

Note: Only the **yo** form of the present tense is irregular: yo **conozco**.

SABER *to know (how)*

	IMPERFECT *knew* *used to know*	PRETERITE *found out* *did find out*	PRESENT *know(s)* *do/does know*	FUTURE *will know*
yo	sabía	**supe**	**sé**	**sabré**
tú	sabías	**supiste**	sabes	**sabrás**
Ud./él/ella	sabía	**supo**	sabe	**sabrá**
nosotros(as)	sabíamos	**supimos**	sabemos	**sabremos**
vosotros(as)	sabíais	**supisteis**	sabéis	**sabréis**
Uds./ellos/ellas	sabían	**supieron**	saben	**sabrán**

Irregularities:

preterite: irregular stem: **sup**- + "combo" endings

present: irregular **yo sé**

future: irregular future stem: **sabr-**

¿Cuándo supiste que ella te quería?

Lo supe cuando me dio su número de teléfono.

18 Tell several things you found out in this class.

EJEMPLO: Supe que Ramón es jugador de tenis.
Supe que hoy es el Día de la Independencia de México.

19 Ask your partner if he or she knows the dates of several holidays.

EJEMPLO: ¿Sabes cuándo es el Día de los Muertos?

 Sí, sé que es el 2 de noviembre.

20 Tell what you will know after reading these books: **Compañeros, Book 2, Las fiestas mundiales, México en un vistazo, Aprender a bailar.**

EJEMPLO: Sabré hablar español.

21 Ask your partner if he or she knows how to do several things.

EJEMPLO: ¿Sabes bailar?

 Sí, sé bailar, pero no sé bailar bien.

22 **Chismes** Ask your partner several questions about himself or herself. Then tell the class what you found out about your partner.

EJEMPLO: Adelina, ¿tienes un novio?

 Sí, tengo un novio. Se llama Ernesto.

Supe que Adelina tiene un novio que se llama Ernesto.

23 Find out when your partner met someone and what he or she knows about that person.

EJEMPLO: ¿Cuándo conociste a Paulina?

La conocí en la fiesta el sábado pasado.

¿Qué sabes de ella?

Sé que es una buena jugadora de vólibol.

24 Ask your partner whom he or she knew at different times in the past. Use the imperfect tense.

EJEMPLO: ¿A quién conocías cuando estabas en la escuela primaria?

Conocía a Juan y a Diego.

25 Tell your partner several cities you know (are acquainted with).

EJEMPLO: Conozco San Antonio, Miami y Baltimore.

26 Read these ads from people who would like pen pals. Choose three whom you would like to know and tell why based on what you know about them.

EJEMPLO: Me gustaría conocer a Diego porque sé que a él le gustan los animales y a mí me gustan. También sé que él tiene un perro y yo tengo un perro. Sé que no tiene muchos amigos y quiero ser su amigo.

Buscamos amigos por correspondencia

¡Hola! Soy Isabelina y soy una estudiante buena en el tercer año de secundaria. Tengo 17 años. Me gusta mucho ir al cine y leer libros de aventura. Soy muy atlética y juego en el equipo de tenis de mi escuela. En mi tiempo libre me gusta ir a los conciertos de música clásica y pasar el tiempo con mi familia.

¿Qué tal, amigos? Me llamo Antonio y tengo 16 años. Soy afro-hispano y vivo en Michigan. Mi familia y yo somos de Panamá. Me gustan los carros deportivos y la música de todos tipos. Quiero hacerme dentista. Soy aficionado de los deportes pero no los juego. En mi tiempo libre trabajo en una tienda de ropa.

Busco un(a) amigo(a) de correspondencia. Soy una chica sincera y bonita y vivo en Tuscon, Arizona. Mi nombre es Maricarmen y tengo 16 años. Asisto a una escuela secundaria y mi clase favorita es el arte. Después de las clases me gusta ir al museo y a la biblioteca. Tengo muchos amigos que desean escribir a otras personas también.

¡Hola! Soy estudiante en una escuela secundaria pero no me gusta estudiar. Prefiero pasar el tiempo con mis compañeros. Me gusta mirar los deportes en la televisión pero no me gusta jugarlos. No sé lo que voy a hacer porque no me gusta trabajar. Mi nombre es Rodolfo y tengo 19 años.

Me llamo Roberto y seré un jugador famoso de béisbol. Me gusta mucho el béisbol y siempre asisto a los partidos de béisbol en mi ciudad. Tengo una colección de cartas de béisbol muy grande. Juego en el equipo de mi escuela. Tengo carteles de jugadores de béisbol en mi alcoba.

SUMMARY OF IRREGULAR VERBS

For most students the best way to learn the irregular verbs is by hearing them and saying them out loud. But it also helps to see similarities in the forms. Here is a summary of the patterns in the irregular verbs you have learned in this book. You will need to add the person endings.

IMPERFECT: there are only three irregular imperfect forms [add the person–time endings]

ir ⟶ IBA   ser ⟶ ERA   ver ⟶ VEÍA

PRETERITE: "COMBO" VERBS

	IRREGULAR STEM	"COMBO" ENDINGS
tener	⟶ TUV-	-E
estar	⟶ ESTUV-	-ISTE
poder	⟶ PUD-	-O
poner	⟶ PUS-	-IMOS
saber	⟶ SUP-	-ISTEIS
venir	⟶ VIN-	-IERON*
hacer	⟶ HIC-	
querer	⟶ QUIS-	*Note: no **i** after **j**
decir	⟶ DIJ-	
traer	⟶ TRAJ-	

OTHER IRREGULAR PRETERITE VERBS:

ser and ir: fui, fuiste, fue, fuimos, fuisteis, fueron
dar: regular **-er/-ir** endings: di, diste, dio, dimos, disteis, dieron

PRESENT: Irregular "YO" forms

-GO
tener ⟶ TENGO*
venir ⟶ VENGO*
hacer ⟶ HAGO
poner ⟶ PONGO
decir ⟶ DIGO*
traer ⟶ TRAIGO
salir ⟶ SALGO
oír ⟶ OIGO
caer ⟶ CAIGO

-OY
ser ⟶ SOY
estar ⟶ ESTOY
dar ⟶ DOY
ir ⟶ VOY

OTHER
ver ⟶ VEO
saber ⟶ SÉ
conocer ⟶ CONOZCO**
haber ⟶ HE

* Stem-changing verbs in remaining forms
** Most verbs ending in **-cer** or **-cir** add **z** before **co (-zco)**.

FUTURE: Irregular stems:

- **drop some letters**

hacer ⟶	HAR-
poder ⟶	PODR-
decir ⟶	DIR-
querer ⟶	QUERR-
saber ⟶	SABR-

- **change the last vowel to d**

tener ⟶	TENDR-
venir ⟶	VENDR-
poner ⟶	PONDR-
salir ⟶	SALDR-

Ser and **ir** are irregular in all tenses except the future:

	IMPERFECT	PRETERITE	PRESENT	FUTURE
ser	era	fui	soy	seré
ir	iba	fui	voy	iré

Haber is irregular in all tenses except imperfect:

haber	había	hube	hé	habré

VERBS WITH MEANING CHANGES IN PRETERITE VS. IMPERFECT

	PRETERITE	IMPERFECT
conocer	*met for the first time*	*acquainted with, knew a person/place*
saber	*found out*	*knew (result of learning)*
poder	*succeeded*	*was able/could*
no poder	*failed*	*was unable/could not*
querer	*tried*	*wanted*
no querer	*refused*	*did not want*

ENCUENTRO PERSONAL

Paulina called her cousin Eduardo, who lives in México, to find out about some of their special celebrations for a report that she is making in Spanish class.

PAULINA: Siempre oímos aquí en los Estados Unidos del Cinco de Mayo pero no sé exactamente lo que es.

EDUARDO: Para nosotros, es una celebración patriótica, más o menos como el 4 de julio para Uds. Pero no se celebra la independencia del país (que es el 16 de septiembre) sino la derrota (*defeat*) de los franceses, que invadieron México en 1863.

PAULINA: ¿Cuál es tu día de fiesta favorito?

EDUARDO: La Navidad, por supuesto. Pero nosotros la celebramos un poco diferentemente que allá en los Estados Unidos. Comenzamos nueve días antes con «Las Posadas», que recuerda cuando María y José buscaban (*searched*) una posada (*inn*). Cada noche vamos a una casa diferente, tocamos a la puerta y cantamos una canción tradicional que se llama «un villancico». En el último día de la Nochebuena hay una gran fiesta. Después todos vamos a la iglesia para la Misa del Gallo.

PAULINA: ¿Y Uds. reciben los regalos de Santa Claus después de la misa?

EDUARDO: No, generalmente esperamos hasta el Día de los Reyes Magos, el 6 de enero, para dar y recibir regalos, porque según (*according to*) la tradición, ése fue el día en que los Reyes le dieron los regalos al niño Jesús.

PAULINA: ¿Hay otro día festivo especial para ti?

EDUARDO: Mi otro día festivo favorito es el Día de los Muertos el 2 de noviembre. Ésta es una fiesta mexicana que se celebraba aún antes de la colonización por los españoles. Es el día en que recordamos a nuestros amigos y parientes muertos. Muchos van al cementerio para poner flores, y a veces comida, en los sepulcros. Algunos cenan allí y recuerdan a los muertos. También en sus casas hacen una ofrenda (*offering*) con fotos, velas y las cosas y comidas favoritas de su familia, porque creen que el espíritu de los muertos está allí durante este día. Pero lo que más me gusta son los dulces y los panes en forma de esqueletos y calaveras.

PAULINA: ¿Hay un día religioso especial para los mexicanos?

EDUARDO: Sí, no debemos olvidar el 12 de diciembre. Es importante porque conmemora la aparición de la Virgen de Guadalupe (la madre de Jesús) a un pobre indio en 1536. La Virgen de Guadalupe es la santa patrona no sólo de México, sino también de toda Latinoamérica.

PAULINA: Gracias, Eduardo, ahora comprendo mejor las celebraciones en tu país.

¿Comprendes?

1. ¿Qué celebran los mexicanos el 5 de mayo?
2. ¿Cuándo es su Día de Independencia?
3. ¿Qué significa «Las Posadas»?
4. ¿Cuándo reciben regalos? ¿Por qué?
5. ¿Por qué es importante el 12 de diciembre?

¡Te toca!

With a partner, compare the celebration of Christmas in the United States and Mexico.

Leemos y contamos

A. María Elena was a Spanish exchange student at Paulina's school last year. She and Paulina are now pen pals. Following is her letter describing the holidays in Spain.

Querida Paulina,

Tú me preguntaste en tu carta acerca de las fiestas que celebramos aquí en España. Pues hay muchas y por eso, te diré las más importantes y bien conocidas.

La fiesta que más me gusta es el Carnaval. En España el Carnaval se celebra los tres días antes del Miércoles de Ceniza (Ash Wednesday), que es cuarenta días antes de la Pascua Florida. Durante el Carnaval, todos se ponen máscaras y disfraces y salen a la calle para bailar y divertirse.

Hay unas grandes celebraciones para la Semana Santa antes de la Pascua Florida. El Jueves y Viernes Santo muchas tiendas se cierran y hay menos tráfico en las ciudades. Hay procesiones por las calles con pasos (estatuas o imágines de Jesucristo y de la Vírgen María) y muchas velas.

Cada región o «patria chica» en España también tiene sus propios días de fiesta. Las Fallas de Valencia, del 12 al 19 de marzo, son muy famosas por sus carros (floats), que se queman (burn) al final de la celebración. Y en Sevilla hay una feria dos semanas después de la Pascua Florida, cuando hay desfiles, circos y muchas diversiones, como bailes flamencos.

En Pamplona, del 7 al 17 de julio se celebra la famosa Fiesta de San Fermín, conocida en todo el mundo por el encierro de los toros. Los toros corren por las calles de la ciudad hacia la plaza de toros, donde luego hay una corrida (bullfight). También hay fuegos artificiales y la gente baila la jota, el baile regional.

¿Cuáles son algunas fiestas que se celebran en tu país?

Con cariño, tu amiga,
María Elena

1. ¿Qué fiesta le gusta más a María Elena? ¿Cuándo es?
2. ¿Cómo celebran la Semana Santa en España?
3. ¿Cómo es la Feria de Sevilla?
4. ¿Por qué es famosa la fiesta de San Fermín?

B. Write to a student in Spain explaining some of your holiday traditions that they do not have: Halloween, Thanksgiving Day, July 4, Memorial Day, etc.

ASÍ ES

La independencia de los países hispanoamericanos

Cada 4 de julio nosotros celebramos nuestra Declaración de Independencia de Inglaterra en 1776. Casi treinta años después, algunas colonias españolas comenzaron su lucha por la independencia de España. El proceso de independencia comenzó en México en 1810 cuando el Padre Hidalgo dio el «Grito de Dolores» (*shout from the town of Dolores*). En Gran Colombia (ahora Venezuela, Colombia, Ecuador y Panamá) el General Simón Bolívar «el libertador» y en el sur el General José de Sucre lucharon por más de diez años contra los españoles. La mayoría de las colonias ganaron su independencia de España para el año 1821. Varios países que existen hoy no se formaron inmediatamente después de la independencia. Panamá, por ejemplo, fue parte de Colombia hasta 1903, cuando se independizó con la ayuda de los Estados Unidos.

Sin embargo, las islas de Cuba y Puerto Rico (en el hemisferio oeste) y las islas de las Filipinas (en el Océano Pacífico) todavía estaban bajo el mando de España. Quedaron así hasta la guerra entre los EE. UU. y España en 1898 cuando Cuba ganó su independencia. Puerto Rico llegó a ser territorio de los Estado Unidos en 1917 y en 1952 se convirtió en un «estado libre asociado» y tiene su propia constitución. Los habitantes de Puerto Rico son ciudadanos americanos.

Aquí están las fechas cuando los países hispanoamericanos recibieron su independencia.

Argentina	el 9 de julio de 1816	Guatemala	el 15 de septiembre de 1821
Bolivia	el 6 de agosto de 1825	Honduras	el 15 de septiembre de 1821
Chile	el 18 de septiembre de 1818	México	el 16 de septiembre de 1810
Colombia	el 20 de julio de 1819	Nicaragua	el 15 de septiembre de 1821
Costa Rica	el 15 de septiembre de 1821	Panamá	el 3 de noviembre de 1903
Cuba	el 20 de mayo de 1902	Paraguay	el 14 y 15 de mayo de 1811
República Dominicana	el 27 de febrero de 1844	Perú	el 28 de julio de 1821
Ecuador	el 3 de octubre de 1822	Uruguay	el 25 de agosto de 1828
El Salvador	el 15 de septiembre de 1821	Venezuela	el 5 de julio de 1821

Miguel Hidalgo y Costilla

Simón Bolívar

Antonio José de Sucre

Los quehaceres

There is always a lot of work to do around the house. Who does these chores at your house?

Vocabulario

Los quehaceres   *Chores*

1. limpiar la casa	*to clean the house*	
• 2. barrer el suelo	*to sweep the floor*	
• 3. fregar el suelo	*to mop the floor*	
4. hacer •la cama	*to make the bed*	
• 5. cambiar las sábanas	*to change the sheets*	
6. lavar la ropa	*to wash the clothes*	
• 7. secar las toallas	*to dry the towels*	
• 8. doblar las toallas	*to fold the towels*	
• 9. planchar las camisas	*to iron the shirts*	
• 10. colgar (ue) la ropa	*to hang up the clothes*	
• 11. pulir los muebles	*to polish the furniture*	
12. quitar* •el polvo	*to dust*	
• 13. sacudir los tapetes	*to shake (out) the rugs*	
14. pasar* •la aspiradora	*to vacuum*	

15. comprar la comida	*to buy food*
16. cocinar la cena	*to cook dinner*
17. poner* la mesa	*to set the table*
18. quitar* la mesa	*to clear the table*
19. lavar los platos	*to wash the dishes*
• 20. fregar las ollas	*to scrub the pots*
21. lavar las ventanas	*to wash windows*
22. reparar el coche	*to repair the car*
23. cortar •el césped	*to cut the lawn*
24. recoger* •las hojas	*to rake the leaves*
25. sacar •la basura	*to take out the garbage*
26. sacar* la nieve	*to shovel the snow*

*The core meaning of these verbs is given below.

quitar	*to take off/away*	poner	*to put*
pasar	*to pass*	sacar	*to take out/off*
recoger	*to gather, to collect*	fregar	*to rub, to scrub*

•Los muebles y otros objetos en los cuartos   *Furniture and other objects in the rooms*

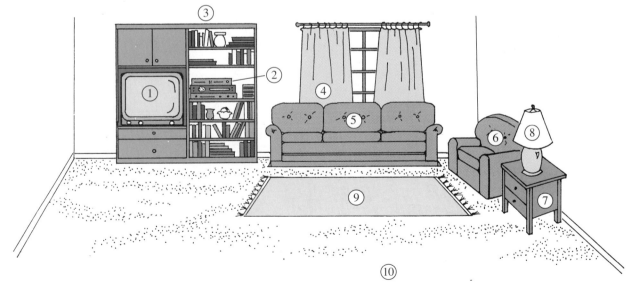

En la sala   *In the living room*

1. el televisor	*television set*		• 6. el sillón	*large chair*
2. el estéreo	*stereo*		• 7. la mesita	*small table*
3. el estante	*bookcase*		• 8. la lámpara	*lamp*
• 4. las cortinas	*drapes, curtains*		• 9. el tapete	*throw rug*
• 5. el sofá	*sofa*		• 10. la alfombra	*carpet*

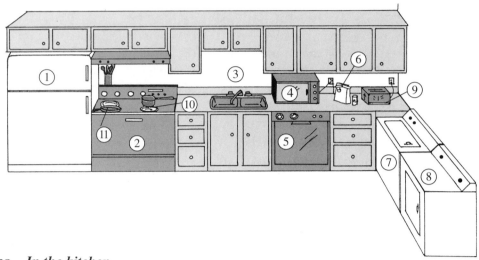

En la cocina   *In the kitchen*

• 1. el refrigerador	*refrigerator*	• 7. la lavadora	*washer*
• 2. la estufa	*stove*	• 8. la secadora	*dryer*
• 3. el fregadero	*sink*	• 9. la tostadora	*toaster*
• 4. el horno de microondas	*microwave oven*	•10. la olla	*pot*
• 5. el lavaplatos*	*dishwasher*	11. la sartén	*frying pan*
• 6. el abrelatas*	*can opener*		

*Words made by joining a verb and a noun use **el** for the singular even though they may end in **s**.

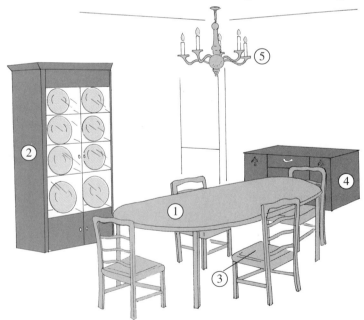

En el comedor   *In the dining room*

1. la mesa	*table*	• 4. el aparador	*buffet*
• 2. el chinero	*china cabinet*	• 5. el candelabro	*chandelier*
3. la silla	*chair*		

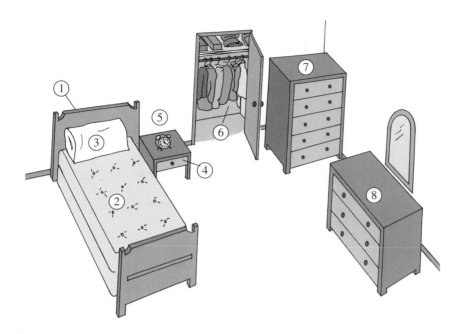

En la alcoba   *In the bedroom*

- 1. la cama   *bed*
- 2. el colchón   *mattress*
- 3. la almohada   *pillow*
- 4. la mesita de noche   *night table*

- 5. el despertador   *alarm clock*
- 6. el armario   *cupboard, closet*
- 7. la cómoda   *chest of drawers*
- 8. el tocador   *dresser, bureau*

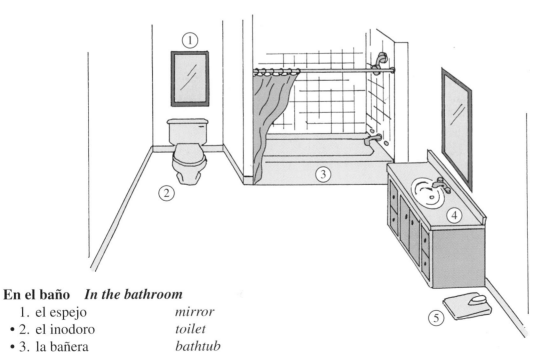

En el baño   *In the bathroom*

- 1. el espejo   *mirror*
- 2. el inodoro   *toilet*
- 3. la bañera   *bathtub*
- 4. el lavabo   *sink*
- 5. la balanza   *scale*

Las cosas para limpiar   *Things for cleaning*

- 1. el cubo   *pail, bucket*
- 2. el jabón líquido   *liquid soap*
- 3. el detergente   *detergent*
- 4. el líquido limpiaventanas   *window cleaner*
- 5. el recogedor de polvo   *dust pan*
- 6. el limpiador en polvo   *cleanser*
- 7. el guardapolvo   *feather duster*
- 8. el papel absorbente   *paper towel*
- 9. el trapo   *rag*
- 10. la escoba   *broom*
- 11. la esponja   *sponge*
- 12. la aspiradora   *vacuum cleaner*
- 13. el fregasuelos*   *mop*

1 Do you have chores to do? Make a list and tell when you do them.

EJEMPLO: Hago mi cama por la mañana todos los días.
            Cambio las sábanas los sábados.

2 What chores do other people in your family do? Make a list and tell what they use to do them.

EJEMPLO: Mi hermano lava la ropa en la lavadora con detergente.
            Mi abuela quita el polvo de los muebles con un guardapolvo.

3 Ask your classmates who does certain chores in their house.

EJEMPLO: ¿Quién saca la basura en tu casa?

                Mi padre generalmente saca la basura.

4 Find a picture of a room in a magazine and describe it and its furnishings in detail. If you prefer, describe one of the rooms in your home.

EJEMPLO: La alcoba es blanca. Tiene cortinas azules. Hay dos camas.

PRESENT PARTICIPLES

To form the present participle of **-ar** verbs, add **-ando** to the stem. To form the present participle of **-er** and **-ir** verbs, add **-iendo** to the stem. The present participle in English ends in *-ing*.

lavar	⟶ lavando	*washing*
barrer	⟶ barriendo	*sweeping*
pulir	⟶ puliendo	*polishing*

The present participle of **-ir** stem-changing verbs has the same change as in the preterite: **e** to **i** and **o** to **u**.

servir	⟶ sirviendo
dormir	⟶ durmiendo

Verbs that have a vowel before **-iendo** change the **i** to **y**.

leer	⟶ leyendo
oír	⟶ oyendo

In many situations where English uses *-ing*, Spanish uses either the infinitive or a clause.

Limpiar la casa es difícil.   *Cleaning the house is difficult.*
Vi a un hombre que leía en el parque.   *I saw a man who was reading in the park.*

ESTAR + PRESENT PARTICIPLE

As you have seen in the verb charts, a Spanish verb can be expressed in various ways in English:

Comes el postre.   *You eat/do eat/are eating dessert.*
Comías el postre.   *You ate/used to eat/were eating dessert.*
Comerás el postre.   *You will eat dessert.*

However, if you want to emphasize that the action <u>was</u>, <u>is</u>, or <u>will be in progress</u> at the time of the sentence, the progressive forms can be used. They are formed using **estar** with the present participle, (the verb stem with the ending **-ando** or **-iendo**). This is like the progressive in English which uses the verb *to be* + *-ing*, but unlike English, it cannot be used for the immediate future.

Compare: Estudio en la biblioteca esta noche.   *I am studying in the library tonight.*

Ir (*to go*) and **venir** (*to come*) are not used in the progressive form.

Voy a la escuela.   *I am going to school.*
Vendré de la tienda.   *I will be coming from the store.*

Esqueleto

ESTAR + *verb stem*	**-ANDO** [*for* -ar]
	-IENDO [*for* -er/-ir]

Estábamos estudiando.   *We were studying.*
Estoy comiendo.   *I am eating.*
Estarán escribiendo.   *They will be writing.*

5 Look around this room and tell what the students are doing right now.

EJEMPLO: Juan está hablando con Susita ahora.
En este momento Susita está escuchando a Juan.

6 *Sit-Con* Your friend telephones to invite you to go to the movies but you cannot go because it's housecleaning day. Tell your friend what everyone is doing.

EJEMPLO: Mi hermana está limpiando el baño.
Mis hermanos están cortando el césped.

7 **Encuesta** Find out what some of your classmates were doing at 7:00 P.M. last night and what they will be doing at 4:30 P.M. this afternoon. Report to the class.

EJEMPLO: Carmen, ¿qué estabas haciendo a las siete anoche?

Yo estaba mirando las noticias en la televisión.

¿Qué estarás haciendo a las cuatro y media esta tarde?

Estaré trabajando en el supermercado.

Reportaje: Anoche Carmen estaba mirando las noticias en la televisión y esta tarde ella estará trabajando en el supermercado.

OBJECT PRONOUNS WITH PROGRESSIVE VERBS

Direct and indirect object pronouns as well as reflexive pronouns are usually attached to the end of the present participle although they can also be placed before **estar**. When attaching the pronoun to the present participle, add an accent over **a** or **e**.

Esqueletos

 (pro)noun + ESTAR + *verb* -ÁNDO/-IÉNDO + *object pronoun*

 (pro)noun + *object pronoun* + ESTAR + *verb* -ANDO/-IENDO

¿La cocina? Estoy limpiándola ahora. OR La estoy limpiando ahora.
The kitchen? I'm cleaning it now.

¿Mi madre? Estaba hablándole hace diez minutos. OR Le estaba hablando.
My mother? I was talking to her ten minutes ago.

¿Mis amigos? Están divirtiéndose en la fiesta. OR Se están divirtiendo.
My friends? They are enjoying themselves at the party.

8 Tell what various people are doing to you right now.

> EJEMPLO: Raúl está hablándome.
> Emilia está mirándome.

9 Look around you to see what other people are doing. Then ask your partner who is doing different things. Use the object pronoun.

> EJEMPLO:  ¿Quién está hablándole a María?
>
> Raúl está hablándole.
>
> ¿Quiénes están durmiéndose?
>
> Amelia y Anita están durmiéndose.

10 *Sit-Con*   Paulina's mother left this list of chores for Paulina, Roberto, Pablo, and Carlota to do after school. She has telephoned to make sure that everyone is doing something that she asked. Tell her who was doing the chore before she called (**antes**), who is doing it right now (**ahora**), or who will be doing it later (**más tarde**).

> EJEMPLO: Madre: ¿Quién está doblando la ropa?
> Tú: Carlota está doblándola.

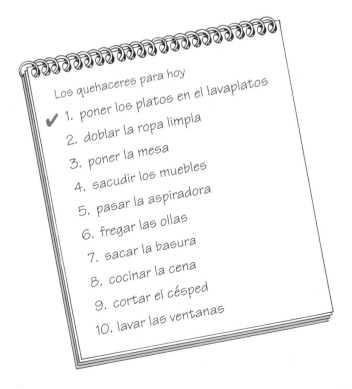

Los quehaceres para hoy
✔ 1. poner los platos en el lavaplatos
2. doblar la ropa limpia
3. poner la mesa
4. sacudir los muebles
5. pasar la aspiradora
6. fregar las ollas
7. sacar la basura
8. cocinar la cena
9. cortar el césped
10. lavar las ventanas

POSSESSIVE ADJECTIVES: LONG FORM

You have already learned the short form of the possessive adjectives: **mi, tu, su**, and **nuestro**. There is also a long form that is often used for emphasis or with demonstrative adjectives (**este, ese**, etc.). The short form goes before the noun, the long form goes after it.

Compare the two sets of possessive adjectives.

SHORT FORM (BEFORE THE NOUN)		LONG FORM (AFTER THE NOUN)	
mi	*my*	mío	*(of) mine*
tu	*your*	tuyo	*(of) yours*
su	*your/his/her/its/their*	suyo	*(of) yours/his/hers/theirs*
nuestro	*our*	nuestro	*(of) ours*
vuestro	*your*	vuestro	*(of) yours*

The possessive adjectives agree with the noun they modify in number and gender.

Mi alcoba es bonita.   *My room is pretty.*
Esta alcoba **mía** es más bonita.   *This room of mine is prettier.*

Sus platos están sucios.   *His plates are dirty.*
¡Los platos **suyos** están sucios!   *His plates are dirty!*

Este coche mío es nuevo.

---

11 Tell about some of your things, using long form possessives.

EJEMPLO: Este coche mío es nuevo.
Esos libros nuestros son interesantes.

12 Tell about some of the people you know, using long form possessives.

EJEMPLO: Los primos nuestros están en San Francisco.
Una amiga mía tiene una alcoba muy bonita.

13 Take turns with your partner telling about and comparing some of your possessions. First use the short form, then the long form of the possessive.

EJEMPLO: Mi libro es viejo. El libro tuyo es menos viejo.

   Nuestra clase es interesante. La clase suya es tan interesante.

POSSESSIVE PRONOUNS

The long form possessive adjectives are made into pronouns by leaving out the noun. They agree in number and gender <u>with the missing noun</u>.

Following are the possessive pronouns:

el mío	la mía	los míos	las mías	*mine*
el tuyo	la tuya	los tuyos	las tuyas	*yours*
el suyo	la suya	los suyos	las suyas	*yours/his/hers/theirs*
el nuestro	la nuestra	los nuestros	las nuestras	*ours*
el vuestro	la vuestra	los vuestros	las vuestras	*yours (in Spain)*

El libro tuyo está aquí. El mío está allí.
Your book is here. Mine is there.

La casa mía es grande. La suya es más grande.
My house is large. Hers is larger.

After forms of **ser**, the article may be omitted.

Las sábanas sucias son suyas.   *The dirty sheets are theirs.*
El espejo es mío.   *The mirror is mine.*

14 Point out some things that belong to different people and identify the owner.

EJEMPLO: Este libro es mío y aquél es suyo.
　　　　　　Esta chaqueta es tuya y ésa es suya.

15 Take turns with your partner telling where something you own is located. Your partner will respond by telling where hers or his is.

EJEMPLO: Mi televisor está en la sala.

El mío está en la cocina.

Mis libros están en mi alcoba.

Los míos están en el sótano.

16 Review the occupations on page 9. Then taking turns with your partner, compare what different members of your families do.

EJEMPLO: Mis hermanas son enfermeras.

La mía es mujer de negocios.

Vocabulario

Las expresiones neutrales y negativas *Neutral and negative expressions*

alguien	*someone, anyone*	nadie	*no one, nobody, not anyone*
algo	*something, anything*	nada	*nothing, not anything*
alguno(a, os, as)*	*some*	ninguno(a, os, as)*	*none, not any, no*
siempre	*always*	nunca	*never, not ever*
también	*also*	tampoco	*neither, not either*
o... o	*either . . . or*	ni... ni	*neither . . . nor . . .*
• de alguna manera	*some way, somehow*	• de ninguna manera	*no way*
• a/en alguna parte	*somewhere*	• a/en ninguna parte	*nowhere*

*Note: **Alguno** and **ninguno** are adjectives that agree in number and gender with the noun they talk about. They drop the **o** before a masculine singular noun, just like **uno**.

algún hombre   *some man*   algunas muchachas   *some girls*
ningún hombre   *no man*   ninguna muchacha   *no girls*

Ninguno is rarely used in the plural.

NEUTRAL AND NEGATIVE EXPRESSIONS

If any part of the sentence is negative, use negative words instead of neutral in the rest of the sentence. **No** or another negative word must be placed before the verb. In English, there can only be one negative word in a sentence; in Spanish if one part of the sentence is negative, the whole sentence is negative. There can be any number of negative words in a sentence.

Nadie hace nada allí.   *No one does anything there.*
Yo nunca compro nada allí tampoco.   *I never buy anything there either.*

Esqueletos

> *negative word + verb*
> **NO** *+ verb + negative word*

Juan <u>nunca</u> va al cine.
Juan <u>no</u> va <u>nunca</u> al cine.   *Juan never goes to the movies.*

17 Have you ever been in a really negative mood? Tell how you act when you are. Use each of the negative words. (Remember to put **no** before the verb if the negative word comes after the verb.)

EJEMPLO: No deseo hablar con nadie.
Nada me hace feliz.
No estoy ni contento ni divertido.

18 There are chores in every household that some people refuse to do. Make a list of chores that various members of your family refuse to do. Try to use all the negative words.

EJEMPLO: Mi hermano nunca saca la basura.
Mi hermanita no hace nada tampoco.

19 **Un día triste**   Have you ever had a disappointing day? Tell what happened, using neutral and negative words.

EJEMPLO: Nadie me visitó.
Alguien me dijo una mentira.

ENCUENTRO PERSONAL

Santiago wants Raúl to go with him to play soccer but Raúl has chores to do. Santiago has an idea for Raúl so that he will be able to accompany him.

SANTIAGO: Raúl, todos vamos al parque ahora. ¿Puedes jugar fútbol con nosotros?

RAÚL: Me gustaría, Santiago, pero en este momento estoy lavando el carro.

SANTIAGO: ¿Qué está haciendo tu hermana ahora? ¿No puede ella lavar el carro?

RAÚL: ¡Qué buena idea! Voy a preguntarle. [En voz alta.] ¡Lina! ¡Oh, Lina! Hazme el favor *(Please)* de terminar de limpiar el carro, ¿OK? Todos los amigos míos van al parque a jugar al fútbol.

LINA: [Una voz desde dentro de la casa.] No puedo hacer nada por ti ahora. ¿Cómo piensas que yo pueda hacer quehaceres tuyos? Tengo que hacer los míos. Ahora estoy preparándonos algo para la cena. Pregúntale a Luis. Él no está haciendo nada ahora.

RAÚL: Luis, mi querido hermano, hazme el favor de limpiar el carro y te prometo sacar la basura el lunes. Estaré limpiando el garaje el lunes y puedo hacerte ese favor en cambio.

LUIS: Está bien, si reparas también mi bicicleta, barres el sótano y pasas la aspiradora en la alfombra de la sala.

RAÚL: ¡De ninguna manera! ¿Crees que soy tan tonto como para hacer todos los quehaceres tuyos de una semana, sólo para que yo pueda jugar al fútbol? Estás tomándome el pelo *(You're kidding me) [literally, "pulling my hair"]*.

SANTIAGO: Vaya, Raúl, dile que sí *(Come on, tell him yes)*. Inés y Paulina estarán jugando con nosotros también y les dije que podemos ir a cenar con ellas después del partido.

RAÚL: Bueno Luis, estoy loco, pero te haré todos los quehaceres tuyos de la semana. Pero espera hasta la próxima vez que me pidas un favor. Te costará un ojo de la cara *(an arm and a leg) [literally, "an eye from the face"]*.

¿Comprendes?

1. ¿Qué están haciendo Santiago y los amigos suyos?
2. ¿Qué está haciendo Raúl? ¿Y Lina?
3. ¿Qué está haciendo Luis en este momento?
4. ¿Qué tiene Raúl que hacer para su hermano para poder ir al parque?
5. ¿Por qué decide Raúl hacer todos los quehaceres de su hermano?

¡Te toca!

Ask each person in the class which chores they like to do or do not like to do.

Leemos y contamos

A. In her last letter, Marisol had asked Paulina about who does the chores in her family. Think of who does these chores in your house as you are reading this part of Paulina's letter, telling Marisol how chores are assigned in her family.

...En mi casa somos más o menos tradicionales pero todos tenemos que ayudar porque mi mamá trabaja como ingeniera. Mi padre repara el carro y la casa. Mi hermano Roberto no hace mucho porque trabaja y también asiste a la universidad por la tarde y estudia mucho por la noche. Él saca la basura y ayuda a Papá cuando tiene tiempo. Mi otro hermano, Pablo, estudia para enfermero y no tiene mucho tiempo tampoco. En casa él tiene que fregar el suelo porque puede hacerlo todo en un día. Los tres hombres de la casa cortan el césped en el verano, recogen las hojas en el otoño y sacan la nieve en el invierno.

Mi mamá generalmente lava y seca la ropa, pero si hay que planchar algo, lo hacemos nosotros mismos porque a mamá no le gusta planchar nada. ¡Aun (Even) papá plancha las camisas suyas! Mamá va también al supermercado para comprar la comida. Mi hermana Carlota y yo le ayudamos a ponerla en los armarios y en el refrigerador cuando llega a casa. También le ayudamos a limpiar la casa. Quitamos el polvo de los muebles y barremos el suelo. Papá pasa la aspiradora en las alfombras porque mamá dice que él lo hace mejor que nadie. Todos nosotros limpiamos nuestras alcobas y hacemos nuestras propias camas; cambiamos las sábanas los sábados y mamá las lava cada semana.

Mamá generalmente cocina cuando llega a casa. Cuando yo no tengo que trabajar en la ropería, Carlota y yo la ayudamos. Yo pelo (peel) las papas y ella prepara la ensalada. Los domingos mi papá cocina. Cuando cocina, usa todas las ollas y sartenes que tenemos. (Cuando papá termina de cocinar, nunca queda ninguna olla limpia.) Le gusta cocinar platos tradicionales con salsas y muchas ingredientes. También papá cocina cuando usamos la parrilla (grill) que está afuera. Carlota pone la mesa y yo la quito. Yo generalmente lavo los platos después de la cena y Carlota los seca con las toallas. Tenemos un lavaplatos, pero no está funcionando en estos días. Alguien tiene que repararlo, pero es difícil arreglarlo porque casi nunca estamos en casa.

Mamá dice que muchas familias en México tienen criadas aun cuando la madre no trabaja fuera de la casa. Pero ella dice que no necesitamos una criada porque todos trabajamos juntos para ayudar a la familia.

1. ¿Qué hace en casa el padre de Paulina?
2. ¿Qué hacen sus hermanos?
3. ¿Qué hace su madre?
4. ¿Qué hace Paulina?
5. ¿Qué hace la hermana de Paulina?
6. ¿Qué opina Paulina sobre la mejor manera de hacer los quehaceres?

B. Write a report about the various chores that everyone in your family does.

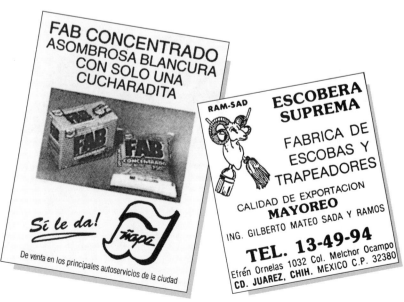

Así es

Los quehaceres

Muchas mujeres hispanas prefieren seguir una vida tradicional, donde la casa y la familia son su primera responsabilidad. Es común que las mujeres trabajen fuera de la casa antes de casarse, pero las mujeres casadas frecuentemente no tienen empleo fuera de la casa. Es la responsabilidad de los hombres ganar el dinero mientras la mujer cuida de la casa y de los hijos.

En muchos países una familia de la clase media frecuentemente tiene criada para ayudar en casa con lavar la ropa, cocinar y hacer otros quehaceres domésticos. Como hay mucha pobreza en algunas áreas del mundo hispano, hay mucha gente que trabaja como criados, aunque ganan muy poco dinero.

En general, la división de los quehaceres en la casa es, para muchas familias, más tradicional que en los EE. UU. Por ejemplo, algunos hombres no desean trabajar en la cocina porque creen que la cocina es el dominio de las mujeres. Pero tales actitudes están cambiando rápidamente en el mundo hispano.

Una fiesta

Following is a list of things we need to do to give a party—before, during, and after.

Vocabulario

Una fiesta   *A party*

Dar una fiesta   *To give a party*

una fiesta de cumpleaños	*a birthday party*
• de aniversario	*anniversary*
• de graduación	*graduation*
• de sorpresa	*surprise*

Antes de la fiesta   *Before the party*

	1. invitar a los amigos	*to invite friends*
•	2. telefonear	*to telephone*
	3. escribir las invitaciones	*to write the invitations*
	4. aceptar la invitación	*to accept the invitation*
	5. ayudar con las preparaciones	*to help with preparations*
	6. comprar los refrescos	*to buy refreshments*
	7. hacer la comida	*to make the food*
•	8. cubrir la mesa	*to cover the table*
	9. poner la mesa	*to set the table*

Vocabulario

En la fiesta   *At the party*

1.	llegar a las siete	*to arrive at seven o'clock*
2.	traer discos compactos	*to bring CDs*
3.	llevar a los amigos	*to take friends*
4.	llevar la ropa buena	*to wear good clothing*
5.	saludar a los invitados	*to greet the guests*
	• al anfitrión	*the host*
	• a la anfitriona	*the hostess*
6.	divertirse (ie, i)	*to have a good time, to have fun, to enjoy oneself*
7.	aburrirse	*to be bored*
8.	bailar	*to dance*
9.	buscar a los amigos	*to look for friends*
10.	ver a un viejo amigo	*to see an old friend*
11.	conocer a una persona nueva	*to meet a new person [first time]*
• 12.	encontrarse (ue) con los amigos	*to meet friends [not first time]*
13.	cantar canciones	*to sing songs*
14.	celebrar un cumpleaños	*to celebrate a birthday*
15.	dar un regalo	*to give a present*
16.	abrir los regalos	*to open the presents*
17.	romper •una piñata	*to break a piñata*
18.	contar (ue) •chistes	*to tell jokes*
19.	charlar con los amigos	*to chat with friends*
20.	escuchar la música	*to listen to music*
21.	mirar la televisión	*to watch television*
22.	tocar la guitarra	*to play the guitar*
23.	tocar música	*to play music*
24.	tomar refrescos	*to drink/have refreshments*
25.	sacar fotos	*to take pictures*

Después de la fiesta   *After the party*

26.	despedirse (i, i)	*to say good-bye*
27.	dar las gracias	*to thank*
28.	volver (ue) a casa	*to return home*

1 Describe for someone who lives in Mexico what a typical party is like where you live. Why do you give parties? Where and when is it held? How are invitations issued? What do you do at the party? Give as much information as you can.

2 *Sit-Con*   You are giving a party to celebrate a friend's birthday. Tell what you will do to get ready for it.

EJEMPLO: Invitaré a nuestros amigos.
Limpiaré el sótano porque la fiesta será allí.

3 Tell what happened at the last party you attended.

EJEMPLO: Llegué a la fiesta a las ocho y media.
Llevé a mi amigo Julián.

PAST PARTICIPLES

To form the past participle of **-ar** verbs, add **-ado** to the stem. To form the past participle of **-er** and **-ir** verbs, add **-ido** to the stem. If the stem ends in a vowel, an accent mark is added to the **-i** of **-ido**. The past participle in English often ends in *-ed* or *-en*.

estudiar	→	**estudiado**	*studied*
comer	→	**comido**	*eaten*
vivir	→	**vivido**	*lived*
caer	→	**caído**	*fallen*
creer	→	**creído**	*believed*

IRREGULAR PAST PARTICIPLES

The following verbs do not form their past participles according to the preceding rule. They must be learned individually. What do most of them end in? What are the exceptions?

abrir	**abierto**	*opened*	poner	**puesto**	*put*
• cubrir	**cubierto**	*covered*	• imponer	**impuesto**	*imposed*
• descubrir	**descubierto**	*discovered*	• componer	**compuesto**	*composed*
decir	**dicho**	*said*	• resolver	**resuelto**	*resolved*
escribir	**escrito**	*written*	romper	**roto**	*broken*
• describir	**descrito**	*described*	ver	**visto**	*seen*
hacer	**hecho**	*made, done*	volver	**vuelto**	*returned*
• deshacer	**deshecho**	*undone*	• devolver	**devuelto**	*returned*
morir	**muerto**	*died*	• envolver	**envuelto**	*wrapped*

USAGE OF PAST PARTICIPLES

Past participles are used as adjectives or with an auxiliary verb to form the passive or perfect forms of the verb.

Adjective:
La comida preparada está en la cocina.   *The prepared food is in the kitchen.*

Passive:
La comida fue preparada por los invitados.   *The food was prepared by the guests.*

Perfect:
Ellos han preparado una buena cena.   *They have prepared a good dinner.*

USING PAST PARTICIPLES AS ADJECTIVES

When the past participle is used as an adjective, the ending agrees with the noun in number and gender.

el estéreo rot<u>o</u>   *the broken stereo*
las flores muert<u>as</u>   *the dead flowers*
la chica aburrid<u>a</u>   *the bored girl*
los platos lavad<u>os</u>   *the washed dishes*

To describe the condition of a noun, use **estar** plus the past participle.

Los platos estarán lavados.

El estéreo estaba roto.   *The stereo was broken.*
Las flores estaban muertas.   *The flowers were dead.*
La chica está aburrida.   *The girl is bored.*
Los platos estarán lavados.   *The dishes will be washed.*

Esqueleto

noun + ESTAR + *verb stem* +	-ADO(A)(OS)(AS)
	-IDO(A)(OS)(AS)

La torta está decorada.   *The cake is decorated.*
Las decoraciones están rotas.   *The decorations are broken.*

4 Describe the object after María did these things to it.

EJEMPLO: María lavó los platos.
            Ahora los platos están lavados.

a. María arregló los libros.
b. María hizo una blusa.
c. María cocinó la cena.
d. María abrió la ventana.

e. María rompió la cámara.
f. María envolvió un regalo.
g. María leyó las invitaciones.
h. María sirvió la comida.

i. María escribió unas cartas.
j. María lavó la ropa.
k. María compró los comestibles.

5 Describe the condition of a house immediately before and after a party.

EJEMPLO: Antes las flores estaban cubiertas con plástico.
            Ahora las flores están muertas.

USING PAST PARTICIPLES IN PASSIVE SENTENCES

Most communication in Spanish is done using active sentences. In an <u>active</u> sentence the subject does the action:

El hombre comió la torta.   *The man ate the cake.*
Ana comprará los libros.   *Ana will buy the books.*

In a <u>passive</u> sentence, the subject receives the action. Use **ser** with the past participle and **por** to indicate the person or thing *(agent)* that does the action. The past participle agrees in number and gender with the subject.

La torta fue comida por el hombre.   *The cake was eaten by the man.*
Los libros serán comprados por Ana.   *The books will be bought by Ana.*

When using the passive to tell what was done in the past, the preterite of **ser** is usually used with the past participle.

Las decoraciones fueron puestas por mi hermano.   *The decorations were put up by my brother.*

If the person doing the action is not stated or implied, the impersonal **se** is preferred instead of the passive.

Se vende pan en esta tienda.   *They sell bread in this store.*

Note: The passive is less common in Spanish than in English and occurs most frequently in writing.

Esqueleto

 | *(pro)noun* + **SER** + *past participle* + **POR** + *person/thing* |

La mesa es puesta por la criada.   *The table is set by the maid.*
Los libros fueron leídos por los estudiantes.   *The books were read by the students.*
La casa será pintada por mi padre.   *The house will be painted by my father.*

La piñata fue hecha en
México por los mexicanos.

6 Rewrite these sentences in the passive.

EJEMPLO: Mis amigos dieron una fiesta.
            La fiesta fue dada por mis amigos.

a. Carlota y Sofía prepararon la comida.
b. Esteban llevó los CDs.
c. Isabel decoró el cuarto.
d. Lidia puso la mesa.
e. Emilio sacó las fotos.

7 Tell the condition of some things you have and tell who made them that way.

EJEMPLO: Mi camisa está planchada.
            Fue planchada por mi madre.

PERFECT TENSES

HABER + *PAST PARTICIPLE*   *to have done something*

To say that something *had/has/will have happened*, use the appropriate form of the helping verb **haber** *(to have)* with the past participle. The past participle always ends in **o** when used with **haber**. **Haber** is only used with a past participle. To say *have* in the sense of possession, use **tener**. Following are the forms of **haber**.

	IMPERFECT *had*	PRETERITE *had*	PRESENT *has/have*	FUTURE *will have*
yo	había	**hube**	**he**	**habré**
tú	habías	**hubiste**	**has**	**habrás**
Ud./él/ella	había	**hubo**	**ha**	**habrá**
nosotros(as)	habíamos	**hubimos**	**hemos**	**habremos**
vosotros(as)	habíais	**hubisteis**	**habéis**	**habréis**
Uds./ellos/ellas	habían	**hubieron**	**han**	**habrán**

Irregularities:
preterite: irregular stem: **hub-** + "combo" endings
present: all forms are irregular, similar to future endings
future: irregular future stem: **habr-**

Note: The preterite form of **haber** is usually found only in literature.

Any form of **haber** plus a past participle (**-ado, -ido** form of a verb) is called a "perfect" tense. The perfect tenses are used in Spanish in much the same way they are used in English. The perfect tenses place the action before a specific time in the past, present, or future.

Ya había visitado a mi tío cuando me viste.   *I had already visited my uncle when you saw me.* [The action took place before another action took place in the past.]

He visto esa película tres veces.   *I have seen that movie three times.* [The action took place at some time before the present.]

Habré ido a México antes de graduarme del colegio.   *I will have gone to Mexico before I graduate from high school.* [The action will take place before another action in the future.]

Esqueleto

> **(pro)noun + HABER + *past participle* + *(rest of sentence)***

Nosotros habíamos visto el avión.   *We had seen the airplane.*
Ellos han comprado los regalos.   *They have bought gifts.*
Tú habrás hecho la tarea.   *You will have done the homework.*

¿Yo he abierto todos mis regalos?

8 Tell some things you have done already today.

EJEMPLO: Ya he mirado la televisión.
            Ya he comido el desayuno.

¿Has hecho la tarea?

Sí, ya la he terminado.

9 Ask your partner if she or he has done the same things as you have today.

EJEMPLO: ¿Has visto a Juan?
¿Has hecho la tarea?

10 Tell your friend some things you had never done before coming to this school.

EJEMPLO: Yo nunca había estudiado en casa.
No nunca había tomado un autobús.

11 Tell some things you will have done before you graduate.

EJEMPLO: Habré viajado por México.
Habré estudiado español por dos años.

12 *Sit-Con*   You are giving a party tonight. Tell what you have done in preparation for it.

EJEMPLO: He limpiado la casa.
He hecho muchos sándwiches.

SUMMARY OF PAST PARTICIPLE USAGE

• as an adjective (showing condition)

(pro)noun + ESTAR + *verb stem*   -ADO(A)(OS)(AS)
-IDO(A)(OS)(AS)

• as a passive (indicating the subject was acted upon)

(pro)noun + SER + *verb stem*   -ADO(A)(OS)(AS)
-IDO(AS)(OS)(AS)   + POR + *person/thing*

• as a perfect tense (relating a previous action to a specific time)

(pro)noun + HABER + *verb stem*   -ADO
-IDO

ENCUENTRO PERSONAL

Paulina and her family are going through a checklist of things to be done before the surprise birthday party for her grandmother at their house. But a problem comes up. How would you handle it?

MAMÁ: Paulina, vamos a ver si todos hemos hecho las tareas. Primero, ¿están hechas todas las camas?

PAULINA: Sí, mamá, todas las camas fueron hechas por nosotros esta mañana.

MAMÁ: Yo sé que los platos están lavados porque yo los había lavado mí misma anoche antes de acostarme. ¿Pero ha puesto alguien la mesa?

PAULINA: Sí, ya está puesta. Yo la he puesto con todos los platos, vasos, tazas y todo…

MAMÁ: A ver, ¿ha sido limpiada toda la casa?

PAULINA: El suelo de la cocina fue barrido y fregado por Carlota, la basura fue sacada por Pablo, el césped fue cortado por papá y yo he lavado las ventanas y he pasado la aspiradora sobre las alfombras. ¿Hemos olvidado algo?

MAMÁ: Creo que no. Yo habré pulido los muebles para esta tarde. Las decoraciones estarán listas, y la comida será preparada por mí también.

PAULINA: Será una fiesta de sorpresa magnífica para la abuelita. Mamá, ¿crees que abuelita haya oído algo de la fiesta?

MAMÁ: Sólo le he hablado de la fiesta a la tía Rosario. Y le había dicho que es una sorpresa
         para la abuelita. A propósito, ¿hemos hecho todas las invitaciones a toda la familia?

TODOS: ¡Yo no las he hecho!

MAMÁ: ¿Quién las ha escrito? ¿Quién les ha informado a todos de la fiesta?
         ¿No ha sido invitado nadie?

PAULINA: Pues, creo que estábamos tan preocupados con las preparaciones que no hemos
         invitado a nadie.

MAMÁ: Todos tendrán que ser invitados por teléfono esta mañana. Pero no vamos a decirle
         nada a la abuelita porque es una fiesta de sorpresa.

¿Comprendes?

1. ¿Quién ha hecho las camas?
2. ¿Quién ha lavado los platos?
3. ¿Está puesta la mesa? ¿Por quién fue puesta?
4. ¿Quién ha hecho qué para limpiar la casa?
5. ¿Qué han hecho los miembros de la familia para limpiar la casa?
6. ¿Qué habrá hecho mamá para la fiesta?
7. ¿Cuál es el problema en las preparaciones para la fiesta?
8. ¿Qué solución tiene la mamá?

¡Te toca!

Ask your classmates if some things have been done in their house and they will tell you by whom they
were done. You might want to refer to the list of household chores on page 333.

Leemos y contamos

A. Paulina is writing to her cousin Eduardo about the party for their grandmother.

Querido Eduardo,

Hemos tenido una gran fiesta para la abuelita, pero hubo un gran problema la mañana de la fiesta. Mamá estaba leyéndonos la lista de preparaciones. Todos ya habíamos hecho las camas, la casa había sido limpiada por mi hermana y yo y la mesa estaba puesta. Mi hermano había sacado la basura, el suelo de la cocina había sido barrido y fregado por mi hermana y mi papá había cortado el césped. Yo ya había lavado las ventanas y había pasado la aspiradora en las alfombras. Las decoraciones estaban listas y la comida estaba preparada. Pero cuando mamá nos preguntó «¿Hemos hecho todas las invitaciones?», cada uno de nosotros respondió «Yo no las he hecho».

De repente habíamos descubierto que nadie había hecho las invitaciones. No habían sido escritas y nadie les había telefoneado a los parientes. Pero al fin todo salió bien. Afortunadamente la semana pasada mi mamá le había dicho a la tía Rosario de la fiesta y ella es muy habladora. Ella les había hablado a todos los parientes durante la semana y les había dicho a todos de los planes para la fiesta, incluso a la abuelita. Por eso todos ya habían oído de la fiesta indirectamente por ella. Por eso cuando todos fueron invitados por fin la mañana de la fiesta, todos pudieron asistir porque ya habían pensado venir.

Todos nos divertimos mucho en la fiesta. Todos los regalos fueron abiertos por la abuelita y, como siempre, ella lloró de alegría. No fue una fiesta de sorpresa para la abuelita, pero ella nos dijo que ya había esperado una fiesta porque tenemos una fiesta para ella cada año.

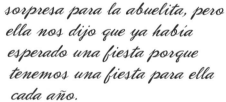

Hasta la próxima vez.
Tu prima que te quiere,
Paulina

1. ¿Quién había hecho qué para preparar para la fiesta?
2. ¿Qué habían descubierto Paulina y su familia antes de la fiesta?
3. ¿Por qué salió todo bien?
4. ¿Qué pasó en la fiesta?
5. ¿Qué les dijo la abuelita de su «fiesta de sorpresa»?

B. Describe the things that had been done to prepare for the last party you went to.

C. Tell what things will have happened before your twenty-fifth birthday.

Así es

La piñata

Para las fiestas de cumpleaños o del Día del Santo para los niños es costumbre romper una piñata. Una piñata es un contenedor en forma de un animal, una estrella u otra figura hecho de barro *(clay)* o *papier mâché* cubierto de papel de seda *(tissue paper)* doblado y cortado para formar una franja *(fringe)*. La piñata está llena de dulces o juguetes pequeños. Se suspende la piñata de una soga *(rope)* en un lugar donde no hay obstrucciones.

Para romper la piñata, se escoge a un niño y se le cubren los ojos con un pañuelo y se le da un palo. Después de girar *(turn around)* al niño, los otros niños gritan instrucciones para llegar a la piñata y le dicen cuando debe golpearla *(strike)* con el palo para romper la piñata. Se puede levantar y bajar la piñata con la soga. Si la piñata no está rota después de tres golpes, le toca a otro niño. Cuando la piñata finalmente se rompe, los dulces y los juguetes caen al suelo y todos corren para recogerlos.

⋘ Unidad IV ⋙

⇒ Unidad IV ⇐
Tools

Vocabulario

Un viaje *A trip*
(Lección 1)

viajar para las vacaciones	*to travel for vacation*
los negocios	*for business*
visitar a la familia	*to visit the family*
estudiar	*to study*
aprender	*to learn*
celebrar una fiesta	*to celebrate a holiday*
asistir a •una boda	*to attend a wedding*
asistir a •un funeral	*to attend a funeral*
hacer un viaje	*to take a trip*

Antes del viaje *Before the trip*

planear un viaje	*to plan a trip*
• la ruta	*the route*
decidir en la destinación	*to decide on the destination*
• escoger un medio de transporte	*to choose a means of transportation*
manejar/•conducir	*to drive*
ir por tren	*to go by train*
por avión	*by airplane*
en coche/automóvil/carro	*by car*
en barco	*by ship*
en autobús	*by bus*
• consultar el horario	*to check the time schedule*
pedir (i, i) información	*to ask for information*
• obtener un pasaporte	*to get/obtain a passport*
un mapa	*a map*
• cheques de viajero	*travelers' checks*
• un boleto	*a ticket*
para •un vuelo sin escalas	*for a nonstop flight*
de ida	*one-way . . .*
de •ida y vuelta	*round-trip . . .*
• reservar un cuarto en un hotel	*to reserve a room in a hotel*
hacer las maletas	*to pack the suitcases*

El viaje   *The trip*

llegar al aeropuerto	*to arrive at the airport*
a la estación	*at the station*
• al puerto	*at the port*
a la destinación	*at the destination*
• facturar el equipaje	*to check in the baggage*
pasar por •la seguridad	*to go through security*
•la aduana	*customs*
• abordar el avión	*to board the airplane*
bajar del avión	*to get off the airplane*
• cambiar aviones	*to change planes*
cambiar dinero	*to exchange money*
recoger el equipaje	*to pick up/claim the baggage*
• llenar el tanque de gasolina	*to fill the gas tank*
comprar recuerdos	*to buy souvenirs*
enviar tarjetas postales	*to send postcards*
• gozar del viaje	*to enjoy the trip*
regresar a casa	*to return home*

Las preposiciones que preceden el infinitivo   *Prepositions that precede the infinitive*
(Lección 1)

antes de	*before*	después de	*after*
en vez de	*instead of*	para	*in order to*
sin	*without*	con	*with*
por	*because of*	hasta	*until*
• al	*on, upon*	• con tal de	*provided*
• en caso de	*in case of*	• a pesar de	*in spite of*

Lo que se hace en el centro comercial   *What one does at the mall*
(Lección 2)

ir de compras	*to go shopping*
• sólo mirar	*to browse, to just look*
gastar dinero	*to spend money*
• reunirse con los amigos	*to meet friends*
comprar cosas	*to buy things*
hallar cosas •en venta	*to find things on sale*
• probarse (ue) ropa	*to try on clothes*
preguntar •el precio	*to ask the price*
pagar en efectivo	*to pay cash*
• con cheque	*with a check*
• con tarjeta de crédito	*with a credit card*
ver •una película	*to see a movie*
comer	*to eat*

caminar	*to walk*
• devolver (ue) algo	*to return something*
• cambiar algo	*to exchange something*
• escoger regalos	*to choose gifts*
jugar (ue) videojuegos	*to play video games*
divertirse (ie, i)	*to have fun*

Las tiendas   *Stores*
(Lección 2)

el almacén	*department store*
• la discotería	*CD store*
la ropería	*clothing store*
la ropa de mujer	*women's clothing*
hombre	*men's . . .*
niño	*children's . . .*
la zapatería	*shoe store*
• la papelería	*stationery store*
la librería	*bookstore*
la juguetería	*toy store*
la tienda de deportes	*sporting goods store*
• la perfumería	*perfume store*
• la mueblería	*furniture store*

La comida   *Food*
(Lección 2)

el restaurante	*restaurant*
la panadería	*bakery*
• la comida rápida	*fast food*
la pastelería	*pastry shop*
la heladería	*ice cream parlor*
la dulcería	*candy store*
la cafetería	*sandwich shop, café*
una tienda de •alimentos naturales	*health food store*

Lugares de •diversión   *Places of entertainment*
(Lección 2)

el cine	*movies*
• la arcada de vídeo	*video arcade*
• la pista de patinaje	*skating arena*
• el gimnasio	*health spa, gym*

Los servicios *Services*
(Lección 2)

• la peluquería	*beauty shop*
• el zapatero	*shoe repairperson*
el banco	*bank*
el optómetra	*optometrist*
los teléfonos públicos	*public telephones*
• los servicios/•el retrete	*restrooms*
… para •caballeros	*men's room*
… para •damas	*ladies' room*
la oficina de •objetos perdidos	*lost and found*
la oficina de •seguridad	*security office*

La ecología *Ecology*
(Lección 3)

• **Las cuestiones**   *Issues*

• amenazar el medioambiente	*to threaten the environment*
• malgastar los recursos naturales	*to waste natural resources*
• el carbón	*coal*
• el petróleo	*oil*
• el agua dulce	*fresh water*
• el malgasto	*waste, misuse*
• destruir el ozono	*to destroy the ozone*
• las selvas tropicales	*tropical jungles/forests*
los bosques	*woods, forest*
• la destrucción	*destruction*
contaminar los lagos	*to pollute the lakes*
los ríos	*the rivers*
los océanos	*the oceans*
• la tierra	*the ground, the soil, the earth*
el aire	*the air*
• la contaminación por…	*pollution by . . .*
• químicos	*chemicals*
• basura	*garbage*
• derrames de petróleo	*oil spills*
• la lluvia ácida	*acid rain*
• el humo de las fábricas	*factory smoke*
• el escape de los automóviles	*auto exhaust*
• consumir	*to consume*
• el consumo	*consumption*
• matar los animales salvajes	*to kill wild animals*
los peces	*fish*
las plantas •en peligro	*endangered plants*

Las soluciones   *Solutions*

pasar •leyes	*to pass laws*
• conservar •electricidad	*to conserve electricity*
• salvar las especies amenazadas	*to save/rescue endangered species*
• eliminar los desperdicios	*to eliminate waste*
• conservar energía	*to conserve energy*
• advertir (ie, i) del problema	*to advise/warn about the problem*
• cortar el agua	*to turn off the water*
• apagar la luz	*to turn out the lights*
• bajar la calefacción	*to lower the heat*
• contribuir a la ecología	*to contribute to ecology*
• reducir el daño	*to reduce the damage*
• echar basura en el basurero	*to throw garbage in the trash can*
• reciclar…	*to recycle . . .*
el papel y •el cartón	*paper and cardboard*
• los contenedores de plástico	*plastic containers*
• la madera	*wood*
• las latas de aluminio	*aluminum cans*
• las botellas de cristal	*glass bottles*
la ropa	*clothing*
• las llantas	*tires*
el metal	*metal*
las pilas	*batteries (flashlight, etc.)*
las baterías	*batteries (car)*
• prohibir el uso de…	*to prohibit the use of . . .*
• los fluorocarburos	*fluorocarbons*
• los químicos	*chemicals*
• los productos de petróleo	*petroleum products*
• los detergentes con •fosfatos	*detergents with phosphates*
• el estirofoma	*Styrofoam*
• el insecticida	*insecticide*
• aumentar el uso de…	*to increase the use of. . .*
el papel •reciclado	*recycled paper*
el gas natural	*natural gas*
los detergentes •biodegradables	*biodegradable detergents*
• los fertilizantes naturales	*natural fertilizers*
• la energía solar	*solar energy*
nuclear	*nuclear*
hidroeléctrica	*hydroelectric*
• del viento	*wind-powered*
aprender de la ecología	*to learn about ecology*
no •perder (ie) tiempo	*to waste no time*

Los verbos irregulares que terminan en «-uir»   *Irregular verbs that end in* -uir
(**Lección 3**)

construir	*to build*	incluir	*to include*
contribuir	*to contribute*	influir	*to influence*
distribuir	*to distribute*	sustituir	*to substitute*
destruir	*to destroy*		

Los verbos irregulares que terminan en «-ducir»   *Irregular verbs that end in* -ducir
(**Lección 3**)

reducir	*to reduce*	producir	*to produce*
conducir	*to drive*	introducir	*to introduce*
traducir	*to translate*		

Verbos y expresiones de persuación   *Verbs and expressions of persuasion*
(**Lección 3**)

aconsejar	*to advise*	mandar	*to command, to order*
decir	*to tell*	pedir (i, i)	*to ask for, to request*
dejar	*to let, to allow*	permitir	*to permit, to allow*
desear	*to wish, to want*	preferir (ie, i)	*to prefer*
esperar	*to hope*	prohibir	*to forbid, to prohibit*
exigir	*to require, to demand*	querer (ie)	*to wish, to want*
hacer	*to make, to cause*	recomendar (ie)	*to recommend*
impedir (i, i)	*to prevent*	rogar (ue)	*to beg, to request*
insistir (en)	*to insist (on)*	sugerir (ie, i)	*to suggest*

(No) Es importante	*It is (not) important*
(No) Es necesario	*It is (not) necessary*
(No) Es esencial	*It is (not) essential*
(No) Es preferible	*It is (not) preferable*
(No) Es urgente	*It is (not) urgent*

Una visita al médico   *A visit to the doctor*
(**Lección 4**)

Las personas   *The people*

el/la médico(a)	*doctor*
el/la enfermero(a)	*nurse*
• el/la especialista	*specialist*
• el/la cirujano(a)	*surgeon*
el/la paciente	*patient*
el/la farmacista	*pharmacist*
el/la recepcionista	*receptionist*
• el/la radiólogo(a)	*radiologist*

Las condiciones médicas y las enfermedades   *Medical conditions and illnesses/diseases*

• enfermarse	*to get sick*
• mejorarse	*to get better*
• empeorarse	*to get worse*
sufrir (de)	*to suffer (from)*
• estar sano(a)	*to be healthy*
estar enfermo(a)	*to be sick*
• estar embarazada	*to be pregnant*
• contraer	*to contract, to catch*
• la diabetes	*diabetes*
• el asma	*asthma*
• la apendicitis	*appendicitis*
• el derrame cerebral	*stroke*
• la fractura de un hueso	*fracture of a bone*
• la torcedura	*sprain*
• la presión arterial alta	*high blood pressure*
• el ataque al corazón	*heart attack*
• el insomnio	*insomnia*
• el cáncer	*cancer*
• la amigdalitis	*tonsillitis*

• la reacción alérgica	*allergic reaction*
la gripe	*flu*
el resfriado	*cold*
• el catarro	*headcold*
• la constipación	*nasal congestion, stuffed nose*
• las paperas	*mumps*
• la rubeola	*three-day measles*
• la varicela	*chicken pox*
• el SIDA	*AIDS*
• el envenenamiento con comida	*food poisoning*
• la mononucleosis	*mononucleosis*
• la bronquitis	*bronchitis*
• la pulmonía	*pneumonia*
• el virus	*virus*
• el sarampión	*measles*
la infección	*infection*
• la conjuntivitis	*"pink-eye"*

• Los síntomas   *Symptoms*

tener…	*to have*
• los mareos	*dizziness*
• el desmayo	*fainting*
• los calambres	*cramps*
• la urticaria	*hives*
• los escalofríos	*chills*
la fiebre (alta)	*(high) fever*
un poco de fiebre	*a little/slight fever*
• el sarpullido	*rash*
un dolor…	*a pain, ache*
de cabeza	*headache*
de estómago	*stomachache*
de garganta	*sore throat*
• de oído	*earache*
• muscular	*muscle pain*
• la diarrea	*diarrhea*
• la náusea	*nausea*
• el estreñimiento	*constipation*

• la picazón	*itch*
• la hinchazón	*swelling*
la tos	*cough*
• la alergia	*allergy*
• vomitar	*to vomit*
• estornudar	*to sneeze*
• desmayarse	*to faint*
• toser	*to cough*
• sonarse (ue) la nariz	*to blow one's nose*
• marearse	*to get dizzy*
• sentirse (ie, i) malo(a)	*to feel bad*
débil	*weak*
• deprimido (a)	*depressed*
enfermo (a)	*sick*
nervioso (a)	*nervous*
cansado (a)	*tired*
• mareado (a)	*dizzy*

El diagnóstico   *Diagnosis*

ir a •la clínica	*to go to the clinic*
a •la sala de emergencia	*emergency room*
al consultorio	*doctor's office*
al hospital	*hospital*
hacer •una cita	*to make an appointment*
• cancelar la cita	*to cancel the appointment*
• llenar una hoja clínica	*to fill out a medical history*
• un formulario de seguro	*an insurance form*
• pesarse	*to weigh oneself*
subirse a •la balanza	*to get on the scale*
• examinar	*to examine*
abrir la boca	*to open one's mouth*
sacar la lengua	*to stick out one's tongue*
escuchar con •un estetoscopio	*to listen with a stethoscope*
• respirar profundamente	*to breathe deeply*
• tragar	*to swallow*
tomarle la temperatura	*to take one's temperature*
• la presión arterial	*blood pressure*
• el pulso	*pulse*
• radiografías	*X rays*
hacerle una prueba de sangre	*to do a blood test*

Los remedios   *Remedies*

• tratar la enfermedad	*to treat the illness*
ponerle •una inyección	*to give a shot to someone*
• ponerle una enyesadura	*to put a cast on*
• recetar	*to prescribe*
recomendar (ie)	*to recommend*
• una pastilla	*a pill*
• un jarabe para la tos	*cough syrup*
• una cápsula	*a capsule*
• unas gotas	*drops*
• un antiácido	*antacid*
• una aspirina	*aspirin*
• un antibiótico	*an antibiotic*
• guardar cama	*to stay in bed*
beber muchos líquidos	*to drink a lot of liquids*
• operar	*to operate*
• curar	*to cure*

Expresiones de duda y negación   *Expressions of doubt and denial*
(Lección 4)

• dudar	*to doubt*	no es •evidente	*it is not evident*
• negar (ie)	*to deny*	no es verdad	*it is untrue*
• es dudoso	*it is doubtful*	no estar seguro	*to not be sure*
no creer	*to not believe*	(no) es posible/imposible	*it's (not) possible/impossible*
no pensar (ie)	*to not think*	(no) es probable/improbable	*it's (not) probable/improbable*
no es •cierto	*it is not certain*		

Expresiones de emoción   *Expressions of emotion*
(Lección 4)

• alegrarse (de)	*to be glad*	sentir (ie, i)	*to be sorry, to regret*
• enojarse	*to be angry*	tener miedo	*to be afraid*
• estar orgulloso(a)	*to be proud*	• temer	*to fear*
• estar encantado(a)	*to be delighted*	gustarle	*to be pleased*
estar triste	*to be sad*	molestarle	*to be bothered*
estar contento(a)	*to be happy*	irritarle	*to be irritated*
• lamentar	*to regret*	sorprenderle	*to be surprised*

Expresiones de juicio   *Expressions of judgment*
(Lección 4)

• Es raro	*It is rare*	Es bueno/malo	*It is good/bad*
Es mejor	*It is better*	Es importante	*It is important*
Es necesario	*It is necessary*	• Es lógico	*It is logical*
• Es preciso	*It is necessary*	• Es ridículo	*It is ridiculous*
Es una lástima	*It is too bad*	• Más vale	*It is better*
• Es increíble	*It is incredible*		

Los automóviles   *Automobiles*
(Lección 5)

•El transporte   *Transportation*

el carro/el automóvil/el coche	*car*	el autobús	*bus*
deportivo	*sports car*	• el camión	*truck*
• descapotable	*convertible*	• la camioneta/•la furgoneta	*pickup truck*
• la ranchera	*station wagon*	la furgoneta/•la combi	*van*
• el remolque	*trailer*	• la caravana	*camper*

Las personas   *People*

• el/la conductor(a)	*driver*	el/la mecánico(a)	*mechanic*
• el/la vendedor(a) de carros	*auto salesperson*	el/la policía	*police officer*
• el/la gerente de la agencia	*agency manager*	• el/la juez	*judge*
• el/la ayudante de gasolinera	*gas station attendant*		

Los automóviles   *Automobiles*
(Lección 5)

• Las piezas de un automóvil   *Parts of a car*

• el acelerador	*accelerator*	• el limpiaparabrisas	*windshield wiper*
• el alambre	*wire*	• la llanta desinflada	*flat tire*
• el asiento	*seat*	• la llanta de repuesta	*spare tire*
• la batería	*battery*	• la manguera	*hose*
• el baúl/el portaequipaje	*trunk*	• la palanca de cambios	*gear shift lever*
• la bujía	*spark plug*	• el parabrisas	*windshield*
• la capota	*hood*	• el parachoques	*bumper*
• el carburador	*carburetor*	• la placa	*license plate*
• el claxón/•la bocina	*horn*	la puerta	*door*
• la compuerta trasera	*tailgate*	• el puño de la puerta	*door handle*
• la correa del ventilador	*fanbelt*	• el radiador	*radiator*
• el embrague	*clutch*	• la rueda	*wheel*
el espejo •retrovisor	*rearview mirror*	• el silenciador	*muffler*
• el farol delantero	*headlight*	• el tanque de gasolina	*gas tank*
• el farol trasero	*taillight*	• el tapacubos	*hubcap*
• el freno	*brake*	• el techo	*roof*
• la guantera	*glove compartment*	• el tubo de escape	*exhaust pipe*
• el guardabarros	*fender*	• la ventanilla	*window*
• la intermitente	*turn signal*	• el volante	*steering wheel*

Las reparaciones   *Repairs*

tener •un accidente	*to have an accident*
• reparar un auto/coche/carro	*to repair a car*
• arreglar un motor descompuesto	*to repair/fix a broken-down engine/motor*
• instalar un silenciador	*to install a muffler*
• llenar el tanque con gasolina	*to fill the tank with gas*
• revisar el aceite y el aire	*to check the oil and air*
• funcionar bien/mal	*to run/work well/badly*

En la carretera   *On the road*

• el tránsito/•la circulación	*traffic*	• la autopista	*expressway, freeway*
• la bocacalle/el cruce	*intersection*	• el carril	*lane*
• el semáforo	*traffic light*	• el arcén	*shoulder (of the road)*
• la glorieta	*traffic circle*	• la cuneta	*ditch*
• el puente	*bridge, overpass*	• la entrada	*entrance*
• la hora punta	*rush hour*	• la salida	*exit*
la carretera	*highway*	• el trébol	*cloverleaf*

Señales de tránsito   *Traffic signs*

• una vía	*one-way*	• cruce de ferrocarriles	*railroad crossing*
• alto/•pare	*stop*	• doble vía	*two-way traffic*
• señal de unión	*merge*	• ceda el paso	*yield*
• prohibido estacionarse	*no parking*	• parada de autobús	*bus stop*
• sobrepasar	*no passing*		
• el giro completo	*no U-turn*		
• doblar a la derecha/izquierda	*no right/left turn*		

La ley de la carretera   *The law of the road*

• abrocharse el cinturón de seguridad	*to buckle your safety belt*
manejar/•conducir con cuidado	*to drive carefully*
• acelerar al límite de velocidad	*to accelerate to the speed limit*
ir más despacio	*to slow down*
parar en la esquina	*to stop at the corner*
poner en •reversa	*to put into reverse*
ponerle •una multa por…	*to give someone a fine/ticket for . . .*
• el exceso de velocidad	*excessive speed, speeding*
• una infracción de la ley	*violation of the law*
manejar sin •licencia	*driving without a license*
• desobedecer una señal de tránsito	*disobeying a traffic signal*
• estacionarse en una zona prohibida	*parking in a no-parking zone*
doblar ilegalmente	*making an illegal turn*
buscar •estacionamiento	*to look for parking*
conseguir un carnet/permiso de conducir	*to get a driver's license*

Expresiones de posibilidad   *Expressions of possibility*
(Lección 5)

• ojalá	*hopefully*
• tal vez	*maybe*
• quizás	*maybe, perhaps*

Conjunciones de resultado incierto   *Conjunctions of uncertain outcome*
(Lección 5)

• para que	*so that*	• con tal que	*provided that*
• sin que	*without*	• en caso (de) que	*in case*
• a menos que	*unless*		

Conjunciones de tiempo   *Conjunctions of time*
(Lección 5)

cuando	*when*	hasta que	*until*
mientras que	*while*	• tan pronto como	*as soon as*
después (de) que	*after*	antes (de) que	*before*

Estructura

VERBS

Conditional tense
(Lección 2)

The person–time endings are attached to the infinitive.

yo		**ía**
tú		**ías**
Ud./él/ella		**ía**
nosotros(as)	**INFINITIVE +**	**íamos**
vosotros(as)		**íais**
Uds./ellos/ellas		**ían**

Irregular conditional stems:

hacer	⟶	har-		poner	⟶	pondr-
saber	⟶	sabr-		salir	⟶	saldr-
haber	⟶	habr-		tener	⟶	tendr-
decir	⟶	dir-		venir	⟶	vendr-
querer	⟶	querr-		poder	⟶	podr-

Past subjunctive
(Lección 2)

Drop **-on** from the **ellos** form of preterite tense, add: **-a, -as, -a, -amos, -ais, -an**.

COMPRAR	COMER	DORMIR (I, I)	TENER	HABER
comprar**on**	comier**on**	durmier**on**	tuvier**on**	hubier**on**
comprar**a**	comier**a**	durmier**a**	tuvier**a**	hubier**a**
comprar**as**	comier**as**	durmier**as**	tuvier**as**	hubier**as**
comprar**a**	comier**a**	durmier**a**	tuvier**a**	hubier**a**
comprá**ramos**	comié**ramos**	durmié**ramos**	tuvié**ramos**	hubié**ramos**
comprá**rais**	comié**rais**	durmié**rais**	tuvié**rais**	hubié**rais**
comprar**an**	comier**an**	durmier**an**	tuvier**an**	hubier**an**

Present subjunctive: regular verbs
(Lección 3)

Drop **-o** from **yo** form of present tense, add:

-AR VERBS	-ER/-IR VERBS
-e	-a
-es	-as
-e	-a
-emos	-amos
-eis	-ais
-en	-an

Verbs ending in **-car, -gar, -zar**, and **-ger** have spelling changes:

-car ⟶ -que   **-gar ⟶ -gue**   **-zar ⟶ -ce**   **-ger ⟶ -ja**

Present subjunctive: stem-changing verbs
(Lección 3)

-AR/-ER VERBS		-IR VERBS	
RESOLVER (UE)		ADVERTIR (IE, I)	
resuelva	resolvamos	advierta	advirtamos
resuelvas	resolváis	adviertas	advirtáis
resuelva	resuelvan	advierta	adviertan

Present subjunctive: irregular verbs
(Lección 3)

HABER	IR	SER	SABER	ESTAR	DAR
haya	vaya	sea	sepa	esté	dé
hayas	vayas	seas	sepas	estés	des
haya	vaya	sea	sepa	esté	dé
hayamos	vayamos	seamos	sepamos	estemos	demos
hayáis	vayáis	seáis	sepáis	estéis	deis
hayan	vayan	sean	sepan	estén	den

Verbs ending in -uir
(Lección 3)

destruir   *to destroy*

	IMPERFECT	PRETERITE	PRESENT	FUTURE
	destroyed	*destroyed*	*destroy(s)*	*will destroy*
	was/were destroying		*am/is/are destroying*	
	used to destroy	*did destroy*	*do/does destroy*	
yo	destruía	destruí	**destruyo**	destruiré
tú	destruías	destruiste	**destruyes**	destruirás
Ud./él/ella	destruía	**destruyó**	**destruye**	destruirá
nosotros(as)	destruíamos	destruimos	destruimos	destruiremos
vosotros(as)	destruíais	destruisteis	destruís	destruiréis
Uds./ellos/ellas	destruían	**destruyeron**	**destruyen**	destruirán

Verbs ending in -ducir
(Lección 3)

reducir   *to reduce*

	IMPERFECT	PRETERITE	PRESENT	FUTURE
	reduced	*reduced*	*reduce(s)*	*will reduce*
	was/were reducing		*am/is/are reducing*	
	used to reduce	*did reduce*	*do/does reduce*	
yo	reducía	**reduje**	**reduzco**	reduciré
tú	reducías	**redujiste**	reduces	reducirás
Ud./él/ella	reducía	**redujo**	reduce	reducirá
nosotros(as)	reducíamos	**redujimos**	reducimos	reduciremos
vosotros(as)	reducíais	**redujisteis**	reducís	reduciréis
Uds./ellos/ellas	reducían	**redujeron**	reducen	reducirán

OTHER STRUCTURES

Using infinitives as nouns
(Lección 1)

As the subject of a sentence
As the object of a preposition

Por *and* para
(Lección 1)

POR	PARA
1. in exchange for *(for)*	1. recipient *(for)*
2. duration of time *(for)*	2. destination *(for, to, toward)*
3. reason *(for, because of)*	3. purpose *(to, in order to, used for)*
4. means of transportation *(by)*	4. deadline *(for, by)*
5. motion *(through, along)*	5. employment *(for)*
6. **por** + infinitive *(because of)*	6. comparison to others *(for)*
	7. **para** + infinitive *(in order to)*

To be going to... /To have just . . .
(Lección 1)

IR A + *infinitive*
ACABAR DE + *infinitive*

Clauses
(Lección 2)

ONE-CLAUSE SENTENCES
   subject + verb
   subject + conjugated verb + infinitive
   subject + conjugated verb + (,/**y/o**) + conjugated verb

TWO-CLAUSE SENTENCES
   subject + verb + conjunction + subject + verb
      MAIN CLAUSE + CONJUNCTION + SECONDARY CLAUSE

   conjunction + subject + verb, + subject + verb
      CONJUNCTION + SECONDARY CLAUSE, + MAIN CLAUSE

Indicative and subjunctive
(Lección 2)

Indicative:
  main clause
  secondary clause when it is a fact or reality

Subjunctive:
  secondary clause when it is not a fact or reality
  secondary clause when the main clause reacts to the secondary clause

Commands
(Lección 3)

Usted, ustedes, and **nosotros** commands:
  Use the present subjunctive forms.
Tú commands
  Affirmative **tú** commands: drop **s** from present indicative **tú** form.
  Negative **tú** commands: use present subjunctive.

Irregular affirmative **tú** commands:
(Use the present subjunctive for negative command.)

tener	⟶ ¡Ten!	poner	⟶ ¡Pon!
venir	⟶ ¡Ven!	salir	⟶ ¡Sal!
decir	⟶ ¡Di!	hacer	⟶ ¡Haz!
ir	⟶ ¡Ve!	ser	⟶ ¡Sé!

Object pronouns with commands
(Lección 3)

Object pronouns are attached to the end of affirmative *(do it!)* commands.
Object pronouns go before negative *(don't do it!)* commands.

Sequence of tenses with the subjunctive
(Lección 4)

MAIN CLAUSE	SECONDARY CLAUSE
PAST or CONDITIONAL	PAST (IMPERFECT) SUBJUNCTIVE PAST PERFECT (PLUPERFECT) SUBJUNCTIVE
PRESENT	{ PRESENT SUBJUNCTIVE PRESENT PERFECT SUBJUNCTIVE PAST (IMPERFECT) SUBJUNCTIVE
FUTURE	PRESENT SUBJUNCTIVE

When to use the subjunctive

1. Relative to the main clause, the secondary clause is not a reality (yet)
   - **como si** clause (Lección 2)
   - **si** clause with conditional in main clause (Lección 2)
   - action hasn't happened yet
     persuasion (Lección 3)
     future time (Lección 5)
     uncertain outcome (Lección 5)
   - uncertain existence (Lección 5)
2. When the emphasis is on the way subject of the main clause reacts to the secondary clause
   - emotional reaction (Lección 4)
   - value judgment (Lección 4)
   - doubt or denial (Lección 4)
3. Softened requests with **querer/poder/deber** (Lección 2)

Esqueletos

Infinitive used as a noun
(Lección 1)

> *infinitive + verb + (rest of sentence)*

Hacer un viaje es divertido. *Taking a trip is fun.*
Planear un viaje es difícil. *Planning a trip is difficult.*

Verbs after a preposition
(Lección 1)

> *subject + verb + preposition + infinitive*

Todo el mundo sueña con viajar a España.
Everyone dreams about traveling to Spain.

Mi prima salió sin decirme adiós.
My cousin left without saying good-bye to me.

One-clause sentences
(Lección 2)

> *subject + verb #1 + verb #2*

Las mujeres desearon comprar un regalo.
The women wanted to buy a gift.

Ellas hallaron y compraron una cafetera.
They found and bought a coffeepot.

Two-clause sentences
(Lección 2)

> *main clause + conjunction + secondary clause*

Mi padre cree que mis amigos son muy simpáticos.
My father thinks (that) my friends are very nice.

Mi hermanastra no sabe si puede ir conmigo.
My stepsister doesn't know if she can go with me.

> *conjunction + secondary clause, + main clause*

Si tengo bastante dinero, iré de compras.
If I have enough money, I will go shopping.

Cuando fui a la tienda, encontré a mis amigos.
When I went to the store, I met my friends.

When to use the subjunctive
(Lección 2)

> *main clause*
> *(indicative)* + **QUE** + *secondary clause*
> *(fact: indicative/not a fact: subjunctive)*

Lucía sabía que las muchachas compraron la blusa.
Lucía knew that the girls bought the blouse.

Lucía insistía que las muchachas compraran la blusa.
Lucía insisted that the girls buy the blouse.

| main clause (reaction) (indicative) | + QUE + | secondary clause (subjunctive) |

Lucía está contenta que las muchachas hayan venido a verla.
Lucía is happy that the girls have come to see her.

Past subjunctive after como si
(Lección 2)

| main clause (indicative) | + COMO SI + | secondary clause (past subjunctive) |

Miguel habla como si viviera en la Casa Blanca.
Miguel talks as if he lived in the White House.

El profesor me miraba como si yo nunca hubiera estudiado.
The teacher looked at me as if I had never studied.

Clauses joined by si
(Lección 2)

| SI + | secondary clause (past subjunctive) | + | main clause (conditional) |

Si yo tuviera tiempo, yo iría al centro comercial.
If I had time, I would go to the shopping center.

| SI + | secondary clause (imperfect indicative) | + | main clause (imperfect) |

Si yo tenía tiempo, yo iba al centro comercial.
If I had time, I used to go to the shopping center.

| SI + | secondary clause (present indicative) | + | main clause (present) |

Si yo tengo tiempo, yo voy al centro comercial.
If I have time, I go to the shopping center.

| SI + | secondary clause (present indicative) | + | main clause (future) |

Si yo tengo tiempo, yo iré al centro comercial.
If I have time, I will go to the shopping center.

Subjunctive with persuasion
(Lección 3)

> *subject #1 + verb + QUE + subject #2 + subjunctive verb*

Yo quería que tú reciclaras el papel.   *I wanted you to recycle the paper.*
Sugerimos que él escriba la carta.   *We suggest that he write the letter.*

Object pronouns with commands
(Lección 3)

> *command + object pronoun(s) [attached]*

¿El libro? Póngalo en la mesa, por favor.
The book? Put it on the table, please.

> **NO** + *object pronoun(s) + command*

¿La música? No la escuche ahora, por favor.
The music? Don't listen to it now, please.

Sequence of tenses
(Lección 4)

> *main clause*
> *(past)* **+ QUE +** *secondary clause*
> *(past subjunctive)*

Yo esperaba que visitaras a tu amigo en el hospital.
I hoped that you visited your friend in the hospital.

> *main clause*
> *(past)* **+ QUE +** *secondary clause*
> *(pluperfect subjunctive)*

Yo esperaba que hubieras visitado a tu amigo en el hospital.
I hoped that you had visited your friend in the hospital.

> *main clause*
> *(conditional)* **+ QUE +** *secondary clause*
> *(past subjunctive)*

Esperaría que visitaras a tu amigo en el hospital.
I would hope that you visit(ed) your friend in the hospital.

| main clause (present) | + QUE + | secondary clause (present subjunctive) |

Espero que visites a tu amigo en el hospital.
I hope that you will visit your friend in the hospital.

| main clause (present) | + QUE + | secondary clause (present perfect subjunctive) |

Espero que hayas visitado a tu amigo en el hospital.
I hope that you (have) visited your friend in the hospital.

| main clause (present) | + QUE + | secondary clause (past subjunctive) |

Espero que visitaras a tu amigo en el hospital.
I hope that you visited your friend in the hospital.

| main clause (future) | + QUE + | secondary clause (present subjunctive) |

Esperaré que visites a tu amigo en el hospital.
I will hope that you visit your friend in the hospital.

¡Buen viaje!

It's not too soon to begin planning for vacation time! What do you want to do this summer? Will you be traveling? Let's start with some vocabulary we can use to describe what we plan to do.

Vocabulario

Un viaje *A trip*

viajar para las vacaciones	*to travel for vacation*
los negocios	*for business*
visitar a la familia	*to visit the family*
estudiar	*to study*
aprender	*to learn*
celebrar una fiesta	*to celebrate a holiday*
asistir a •una boda	*to attend a wedding*
asistir a •un funeral	*to attend a funeral*
hacer un viaje	*to take a trip*

Antes del viaje *Before the trip*

planear un viaje	*to plan a trip*
• la ruta	*the route*
decidir en la destinación	*to decide on the destination*
• escoger un medio de transporte	*to choose a means of transportation*
manejar/•conducir	*to drive*
ir por tren	*to go by train*
por avión	*by airplane*
en coche/automóvil/carro	*by car*
en barco	*by ship*
en autobús	*by bus*
• consultar el horario	*to check the time schedule*
pedir (i, i) información	*to ask for information*
• obtener • un pasaporte	*to get/obtain a passport*
un mapa	*a map*
• cheques de viajero	*travelers' checks*
• un boleto	*a ticket*
para •un vuelo sin escalas	*for a nonstop flight*
de •ida	*one way . . .*
de •ida y vuelta	*round-trip . . .*
• reservar un cuarto en un hotel	*to reserve a room in a hotel*
hacer las maletas	*to pack the suitcases*

El viaje   *The trip*

llegar al aeropuerto	*to arrive at the airport*
a la estación	*at the station*
• al puerto	*at the port*
a la destinación	*at the destination*
• facturar el equipaje	*to check in the baggage*
pasar por • la seguridad	*to go through security*
• la aduana	*customs*
• abordar el avión	*to board the airplane*
bajar del avión	*to get off the airplane*
• cambiar aviones	*to change planes*
cambiar dinero	*to exchange money*
recoger el equipaje	*to pick up/claim the baggage*
• llenar el tanque de gasolina	*to fill the gas tank*
comprar recuerdos	*to buy souvenirs*
enviar tarjetas postales	*to send postcards*
• gozar del viaje	*to enjoy the trip*
regresar a casa	*to return home*

TURISMO AL DIA
Premio INTRE
LA MAS COMPLETA INFORMACION
del turismo local e internacional.
Viaje por el mundo y entérese cómo hacerlo.
Tarifas, países, excursiones, hoteles, cruceros y mucho más.
Todos los domingos en vivo de 2:00 a 3:00 P.M.
Moderador *RICARDO CALVO*

1 Tell your partner about some trips you have taken. Tell where you went, when, why, and how you got there.

EJEMPLO: Durante mis vacaciones de invierno, fui a México para visitar a mis primos. Fui por avión.

2 Plan a trip with your partner. Decide on a place you would like to visit and tell what you will do to get there.

EJEMPLO: Vamos a España. Tenemos que obtener un pasaporte.
Decidimos viajar por avión…

In Spanish, infinitives (**-ar, -er,** and **-ir**) are used in many situations where *-ing* is used in English.

USING INFINITIVES AS NOUNS—Part I

AS THE SUBJECT OF A SENTENCE

When an action is used as the subject of a sentence, the infinitive form of the verb is used.

Esqueleto

infinitive + verb + (rest of sentence)

Hacer un viaje es divertido.   *Taking a trip is fun.*
Planear un viaje es difícil.   *Planning a trip is difficult.*

3 With your partner, make a list of five activities that are fun and five activities that are boring.

EJEMPLO: Bailar es divertido.
Limpiar la casa es aburrido.

4 What do you want to do this summer? Make a list and tell why.

EJEMPLO: Quiero leer. Leer es interesante.
Quiero ganar dinero. Ganar dinero es necesario.

USING INFINITIVES AS NOUNS—Part II

AFTER A PREPOSITION

The infinitive form of the verb is used when it follows a preposition.

Esqueleto

subject + verb + preposition + infinitive

Todo el mundo sueña con viajar a España.
Everyone dreams about traveling to Spain.

Mi prima salió sin decirme adiós.
My cousin left without saying good-bye to me.

Vocabulario

Las preposiciones que preceden el infinitivo *Prepositions that precede the infinitive*

antes de	*before*	después de	*after*
en vez de	*instead of*	para	*in order to*
sin	*without*	con	*with*
por	*because of*	hasta	*until*
• al	*on, upon*	• con tal de	*provided*
• en caso de	*in case of*	• a pesar de	*in spite of*

5 Tell some things that you and your friends do together and tell how, when, and why.

EJEMPLO: Recibimos buenas notas sin estudiar mucho.
Hablamos español mucho para aprenderlo.
Esquiamos en vez de jugar al fútbol.

You may have noticed that **por** and **para** have many uses and equivalents in English. Even though these two prepositions share the same translations *(for, by)*, they always have different meanings.

POR AND PARA

Study this chart which shows some of the most common uses of **por** and **para**.

POR	PARA
1. in exchange for *(for)*	1. recipient *(for)*
2. duration of time *(for)*	2. destination *(for, to, toward)*
3. reason *(for, because of)*	3. purpose *(to, in order to, used for)*
4. means of transportation *(by)*	4. deadline *(for, by)*
5. motion *(through, along)*	5. employment *(for)*
6. **por** + infinitive *(because of)*	6. comparison to others *(for)*
	7. **para** + infinitive *(in order to)*

EXAMPLES USING POR

1. in exchange for *(for)*
    Lo compré por tres dólares.
        I bought it for three dollars.
    Te daré mi libro por tu revista.
        I'll give you my book for your magazine.

2. duration of time *(for)*
    Estoy aquí por cinco días.   *I'm here for five days.*
    Estudié por tres horas.   *I studied for three hours.*

3. reason *(for, because of)*
    Él lo hizo por amor.   *He did it for love.*
    No fuimos por la lluvia.   *We did not go because of the rain.*

4. means of transportation *(by)*

    Fuimos por avión.   *We went by plane.*

5. motion *(through, along)*

    Caminamos por el parque.   *We walked through the park.*
    Caminamos por el río.   *We walked along the river.*

6. **por** + infinitive *(because of)*

    Por haber estudiado, Juan salió bien en el examen.
      Because of having studied, Juan did well on the exam.

    No fuimos por la lluvia.
      We did not go because of the rain.

Por is also used in many expressions that need to be memorized.

por favor *please*	¿por qué? *why*?
por la mañana *in the morning*	por lo menos *at least*
por la tarde *in the afternoon*	por teléfono *on the phone*
por la noche *at night*	por aquí *around here*
por ejemplo *for example*	por allí *over there*

EXAMPLES USING PARA

Para is used to indicate a goal, use, purpose, or destination. This is easier to remember if you associate the **a** in **para** with its meaning *to* as when pointing toward ⟶ a goal.

1. recipient *(for)*
   Tengo un regalo para ti.   *I have a gift for you.* ⟶ *you*

2. destination *(for, to, toward)*
   Salgo para Texas hoy.   *I am leaving for Texas today.* ⟶ *Texas*

3. purpose *(to, in order to, used for)*
   Estudiamos para aprender.   *We study (in order) to learn.* ⟶ *learning*
   Es una taza para té.   *It is a teacup (cup for tea).* ⟶ *tea*

4. deadline *(for, by)*
   Lo necesito para el viernes.   *I need it for (by) Friday.* ⟶ *Friday*

5. employment *(for)*
   Ella trabaja para su padre.   *She works for her father.* ⟶ *father*

6. comparison to others *(for)*
   Es fácil para mí.   *It's easy for me.* ⟶ *me*

7. **para** + infinitive *(in order to)*
   Estudia para recibir buenas notas.   *He studies in order to get*
   good grades. ⟶ *good grades*

Note: There are other meanings for **por** and **para** that are less frequently used. If you find one, you may ask your teacher for its meaning.

6 **Mis vacaciones** Answer these questions about your vacation plans.

   a. ¿Para dónde irás de vacaciones? *(destination)*
   b. ¿Por dónde irás para llegar allí? *(motion/through)*
   c. ¿Por medio de qué transporte irás? *(transportation)*
   d. ¿Por qué irás a tu destinación? *(reason/because)*
   e. ¿Para qué irás? *(purpose/in order to)*
   f. ¿Para quién comprarás regalos? *(recipient)*
   g. ¿Cuánto pagarás por los regalos? *(exchange)*
   h. ¿Por cuánto tiempo estarás allí? *(duration)*
   i. ¿Para cuándo regresarás? *(deadline)*

7 Find out about someone else's vacation plans by asking her or him the questions in Activity 6.

8 Why do your friends travel? Tell the reasons.

   EJEMPLO: María viaja para divertirse.

9 Tell some things your friends were able to do and why they were successful.

   EJEMPLO: Por hablar español Susana obtuvo el trabajo.

10 Tell some things that your friends do or did and why.

   EJEMPLO: Mis amigos trabajan en un restaurante para ganar dinero.
   Miguel compró un coche para ir a la escuela.

11 Ask your friends what they bought while on vacation, who they bought it for, and how much they paid for it.

   EJEMPLO: ¿Qué compraste, para quién y por cuánto dinero?

   Compré unos pendientes para mi novia por diez dólares.

IR A + *INFINITIVE* / ACABAR DE + *INFINITIVE*
TO BE GOING TO... / TO HAVE JUST...

¡Acabo de llegar!

Ir a + *infinitive* indicates that an action will take place within a short time.
Acabar de + *infinitive* indicates that an action took place in the recent past.
(It is the equivalent of *to have just done something*.)

Voy a escribir la tarea.   *I am going to do the homework.*
Acabamos de aprender algo nuevo.   *We just learned something new.*

---

12 Tell some things that you just did and other things that you are going to do.

   EJEMPLO: Acabo de escribir la tarea y voy a mirar la televisión.
   Acabamos de aprender la lección y vamos a tomar un examen.

ENCUENTRO PERSONAL

Paulina and her friends Inés and Rosita are talking about the trips they are planning for the summer.

PAULINA: ¿Tienen Uds. planes de viajar este verano?

INÉS: Este verano pienso viajar en avión a Puerto Rico para visitar a mis amigos. Planeamos pasar una semana en el este del país en el parque nacional que se llama El Yunque *(anvil)*. Es una selva tropical con todo tipo de animales y pájaros. Hace dos años que fui por allí y me impresionó mucho.

PAULINA: Me parece un plan magnífico, Inés. ¿Qué preparaciones tienes que hacer antes de hacer el viaje?

INÉS: Hace una semana que compré los boletos de avión de Nueva York a San Juan, pero todavía tengo que consultar el horario de autobuses para llegar a tiempo a Nueva York. Afortunadamente no tengo que cambiar dinero ni obtener un pasaporte porque, como tú ya sabes, Puerto Rico está asociado con los Estados Unidos. Y tú, Rosita, qué planes tienes para el verano?

ROSITA: ¿Yo? Pues el único viaje que tengo planeado ahora es asistir a la boda de mi prima en Monterrey, en el norte de México. Vamos en carro porque tenemos mucho tiempo y queremos ver un poco de los Estados Unidos. Para nosotros será una combinación de visita y vacaciones.

PAULINA: Y, ¿qué preparaciones tienen que hacer antes de salir?

ROSITA: Este *(um)*, a ver *(let me see)*, no tenemos que decidir en la destinación ni escoger un medio de transporte. Solamente tenemos que llenar el tanque con gasolina y manejar hasta Laredo, en la frontera con México. Allí cruzamos el Río Grande y pasamos por la aduana en Nuevo Laredo. Luego manejamos varias horas hacia el sur, hasta llegar a Monterrey.

PAULINA: ¿No tienen que obtener pasaportes y cambiar dinero antes de ir?

ROSITA: No, es mejor cambiar el dinero en un banco allí en México y no es necesario tener pasaporte para ir al norte de México por tan poco tiempo. Pero sí tenemos que comprar seguro *(insurance)* contra accidentes porque la póliza *(policy)* que tenemos no es válida para México. Y tú, Paulina, ¿qué vas a hacer este verano?

PAULINA: ¿Recuerdan a Salvador, mi novio de hace un año? Me invitó a visitarlos a él y a su familia en Santo Domingo. Mamá dice que puedo ir si pago mis boletos de avión. Y puedo comprar la ropa que necesitaré en la tienda donde trabajo con un descuento. Tendré que conseguir un pasaporte y cheques de viajero.

INÉS: ¿Qué dice Santiago de tu plan de visitar a tu ex-novio?

PAULINA: No está muy contento, Inés, pero dice que todavía seremos novios cuando yo regrese *(I return)*.

ROSITA: ¡Qué bueno que ya sabemos hablar español! ¿No? Podemos divertirnos mejor y gozar de los viajes al máximo.

INÉS: Tienes razón, Rosita. ¡Buen viaje!

¿Comprendes?

1. ¿Para dónde piensa viajar Inés?
2. ¿Cuánto tiempo hace que fue allí? ¿Qué va a hacer allí?
3. ¿Qué preparaciones tiene que hacer antes de ir?
4. ¿Adónde va Rosita? ¿Por qué va allí?
5. ¿Qué medio de transporte va a utilizar?
6. ¿Qué preparaciones tiene que hacer antes de ir?
7. ¿Tiene Rosita que cambiar dinero y obtener pasaporte? ¿Por qué no?
8. ¿Qué va a hacer Paulina?
9. ¿Qué tiene que hacer antes de viajar?
10. ¿Qué dice Santiago de sus planes?
11. ¿Por qué dice Rosita que ellos pueden gozar mucho de los viajes?

¡Te toca!

Talk with your classmates about the trips you plan to take this summer, the reason for the trips, and what preparations you have to make before leaving.

Leemos y contamos

A. Raúl's cousin Alberto, who goes to another school, went to Spain with his class. Would you like to take a trip like this also?

Hola Raúl,

Quiero hablarte de algo que hice y que me gustó muchísimo.

Hace unas semanas, durante las vacaciones de primavera, yo hice un viaje a España por una semana. Fui con mi profesora de español y otros ocho estudiantes. Había dos razones principales para el viaje: para estudiar un poco la cultura del país y para practicar y aprender más el español. Pero resultó que nosotros nos divertimos mucho también, como verán en seguida.

Las preparaciones para el viaje comenzaron en octubre. Por muchos meses trabajábamos para juntar (get together) dinero para el viaje. Nosotros vendimos decoraciones de Navidad hechas a mano por nosotros. Vendimos pasteles hechos por nosotros en la cafetería cada viernes. Y en la primavera lavamos carros. También tuvimos que obtener pasaportes y hacer las maletas. La compañía de excursiones compró boletos e hizo reservaciones para los hoteles.

Por fin llegó el día para salir. En el aeropuerto facturamos el equipaje y abordamos el avión. Fue un vuelo sin escalas, directo a Madrid. Pasamos un día en ver un poco de la ciudad. El Museo del Prado y El Escorial me impresionaron mucho por su grandeza e historia. El día siguiente subimos a un autobús para hacer una gira (tour) rápida del país comenzando con Sevilla, en el sur de España. Visitamos el sitio de la Feria Mundial de 1992 en una isla en el Río Guadalquivir y la famosa Catedral de la Sagrada Familia. De allí fuimos en autobús por las montañas a Granada, donde visitamos La Alhambra, el famoso palacio de los moros. De allí fuimos a las fabulosas playas de la Costa del Sol y a la ciudad de Valencia. Terminamos la gira en la ciudad de Barcelona, sitio de los Juegos Olímpicos de 1992. Abordamos el avión en Barcelona para un vuelo breve a Madrid; allí cambiamos aviones para regresar a casa.

Fue un viaje magnífico, y no puedo mencionar todo lo que vimos o hicimos allí. Pero conocí a muchas personas simpáticas y vi muchos lugares inolvidables. Quiero volver a España muy pronto—y esta vez espero pasar muchas semanas o meses allí.

Con cariño,
Tu primo Alberto

1. ¿Quiénes fueron, adónde y por qué?
2. ¿Por cuánto tiempo fue el viaje?
3. ¿Por cuánto tiempo hacían las preparaciones para el viaje?
4. ¿Qué preparaciones hacían?
5. ¿Qué partes de España visitaron y qué vieron?
6. ¿Qué comentarios hace el estudiante sobre su viaje?

B. Describe a trip that you have taken. Why did you take the trip? What did you have to do in order to get ready?

C. What is your goal *(meta)* in life? Explain how you hope to be able to attain it. What will you have to do?

ASÍ ES

El transporte

En los países de Hispanoamérica y en España, los carros son muy caros y la gasolina cuesta mucho más que aquí. Por eso la gente depende más de otros medios de transporte, especialmente del tren y del autobús, y en las ciudades grandes, del taxi y del metro *(subway)*.

En España hay un sistema nacional de trenes que se llama «la Red de Ferrocarriles Españoles» *(Network of Spanish Railroads)* o RENFE. Hay varias categorías de trenes, incluso trenes ultrarrápidos que conectan las ciudades grandes de España con el resto de Europa. En Hispanoamérica, el tren es una forma eficiente de viajar largas distancias y es mucho más barato que volar en avión.

Hablando en términos generales, hay dos tipos de autobuses en el mundo hispano: los autobuses locales que tienen rutas dentro de una ciudad y los autobuses «express» de primera clase, que viajan entre las ciudades grandes con escalas limitadas. Éstos frecuentemente son muy modernos, con aire acondicionado y baños abordo. Los autobuses de segunda clase son a veces viejos autobuses escolares de los EE. UU. que llevan a los habitantes del campo a los mercados de la ciudad con sus cosechas *(crops)* en cestas y animales en jaulas.

Muchas ciudades grandes del mundo hispano tienen muy modernos sistemas de metro. México D.F. (Distrito Federal), por ejemplo, tiene un metro muy limpio, cómodo, rápido y económico. También hay autobuses y taxis en las ciudades grandes. Siempre es una buena idea preguntar cuánto costará el viaje en taxi antes de subir porque no siempre hay tasas fijas *(fixed rates)*.

En el centro comercial

Do you and your friends like going to the shopping center? What do you do when you are there? Do you have to make choices about where you go and what you can buy?

Vocabulario

Lo que se hace en el centro comercial *What one does at the mall*

ir de compras	*to go shopping*	ver •una película	*to see a movie*
• sólo mirar	*to browse, to just look*	comer	*to eat*
gastar dinero	*to spend money*	caminar	*to walk*
• reunirse con los amigos	*to meet friends*	• devolver (ue) algo	*to return something*
comprar cosas	*to buy things*		
hallar cosas •en venta	*to find things on sale*	• cambiar algo	*to exchange something*
• probarse (ue) ropa	*to try on clothes*		
preguntar •el precio	*to ask the price*	• escoger regalos	*to choose gifts*
pagar en efectivo	*to pay cash*	jugar (ue) videojuegos	*to play video games*
• con cheque	*with a check*		
• con tarjeta de crédito	*with a credit card*	divertirse (ie, i)	*to have fun*

Las tiendas *Stores*

1. el almacén — *department store*
- 2. la discotería — *CD store*
3. la ropería — *clothing store*
4. la ropa de mujer — *women's clothing*
5.   hombre — *men's . . .*
6.   niño — *children's . . .*
7. la zapatería — *shoe store*

- 8. la papelería — *stationery store*
9. la librería — *bookstore*
10. la juguetería — *toy store*
11. la tienda de deportes — *sporting goods store*
- 12. la perfumería — *perfume store*
- 13. la mueblería — *furniture store*

La comida *Food*

1. el restaurante — *restaurant*
2. la panadería — *bakery*
- 3. la comida rápida — *fast food*
4. la pastelería — *pastry shop*
5. la heladería — *ice cream parlor*
6. la dulcería — *candy store*
7. la cafetería — *sandwich shop, café*
8. una tienda de •alimentos naturales — *health food store*

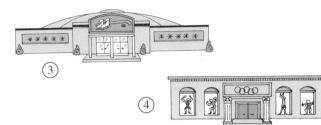

Lugares de •diversión   *Places of entertainment*

1. el cine — *movies*
• 2. la arcada de vídeo — *video arcade*

• 3. la pista de patinaje — *skating arena*
• 4. el gimnasio — *health spa, gym*

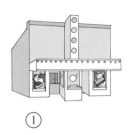

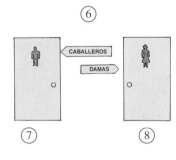

Los servicios   *Services*

• 1. la peluquería — *beauty shop*
2. el zapatero — *shoe repairperson*
3. el banco — *bank*
• 4. el optómetra — *optometrist*
5. los teléfonos públicos — *public telephones*

• 6. los servicios/•el retrete — *restrooms*
7. … para •caballeros — *men's room*
8. … para •damas — *ladies' room*
9. la oficina de •objetos perdidos — *lost and found*
10. la oficina de •seguridad — *security office*

1 Describe the stores and services at a shopping center near where you live.

EJEMPLO: Northland es un centro comercial cerca de mi casa. Hay muchas zapaterías, dos librerías…

2 Tell about a recent trip to a shopping center: where you went, what you bought, and what the people with you bought.

EJEMPLO: El sábado pasado, fui al centro comercial con mis amigas. Yo compré una falda roja y mi amiga compró zapatos tenis.

3 Make a list of your favorite stores. Tell what kind of stores they are and what you will buy the next time you go there.

EJEMPLO: *Duke and Smith* es una ropería para mujeres. Compraré vestidos allí.
Beck and Call es una papelería. Compraré una tarjeta de cumpleaños para mi madrastra.

THE CONDITIONAL TENSE

The conditional tense tells what would happen under certain conditions.

Mi hermano compraría un nuevo carro pero no tiene bastante dinero.
My brother would buy a new car but he doesn't have enough money.

Do not confuse the conditional *would* with the imperfect tense *would* that means *used to.*

The conditional tense is formed in the same way as the future but with different endings.

FORMING THE CONDITIONAL TENSE

The conditional person–time endings are attached to the infinitive. Notice that they are the same endings as the **-er/-ir** imperfect.

yo		**-ía**
tú		**-ías**
Ud./él/ella		**-ía**
nosotros(as)	INFINITIVE +	**-íamos**
vosotros(as)		**-íais**
Uds./ellos/ellas		**-ían**

The conditional has the same irregular stems as the future.

hacer	⟶	har-	poner ⟶	pondr-
saber	⟶	sabr-	salir ⟶	saldr-
haber	⟶	habr-	tener ⟶	tendr-
decir	⟶	dir-	venir ⟶	vendr-
querer	⟶	querr-	poder ⟶	podr-

4 If you and your friends were at the mall, what would you buy? What would your friends buy?

EJEMPLO: Yo compraría una falda larga de algodón rosado.
Mi amigo Carlos compraría un disco compacto de música popular.

5 Ask a classmate which store he or she would go to to buy various items. Refer to the lists of clothing or other items from the vocabulary lists on pages 13, 16, and 146.

EJEMPLO: ¿Adónde irías para comprar una falda?

Yo iría a la ropería para comprar una falda.

6 Find out which shopping center your classmates would like to go to this weekend and what they would do there.

EJEMPLO: ¿A cuál centro comercial te gustaría ir este fin de semana?

Iría a Northland.

¿Qué harías allí?

Me encontraría con mis amigos.

Los compraría pero no tengo bastante dinero.

7 Tell some things that you would do but cannot and tell the reason.

EJEMPLO: Iría al cine pero debo estudiar.
Compraría este libro pero no tengo bastante dinero.

ONE-CLAUSE SENTENCES

A clause is a group of words containing a subject and a verb. If there is one subject and two verbs, the infinitive is used for the second verb unless the two verbs are joined by a comma, **y**, or **o**.

Mis amigos <u>van</u> al cine.   *My friends are going to the movies.*
Mis amigos <u>desean ver</u> una película.   *My friends want to see a movie.*
Ellos <u>mirarán</u> la película <u>y comerán</u> dulces.   *They will watch the movie and eat candy.*

Esqueleto

subject + verb #1 + verb #2

Las mujeres desearon comprar un regalo.
The women wanted to buy a gift.

Ellas hallaron y compraron una cafetera.
They found and bought a coffeepot.

TWO-CLAUSE SENTENCES

If a sentence has more than one clause, it must be joined with a joining word called a *conjunction*. Some common conjunctions are **y, o, que, pero, si**, and **porque**. The clause that follows the conjunction is called the secondary (or dependent) clause. The other clause is the main (or independent) clause.

subject + verb + conjunction + subject + verb
MAIN CLAUSE + CONJUNCTION + SECONDARY CLAUSE

If the secondary clause precedes the main clause, the two clauses are separated with a comma.

conjunction + subject + verb, + subject + verb
CONJUNCTION + SECONDARY CLAUSE, + MAIN CLAUSE

Esqueletos

main clause + conjunction + secondary clause

Mi padre cree <u>que</u> mis amigos son muy simpáticos.
My father thinks (that) my friends are very nice.

Mi hermanastra no sabe <u>si</u> puede ir conmigo.
My stepsister doesn't know if she can go with me.

conjunction + secondary clause, + main clause

<u>Si</u> tengo bastante dinero, iré de compras.
<u>If</u> I have enough money, I will go shopping.

<u>Cuando</u> fui a la tienda, encontré a mis amigos.
<u>When</u> I went to the store, I met my friends.

THE CONJUNCTION QUE

Que *(That)* is frequently used to join clauses. **Que** or another conjunction must be used to join two clauses. Notice that in English, *that* is often omitted.

> Mi padre sabe que yo nado bien. *My father knows (that) I swim well.*

Que can also mean *which* or *who(m)* when it introduces a clause that describes a noun.

> Compré zapatos que puedo llevar a la fiesta.
> *I bought shoes which I can wear to the party.*

> Esa mujer que tiene pelo largo es muy simpática.
> *That woman who has long hair is very nice.*

8 Tell some things you know about your favorite shopping center. Use sentences that have two clauses.

EJEMPLO: Sé que Fernwood tiene doscientos cuarenta tiendas.
No sé si tiene la mejor arcada de videojuegos en la ciudad.

S U P E R M E R C A D O

J. FAUSTINO BARRIGA T.
Paracho Mich.   Nicolas Bravo No. 219
Fabricante de Guitarras Finas y Comerciales. se Surten Pedidos
en Cualquier Parte del Pais y del Extranjero
EXPOSICION DE ARTESANIAS

La Ciudadela Stand 55 y No. 20   Tel. 512-90-89
Balderas y Plaza de la Ciudadela   México 1 D. F.

★ ★
UNIÓN EUROPEA
★ ★ ★

PARA EL MEJOR SERVICIO AL AMA DE CASA.

SITRAM & **VITREX**

EL ACERO INOXIDABLE FRANCES Y EL ESMALTE VITRIFICADO ESPAÑOL,
AL SERVICIO DE LA COCINA EUROPEA.

Dos lideres europeos en menaje de cocina, unen sus esfuerzos técnicos y comerciales para satisfacer las exigencias del ama de casa española. La experiencia técnica y comercial de ambas sociedades permite a nivel domés-tico y profesional, una alta calidad en los productos y plena satisfacción en la condimentación y elaboración de los alimentos. Sus fabricados son utilizables en las más modernas energias de la cocina especialmente vitrocerámicas e inducción.

THE SUBJUNCTIVE

Up to this point, all the verb forms you have used indicate facts or what is perceived as reality. They are called *indicative* verb forms and include imperfect, preterite, present, future, and conditional and the perfect tenses with the same tenses of **haber**.

Es un hecho que...		It is a fact that . . .
cantaba	*[imperfect]*	I used to sing
canté	*[preterite]*	I sang
canto	*[present]*	I sing
cantaré	*[future]*	I will sing
cantaría	*[conditional]*	I would sing

There is another set of verb forms called the *subjunctive*. They are used when the situation expressed in the secondary clause is *not a fact or reality* relative to the main clause or when the main clause expresses a *reaction* to the secondary clause.

WHEN TO USE THE SUBJUNCTIVE

The <u>indicative</u> is always used in the main clause. It is also used in a secondary clause when it expresses a fact or reality (unless a reaction to reality is involved; see page 448).

The <u>subjunctive</u> is used in a secondary clause when it is not a fact or reality or when the main clause reacts to the secondary clause.

SUBJUNCTIVE TENSES

There are only two simple tenses of the subjunctive: past (sometimes called the imperfect subjunctive) and present. The present subjunctive of **haber (haya)** plus the past participle is called the present perfect subjunctive. Likewise, the past subjunctive of **haber (hubiera)** plus the past participle is called the past perfect (pluperfect) subjunctive.

Esqueletos

| main clause (indicative) | + QUE + | secondary clause (fact: indicative/not a fact: subjunctive) |

Lucía sabía que las muchachas <u>compraron</u> la blusa.
Lucía knew that the girls bought the blouse.

Lucía insistía que las muchachas <u>compraran</u> la blusa.
Lucía insisted that the girls buy the blouse.

| main clause (reaction) (indicative) | + QUE + | secondary clause (subjunctive) |

Lucía está contenta que las muchachas <u>hayan venido</u> a verla.
Lucía is happy that the girls have come to see her.

In this lesson we will use the past subjunctive after **como si** *(as if)* and nonfactual **si** *(if)* clauses, so let's learn how to form the past subjunctive.

FORMING THE PAST SUBJUNCTIVE

To form the past (imperfect) subjunctive, drop the **-on** from the third person plural form of the preterite (**Uds./ellos/ellas** form) and add **-a** plus the person endings (**-s, -mos, -n**). The **nosotros** form will require an accent on the third vowel from the end. This rule will work for *all* verbs.

COMPRAR	COMER	DORMIR (i, i)	TENER	HABER
comprar**on**	comier**on**	durmier**on**	tuvier**on**	hubier**on**
comprar**a**	comier**a**	durmier**a**	tuvier**a**	hubier**a**
comprar**as**	comier**as**	durmier**as**	tuvier**as**	hubier**as**
comprar**a**	comier**a**	durmier**a**	tuvier**a**	hubier**a**
compr**áramos**	comi**éramos**	durmi**éramos**	tuvi**éramos**	hubi**éramos**
compr**árais**	comi**érais**	durmi**érais**	tuvi**érais**	hubi**érais**
comprar**an**	comier**an**	durmier**an**	tuvier**an**	hubier**an**

The past perfect subjunctive is formed using the past subjunctive of **haber** (**hubiera** + the person endings) with the past participle.

Hablaban como si ya <u>hubieran</u> terminado.
They talked as if they had already finished.

Note: An alternate method of forming the past subjunctive is to drop the **-ron** and add **-se** plus the person ending.

compraron –**ron** + endings = comprase, comprases, comprase, comprásemos, compráseis, comprasen

The two forms are interchangeable but the **-ra** forms are used more frequently. For this reason, examples are given using the **-ra** forms.

PAST SUBJUNCTIVE AFTER COMO SI

When **como si** *(as if)* is used to join two clauses, the verb after it is always past subjunctive. The information in this clause is not reality.

Mi esposa gasta dinero como si fuéramos millonarios.

Esqueleto

| main clause (indicative) | + COMO SI + | secondary clause (past subjunctive) |

Miguel habla <u>como si viviera</u> en la Casa Blanca.
Miguel talks <u>as if he lived</u> in the White House.

El profesor me miraba <u>como si yo nunca hubiera estudiado.</u>
The teacher looked at me <u>as if I had never studied.</u>

9 Sometimes people act differently from the way they really are. Tell some ways your friends act that are different from reality.

EJEMPLO: Javier se porta como si nunca estudiara.
Elena se porta como si nadie la invitara nunca a las fiestas.

Se porta como si viera un fantasma.

CLAUSES JOINED BY SI

The past subjunctive is used in clauses beginning with **si** *(if)* when the main clause is in the conditional tense. When the main clause is imperfect, preterite, present, or future tense, the secondary clause is indicative. The **si** clause can be first or last in the sentence.

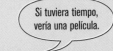

Si tuviera tiempo,
vería una película.

Si tuviera tiempo, iría al centro comercial.
If I had time, I would go to the shopping center.

Iría al centro comercial si tuviera tiempo.
I would go to the shopping center if I had time.

The perfect forms can also be used with **si** clauses.

Habría ido al centro comercial si hubiera tenido tiempo.
I would have gone to the shopping center if I had had time.

Esqueletos

| SI + | secondary clause *(past subjunctive)* | + | main clause *(conditional)* |

Si yo tuviera tiempo, yo iría al centro comercial.
If I had time, I would go to the shopping center.

| SI + | secondary clause *(imperfect indicative)* | + | main clause *(imperfect)* |

Si yo tenía tiempo, yo iba al centro comercial.
If I had time, I used to go to the shopping center.

| SI + | secondary clause *(present indicative)* | + | main clause *(present)* |

Si yo tengo tiempo, yo voy al centro comercial.
If I have time, I go to the shopping center.

| SI + | secondary clause *(present indicative)* | + | main clause *(future)* |

Si yo tengo tiempo, yo iré al centro comercial.
If I have time, I will go to the shopping center.

10 **Encuesta**   Ask your classmates what they do after school if they don't have any homework.

EJEMPLO: ¿Qué haces después de las clases si no tienes tarea?

Si no tengo tarea, voy a la casa de mi amigo.

11 **Encuesta**   Find out what your classmates will do if they finish their homework early.

EJEMPLO: ¿Qué harás si terminas tu tarea temprano?

Si termino mi tarea temprano, miraré una película en la televisión.

12 **Encuesta**   Ask your classmates what they would do if they won the lottery. Use the past subjunctive after **si** since the main clause is conditional.

EJEMPLO: ¿Qué harías si ganaras la lotería?

Si yo ganara la lotería, compraría una casa grande.

Si yo ganara la lotería, viajaría a España.

Si yo ganara la lotería, compraría una casa grande.

13 Tell under what circumstances you would learn to fly an airplane.

EJEMPLO: Si tuviera veinte y un años, aprendería a volar un avión.
Si viviera cerca de un aeropuerto, aprendería.

14 **Encuesta**   Find out from your classmates what they would do in the following situations at the shopping center. Then report the results of your survey.

EJEMPLO: ¿Qué harías si hallaras un bolso de pasteles?

Yo comería los pasteles.

Reportaje: Elena comería los pasteles.

a. si hallara un bolso de pasteles
b. si encontrara a un niño perdido *(lost)*
c. si perdiera un papel importante
d. si conociera a una persona muy famosa
e. si una persona pasara delante en una cola *(line)*

SOFTENED REQUESTS

The conditional form or the past subjunctive are often used with **querer, poder,** and **deber** to soften the effect of an order or request.

Compare the following:

Quiero saber el precio.	*I want to know the price.*
<u>Querría</u> saber el precio. OR <u>Quisiera</u> saber el precio.	*I would like to know the price.*
¿Puede Ud. ayudarme?	*Can you help me?*
¿<u>Podría</u> Ud. ayudarme? OR ¿<u>Pudiera</u> Ud. ayudarme?	*Could you help me?*
Debemos ir de compras.	*We ought to go shopping.*
<u>Deberíamos</u> ir de compras. OR <u>Debiéramos</u> ir de compras.	*We should go shopping.*

15 **Sit-Con**   You are shopping for a gift for someone's birthday. With your partner, recreate the conversation you have with the salesperson. Use the conditional forms of the verb for some and the past subjunctive for others to soften the request.

EJEMPLO: — Me gustaría comprarle una bufanda a mi hermana para su cumpleaños. ¿Podría mostrarme algunas?

— ¿Hay aquí una bufanda que le gustaría ver?

— Quisiera ver ésa. ¿Pudiera decirme el precio?

— El precio es quince dólares.

— Bueno, me gustaría comprarla. Aquí está mi tarjeta de crédito.

¿Pudiera Ud. ayudarme? Quisiera saber el precio.

ENCUENTRO PERSONAL

Paulina heard that Santiago found some money in the mall. She and his friends are discussing how they would spend the money if <u>they</u> found some money.

SANTIAGO:　¿Qué harías tú, Paulina, si encontraras dinero en el centro comercial?

PAULINA:　Si yo encontrara dinero en el centro comercial, yo iría de compras en todas mis tiendas preferidas. Primero iría al departamento de ropa femenina en un almacén para probarme un vestido rojo. Y luego miraría una película en el cine del centro.

SANTIAGO:　Y tú, Sean, ¿qué harías?

SEAN:　Yo no me compraría ninguna ropa ni vería ninguna película tampoco. Lo que me interesan son los videojuegos. Primero jugaría en la arcada de vídeo, y luego iría a la tienda para comprarme unos juegos nuevos para jugar en casa. ¿Qué harías tú, Rosita?

ROSITA:　Si yo tuviera un poco de dinero ahora, yo entraría en un restaurante y pediría un bistec. Y luego iría a la heladería para comer algunos postres. ¡Tengo mucha hambre! ¿Y tú, Inés?

INÉS: Todos Uds. hablan como si fueran ladrones. Yo no haría nada con el dinero; no compraría ninguna ropa, ni jugaría ningunos videojuegos ni comería nada con el dinero. Yo no podría dormir si hiciera cosas tan malas. Si yo encontrara dinero en el centro comercial, lo que haría es ir directamente a la oficina de seguridad y se lo daría a la policía. Ellos encontrarían a la persona que lo perdió y se lo devolverían.

PAULINA: Sí, claro, Inés. Tienes razón. En realidad yo tendría que hacer lo mismo. Solamente estábamos soñando, pero no somos ningunos ladrones.

¿Comprendes?

1. ¿Qué dice Paulina que haría si encontrara dinero en el centro comercial?
2. ¿Y qué haría Sean? ¿Y Rosita?
3. En la opinión de Inés, ¿cómo hablan ellos? ¿Cómo se sentiría ella si hiciera lo mismo?
4. ¿Qué haría Inés con el dinero si lo encontrara?
5. ¿Está Paulina de acuerdo con Inés?
6. ¿Y qué harías tú si encontraras el dinero perdido en el centro?

¡Te toca!

Discuss with your friends what you would do if you won a $100 gift certificate to spend at the mall.

Leemos y contamos

A. Now that Paulina is coming to visit, Salvador is making plans for things they can do. Read his letter to her.

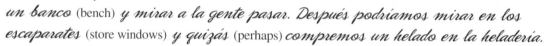

Querida Paulina:

¡Sabes lo que echo de menos (miss) más de no vivir en tu ciudad? No hay ningunos centros comerciales cerca de nosotros. Si estuviera contigo ahora, iríamos otra vez al centro comercial para ir de compras, o si no tuviéramos mucho dinero extra, podríamos sentarnos en un banco (bench) y mirar a la gente pasar. Después podríamos mirar en los escaparates (store windows) y quizás (perhaps) compremos un helado en la heladería.

Yo sé que estoy hablando como si no pudiéramos ir de compremos. No es así. Podríamos ir al centro donde hay un almacén y muchas tiendas y podríamos comprar de todo. Te compraría dulces en la dulcería, helado en la heladería y un anillo en la joyería. Iríamos al cine o escucharíamos a los músicos en la plaza. También podríamos ir al mercado al aire libre para comprar cosas allí. Nos divertiríamos porque estaríamos juntos. Pero me gustan más los centros comerciales porque todo está bajo el mismo techo y hay aire acondicionado.

Hace muy buen tiempo hoy y hace calor. Si estuvieras aquí ahora, nadaríamos en la playa con mis amigos. O si fuéramos a las montañas, montaríamos a caballo. No tendrías que tener miedo porque no hay animales feroces allí. Me gustaría mucho llevarte al rancho de mi familia, donde tenemos muchas vacas.

Mi abuela dice que puedo organizar una fiesta en tu honor y todos mis amigos dicen que si hay un espectáculo en el teatro o un concierto en el parque, irán con nosotros. También dicen que si queremos ir, nos acompañarán a la ciudad para ir a un centro comercial o para ver una película.

Estoy haciendo muchos planes, como si tú llegaras mañana. No puedo esperar tu llegada en julio para mirar tus ojos bonitos...

Tu fiel amigo,
Salvador

1. ¿Por qué ya no va Salvador a ningunos centros comerciales?
2. Si Salvador estuviera con Paulina hoy, ¿qué harían ellos?
3. ¿Qué podrían hacer si fueran a las montañas?
4. ¿Adónde querría llevarla?
5. ¿Qué harán con sus amigos?

B. Describe a recent trip to a shopping mall. Tell who went with you and what you did there.

Así es

Vamos de compras

Si viajaras a un país hispano, tarde o temprano querrías ir de compras. ¿Cuáles son las opciones que tendrías?

En las ciudades de los países hispanos hay grandes almacenes donde puedes comprar de todo—ropa, joyas, juguetes, libros, discos compactos, cosas para la casa, etc. También hay tiendas especializadas como zapaterías, roperías, joyerías, etc., que venden solamente una cosa. En las afueras de las ciudades hay centros comerciales donde hay almacenes y también tiendas especializadas, restaurantes, servicios y más, todos bajo un solo techo. Pero tienes que recordar que si fueras de compras en una tienda de este tipo, no podrías regatear *(bargain)*. Se paga el precio en la etiqueta *(ticket)*.

Pero si estuvieras en un pueblo, tendrías que buscar lo que quieres en el mercado al aire libre. En los pueblos pequeños el día del mercado tiene lugar uno o dos días por semana. Los vendedores llevan sus mercancías *(merchandise)* y las venden de un puesto *(stall)* o a veces de su camión. Se puede comprar todo tipo de comestibles, ropa, artesanías *(crafts)* y animales en el mercado. En el mercado regatearías porque es la costumbre.

Probablemente querrías comprar recuerdos *(souvenirs)* del país. En muchos países, el gobierno tiene centros turísticos donde los turistas pueden comprar artesanías. Aquí los precios son fijos *(fixed)* y podrías comprar recuerdos para todos tus amigos.

¡Salvemos la tierra!

It seems that almost everyone is concerned with the environment. Are you? In this lesson we will talk about environmental issues and discuss what to do about them.

Vocabulario

La ecología   *Ecology*

- **Las cuestiones**   *Issues*
- amenazar el medioambiente   *to threaten the environment*
- malgastar los recursos naturales   *to waste natural resources*
  - el carbón   *coal*
  - el petróleo   *oil*
  - el agua dulce   *fresh water*
- el malgasto   *waste, misuse*
- destruir* el ozono   *to destroy the ozone*
  - las selvas tropicales   *tropical jungles/forests*
    los bosques   *woods, forest*
- la destrucción   *destruction*
- contaminar los lagos   *to pollute the lakes*
    los ríos   *the rivers*
    los océanos   *the oceans*
  - la tierra   *the ground, the soil, the earth*
    el aire   *the air*
- la contaminación por…   *pollution by . . .*
  - químicos   *chemicals*
  - basura   *garbage*
  - derrames de petróleo   *oil spills*
  - la lluvia ácida   *acid rain*
  - el humo de las fábricas   *factory smoke*
  - el escape de los automóviles   *auto exhaust*
- consumir   *to consume*
- el consumo   *consumption*
- matar los animales salvajes   *to kill wild animals*
    los peces   *fish*
    las plantas •en peligro   *endangered plants*

*Irregular verb; see page 422.

El aceite de motor afecta las plantas de tratamiento de aguas.

Autoridad de Desperdicios Sólidos
1-800-981-RECI

Vocabulario

Las soluciones   *Solutions*

pasar •leyes	*to pass laws*
• conservar •electricidad	*to conserve electricity*
• salvar las especies amenazadas	*to save/rescue endangered species*
• eliminar los desperdicios	*to eliminate waste*
• conservar energía	*to conserve energy*
• advertir (ie, i) del problema	*to advise/warn about the problem*
• cortar el agua	*to turn off the water*
• apagar la luz	*to turn out the lights*
• bajar la calefacción	*to lower the heat*
• contribuir* a la ecología	*to contribute to ecology*
• reducir** el daño	*to reduce the damage*
• echar basura en el basurero	*to throw garbage in the trash can*
• reciclar…	*to recycle . . .*
el papel y •el cartón	*paper and cardboard*
• los contenedores de plástico	*plastic containers*
• la madera	*wood*
• las latas de aluminio	*aluminum cans*
• las botellas de •cristal	*glass bottles*
la ropa	*clothing*
• las llantas	*tires*
el metal	*metal*
las pilas	*batteries (flashlight, etc.)*
las baterías	*batteries (car)*

• prohibir el uso de…	*to prohibit the use of . . .*
• los fluorocarburos	*fluorocarbons*
• los químicos	*chemicals*
• los productos de petróleo	*petroleum products*
• los detergentes con fosfatos	*detergents with phosphates*
• el estirofoma	*Styrofoam*
• el insecticida	*insecticide*
• aumentar el uso de…	*to increase the use of . . .*
el papel •reciclado	*recycled paper*
el gas natural	*natural gas*
los detergentes •biodegradables	*biodegradable detergents*
• los fertilizantes naturales	*natural fertilizers*
• la energía solar	*solar energy*
nuclear	*nuclear*
hidroeléctrica	*hydroelectric*
• del viento	*wind-powered*
aprender de la ecología	*to learn about ecology*
no •perder (ie) tiempo	*to waste no time*

*Irregular verb; see page 422.

**Irregular verb; see page 423.

1 Tell some things that you are aware of in your area that are destructive to the environment.

EJEMPLO: Hay contaminación de los océanos por los derrames de petróleo.

2 Tell some of the ways in which you and your community are helping to save the planet.

EJEMPLO: Yo reduzco mi uso de electricidad.
Nosotros reciclamos el papel.

No dejes
para mañana,
lo que puedas
hacer hoy.
Apoya el reciclaje.

Hoy

Mañana

AUTORIDAD DE DESPERDICIOS SOLIDOS
Recicla hoy para un mejor mañana

Following are the forms for the verb **destruir** (*to destroy*). Most verbs that end in **-uir** follow this pattern.

DESTRUIR *to destroy*

	IMPERFECT	PRETERITE	PRESENT	FUTURE
	destroyed *was/were destroying* *used to destroy*	*destroyed* *did destroy*	*destroy(s)* *am/is/are destroying* *do/does destroy*	*will destroy*
yo	destruía	destruí	**destruyo**	destruiré
tú	destruías	destruiste	**destruyes**	destruirás
Ud./él/ella	destruía	**destruyó**	**destruye**	destruirá
nosotros(as)	destruíamos	destruimos	destruimos	destruiremos
vosotros(as)	destruíais	destruisteis	destruís	destruiréis
Uds./ellos/ellas	destruían	**destruyeron**	**destruyen**	destruirán

Irregularities:
preterite: i ⟶ y between vowels
present: **y** added to "boot" forms

Vocabulario

Los verbos irregulares que terminan en «-uir»   *Irregular verbs that end in -uir*

construir	*to build*	incluir	*to include*
contribuir	*to contribute*	influir	*to influence*
distribuir	*to distribute*	sustituir	*to substitute*
destruir	*to destroy*		

3 Tell about the destruction of the environment in the area where you live.

EJEMPLO: Las fábricas destruyeron el aire con el humo.
Los hombres de negocios construyen muchos edificios.

Verbs ending in **-ducir** follow the same pattern as **reducir** below.

VERBS ENDING IN -DUCIR

REDUCIR *to reduce*

	IMPERFECT *reduced* *was/were* *reducing* *used to reduce*	PRETERITE *reduced* *did reduce*	PRESENT *reduce(s)* *am/is/are* *reducing* *do/does reduce*	FUTURE *will reduce*
yo	reducía	**reduje**	**reduzco**	reduciré
tú	reducías	**redujiste**	reduces	reducirás
Ud./él/ella	reducía	**redujo**	reduce	reducirá
nosotros(as)	reducíamos	**redujimos**	reducimos	reduciremos
vosotros(as)	reducíais	**redujisteis**	reducís	reduciréis
Uds./ellos/ellas	reducían	**redujeron**	reducen	reducirán

Irregularities:
preterite: "combo" verb, no **i** in **ellos** form.
present: **yo** form ends in **-zco**

Vocabulario

Los verbos irregulares que terminan in «-ducir»   *Irregular verbs that end in -ducir*

reducir	*to reduce*	producir	*to produce*
conducir	*to drive*	introducir	*to introduce*
traducir	*to translate*		

4  Tell about ways that the destruction of the environment has been reduced.

EJEMPLO: Las amas de casa reducen la contaminación del agua cuando usan detergentes
sin fosfatos.
Yo reduzco el uso de papel escribiendo en los dos lados.

In some situations when the main clause of a two-clause sentence is in the present or future tense, the present subjunctive may have to be used. First we will learn to form the present subjunctive; then we will learn when to use it.

PRESENT SUBJUNCTIVE: REGULAR VERBS

To form the present subjunctive, begin with the **yo** form of present indicative and remove **-o**. Then add the following endings:

-AR VERBS	-ER/-IR VERBS
-e	-a
-es	-as
-e	-a
-emos	-amos
-eis	-ais
-en	-an

Note: Verbs ending in **-car, -gar, -zar,** and **-ger** will have spelling variations.

-car ⟶ **-que**   **-gar** ⟶ **gue**   **-zar** ⟶ **-ce**   **-ger** ⟶ **-ja**

-AR VERBS	-ER/-IR VERBS	SPELLING VARIATION	IRREGULAR YO
SALVAR = yo salvo	CONSUMIR = yo consumo	BUSCAR = yo busco	REDUCIR = yo reduzco
salve	consuma	busque	reduzca
salves	consumas	busques	reduzcas
salve	consuma	busque	reduzca
salvemos	consumamos	busquemos	reduzcamos
salvéis	consumáis	busquéis	reduzcáis
salven	consuman	busquen	reduzcamos

PRESENT SUBJUNCTIVE: STEM-CHANGING VERBS

-Ar and **-er** stem-changing verbs change in the "boot" forms only. There is no change in the **nosotros(as)** and **vosotros(as)** forms. **-Ir** stem-changing verbs have <u>both</u> stem changes, the first stem change in the "boot" forms and the second change in the **nosotros(as)** and **vosotros(as)** forms.

-AR/-ER VERBS		-IR VERBS	
RESOLVER (UE)		ADVERTIR (IE, I)	
resuelva	resolvamos	advierta	advirtamos
resuelvas	resolváis	adviertas	advirtáis
resuelva	resuelvan	advierta	adviertan

PRESENT SUBJUNCTIVE: IRREGULAR VERBS

There are only six verbs that are irregular because their present tense **yo** form does not end in **o**. If you remember that the first letter of each forms the word "HISSED," it will be easier to remember them.

HABER	IR	SER	SABER	ESTAR	DAR
haya	vaya	sea	sepa	esté	dé
hayas	vayas	seas	sepas	estés	des
haya	vaya	sea	sepa	esté	dé
hayamos	vayamos	seamos	sepamos	estemos	demos
hayáis	vayáis	seáis	sepáis	estéis	deis
hayan	vayan	sean	sepan	estén	den

Notice the accents on some forms of **estar** and **dar**.

Vocabulario

There are many ways of trying to persuade or influence others to do something. Here are some of them. Can you think of others?

Verbos y expresiones de persuación   *Verbs and expressions of persuasion*

aconsejar	*to advise*	mandar	*to command, to order*
decir	*to tell*	pedir (i, i)	*to ask for, to request*
dejar	*to let, to allow*	permitir	*to permit, to allow*
desear	*to wish, to want*	preferir (ie, i)	*to prefer*
esperar	*to hope*	prohibir	*to forbid, to prohibit*
exigir	*to require, to demand*	querer (ie)	*to wish, to want*
hacer	*to make, to cause*	recomendar (ie)	*to recommend*
impedir (i, i)	*to prevent*	rogar (ue)	*to beg, to request*
insistir (en)	*to insist (on)*	sugerir (ie, i)	*to suggest*

(No) Es importante	*It is (not) important*
(No) Es necesario	*It is (not) necessary*
(No) Es esencial	*It is (not) essential*
(No) Es preferible	*It is (not) preferable*
(No) Es urgente	*It is (not) urgent*

INFINITIVE VS. SUBJUNCTIVE WITH PERSUASION

When we persuade someone, we are telling them what we want them to do. If this is done in a general sense, the infinitive is used for the second verb.

Es importante salvar la tierra.   *It's important to save the Earth.*

When one subject is trying to persuade another to do (or not do) something, the subjunctive is used because when the people who are being persuaded are mentioned, a secondary clause is created. The main clause and the secondary clause will have different subjects. Since, at the time of the main clause, they have not yet responded to the request, the secondary clause is not a fact or a reality so the subjunctive is used.

If the main clause is in the past or conditional, the verb in the secondary clause is in the past subjunctive. If the verb in the main clause is in the present or future, use the present subjunctive in the secondary clause.

Note: In a statement using these verbs and expressions where there is only one clause, the infinitive is used for the second verb.

Queremos salvar las especies en peligro.   *We want to save endangered species.*

Esqueleto

> *subject # 1 + verb + QUE + subject # 2 + subjunctive verb*

Yo quería que tú reciclaras el papel. *I wanted you to recycle the paper.*
Sugerimos que él escriba la carta. *We suggest that he write the letter.*

5 With your classmates, brainstorm ways to save the planet.

EJEMPLO: Es necesario prohibir el uso de fluorocarburos.
Recomendamos reciclar el papel.

6 Working with your partner, tell what your recommendations are for saving the Earth.

EJEMPLO: Recomendamos echar basura en los basureros.
Sugerimos bajar la calefacción durante el invierno.

7 Using the expressions of persuasion, take turns with your partner telling him or her what is necessary, important, essential, urgent, or preferable for him or her to do to save the Earth. Since there is a second subject mentioned, the subjunctive will be used in the secondary clause.

EJEMPLO: Es necesario que tú eches papel en el basurero.
Es esencial que tú cortes el agua.

8 *Sit-Con* Tell your representative in Congress what you want, hope, and suggest, insist, etc., that he or she do to protect the environment.

EJEMPLO: Deseo que Ud. pase leyes para proteger los bosques.
Insisto en que Ud. prohiba el uso de fluorocarburos.

9 Tell your parents some things that you advise, request, ask, etc., that they do to be more ecological.

EJEMPLO: Sugiero que Uds. no usen detergentes con fosfatos.
Pido que Uds. compren contenedores de papel en
vez de plástico.

Tell some things that you recommend, suggest, demand, etc., we all do to save natural resources.

EJEMPLO: Es esencial que apaguemos las luces al salir del cuarto.
Es importante que salvemos los océanos.

COMMANDS—Part I

An affirmative command tells someone to do something and a negative command tells someone not do something. Commands can be given to one person or to a group.

USTED, USTEDES, AND NOSOTROS COMMANDS

These commands use the present subjunctive forms.

¡No eche (Ud.) basura en el suelo!   *Don't throw garbage on the floor!*
¡Sepan (Uds.) las opciones!   *Know the options!*
¡Reduzcamos la contaminación!   *Let's reduce pollution!*

Note: Subject pronouns are not necessary with commands but **Ud.** or **Uds.** may be placed after the verb.

The **nosotros** command of **ir** is **Vamos** *(Let's go)* and **No vayamos** *(Let's not go)*.

---

11 Tell your senator what should be done to help the environment. Use **Ud.** commands.

EJEMPLO: Controle las emisiones de humo de las fábricas.
No permita el uso de fluorocarburos.

12 Tell your parents what they can do to help the environment. Use **Uds.** commands.

EJEMPLO: Usen detergentes degradables para lavar la ropa.
Reciclen los periódicos.

13 In a group, decide on at least ten ways you can help to reduce pollution. Use **nosotros** commands.

EJEMPLO: Tomemos menos exámenes para usar menos papel.
Reciclemos nuestra ropa vieja.

COMMANDS—Part II

TÚ COMMANDS

Affirmative *(Do it!)* **tú** commands drop the **s** from the present indicative **tú** form.
Negative *(Don't do it!)* **tú** commands use the present subjunctive.

SALVAR	¡Salva!	*Save!*	¡No salves!	*Don't save!*
REDUCIR	¡Reduce!	*Reduce!*	¡No reduzcas!	*Don't reduce!*
ADVERTIR	¡Advierte!	*Advise!*	¡No adviertas!	*Don't advise!*

IRREGULAR AFFIRMATIVE **TÚ** COMMANDS

These verbs have irregular affirmative **tú** *(Do it!)* commands but they use the present
subjunctive for the negative *(Don't do it!)* command.

tener ⟶	¡Ten!	*Have!*	poner ⟶	¡Pon!	*Put!*
venir ⟶	¡Ven!	*Come!*	salir ⟶	¡Sal!	*Leave!*
decir ⟶	¡Di!	*Say/Tell!*	hacer ⟶	¡Haz!	*Do/Make!*
ir ⟶	¡Ve!	*Go!*	ser ⟶	¡Sé!	*Know!*

Pon el papel en el cesto.   *Put the paper in the basket.*
No pongas el papel en el suelo.   *Don't put the paper on the floor.*

14 What are some ways your friends pollute the environment? Tell them what they should and
should not do to help the environment. Use **tú** commands.

EJEMPLO: Marta, corta el agua mientras te cepillas los dientes.
No uses sacos de plástico para la basura.

15 Make a list of ten things your friends do that hurt the environment. Tell them not to do them
any more.

EJEMPLO: (Marisol tira la basura en la calle.)
Marisol, ¡no tires la basura en la calle!

(Todos mis amigos usan mucho papel.)
¡No usen Uds. tanto papel!

Marisol, ¡no tires la basura en la calle.

OBJECT PRONOUNS WITH COMMANDS

Object pronouns are attached to the end of affirmative *(Do it!)* commands. Remember to put the accent mark on the command if needed to keep the stress in the right place.

Dímelo.   *Tell it to me.*
Pónganla allí.   *Put it there.*
Démelo, por favor.   *Give it to me, please.*

Object pronouns go before negative *(Don't do it!)* commands.

¡No lo digas!   *Don't say it!*
¡No la pongan allí!   *Don't put it there!*

¡Démelo, por favor!

¡No me lo dé!

Esqueletos

command + object pronoun(s) [attached]

¿El libro? Póngalo en la mesa, por favor.
The book? Put it on the table, please.

NO + object pronoun(s) + command

¿La música? No la escuche ahora, por favor.
The music? Don't listen to it now, please.

16 *Sit-Con*   You and a friend are writing to your state representative to encourage him or her to help save the environment. You both have a lot of suggestions, but have decided not to put all of them in your letter. First make a list of ten things you think should be done, then decide on the five most important suggestions to put in the letter. Tell your friend which suggestions to put in and which not to put in the letter.

EJEMPLO: Prohibamos el uso de fosfatos.   ¡Pónlo en la carta!
Reciclemos la ropa.   ¡No lo pongas en la carta!
No malgastemos el petróleo.   ¡No lo pongas en la carta!

17 *Sit-Con*   Your community has begun a recycling project for plastics, glass, and paper and is providing each household with a container **(contenedor)** for each. Tell one of your family members where to put each of the following items. (Use object pronouns with **tú** commands.)

EJEMPLO: (una botella de salsa de tomate):
Pónla en el contenedor de cristal.
No la pongas en el basurero.
(una caja de detergente)
Pónla en el contenedor de papel.

a. un periódico
b. una botella de jugo
c. unas tarjetas de Navidad
d. unos cartones de leche
e. una botella de champú
f. una caja de un regalo
g. un saco del supermercado
h. una botella de refrescos

18 **¿Qué debemos hacer con... ?**   Tell your friends what to do about the following environmental problems. (Use object pronouns with **Uds.** commands.)

EJEMPLO: Las selvas tropicales desaparecen.
　　　　　　　¡Consérvenlas!
　　　　　　Usamos mucho papel.
　　　　　　　¡No lo malgasten!

a. Los fluorocarburos destruyen el ozono.
b. Los pajáros mueren en los derrames de petróleo.
c. Hay mucha alga *(algae)* en los ríos a causa de los fosfatos.
d. Los árboles desaparecen para hacer papel.
e. Sufrimos por el humo de las fábricas.
f. Hay latas y botellas de refrescos al lado de los caminos.
g. Usamos mucho carbón para producir electricidad.

ENCUENTRO PERSONAL

Paulina and her classmates are discussing their plans for Earth Day at their school.

TODOS: Paulina, tú eres la presidenta del Club de la Tierra. Dinos qué debemos hacer.

PAULINA: Para salvar la tierra, comencemos aquí en la escuela. Celebremos un Día de la Tierra y así podemos dar información sobre las cuestiones y los remedios para mejorar el mundo.

ROSITA: ¡Qué buena idea, Paulina! Comencemos ahora mismo a planearlo. ¿Qué es necesario que hagamos primero?

PAULINA: Pues, Rosita, primero es esencial que planeemos la publicidad para el Día de la Tierra. Carlos, sugiero que llames las estaciones de radio e invita al público. Rosita, quiero que escribas un artículo para el periódico y mándaselo inmediatamente. Es urgente que reciba el artículo mañana. Sean y Melinda, hagan carteles para los pasillos de la escuela. Y díganles todos a sus familias de nuestra producción. Santiago, tú estás encargado *(in charge)* de las exhibiciones. Dinos qué debemos hacer.

SANTIAGO: Es importante que ayudemos a todos a preparar exhibiciones de información. Tomás y Miguel, construyan Uds. unos muros altos en la sala y Tanya, te pido que tú pintes un mapa del mundo. Antonio, Luis y Sean, lleven Uds. las mesas de la cafetería y pónganlas en la sala de conferencias. Y Marisela y Jasmina, hagan Uds. decoraciones para la sala.

RAÚL: No olvidemos llevar libros y vídeos con información sobre el medioambiente. Sugiero que Uds. traigan todos los libros que tienen a la cafetería el sábado. Inés, ve a la biblioteca y saca los vídeos que necesitamos. Tráemelos a mi casa esta noche. Paulina, dinos dónde debemos estar y cuándo debemos comenzar el trabajo.

PAULINA: No se preocupen Uds. Tenemos dos semanas para preparar. Pero es esencial que vengan Uds. todos mañana después de la escuela y comencemos el trabajo entonces.

¿Comprendes?

1. ¿Quién es la presidenta del Club de la Tierra?
2. ¿Qué idea propone ella?
3. ¿Que órdenes les da Paulina a los miembros del club?
4. ¿Qué dicen Santiago y Raúl que hagan los estudiantes?
5. ¿Cuando será el Día de la Tierra y cuando comenzarán a trabajar?

¡Te toca!

Plan your own Earth Day and decide what could be done to make it work.

Leemos y contamos

A. For Earth Day, Paulina's class made a report of the environmental problems in their community and a list of suggestions for various people to improve the environment.

Los problemas del medioambiente en nuestra comunidad

a. **El malgasto de energía**   Los carros usan demasiada gasolina, las casas usan demasiada agua y electricidad y los individuos consumen demasiado de todo.

b. **La contaminación del aire**   El escape de los autos y de las fábricas crea humo y lluvia ácida que amenazan la salud de los habitantes y matan los árboles.

c. **El maluso de químicos**   Insecticidas, fertilizantes y detergentes con fosfatos contaminan el agua de los ríos y lagos.

d. **Basura y desperdicios en las calles**   Las personas maleducadas no echan papeles, botellas y envolturas *(wrappers)* en los basureros.

Soluciones para nuestra comunidad

a. Para conservar energía compre carros, máquinas y aparatos eléctricos más eficientes. Apague las luces y corte el agua cuando posible. Investigue otras formas de energía, por ejemplo: energía solar, nuclear, hidroeléctrica y del viento.

b. Cree leyes *(laws)* que controlan la cantidad de contaminantes que pueden emitir los autos y fábricas y pongan multas *(fines)* para infracciones.

c. Elimine el uso de químicos innecesarios y utilice insecticidas y fertilizantes naturales. Aumente el uso de detergentes sin fosfatos.

d. Eche la basura en los basureros y no eche desperdicios en las aceras o en la calle. Limpie las calles en frente de su casa y en su vecindad.

---

1. ¿Cuáles son los cuatro tipos de problemas que hay en la comunidad?
2. ¿Cuáles son las sugerencias que hacen los estudiantes para cada problema?
3. ¿Hay algunos de los mismos problemas en tu comunidad? ¿Cuáles son?
4. ¿Cuáles son algunos remedios para estos problemas?
5. ¿Tienes tú mucho o poco interés en el medioambiente? ¿Por qué?

B. Write a report about the problems of pollution in your community. Then offer some solutions to the problem.

C. Make a list of twenty things we should do to eliminate the problem of polluting our planet. (Use the **nosotros** commands.)

Así es

La ecología

La protección del ambiente es una meta *(goal)* internacional, pero a pesar de *(in spite of)* conferencias y proclamas entre los líderes, mucha gente hace poco para eliminar la amenaza. Hay muchas razones por las cuales no hemos eliminado los problemas.

Para los países pobres de la América del Sur, la venta *(sale)* de sus recursos naturales ayuda la economía. Por ejemplo, las selvas tropicales de Brasil, Perú, Colombia y otros países producen madera *(wood)* que usamos para los muebles. Cuando cortan los árboles, destruyen el balance ecológico de la selva. La minas también hacen daño a la tierra pero la venta de estos recursos representa trabajo y dinero para mejorar la vida de la gente.

En nuestro país, destruimos bosques para producir papel y materiales para construir casas. Los animales y las plantas que viven en los bosques sufren y desaparecen mientras la cosecha *(harvesting)* de árboles provee *(provides)* trabajo para miles de personas. La conservación de papel ayudaría la conservación de los bosques pero malgastamos papel en abundancia.

Salvar nuestra planeta no es el trabajo de algunas pocas personas. Es urgente que todo el mundo haga su parte. Es importante que conservemos los recursos, que no malgastemos nada y que busquemos mejores maneras de disminuir *(lessen)* el daño que hemos hecho hasta ahora.

Una visita al médico

In this lesson we'll learn what to say in the doctor's office and also how to talk about influencing, emotion, and doubt.

Vocabulario

Una visita al médico   *A visit to the doctor*

Las personas   *The people*

el/la médico(a)	*doctor*	el/la paciente	*patient*
el/la enfermero(a)	*nurse*	el/la farmacista	*pharmacist*
• el/la especialista	*specialist*	el/la recepcionista	*receptionist*
• el/la cirujano(a)	*surgeon*	• el/la radiólogo(a)	*radiologist*

Las condiciones médicas y las enfermedades   *Medical conditions and illnesses/diseases*

• enfermarse	*to get sick*	• estar sano(a)	*to be healthy*
• mejorarse	*to get better*	estar enfermo(a)	*to be sick*
• empeorarse	*to get worse*	• estar embarazada*	*to be pregnant*
sufrir (de)	*to suffer (from)*	• contraer	*to contract, to catch*

* Note: **Embarazada** is a false cognate. To say "embarrassed," use **avergonzado**.

- la diabetes — *diabetes*
- el asma — *asthma*
- la apendicitis — *appendicitis*
- el derrame cerebral — *stroke*
- la fractura de un hueso — *fracture of a bone*
- la torcedura — *sprain*
- la presión arterial alta — *high blood pressure*
- el ataque al corazón — *heart attack*
- el insomnio — *insomnia*
- el cáncer — *cancer*
- la amigdalitis — *tonsillitis*
- la reacción alérgica — *allergic reaction*
- la gripe — *flu*
- el resfriado — *cold*
- el catarro — *headcold*
- la constipación — *nasal congestion, stuffed nose*
- las paperas — *mumps*
- la rubeola — *three-day measles*
- la varicela — *chicken pox*
- el SIDA — *AIDS*

- el envenenamiento con comida   *food poisoning*
- la mononucleosis   *mononucleosis*
- la bronquitis   *bronchitis*
- la pulmonía   *pneumonia*
- el virus   *virus*
- el sarampión   *measles*
  la infección   *infection*
- la conjuntivitis   *"pink-eye"*

- **Los síntomas**   *Symptoms*
  tener…   *to have*
    (omit the article unless followed by an adjective)
  - los mareos   *dizziness*
  - el desmayo   *fainting*
  - los calambres   *cramps*
  - la urticaria   *hives*
  - los escalofríos   *chills*
    la fiebre (alta)   *(high) fever*
    un poco de fiebre   *a little/slight fever*
  - el sarpullido   *rash*
    un dolor…   *a pain, ache*
      de cabeza   *headache*
      de estómago   *stomachache*
      de garganta   *sore throat*
    - de oído   *earache*
    - muscular   *muscle pain*
  - la diarrea   *diarrhea*
  - la náusea   *nausea*
  - el estreñimiento   *constipation*
  - la picazón   *itch*
    la hinchazón   *swelling*
    la tos   *cough*
  - la alergia   *allergy*
- vomitar   *to vomit*
- estornudar   *to sneeze*
- desmayarse   *to faint*
- toser   *to cough*
- sonarse (ue) la nariz   *to blow one's nose*
- marearse   *to get dizzy*
- sentirse (ie, i) malo(a)   *to feel bad*
        débil   *weak*
    - deprimido(a)   *depressed*
      enfermo(a)   *sick*
      nervioso(a)   *nervous*
      cansado(a)   *tired*
    - mareado(a)   *dizzy*

Vocabulario

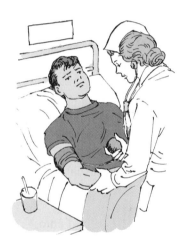

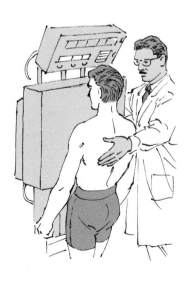

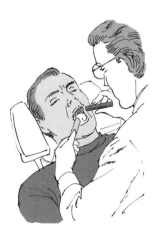

El diagnóstico   *Diagnosis*

ir a •la clínica	*to go to the clinic*
a •la sala de emergencia	*emergency room*
al consultorio	*doctor's office*
al hospital	*hospital*
hacer •una cita	*to make an appointment*
• cancelar la cita	*to cancel the appointment*
• llenar una hoja clínica	*to fill out a medical history*
• un formulario de seguro	*an insurance form*
• pesarse	*to weigh oneself*
subirse a •la balanza	*to get on the scale*
• examinar	*to examine*
abrir la boca	*to open one's mouth*
sacar la lengua	*to stick out one's tongue*
escuchar con •un estetoscopio	*to listen with a stethoscope*
• respirar profundamente	*to breathe deeply*
• tragar	*to swallow*
tomarle* la temperatura	*to take one's temperature*
• la presión arterial	*blood pressure*
• el pulso	*pulse*
• radiografías	*X rays*
hacerle* una prueba de sangre	*to do a blood test*

*Note: use indirect object pronouns with these expressions.

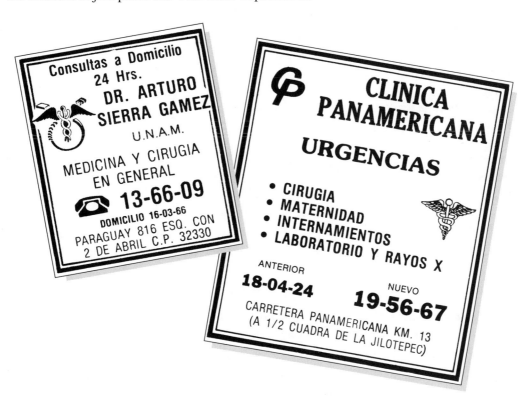

Consultas a Domicilio
24 Hrs.
**DR. ARTURO
SIERRA GAMEZ**
U.N.A.M.
MEDICINA Y CIRUGIA
EN GENERAL
☎ **13-66-09**
DOMICILIO 16-03-66
PARAGUAY 816 ESQ. CON
2 DE ABRIL C.P. 32330

**CLINICA
PANAMERICANA**
URGENCIAS
• CIRUGIA
• MATERNIDAD
• INTERNAMIENTOS
• LABORATORIO Y RAYOS X
ANTERIOR
18-04-24
NUEVO
19-56-67
CARRETERA PANAMERICANA KM. 13
(A 1/2 CUADRA DE LA JILOTEPEC)

Los remedios   *Remedies*

- tratar la enfermedad — *to treat the illness*
  ponerle* •una inyección — *to give a shot to someone*
  ponerle*una enyesadura — *to put a cast on*
- recetar — *to prescribe*
  recomendar (ie) — *to recommend*
    - una pastilla — *a pill*
    - un jarabe para la tos — *cough syrup*
    - una cápsula — *a capsule*
    - unas gotas — *drops*
    - un antiácido — *antacid*
    - una aspirina — *aspirin*
    - un antibiótico — *an antibiotic*
- guardar cama — *to stay in bed*
  beber muchos líquidos — *to drink a lot of liquids*
- operar — *to operate*
- curar — *to cure*

*Note: use indirect object pronouns with these expressions.

Remember to use **el/la/los/las** instead of posessive pronouns with parts of the body.
An indirect object pronoun is used when someone is doing something to someone else.

La paciente sacó <u>la</u> lengua.   *The patient stuck out her tongue.*
La enfermera **le** toma la temperatura al paciente.   *The nurse is taking the patient's temperature.*

1 Describe how you felt the last time you were sick. What was the cause?

EJEMPLO: Hace dos semanas tuve la gripe. Tuve dolor de cabeza, una fiebre alta y tosí mucho.

2 Tell what the doctor does when you go for a physical exam.

EJEMPLO: Cuando el médico me examina, escucha mis pulmones y mi corazón con el
estetoscopio.

3 *Sit-Con*   You are Doctor Molino. Several people come to you during your office hours. They describe their symptoms and you make a diagnosis. Since you are not a real doctor, don't worry if you give the wrong diagnosis.

4 *Sit-Con*   A group of hypochondriacs meet after seeing their doctors and describe their symptoms and their illnesses.

SEQUENCE OF TENSES WITH THE SUBJUNCTIVE

The sequence of tenses in Spanish follows the English pattern with only two exceptions:

1 If the action of the secondary clause is in the future, use the present subjunctive.

2. If the verb in the main clause is in the conditional, use past subjunctive in the secondary clause.

MAIN CLAUSE	SECONDARY CLAUSE
PAST or CONDITIONAL	PAST (IMPERFECT) SUBJUNCTIVE PAST PERFECT (PLUPERFECT) SUBJUNCTIVE
PRESENT	PRESENT SUBJUNCTIVE PRESENT PERFECT SUBJUNCTIVE PAST (IMPERFECT) SUBJUNCTIVE
FUTURE	PRESENT SUBJUNCTIVE

Remember: Use the infinitive for the second verb if there is only one subject.

Yo espero <u>visitar</u> a mi amigo en el hospital.   *I hope to visit my friend in the hospital.*

Esqueletos

main clause (past) + QUE + secondary clause (past subjunctive)

Yo esperaba que visitaras a tu amigo en el hospital.
I hoped that you visited your friend in the hospital.

main clause (past) + QUE + secondary clause (pluperfect subjunctive)

Yo esperaba que hubieras visitado a tu amigo en el hospital.
I hoped that you had visited your friend in the hospital.

| main clause (conditional) | + QUE + | secondary clause (past subjunctive) |

Esperaría que visitaras a tu amigo en el hospital.
I would hope that you visit(ed) your friend in the hospital.

| main clause (present) | + QUE + | secondary clause (present subjunctive) |

Espero que visites a tu amigo en el hospital.
I hope that you will visit your friend in the hospital.

| main clause (present) | + QUE + | secondary clause (present perfect subjunctive) |

Espero que hayas visitado a tu amigo en el hospital.
I hope that you (have) visited your friend in the hospital.

| main clause (present) | + QUE + | secondary clause (past subjunctive) |

Espero que visitaras a tu amigo en el hospital.
I hope that you visited your friend in the hospital.

| main clause (future) | + QUE + | secondary clause (present subjunctive) |

Esperaré que visites a tu amigo en el hospital.
I will hope that you visit your friend in the hospital.

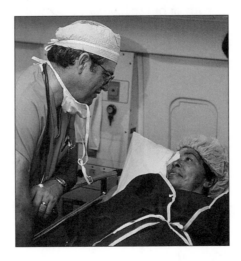

Vocabulario

Expresiones de duda y negación   *Expressions of doubt and denial*

- dudar   *to doubt*
- negar (ie)   *to deny*
- es dudoso   *it is doubtful*
  no creer   *to not believe*
  no pensar (ie)   *to not think*
  no es •cierto   *it is not certain*

no es •evidente   *it is not evident*
no es verdad   *it is not true*
no estar seguro   *to not be sure*
(no) es posible/imposible *it's (not) possible/impossible*
(no) es probable/improbable *it's (not) probable/improbable*

SUBJUNCTIVE WITH DOUBT AND DENIAL

The subjunctive is used when the main clause expresses doubt or denial, because the subject of the main clause does not believe the secondary clause is reality or fact (even if it may actually be so). Many expressions of doubt and denial can be changed to show fact or certainty by changing from or to the negative form. When this happens, the indicative is used.

No creo que <u>sea</u> médico.   *I don't believe that he's a doctor.*
[Since I don't believe it, it's not a fact for me.]

Creo que él <u>es</u> médico.   *I believe he's a doctor.*
[For me it's a fact that he is a doctor.]

No estoy seguro que <u>sea</u> médico.   *I'm not sure he is a doctor.*
[Since I'm not sure, there is doubt for me.]

Estoy seguro que <u>es</u> médico.   *I'm sure he is a doctor.*
[Since I'm sure, it's fact for me.]

Es posible, es imposible, es probable, and **es improbable** always require the subjunctive in the second clause even if used in a negative sense, since they express a reaction to a situation (see page 408).

No es posible que te hayas roto el brazo.   *It's not possible that you have broken your arm.*
Es probable que mejore en seis semanas.   *It's probable that it will be better in six weeks.*

5 Tell some things you are uncertain about.

EJEMPLO: Dudo que tengas fiebre.
No creo que haya un remedio para un resfriado.

6 Tell some things you are certain about.

EJEMPLO: No dudo que la buena salud es lo más importante.

7 Ask your classmates if they believe different things.

EJEMPLO: ¿Crees que encuentren una cura para el catarro?

No, no creo que encuentren una cura.

Sí, creo que encontrarán una cura.

8 **Encuesta** Make a list of several things that you doubt will happen in the future. Ask several classmates their opinions. How many of them share yours? Be careful to use subjunctive only where there is not a fact.

EJEMPLO: ¿Es posible que los humanos vayan a vivir en otras planetas?

Estoy seguro de que van a vivir allí.

No creo que vayan a vivir en otras planetas.

Another situation where the subjunctive is used is when the main clause reacts to the secondary clause with an emotion or a value judgment. In these cases, the subjunctive is used in the secondary clause *even though the situation may be a fact.*

Vocabulario

Expresiones de emoción *Expressions of emotion*

• alegrarse (de)	*to be glad*	sentir (ie, i)	*to be sorry, to regret*
• enojarse	*to be angry*	tener miedo	*to be afraid*
• estar orgulloso(a)	*to be proud*	• temer	*to fear*
• estar encantado(a)	*to be delighted*	gustarle	*to be pleased*
estar triste	*to be sad*	molestarle	*to be bothered*
estar contento(a)	*to be happy*	irritarle	*to be irritated*
• lamentar	*to regret*	sorprenderle	*to be surprised*

Expresiones de juicio *Expressions of judgment*

These expressions are generally impersonal expressions using **ser**. Any tense of **ser** can be used.

• Es raro	*It is rare*	Es bueno/malo	*It is good/bad*
Es mejor	*It is better*	Es importante	*It is important*
Es necesario	*It is necessary*	• Es lógico	*It is logical*
• Es preciso	*It is necessary*	• Es ridículo	*It is ridiculous*
Es una lástima	*It is too bad*	• Más vale	*It is better*
• Es increíble	*It is incredible*		

SUBJUNCTIVE WITH EMOTIONAL REACTION AND VALUE JUDGMENT

When the subject of the main clause reacts positively or negatively to the secondary clause with emotion or a value judgment, the subjunctive is used in the secondary clause *even though the secondary clause may be a fact.*

Juan se alegra de que estés aquí.   *Juan is happy that you are here.*

[It is a fact that you are here, but the subjunctive is used because it expresses Juan's reaction to the situation.]

Era una lástima que el médico no pudiera verlo ayer.   *It's too bad that the doctor couldn't see him yesterday.*

[It is a fact that the doctor couldn't see him yesterday, but the subjunctive is used because **Era una lástima** expresses a value judgment about the situation.]

Remember to use the infinitive for the second verb if there is only one subject and two verbs.

Me alegro de estar aquí.   *I am happy to be here.*

---

9 Tell some situations about which you are happy.

EJEMPLO: Me alegro de que mi familia esté sana.

10 Tell some situations about which you are angry.

EJEMPLO: Me molesta que haya tantos pacientes en el hospital.

11 Following are some things that your friends are doing or did. Tell how you feel about them. (Pay attention to the tense of the subjunctive.)

EJEMPLO: Tu amigo ha estado muy enfermo pero ahora se mejora.
Me alegro de que mi amigo se mejore.

a. Tu amigo ganó un premio en la lotería.
b. Tu amiga va a vivir en otra ciudad.
c. Tu amigo se rompió la pierna.
d. Tu amiga sale con tu novio (o tu amigo sale con tu novia).
e. Tus amigos organizan una fiesta para tu cumpleaños.
f. Tus amigos recibieron buenas notas en la clase de español.
g. Tu amigo perdió su chaqueta nueva.
h. Tus amigos te invitaron a un restaurante elegante para la cena.

12 Tell some situations that you are sorry about.

EJEMPLO: Siento que Diego no haya podido ir a la fiesta.

13 Tell what other people do or do not do that bothered you.

EJEMPLO: Me molestaba que mis padres no me comprendieran.

14 Give your opinion about some things people used to do, did, do, or will do.

EJEMPLO: Es bueno que el médico haya curado al niño.
Es una lástima que Luisa no esté bien.

15 Tell your reaction to some of the things that are happening in the world today.

EJEMPLO: Es increíble que el gobierno no pueda eliminar la pobreza.
Es terrible que los camiones creen tanta contaminación.

16 *Sit-Con*   A friend will be going to live in another country. Tell your reaction and your opinion about what he or she should do to get ready and after arriving.

EJEMPLO: Me alegro de que vayas a España para estudiar.
Es importante que me escribas.

ASDRUBAL GUTTY
ENFERMEDADES CRONICAS
PIEL-CABELLO. Son curables: inútil tratamiento externo, cúrese orgánicamente sin antibióticos. Acné, manchas, calvicie prematura, caspa, piquiña, seborrea, pecas seniles, arrugas, hongos, psoriasis, alergias, verrugas, cicatrices, úlcera varicosa, várices, gota. Ejecutivos y casos especiales consultas privadas a domicilio. Cualquier ciudad. Garantía fotográfica de curación. Cra. 16 N° 39-A-85. Teleinformación: 2880785, 2850110.

ENCUENTRO PERSONAL

While Inés was on a trip to Puerto Rico, she became ill and went to the emergency room to be examined.

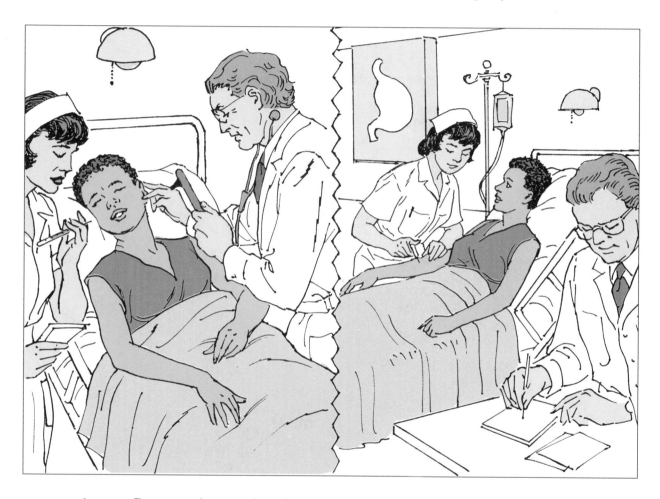

MÉDICO:	Buenas tardes, señorita. ¿Qué tiene?
INÉS:	No sé, doctor, pero tengo dolor de estómago y creo que tengo fiebre. Temo haber comido algo malo. Me siento muy mal.
MÉDICO:	¿Está Ud. vomitando o tiene náusea o diarrea?
INÉS:	No, doctor, pero tengo escalofríos.
MÉDICO:	Abra la boca y saque la lengua, por favor. Ahora respire profundamente mientras yo le escucho el corazón y los pulmones con el estetoscopio. Ahora voy a mirarle los oídos. A veces el dolor de estómago resulta de una infección de los oídos. Hummmmm. Me parece que hay un poco de inflamación.
INÉS:	¿Es serio?

MÉDICO: No puedo decirle ahora, pero no creo que Ud. esté enferma del estómago. *[A la enfermera]* Vamos a tomarle la temperatura y la presión arterial. También quiero que hagan un análisis de sangre y que hagan una radiografía del torso para saber si puede ser que tenga algo en el estómago.

ENFERMERA: Señorita, no tenga Ud. miedo. Es posible que sea solamente la gripe.

            [Después de media hora.]

MÉDICO: Tengo aquí los resultados de las pruebas. Ud. tiene mucha suerte, señorita. La radiografía del estómago resultó negativa. Es probable que esté enferma con una infección de oídos. ¿Es Ud. alérgica a la penicilina?

INÉS: No que yo sepa, doctor.

MÉDICO: Ojalá podamos tratarla con píldoras o una inyección. Si no la sana el antibiótico, es posible que tengamos que hacerle más pruebas, pero dudo que sea necesario. Aquí está su receta. Recomiendo que Ud. descanse en casa hasta que la fiebre se baje. Tome la medicina por diez días y venga a verme en dos semanas.

INÉS: Gracias, doctor. Creía que tenía la apendicitis. Me alegro de que no sea necesario que me operen.

¿Comprendes?

1. ¿Cuáles eran los síntomas que tenía Inés?
2. ¿Cómo se sentía y que temía ella?
3. ¿Qué hizo el médico para examinarla?
4. ¿Qué pruebas quería el médico que la enfermera le hiciera?
5. ¿Qué dice la enfermera que es posible que sea?
6. ¿Y qué cree el médico que pueda ser?
7. ¿Cuál es la diagnosis y que recomienda el médico?

¡Te toca!

Role-play with your classmates: One of you is a patient who complains about certain symptoms. Another one is a doctor and one is a nurse. Decide on a course of treatment.

SERVICIO MEDICO-URGENTE
DIA Y NOCHE
Emergencias Médicas
Consulta General
Cirugía - Partos
Niños - Sueros
SIEMPRE HAY UN MEDICO VELANDO POR SU SALUD LAS 24 HORAS
Tel. 12-73-10
AV. 16 DE SEPTIEMBRE 1128 OTE.
(EN SEGUIDA FARMACIA IRIS)

Leemos y contamos

A. Paulina is writing a letter to her friend Maricela about an interesting experience she had recently.

Querida Maricela,

Esta semana yo tuve una experiencia muy agradable. Una enfermera que conozco me llamó y me preguntó si podría traducir para una mujer hispana en una clínica de la vecindad. Dije que sí, aunque dudaba que pudiera ayudar mucho. Cuando llegué, conocí a Marina, una mujer simpática de cuarenta años que no hablaba ni una palabra de inglés. Ella tenía una infección de los pulmones y quería que yo le dijera al médico los síntomas que tenía. Le ayudé a llenar la hoja clínica y la acompañé mientras hacían varias pruebas. El médico le escuchó los pulmones con el estetoscopio y le tomaron radiografías. La enfermera la pesó en la balanza y le tomó el pulso y la presión arterial. La mujer temía tener algo serio como bronquitis o pulmonía. El médico dijo que no creía que fuera pulmonía. Pero dijo que ella tenía una infección seria y que debería tomar unas píldoras y guardar cama.

Durante este tiempo llegué a conocer a Marina. Ella me contaba mucho de su vida en Honduras y de su familia que vive allí. Ella quería que yo fuera a visitarla en su casa después de curarse. Le dije que con mucho gusto iría a su casa. Me dio mucho placer poder ayudarla y también al mismo tiempo conocer a una persona tan simpática.

1. ¿Por qué fue Paulina a la clínica?
2. ¿Cómo era Marina y cómo estaba?
3. ¿Qué pruebas le hicieron el médico y la enfermera?
4. ¿Qué temía Marina que fuera la enfermedad?
5. ¿Qué creía el médico que tenía y cuáles eran sus recomendaciones?
6. ¿Qué quería Marina que hiciera Paulina?

B. Write about one of your own experiences in a doctor's office or hospital.

ASÍ ES

Asistencia médica en Hispanoamérica

Es frecuente que el viajero en Hispanoamérica encuentre riesgos a la salud que no son comunes en los EE. UU., por ejemplo, la malaria y otras enfermedades tropicales. Si se enferma, se puede ir a un hospital en una ciudad grande o buscar un médico o una clínica recomendados por la Embajada de los Estados Unidos. Así se puede recibir tratamiento moderno con antibióticos o cirugía, si es necesario.

Aunque hay buena asistencia médica en las ciudades grandes de Hispanoamérica, en las regiones rurales no hay tantos médicos ni hospitales modernos y la gente frecuentemente tiene que utilizar tratamientos tradicionales, por ejemplo, el uso de remedios herbales. A veces les sorprende a los viajeros ver la variedad de medicamentos que se puede comprar sin receta en las farmacias. Y en muchos países los farmacistas también pueden poner inyecciones.

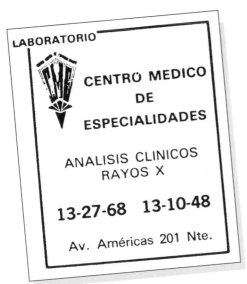

El automóvil y el conducir

In this lesson, we'll be learning about cars and driving. We will also learn more about the subjunctive.

Vocabulario

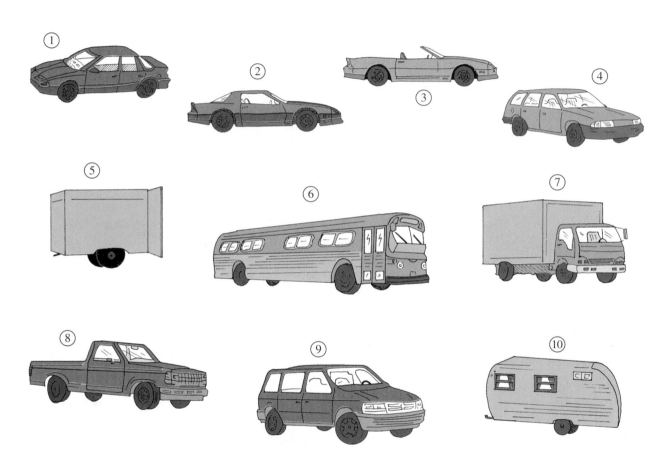

Los automóviles *Automobiles*

- **El transporte** *Transportation*

1. el carro/el automóvil/el coche	car	6. el autobús	bus
2. deportivo	sports car	• 7. el camión	truck
• 3. descapotable	convertible	• 8. la camioneta/•la furgoneta	pickup truck
4. la ranchera	station wagon	9. la furgoneta/•la combi	van
5. el remolque	trailer	• 10. la caravana	camper

Las personas   *People*

- 1. el/la conductor(a) — *driver*
- 2. el/la vendedor(a) de carros — *auto salesperson*
- 3. el/la gerente de la agencia — *agency manager*
- 4. el/la ayudante de la gasolinera — *gas station attendant*
- 5. el/la mecánico(a) — *mechanic*
- 6. el/la policía* — *police officer*
- 7. el/la juez — *judge*

*Note: **la policía** also means *the police*.

Vocabulario

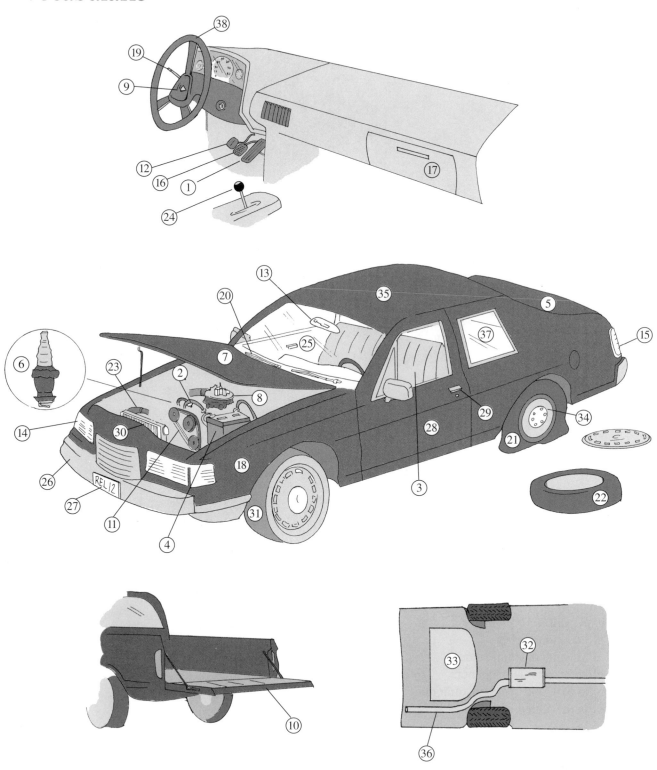

• Las piezas de un automóvil   *Parts of a car*

• 1. el acelerador	*accelerator*		• 20. el limpiaparabrisas	*windshield wiper*
• 2. el alambre	*wire*		• 21. la llanta desinflada	*flat tire*
• 3. el asiento	*seat*		• 22. la llanta de repuesta	*spare tire*
• 4. la batería	*battery*		• 23. la manguera	*hose*
• 5. el baúl/el portaequipaje	*trunk*		• 24. la palanca de cambios	*gear shift lever*
• 6. la bujía	*spark plug*		• 25. el parabrisas	*windshield*
• 7. la capota	*hood*		• 26. el parachoques	*bumper*
• 8. el carburador	*carburetor*		• 27. la placa	*license plate*
• 9. el claxón/•la bocina	*horn*		• 28. la puerta	*door*
• 10. la compuerta trasera	*tailgate*		• 29. el puño de la puerta	*door handle*
• 11. la correa del ventilador	*fanbelt*		• 30. el radiador	*radiator*
• 12. el embrague	*clutch*		• 31. la rueda	*wheel*
• 13. el espejo •retrovisor	*rearview mirror*		• 32. el silenciador	*muffler*
• 14. el farol delantero	*headlight*		• 33. el tanque de gasolina	*gas tank*
• 15. el farol trasero	*taillight*		• 34. el tapacubos	*hubcap*
• 16. el freno	*brake*		• 35. el techo	*roof*
• 17. la guantera	*glove compartment*		• 36. el tubo de escape	*exhaust pipe*
• 18. el guardabarros	*fender*		• 37. la ventanilla	*window*
• 19. la intermitente	*turn signal*		• 38. el volante	*steering wheel*

Las reparaciones   *Repairs*

   1. tener •un accidente
   • 2. reparar un auto/coche/carro
   • 3. arreglar un motor descompuesto
   • 4. instalar un silenciador
   • 5. llenar el tanque con gasolina
   • 6. revisar el aceite y el aire
   • 7. funcionar bien/mal

to have an accident
to repair a car
to repair/fix a broken-down engine/motor
to install a muffler
to fill the tank with gas
to check the oil and air
to run/work well/badly

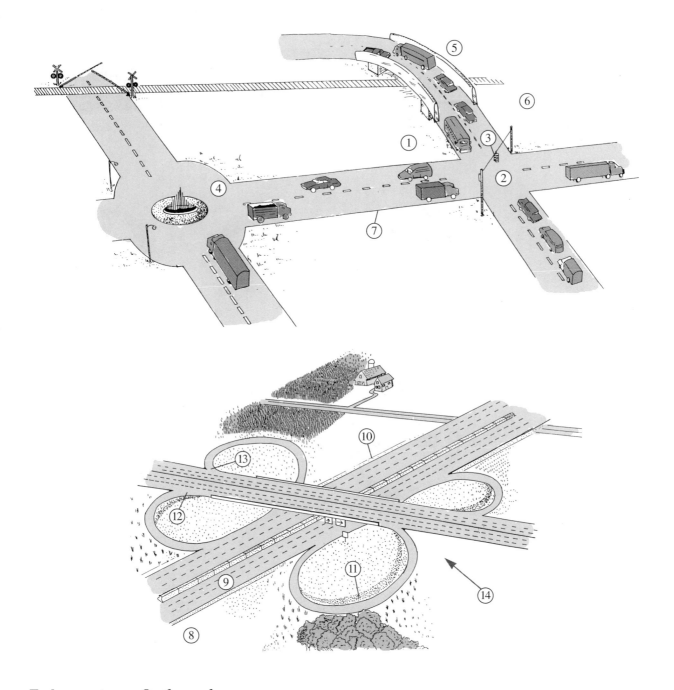

En la carretera   *On the road*

- 1. el tránsito/•la circulación — *traffic*
- 2. la bocacalle/el cruce — *intersection*
- 3. el semáforo — *traffic light*
- 4. la glorieta — *traffic circle*
- 5. el puente — *bridge, overpass*
- 6. la hora punta — *rush hour*
- 7. la carretera — *highway*
- 8. la autopista — *expressway, freeway*
- 9. el carril — *lane*
- 10. el arcén — *shoulder (of the road)*
- 11. la cuneta — *ditch*
- 12. la entrada — *entrance*
- 13. la salida — *exit*
- 14. el trébol — *cloverleaf*

Señales de tránsito   *Traffic signs*

- una vía   *one-way*
- alto/•pare   *stop*
- señal de unión   *merge*
- prohibido estacionarse   *no parking*
    - sobrepasar   *no passing*
    - el giro completo   *no U-turn*
    - doblar la derecha/izquierda   *no right/left turn*
- cruce de •ferrocarriles   *railroad crossing*
- doble vía   *two-way traffic*
- ceda el paso   *yield*
- parada de autobús   *bus stop*

La ley de la carretera   *The law of the road*

• abrocharse el cinturón de seguridad	*to buckle your safety belt*
manejar/•conducir con cuidado	*to drive carefully*
• acelerar al límite de velocidad	*to accelerate to the speed limit*
ir más despacio	*to slow down*
parar en la esquina	*to stop at the corner*
poner en •reversa	*to put into reverse*
ponerle •una multa por…	*to give someone a fine/ticket for . . .*
• el exceso de velocidad	*excessive speed, speeding*
• una infracción de la ley	*violation of the law*
manejar sin •licencia	*driving without a license*
• desobedecer una señal de tránsito	*disobeying a traffic signal*
• estacionarse en una zona prohibida	*parking in a no-parking zone*
• doblar ilegalmente	*making an illegal turn*
buscar •estacionamiento	*to look for parking*
conseguir un carnet/permiso de conducir	*to get a driver's license*

1 Find a picture of a car or other vehicle in a magazine or draw one of your own. Label the parts.

2 *Sit-Con*   You are having trouble with your car. Describe the difficulty to the mechanic and arrange to have it repaired.

EJEMPLO: Mi coche no funciona bien.

            ¿Cuál es el problema?

3 Your friend is learning to drive. Explain what he or she should do to get to your house from school. Use roadway markings and driving instructions.

EJEMPLO: Cuando llegues a la calle del estacionamiento, dobla a la derecha y ve al semáforo en el cruce de Lincoln y Adams…

4 *Sit-Con*   Your friend just had a traffic accident. Find out what happened.

EJEMPLO: Acabo de tener un accidente con mi carro.

            Espero que no te hayas hecho daño *(get hurt)*.

            No, pero…

You have already learned that the subjunctive is used with persuasion because the secondary clause is not a fact in relation to the main clause. Following are some other situations where the subjunctive is used when the statement of the secondary clause is not a fact or reality:

- with the expressions **ojalá** *(hopefully)* and **tal vez** or **quizás** *(maybe, perhaps)*

- when the outcome is uncertain

- when the event has not happened yet

- when the existence of an item is uncertain

Now let's look at some expressions for each of these situations that may require the subjuctive.

OJALÁ, TAL VEZ, AND QUIZÁS

The expressions **ojalá (que)** *(hopefully)*, **tal vez** or **quizás** *(maybe, perhaps)* always take the subjunctive because the statement that follows them is not a fact. These expressions do not require a two-clause sentence. The use of **que** with **ojalá** is optional.

Ojalá (que) venga a la fiesta.   *Hopefully he'll come to the party.*
Ojalá (que) viniera a la fiesta.   *Hopefully he came to the party.*
Quizás (Tal vez) sea el silenciador.   *Maybe it's the muffler.*

5 *Sit-Con*   Your parents have told you that they bought a car for your birthday but they won't tell you anything about it. Tell your friend what you hope the car will be like.

EJEMPLO: Ojalá que sea rojo. Tal vez tenga un CD.

6 Use the preceding expressions to tell what you think might happen to you in the future.

EJEMPLO: Ojalá que yo vaya a la universidad.
            Tal vez yo viva en otra ciudad.

Vocabulario

Conjunciones de resultado incierto   *Conjunctions of uncertain outcome*

- para que   *so that*
- sin que   *without*
- a menos que *unless*

- con tal que   *provided that*
- en caso (de) que   *in case*

SUBJUNCTIVE WITH UNCERTAIN OUTCOME

When the outcome of the action of the main clause is not certain, the subjunctive is used in the secondary clause. The conjunctions of uncertain outcome <u>always</u> require the subjunctive.

Trabajo <u>para que</u> compremos un carro.   *I'm working <u>so that</u> we may buy a car.*

Pagó la multa <u>sin que</u> sus padres lo supieran.   *She paid the fine <u>without</u> her parents knowing about it.*

Repararemos el carro <u>a menos que</u> ya no existan las piezas.   *We'll repair the car <u>unless</u> the parts no longer exist.*

Mis padres me comprarán un carro <u>con tal que</u> yo pague los seguros.   *My parents will buy me a car <u>provided</u> I pay the insurance.*

Te llamaré <u>en caso que</u> mi hermana conduzca a la fiesta.   *I'll call you <u>in case</u> my sister drives to the party.*

When both clauses have the same subject, the preposition followed by an infinitive is used instead of a conjunction with a clause.

Trabajo para comprar un carro.   *I'm working to buy a car.*

Pagó la multa sin sacar dinero del banco.   *She paid the fine without taking money out of the bank.*

---

7 Tell some things that will happen provided something else happens first.
Use **con tal que** + *subjunctive.*

EJEMPLO: Compraré un coche con tal que mis padres me den dinero para mi cumpleaños.
Tendremos una fiesta en clase con tal que todos traigan la comida.

8 Tell the reason why some things are done. Use **para que** + *subjunctive.*

EJEMPLO: El policía se estaciona en la esquina para que todos puedan verlo.
Mi hermana vive en el campo para que su familia tenga muchos animales.

9 Tell what people did, do, or will do without something else happening. Use **sin que** + *subjunctive.*

EJEMPLO: Mi primo salió sin que yo lo supiera.
Los estudiantes hablan sin que el profesor los oiga.
Sus hijos organizarán una fiesta sin que ella los ayude.

10 Tell some things that will happen unless something else happens. Use a **menos que** + *subjunctive.*

EJEMPLO: Obtendré los mapas para el viaje a menos que la oficina esté cerrada.
Nos reuniremos en México a menos que mi amigo no pueda viajar.

AUNQUE

Aunque *(although, even though)* is followed by the subjunctive when the action is not a reality (from the speaker's point of view) and the indicative when it is viewed as a reality.

Yo lo ayudaré aunque él <u>es</u> tacaño.
I will help him although/even though he <u>is</u> stingy. [I already know he's stingy.]

Yo lo ayudaré aunque él <u>sea</u> tacaño.
I will help him even though he <u>may be</u> stingy. [I don't know if he is or isn't stingy.]

11 Tell some things that will happen even though the situation may not be a fact.
Use **aunque** + *subjunctive.*

EJEMPLO: Lo haré aunque no sea correcto.

12 Tell some things that did not happen even though what someone did was a fact.
Use **aunque** + *indicative.*

EJEMPLO: Aunque me pidió ayuda, no lo ayudé.

Vocabulario

Conjunciones de tiempo   *Conjunctions of time*

cuando	*when*
mientras que	*while*
después (de) que	*after*
hasta que	*until*
• tan pronto como	*as soon as*
antes (de) que	*before*

SUBJUNCTIVE WITH A FUTURE EVENT

When time conjunctions join two clauses, the subjunctive is used in the secondary clause when the event is in the future relative to the main clause. If the event has already occurred relative to the main clause, the indicative is used in the secondary clause.

Compare these sentences:

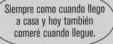

Siempre como cuando llego a casa y hoy también comeré cuando llegue.

Comeré <u>cuando</u> **llegue** a casa.   *I will eat <u>when</u> I arrive home.*
  [I haven't arrived yet; it's not a reality.]
Siempre como <u>cuando</u> **llego** a casa.   *I always eat <u>when</u> I arrive home.*
  [My arriving is a reality.]
Ayer yo comí <u>cuando</u> **llegué** a casa.   *Yesterday I ate when I*
  arrived home.   [It's a reality that I arrived.]

Mañana hablaremos <u>mientras</u> el mecánico **trabaje**.
  Tomorrow we'll talk <u>while</u> the mecanic works.
Siempre hablamos <u>mientras</u> el mecánico **trabaja**.
  We always talk <u>while</u> the mechanic works.

Mañana hablaremos mientras el mecánico trabaje.

Pablo no dormirá <u>después</u> que le **digamos** lo que pasó.
  Pablo won't sleep <u>after</u> we tell him what happened.
Pablo no durmió <u>después</u> que le **dijimos** lo que pasó.
  Pablo didn't sleep <u>after</u> we told him what happened.

No saldré <u>hasta que</u> **termine**.   *I won't leave <u>until</u> he finishes.*
No salí <u>hasta que</u> **terminó**.   *I didn't leave <u>until</u> he finished.*

Venderé la casa <u>tan pronto como</u> **pueda**.   *I will sell the house <u>as soon as</u> I can.*
Vendí la casa <u>tan pronto como</u> **pude**.   *I sold the house <u>as soon as</u> I could.*

Venderé la casa tan pronto como pueda.

Antes (de) que (Before) <u>always</u> takes subjunctive because its meaning puts the action in the future in relation to the main verb.

Mi mamá me besará <u>antes de que</u> yo **salga**.   *My mom will kiss me <u>before</u> I leave.*
Mi mamá me besa <u>antes de que</u> yo **salga**.   *My mom kisses me <u>before</u> I leave.*
Ella me besó <u>antes de que</u> yo **saliera**.   *She kissed me <u>before</u> I left.*

13 Write about some things that may happen in the future. Use the preceding conjunctions (joining words) so that you need the subjunctive for the secondary verb.

EJEMPLO: Pagaré la multa tan pronto como llegue mi cheque.
Mis parientes en Arizona me visitarán después de que yo llegue a Tucson.

14 What are some things you did and will do before other people? Use **antes de que** + *subjunctive*.

EJEMPLO: Recibí mi permiso antes de que Roberto recibiera el suyo.
Aprenderé a nadar antes de que mi amiga aprenda.

15 Tell some things that happened when something else was happening. Use the indicative because these events are reality.

EJEMPLO: Sus padres le compraron un carro cuando cumplió diez y ocho años.
Mi carro no funcionó cuando necesitó una batería.

16 Tell some things that happen when something else happens. Use the indicative because you are talking about reality.

EJEMPLO: Tomo el autobús cuando mis padres no me llevan en carro.
Duermo en la sala cuando mi tía nos visita.

17 Tell some things that will happen when something else happens. Remember to use the subjunctive since the second event is not a fact yet.

EJEMPLO: Iré a casa cuando venga el autobús.
Ana aprenderá a conducir cuando su padre le enseñe.

SUBJUNCTIVE WITH UNCERTAIN EXISTENCE

When the existence of a person or an item is uncertain from the speaker's point of view, the subjunctive is used. When it is known that the thing or person exists, then the indicative is used.

Busco un libro que tenga muchas fotos de animales.
I'm looking for a book that has a lot of photographs of animals.

Tengo un libro que tiene muchas fotos de animales.
I have a book that has a lot of photographs of animals.

The following verbs in the main clause often introduce a secondary clause of uncertain existence.

buscar   *to look for*
preferir   *to prefer*
necesitar   *to need*
querer, desear   *to want*
gustaría   *would like*
no había/hay/habrá   *there wasn't/isn't/won't be*
¿Había/Hay/Habrá?   *Was there/Is there/Will there be?*
no tener   *to not have*

When **nadie, nada,** or **ninguno** is used in the main clause, the subjunctive is used in the secondary clause because the person or thing does not exist.

No hay nadie que pueda hacerlo.   *There is no one who can do it.*

No leímos nada que explicara este asunto.   *We didn't read anything that explained this matter.*

The **personal a** is used only with an existing person.

Buscarán un hombre que pueda repararlo.   *They will look for a man who can repair it.*
Buscarán al hombre que puede repararlo.   *They will look for the man who can repair it.*

18 Compare these sentences and tell why the indicative or subjunctive is used for each.

a. Necesitamos un carro que <u>funcione</u> bien.
   Necesitamos el carro que <u>funciona</u> bien.
b. Busco una casa que <u>esté</u> en la playa.
   Busco la casa que <u>está</u> en la playa.
c. Antonio prefiere una amiga que le <u>diga</u> la verdad.
   Antonio prefiere a la amiga que le <u>dice</u> la verdad.
d. Deseo un mecánico que <u>sepa</u> mucho.
   Deseo al mecánico que <u>sabe</u> mucho.
e. Me gustaría un carro que <u>sea</u> económico.
   Me gustaría el carro que <u>es</u> económico.

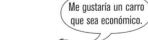

Me gustaría un carro que sea económico.

f. Hay un mecánico que <u>sabe</u> repararlo.
¿Hay un mecánico que <u>sepa</u> repararlo?
No hay mecánico que <u>sepa</u> repararlo.

g. Tengo un mecánico que <u>sabe</u> mucho.
No tengo un mecánico que <u>sepa</u> mucho.

h. ¿Conoces un mecánico que <u>pueda</u> reparar tu carro?
Sí, conozco a alguien que <u>puede</u> repararlo.
No, no conozco a nadie que <u>pueda</u> repararlo.

19 Tell your partner what kind of car you would like to have in the future. Use the subjunctive since the car is not a reality for you yet.

EJEMPLO: Quiero un carro que tenga un radio estéreo.
Quiero un carro que use electricidad en vez de gasolina.

20 Have you thought about the kind of person you would like to marry? Take turns with your partner, telling the qualities you are looking for in your future husband or wife.

EJEMPLO: Quiero un(a) esposo(a) que hable español.
Busco alguien que sepa cocinar.

21 Create the perfect school. Take turns with your partner, telling the things you would want to have in an ideal school.

EJEMPLO: Me gustaría una escuela que tenga una piscina olímpica.
Quisiera profesores que den exámenes fáciles.

22 *Sit-Con*   You and a friend want to get part-time jobs for the summer. Take turns telling some of the things that you would like to have in the job.

EJEMPLO: Me gustaría tener un trabajo que me pague bien.
Necesito un trabajo donde la gente sea simpática.

23 Ask your partner if various things exist. Your partner will respond according to his or her knowledge of the thing's existence.

EJEMPLO: ¿Hay carros que tengan el volante a la derecha?

Sí, hay carros que tienen el volante a la derecha. / No, no hay carros que tengan el volante a la derecha.

SUMMARY OF SUBJUNCTIVE USAGE

SENTENCE PATTERN

main clause + QUE + *secondary clause* ⟨ indicative / subjunctive

SEQUENCE OF TENSES

MAIN CLAUSE	SECONDARY CLAUSE
PAST or CONDITIONAL	PAST (IMPERFECT) SUBJUNCTIVE PAST PERFECT (PLUPERFECT) SUBJUNCTIVE
PRESENT	PRESENT SUBJUNCTIVE PRESENT PERFECT SUBJUNCTIVE PAST (IMPERFECT) SUBJUNCTIVE
FUTURE	PRESENT SUBJUNCTIVE

WHEN TO USE THE SUBJUNCTIVE

1. Relative to the main clause, the secondary clause is not a reality (yet)
   - **como si** clause
   - **si** clause with conditional
   - action in the future
       persuasion
       future time
       uncertain outcome
   - uncertain existence

2. when the emphasis is on the way the subject of the main clause reacts to the secondary clause
   - doubt or denial
   - emotional reaction
   - value judgment

3. softened requests with **querer/poder/deber**

ENCUENTRO PERSONAL

Shortly after she got her driver's license, Rosita bought an old car. Now it isn't running properly and she takes it to a garage for repairs.

ROSITA: Buenos días, señor. Busco un mecánico que pueda arreglar mi coche.

MECÁNICO: A su servicio, señorita. ¿Qué problema tiene?

ROSITA: No creo que sea nada muy serio. Sale mucho humo del escape y el silenciador hace ruido. Es posible que los frenos no funcionen bien tampoco. Hay una vibración en el volante y la intermitente no funciona todo el tiempo. ¿Cree Ud. que pueda repararlo?

MECÁNICO: Sí, cómo no, señorita. ¿Para cuándo necesita el coche?

ROSITA: Esperaba que Uds. terminaran esta mañana. Pensaba ir de compras esta tarde.

MECÁNICO: Lo siento, señorita, pero no creo que sea posible arreglarlo en medio día. Es probable que Ud. necesite un nuevo silenciador y que yo tenga que instalarle nuevos frenos. En cuanto al humo, es necesario que revisemos el motor antes de que yo sepa la causa. La vibración puede ser causada por una llanta defectuosa, y es posible que la intermitente tenga un alambre roto. Preferimos que Ud. deje el carro aquí hasta que pueda revisarlo para que tengamos tiempo suficiente.

ROSITA: ¡Dios mío! Ojalá mi amiga pueda prestarme su bicicleta hasta que Uds. me devuelvan el coche.

MECÁNICO: No se preocupe Ud., señorita. La llamaremos tan pronto como terminemos con el trabajo. Recomendamos que Ud. busque a alguien que le preste otro carro en caso de que no podamos terminar para mañana.

ROSITA: Ojalá mi amiga me preste su coche. ¡Es imposible ir al banco sin coche!

¿Comprendes?

1. ¿Qué busca Rosita?
2. ¿Cuáles son los problemas que tiene su coche?
3. ¿Para cuándo quiere Rosita el coche? ¿Por qué?
4. ¿Qué le dice el mecánico?
5. ¿Qué recomienda el mecánico?
6. ¿Qué espera Rosita? ¿Por qué?

¡Te toca!

Describe real or imaginary problems of your car with a classmate and see if you can agree on what to do.

Leemos y contamos

A. Rosita is writing about the misadventure she had when she went to the bank in a car she borrowed.

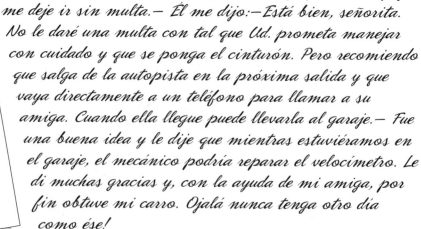

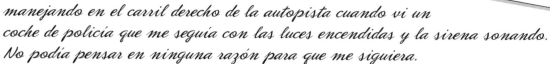

¡Qué día más terrible! Porque mi carro estaba con el mecánico, yo necesitaba alguien que me prestara un carro. Cuando mi amiga Inés oyó de los problemas con mi carro, me prestó el suyo para que yo pudiera ir al banco. El mecánico no repararía mi carro sin que le diera un depósito. Después de salir del banco con cien dólares para que el mecánico pudiera empezar a arreglar mi coche, estaba manejando en el carril derecho de la autopista cuando vi un coche de policía que me seguía con las luces encendidas y la sirena sonando. No podía pensar en ninguna razón para que me siguiera.

Cuando detuve el carro en el arcén, el policía me dijo: —Lo siento, señorita, pero temo que tenga que ponerle una multa por exceso de velocidad. ¿Me permite ver su carnet de conducir?— Yo estaba muy avergonzada. Nunca había recibido una multa. Entonces el policía me dijo: —Siento decirle que la placa está expirada y que tengo que darle otra multa por no abrocharse el cinturón de seguridad.— Le expliqué que no era mi coche y que no funcionaba el velocímetro. Además le dije que no estaba acostumbrada a abrocharme en ese coche y que acababa de sacar dinero para pagar las reparaciones de mi coche.

Le dije: —Señor policía, yo sé que Ud. debe darme unas multas, pero generalmente manejo con mucho cuidado. Espero que Ud. tenga paciencia y que me deje ir sin multa.— Él me dijo:—Está bien, señorita. No le daré una multa con tal que Ud. prometa manejar con cuidado y que se ponga el cinturón. Pero recomiendo que salga de la autopista en la próxima salida y que vaya directamente a un teléfono para llamar a su amiga. Cuando ella llegue puede llevarla al garaje.— Fue una buena idea y le dije que mientras estuviéramos en el garaje, el mecánico podría reparar el velocímetro. Le di muchas gracias y, con la ayuda de mi amiga, por fin obtuve mi carro. Ojalá nunca tenga otro día como ése!

1. ¿Dónde estaba Rosita cuando vio el policía?
2. ¿Qué hizo ella cuando lo vio?
3. ¿Qué le dijo el policía?
4. ¿Qué infracciones de la ley mencionó el policía?
5. ¿Qué excusas tenía Rosita?
6. ¿Qué le recomendó el policía que hiciera Rosita?

B. Write about one of your own experiences with traffic violations or car repairs.

Así es

Palabras regionales

En varias partes del mundo, personas que hablan la misma lengua frecuentemente usan distintas palabras para referirse a las mismas cosas y a veces hablan con una pronunciación diferente. Por ejemplo, en México se dice «carro» pero en España prefieren «coche», y «auto» se comprende en todas partes. Lo mismo ocurre con «autobús» que es la palabra que se usa en la mayor parte del mundo hispanoparlante. Pero en México se dice «camión» y en Cuba se dice «guagua».

¿Qué podemos hacer con tantas diferencias? No es posible aprender todos los variantes de una palabra para cada dialecto. Es recomendable aprender una palabra de uso más general y si viajas a un lugar donde se usa otra palabra, puedes aprender la palabra en el dialecto local.

HISPANOAMÉRICA	ESPAÑA
alberca, pileta	piscina
ándele	venga
anteojos, lentes	gafas
apartamento	piso
apurarse	darse prisa
auto, carro	coche
baño	servicio
boleto, pasaje	billete
enojado	enfadado
omnibús, camión	autobús
cabellos	pelo
cacahuate, maní	cacahuete
compadre	amigo
cuadra	manzana
chícharo	guisante
descomponerse	estropearse
empacar	hacer la maleta

Vocabulary

⚛ Spanish-English ⚛

This glossary contains all the vocabulary introduced in **Compañeros, Spanish for Communication, Books 1 and 2.** The reference number in bold following each entry indicates the unit and lesson in which each word or expression first appears in Book 2. The second number indicates the unit and lesson in which each word or expression first appeared in Book 1.

A

a   to, at   **I.1,** I.9
a casa   home   **II.4**
a la derecha de   to the right of   **II.1,** III.2
a la izquierda de   to the left of   **II.1,** III.2
a menos que   unless   **IV.5**
a menudo   often   **II.5**
a pesar de   in spite of   **IV.1**
a pie   on foot   **II.1,** III.4
¿A qué hora es...   What time is . . . ?   **I.1**
a rayas   striped   **II.2**
a través de   across   **II.1,** III.3
a veces   sometimes   **II.5,** I.5
la **abeja**   bee   **I.5,** III.6
abierto(a)   open(ed)   **III.5**
el/la **abogado(a)**   lawyer   **I.2,** II.5
abordar   to board   **IV.1**
abrazar   to hug   **III.2**
el **abrazo**   hug   **III.2,** I.1
el **abrelatas**   can opener   **III.4**
el **abrigo**   coat   I.5
abril   April   **I.1,** I.9
abrir   to open   **I.1,** IV.3
abrocharse   to fasten   **IV.5**
la **abuela**   grandmother   **I.2,** I.3
el **abuelo**   grandfather   **I.2,** I.3
los **abuelos**   grandparents   **I.2,** I.3
aburrido(a) (estar)   bored   **I.3,** III.1
aburrido(a) (ser)   boring   **I.2,** II.2
aburrirse   to get bored   **III.2**
acabar de   to have just   **II.5,** IV.2
aceptar   to accept   IV.1
el **accidente**   accident   **IV.5**
el **aceite**   oil   **IV.5**
el **acelerador**   accelerator   **IV.5**
acelerar   to accelerate   **IV.5**
aceptar   to accept   **III.5,** IV.1
Achís   Achoo   I.4
ácido(a)   acid   **IV.3**
aconsejar   to advise   **IV.3**
el **acordeón**   accordion   **III.1**

acostarse (ue)   to go to bed   **III.2,** IV.5
la **actividad**   activity   **I.1,** IV.1
el **actor**   actor   **I.2,** II.5
la **actriz**   actress   **I.2,** II.5
acuático(a)   aquatic   **I.5,** III.6
adelante   straight ahead   **II.4**
Adiós   Good-bye   **I.1,** I.1
admirar   to admire   **II.2**
¿Adónde?   Where (to)?   **II.1,** I.8
la **aduana**   customs   **IV.1**
advertir (ie, i)   to warn   **IV.3**
el/la **aeromozo(a)**   flight attendant   **I.2**
el **aeropuerto**   airport   **II.1**
el **aerosol**   aerosol   **IV.3**
afeitarse   to shave   **III.2,** IV.5
las **afueras**   suburbs   **II.1,** III.3
la **agencia**   agency   **IV.5**
el/la **agente**   agent   **I.2,** II.5
agitado(a)   upset   **I.3,** III.1
agosto   August   **I.1,** I.9
el/la **agricultor(a)**   farmer   **I.2,** II.5
el **agua** *(f.)*   water   **I.5,** I.6
el **agua dulce** *(f.)*   fresh water   **IV.3**
el **aguacate**   avocado   **II.3**
la **ahijada**   goddaughter   **I.2,** II.4
el **ahijado**   godson   **I.2,** II.4
ahora   now   **II.5,** I.3
ahumar   to smoke (food)   **II.3**
el **aire**   air   **IV.3,** IV.6
el **ajedrez**   chess   **III.1**
el **ajo**   garlic   **II.3,** IV.2
al (a+el)   to the   **II.1,** III.4
al + *infinitive*   on, upon, while   **II.1**
al lado de   beside, next to   **II.1,** III.2
al otro lado de   on the other side of   **II.1,** III.2
al vapor   steamed   **II.3**
el **alambre**   wire   **IV.5**
el **albañil**   bricklayer   **I.2**
la **albóndiga**   meatball   **II.3**
la **alcoba**   bedroom   **II.1,** I.7
alegrarse (de)   to be happy   **III.2**
alegre   cheerful, happy   **I.2,** II.2

el **alemán**   German (language)   **I.5**, II.3
Alemania   Germany   II.3
la **alergia**   allergy   **IV.4**
alérgico(a)   allergic   **IV.4**
el **alfabeto**   alphabet   **I.1**, I.2
el **alfiler de corbata**   tie tack   **II.2**
la **alfombra**   carpet   **III.4**
el **álgebra** *(f.)*   algebra   **I.5**, IV.4
algo   something   **II.5**, I.10
el **algodón**   cotton   **II.2**
alguien   someone   **I.1**, IV.4
alguna manera (de…)   some way   **III.4**
alguna parte   somewhere   **III.4**
alguna vez   some time   **II.5**
algunas veces   sometimes   **II.5**, II.1
alguno(a)   some   **III.4**, IV.4
alimentar   to feed   **IV.6**
el **alimento**   food   **IV.2**
allí   there   **I.1**, I.3
el **almacén**   department store   **II.1**, III.2
la **almeja**   clam   **I.5**, III.6
la **almohada**   pillow   **III.4**
almorzar (ue)   to eat lunch   **II.3**, IV.2
el **almuerzo**   lunch   **II.3**, I.6
la **alpaca**   alpaca   **II.2**
alrededor de   around, surrounding   **II.1**, III.2
alto(a)   high, tall (in height)   **I.1**, I.7
alto(a)   loud   **I.1**, I.1
alto (street sign)   stop   **IV.5**
la **altura**   altitude, height   **III.3**
el **aluminio**   aluminum   **IV.3**
el/la **alumno**   pupil   **I.2**
el **ama de casa** *(f.)*   homemaker   **I.2**, II.5
amable   courteous, kind   **I.2**, II.2
amarillo(a)   yellow   **I.4**, I.7
ambiciosamente   ambitiously   **II.5**
ambicioso(a)   ambitious   **I.2**, II.2
amenazado(a)   endangered, threatened   **IV.3**
amenazar   to endanger, to threaten   **IV.3**
el/la **americano(a)**   American   II.3
la **amigdalitis**   tonsillitis   **IV.4**
el/la **amigo(a)**   friend   **I.2**, I.2
amistoso(a)   friendly   **I.2**, II.2
anaranjado(a)   orange   **I.4**, I.7
ancho(a)   wide   **I.4**, I.7
el **anfibio**   amphibian   **I.5**, III.6
el/la **anfitrión(ona)**   host, hostess   **III.5**
el **anillo**   ring   **I.5**
el **animal**   animal   **I.5**, I.6
el **aniversario**   anniversary   **III.5**
anteayer   day before yesterday   **II.5**, I.9
los **anteojos**   glasses (eye)   **II.2**
antés (de)   before   **II.1**, II.1
antes de que   before   **IV.5**

el **antiácido**   antacid   **IV.4**
el **antibiótico**   antibiotic   **IV.4**
antiguo(a)   ancient, old, former   **I.4**, IV.3
antipático(a)   mean, not nice   **I.2**, II.2
añadir   to add   **II.3**, IV.2
el **año**   year, grade in school   **I.1**, I.3
el **Año Nuevo**   New Year   **III.3**
el **año pasado**   last year   II.1
apagar   to turn off   **IV.3**
el **aparador**   buffet   **III.4**
el **apartamento**   apartment   **II.1**, I.7
el **apellido**   last name   **I.1**, I.2
la **apendicitis**   appendicitis   **IV.4**
el **apio**   celery   **II.3**, IV.2
aprender   to learn   **II.5**, I.10
aprobar (ue)   to pass (a test, an exam)   **II.5**, IV.4
los **apuntes**   notes (information)   **II.5**, IV.4
aquel(la)   that (far)   **I.4**, III.3
aquello   that *(indefinite)*   **I.4**, III.3
aquellos(as)   those   **I.4**, III.3
aquí   here   **I.1**, I.3
la **araña**   spider   **I.5**, I.6
el **arándano**   blueberry   **II.3**, IV.2
el **árbol**   tree   **III.3**, IV.5
la **arcada de vídeo**   arcade   **IV.2**
el **arcén**   shoulder of road   **IV.5**
el **archivador**   file cabinet   **I.4**, I.8
el **arco iris**   rainbow   **II.1**
la **ardilla**   squirrel   **I.5**, I.6
la **arena**   sand   **III.5**
la **aritmética**   arithmetic   **I.5**
el **armario**   closet, locker, cabinet   **I.4**, I.8
la **arquería**   archery   **III.1**
el/la **arquitecto(a)**   architect   **I.2**, II.5
arreglar   to arrange   **III.2**; to fix   **IV.5**
arreglar(se)   to fix up (oneself)   **III.2**
el **arroz**   rice   **II.3**, IV.2
el **arte** *(f.)*   art   **I.5**, I.9
el/la **artista**   artist   **I.2**, II.5
asado(a)   broiled   **II.3**
asar   to broil   **II.3**
el **ascensor**   elevator   **II.1**
así   so, thus   **I.1**, I.1
así, así   so-so   I.1
¡Así es!   That's the way it is!   **I.1**, I.1
el **asiento**   seat   **IV.5**
asistir (a)   to attend   **II.5**, IV.3
el **asma**   asthma   **IV.4**
la **aspiradora**   vacuum cleaner   **III.4**
la **aspirina**   aspirin   **IV.4**
asustado(a)   frightened   **I.3**
el **ataque al corazón**   heart attack   **IV.4**
atlético(a)   athletic   **I.2**, II.2

atrás behind, in back of **III.1**
atravesar (ie) to cross (a street) **III.1**
el **atún** tunafish **II.3**
el **aula** (*f.*) classroom **I.4**, I.8
aumentar to add to **IV.3**
aunque although **IV.5**, IV.3
el **auto** car **II.1**, I.8
el **autobús** bus **II.1**, I.8
el **automóvil** automobile **IV.1**, II.2
la **autopista** expressway **II.4**
la **avena** oats **II.3**, IV.2
la **avenida** avenue **II.4**, IV.3
avergonzado(a) embarrassed **IV.4**
el **avión** airplane **II.1**, I.8
ayer yesterday **II.5**, I.9
el/la **ayudante** attendant **I.2**
ayudar (a) to help **II.5**, IV.1
la **azotea** attic **II.1**
el **azúcar** (*f.*) sugar **II.3**, IV.2
la **azucarera** sugar bowl **II.3**
azul blue **I.4**, I.7

B

el **badminton** badminton **III.1**
bailar to dance **III.5**, I.10
el **baile** dance **III.3**
bajar to go down, to get off **II.4**, IV.3;
    to lower **IV.3**
bajar de to get off **IV.3**
bajo(a) low, short (in height) **I.2**, I.7
la **balanza** scale **IV.4**
la **ballena** whale **I.5**, III.6
el **baloncesto** basketball **III.1**
el **banco** bank, bench **III.2**
la **bandera** flag I.8
el/la **banquero(a)** banker **II.5**
bañarse to bathe, to take a bath **III.2**, IV.5
el **banco** bank, bench **II.1**, III.2
la **bandera** flag **I.4**, I.8
la **bañera** bathtub **III.4**
el **baño** bathroom **I.1**, I.7
barato(a) inexpensive **I.4**, II.6
la **barba** beard **I.3**, III.1
el/la **barbero** barber **I.2**
el **barco** boat **II.1**, III.4
el **barquillo** waffle **II.3**
barrer to sweep **III.4**
el **barrio** neighborhood **II.4**, IV.3
el **básquetbol** basketball I.10
bastante fairly, quite, enough **I.2**, I.7
la **basura** garbage **III.4**
el **basurero** garbage can **IV.3**
la **bata** robe **II.2**

la **batata** sweet potato **II.3**, IV.2
el **bate** bat (sports) **I.5**, III.5
la **batería** battery (car) **IV.5**
el **baúl** trunk **IV.5**
el/la **bebé** baby **I.2**, I.2
beber to drink **II.3**, I.6
la **bebida** beverage **II.3**, IV.2
el **béisbol** baseball **III.1**, I.10
besar to kiss **III.2**
el **beso** kiss **III.2**, I.1
la **biblioteca** library **II.1**, I.8
la **bicicleta (en...)** bicycle (by . . .) **I.5**, I.8
bien well **I.1**, I.1
el **bigote** mustache **I.3**, III.1
el **billete** ticket **IV.1**, IV.6
biodegradable biodegradable **IV.3**
la **biología** biology **I.5**, IV.4
el **bistec** steak **II.3**
blanco(a) white **I.4**, I.7
blando(a) soft **I.4**, II.6
el **bloque** block (of wood) **I.5**, III.5
la **blusa** blouse **II.2**, I.5
la **boca** mouth **I.3**, I.4
la **bocacalle** intersection **IV.5**
el **bocadito** snack food **II.3**
la **bocina** horn of a car **IV.5**
la **boda** wedding **IV.1**
el **boleto** ticket **IV.1**
el **bolígrafo** ballpoint pen **I.4**, I.8
los **bolitos** polka dots **II.2**
los **bolos** bowling **III.1**
la **bolsa** purse **II.2**, IV.6
el **bolsillo** pocket **II.2**
el/la **bombero(a)** firefighter **I.2**, II.5
bonito(a) pretty **I.2**, II.1
bordado(a) embroidered **II.2**
el **borrador** eraser (chalkboard) **I.4**, I.8
el **bosque** forest **I.5**, III.6
la **bota** boot **II.2**, IV.6
la **botella** bottle **IV.3**
el **botón** button **II.2**
el **brazalete** bracelet **II.2**
el **brazo** arm **I.3**, I.4
el **broche** pin **II.2**
el **bróculi** broccoli **II.3**
broncearse to sunbathe **III.1**, IV.6
la **bronquitis** bronchitis **IV.4**
la **bruja** witch **III.3**
el **buen tiempo** nice weather **II.1**, I.5
Buenas noches Good evening, Good night
    I.1, I.1
Buenas tardes Good afternoon I.1
bueno(a) good **I.1**, I.1
Bueno OK I.9

Buenos días   Good morning   **I.1**, I.1
el **búfalo**   buffalo   **I.5**, III.6
la **bufanda**   scarf   **II.2**
la **bujía**   spark plug   **IV.5**
burlarse de   to make fun of   **III.2**
el **burro**   donkey   **I.5**, I.6
buscar   to look for   **III.5**, IV.1

C

el **caballero**   gentleman   **IV.2**
el **caballo**   horse   **I.5**, I.6
el **caballo balancín**   rocking horse   **I.5**, III.5
la **cabeza**   head   **I.3**, I.4
la **cabra**   goat   **I.5**, III.6
el **cacahuete**   peanut   **I.3**, IV.2
la **cachemira**   paisley   **II.2**
cada   each   **III.4**
la **cadena**   chain   **II.2**
el **café**   coffee   **II.3**, I.6
la **cafetera**   coffeepot   **II.3**
la **cafetería**   cafeteria   **II.5**, IV.2
la **caja**   box   **III.3**, IV.2
el/la **cajero(a)**   cashier   **I.2**
el **cajón de arena**   sandbox   **I.5**, III.5
la **calabaza**   pumpkin   **III.3**
los **calambres**   cramps   **IV.4**
la **calavera**   skull   **III.3**
los **calcetines**   socks   **II.2**, I.5
la **calculadora**   calculator   **I.4**, I.8
calcular   to do arithmetic   **II.5**, IV.4
el **cálculo**   calculus   **I.5**, IV.4
la **calefacción**   heat, heating (building)   **IV.3**
el **calendario**   calendar   **I.1**, I.9
callado(a)   quiet   **I.2**, II.2
callarse   to be quiet   **III.2**
la **calle**   street   **II.4**, IV.3
el **calor**   heat   **I.3**, I.5
calor (tener…)   to be warm/hot   I.5
calvo(a)   bald   **I.2**, II.1
los **calzoncillos**   undershorts   **II.2**
la **cama**   bed   **III.4**
el/la **camarero(a)**   waiter, waitress   **I.2**
los **camarones**   shrimp   **II.3**, IV.2
cambiar   to change   **III.4**
el **camello**   camel   **I.5**, III.6
caminar   to walk   **IV.2**, I.10
el **camino**   road   **II.4**, IV.3
el **camión**   truck, bus   **I.2**
la **camioneta**   pickup truck   **IV.5**
la **camisa**   shirt   **II.2**, I.5
la **camiseta**   T-shirt   **II.2**, IV.6
el **camisón**   nightgown   **II.2**
el **campo**   countryside   **II.1**, III.3

la **canasta**   basket   **III.3**
cancelar   to cancel   **IV.4**
el **cáncer**   cancer   **IV.4**
la **canción**   song   **III.5**, I.10
el **candelabro**   chandelier   **III.4**
el **candelero**   candlestick   **II.3**
el **cangrejo**   crab   **I.5**, III.6
el **canguro**   kangaroo   **I.5**, III.6
las **canicas**   marbles   **I.5**, III.5
canoso(a)   gray-haired   **I.2**, II.1
cansado(a)   tired   **I.3**, III.1
cansarse   to get tired   **III.2**
cantar   to sing   **III.5**, I.10
la **capital**   capital city   **II.1**, III.3
la **capota**   hood   **IV.5**
la **cápsula**   capsule   **IV.4**
la **cara**   face   **I.3**, I.4
la **característica**   characteristic   **I.2**
la **caravana**   camper   **IV.5**
el **carbón**   coal   **IV.3**
el **carburador**   carburetor   **IV.5**
la **cárcel**   jail   **II.1**
el **Carnaval**   Carnaval (Mardi Gras)   **III.3**
cariñosamente   affectionately   II.2
la **carne**   meat   **II.3**, IV.2
la **carne molida**   ground meat   **II.3**, IV.2
la **carnicería**   butcher shop   **II.1**, III.2
caro(a)   expensive   **I.4**, II.6
el/la **carpintero(a)**   carpenter   **I.2**
la **carrera**   career   **I.2**, IV.4
la **carreta**   wagon   **I.5**, III.5
la **carretera**   highway   **II.4**
el **carril**   lane   **IV.5**
el **carro**   car   **II.1**, I.8
el **carro alegórico**   float   **III.3**
la **carta**   letter (mail)   **I.5**, I.8
la **cartera**   briefcase   **I.4**, I.8; wallet   **II.2**, IV.6
el/la **cartero(a)**   mail carrier   **I.2**
el **cartón**   cardboard   **IV.3**
la **casa**   house   **II.1**, I.3
la **casa de muñecas**   dollhouse   **I.5**, III.5
casado(a) (estar)   married   **I.3**, III.1
casarse   to get married   **III.2**
el **casete**   cassette   **I.4**, II.6
el **casimir**   cashmere   **II.2**
el **catarro**   cold (headcold)   **IV.4**, I.4
catorce   fourteen   **I.1**, I.3
el **catsup**   ketchup   **II.3**
la **cebada**   barley   **II.3**
la **cebolla**   onion   **II.3**, IV.2
la **cebra**   zebra   **I.5**, III.6
ceder el paso   to yield   **IV.5**
la **ceja**   eyebrow   **I.3**
celebrar   to celebrate   **III.5**, IV.1

celoso(a) jealous **I.3,** III.1

el **cementerio** cemetery **III.3**

la **cena** dinner, evening meal, supper **II.3,** I.6

cenar to eat dinner **II.3,** IV.2

el **centro** center, downtown **II.1,** III.3

el **centro comercial** shopping mall **II.1,** III.2

el **centro de flores** floral centerpiece **II.3**

cepillar(se) to brush **III.2,** IV.5

cerca (de) near **II.1,** III.2

el **cerdo** pig **I.5,** I.6; pork IV.2

el **cereal** cereal **II.3,** IV.2

el **cerebro** brain **I.3,** III.1

la **cereza** cherry **II.3,** IV.2

cero zero **I.1,** I.3

cerrar (ie) to close **I.1,** IV.4

el **césped** lawn **III.4**

el **chaleco** vest **II.2**

la **chaqueta** jacket **II.2,** I.5

charlar to chat **III.5,** IV.1

el **charol** patent leather **II.2**

¡Chau! Bye! **I.1,** I.1

el **cheque de viajero** traveler's check **IV.1**

el **chicle** chewing gum **II.3**

el/la **chico(a)** teenager **I.2**

el **chinero** china closet **III.4**

el **chino** Chinese (language) **I.5,** IV.4

el **chiste** joke **III.5**

chistoso(a) funny **I.2**

el **chocolate** chocolate **II.3,** I.6

la **chuleta** chop **II.3,** IV.2

cien(to) hundred **I.1,** I.10

la **ciencia** science **I.5,** I.9

el/la **científico(a)** scientist **I.2**

cierto(a) certain **IV.4**

el **ciervo** deer **I.5,** III.6

cinco five **I.1,** I.3

cincuenta fifty **I.1,** I.3

el **cine** movie theater **II.1,** I.10

la **cinta** tape **I.4,** I.8

el **cinturón** belt **II.2,** IV.6

el **cinturón de seguridad** seat belt **IV.5**

el **circo** circus **III.3,** IV.2

la **circulación** traffic **IV.5**

circular circular **I.4,** I.7

el/la **cirujano(a)** surgeon **IV.4**

la **cita** appointment, date **IV.4**

la **ciudad** city **II.1,** I.5

el/la **ciudadano(a)** citizen III.3

el **clarinete** clarinet **III.1**

claro(a) clear **II.1,** I.5; light (in color) **I.4,** I.7

¡Claro! Of course! I.5

la **clase** class **I.5,** I.9

la **clase de tecleo** keyboarding IV.4

el **claxón** horn **IV.5**

la **clínica** clinic **IV.4**

el **coche** car **I.5,** I.8

cocido(a) cooked **II.3**

la **cocina** kitchen **II.1,** I.7

cocinar to cook **II.3,** I.10

el/la **cocinero(a)** cook, chef **I.2**

el **codo** elbow **I.3,** I.4

el **col** cabbage **II.3**

el **colchón** mattress **III.4**

coleccionar to collect **III.1**

el **colegio** high school **I.5**

colgar (ue) to hang up **III.4**

la **coliflor** cauliflower **II.3,** IV.2

la **colina** hill **II.1**

el **collar** necklace **II.2**

el **color** color **I.4,** I.7

el **columpio** swing **I.5,** III.5

el **combi** van **IV.5**

la **combinación** slip **II.2**

el **comedor** dining room **II.1,** I.7

comenzar (ie) to begin, to start **III.1,** IV.1

comer to eat **II.3,** I.6

el **comercio** business **I.5,** IV.4

la **cometa** kite **I.5,** III.5

la **comida** dinner, midday main meal, food, meal **II.3,** I.6

la **comida rápida** fast food **IV.2**

como as, like **II.2,** I.3

¿Cómo? How? **I.1,** I.1

¿Cómo está(n)… ? How is (are) . . . ? **I.1,** I.1

¿Cómo está Ud.? How are you? **I.1,** I.1

¿Cómo estás? How are you? **I.1,** I.1

¿Cómo se dice... ? How do you say . . . ? **I.1,** I.1

¿Cómo se escribe… ? How do you spell . . . ? **I.1,** I.2

¿Cómo se llama Ud.? What's your name? **I.1,** I.2

como si as if **IV.2**

¿Cómo te llamas? What's your name? **I.1,** I.2

la **cómoda** chest of drawers **III.4**

cómodamente comfortably **II.5**

cómodo(a) comfortable **I.3,** IV.5

el/la **compañero(a)** friend, classmate I.2

la **competencia** competition IV.4

componer to compose **III.5**

comprar to buy **II.2,** I.10

comprender to understand **I.1,** I.1

comprometerse to become engaged **III.2**

la **compuerta trasera** tailgate **IV.5**

compuesto(a) composed **III.5**

la **computadora** computer **I.V,** I.8

cuidadosamente   carefully   **II.5**
cuidar   to take care of   **III.1,** I.10
cuidar de los niños   to babysit   **III.1,** I.10
el **cumpleaños**   birthday   **I.1,** I.9
la **cuñada**   sister-in-law   **I.2,** II.4
el **cuñado**   brother-in-law   **I.2,** II.4
la **cuneta**   ditch   **IV.5**
Cupido   Cupid   **III.3**
curar   to cure   **IV.4**
curioso(a)   curious   **I.2**

D

la **dama**   lady   **IV.2**
las **damas**   checkers   **III.1,** III.5
el **daño**   damage   **IV.3**
dar   to give   **II.2,** I.10
dar las gracias   to give thanks, to thank   **III.3,** IV.1
dar un paseo   to go for a walk   **III.1,** IV.6
dar una vuelta   to make a turn   **IV.5**
darse cuenta   to realize   **III.2**
de   from   **I.1,** II.3; of, about   **I.1,** II.4
de compras (ir...)   shopping (to go . . .)   **III.1**
¿De dónde es... ?   Where is . . . from?   II.3
de hecho   in fact   III.3
De nada   You're welcome   **I.1,** I.1
de niño(a)   as a child   **II.5,** II.1
de nuevo   again   **II.5**
¿De quién?   Whose?   I.5
de repente   suddenly   **II.5,** II.1
de una vez   all at once   **II.5,** II.1
de vez en cuando   from time to time   **II.5,** II.1
de viejo(a)   as an old person   **II.5,** II.1
debajo (de)   under   **II.1,** III.2
deber   to owe   **IV.2**
deber + *infinitive*   should/ought to + *verb*   **II.5,** IV.2
debiera   should   **IV.2**
débil   weak   **I.2,** II.1
decidir   to decide   **IV.1,** IV.6
décimo(a)   tenth   **II.4,** IV.3
decir   to say, to tell   **III.3,** IV.6
el **dedo (de la mano)**   finger   **I.3,** I.4
el **dedo del pie**   toe   **I.3,** I.4
dejar   to allow, to let   **IV.3**
del (de + el)   of the, from the   **I.2,** I.2
delante de   in front of   **II.1,** III.2
delgado(a)   thin   **I.2,** II.1
demasiado   too much   **I.5**
el/la **dentista**   dentist   **I.2,** II.5
dentro (de)   inside of   **II.1,** III.2
el **deporte**   sport   I.10
deportivo(a)   sport   **II.2,** IV.6

deprimido(a)   depressed   **IV.4**
la **derecha**   right   **II.1,** III.2
el **derrame**   spill   **IV.3**
el **derrame cerebral**   stroke   **IV.4**
desayunar   to eat breakfast   **III.3,** IV.2
el **desayuno**   breakfast   **II.3,** I.6
descansar   to rest   **III.1,** IV.1
el **descapotable**   convertible   **IV.5**
descompuesto   broken down   **IV.5**
descortés   discourteous, rude   **I.2**
describir   to describe   **II.4**
descrito(a)   described   **III.5**
descubierto(a)   discovered   **III.5**
descubrir   to discover   **III.5**
la **descripción**   description   II.1
desde   from (time), since   **II.1,** IV.4
desear   to desire, to want   **II.5,** IV.1
el **desfile**   parade   **III.3**
desgarrar   to rip, to tear   **II.2**
deshacer   to undo, to destroy, to damage   **III.5,** IV.6
deshecho(a)   undone   **III.5**
el **desierto**   desert   **II.1,** III.3
desinflado(a)   flat (tire)   **IV.5**
desmayarse   to faint   **IV.4**
el **desmayo**   faintness   **IV.4**
desobedecer   to disobey   **IV.5**
despacio   slowly   **I.1,** I.1
despedirse (i, i) (de)   to say good-bye (to)   **III.2,** IV.5
el **desperdicio**   waste   **IV.3**
el **despertador**   alarm clock   **I.5,** IV.5
despertarse (ie)   to wake up   **III.2,** IV.5
después (de) (que)   after   **II.1,** II.1
la **destinación**   destination   **IV.1,** IV.6
la **destrucción**   destruction   **IV.3**
destruir   to destroy   **IV.3**
el **desván**   attic   **II.1,** I.7
el **detergente**   detergent   **III.4**
detrás de   behind   **II.1,** III.2
devolver (ue)   to return (something)   **III.1**
devuelto(a)   returned   **III.5**
el **día**   day   **I.1,** I.1
el **Día de Acción de Gracias**   Thanksgiving   **III.3**
el **Día de las Brujas**   Halloween   **III.3**
la **diabetes**   diabetes   **IV.4**
el **diagnóstico**   diagnosis   **IV.4**
la **diarrea**   diarrhea   **IV.4**
dibujar   to draw   **III.1,** I.8
el **diccionario**   dictionary   **I.4,** I.8
dicho(a)   said   **III.5**
diciembre   December   **I.1,** I.9
el **diente**   tooth   **I.3,** I.4

diez   ten   **I.1,** I.3
difícil   difficult   **I.4,** III.1
el **dinero**   money   **IV.1,** I.10
la **dirección**   address, direction   **II.4,** IV.3
el **disco compacto**   compact disc, CD   **I.5,** I.8
la **discotería**   record store   **IV.2**
discutir   to argue, to discuss   **II.5,** IV.3
el **diseño**   pattern   **II.2**
el **disfraz**   costume   **III.3**
disgustar   to annoy, to displease   **II.3**
la **diversión**   amusement   **III.3**
divertido(a)   fun   **I.2**
divertirse (ie, i)   to enjoy oneself, to have a good time, to have fun   **III.1,** IV.5
dividido(a) por   divided by   **I.4,** I.3
dividir   to divide   **II.5,** IV.4
divorciarse   to get divorced   **III.2**
doblar   to fold, to   **III.4;** to turn   **II.4**
la **doble vía**   two-way   **IV.5**
doce   twelve   **I.1,** I.3
el/la **doctor(a)**   doctor   **I.1**
doler (ue)   to hurt,   **I.3,** I.4
el **dolor**   ache,   **I.3,** III.1; pain   **IV.4,** III.1
doméstico(a)   domestic   **I.5,** III.6
domingo   Sunday   **I.1,** I.9
los **dominós**   dominos   **III.1**
don   title of respect   **I.1,** I.2
doña   title of respect   **I.1,** I.2
¿Dónde?   Where?   **I.2,** I.3
dorado(a)   gold   **I.4,** II.6
dormir (ue, u)   to sleep   **III.1,** I.10
dormirse (ue, u)   to go to sleep, to fall asleep   **III.2,** IV.5
dos   two   **I.1,** I.3
dos veces   twice   **II.5,** II.1
doscientos   two hundred   **I.4,** I.10
el **drama**   drama, acting   **I.5**
el **dril**   denim   **II.2**
ducharse   to (take a) shower   **III.2,** IV.5
dudar   to doubt   **IV.4**
dudoso(a)   doubtful   **IV.4**
el **duende**   goblin   **III.3**
la **dulcería**   candy store   **II.1,** III.2
los **dulces**   candy   **II.3,** IV.2
los **dulces de goma**   gumdrops   **III.3**
el **durazno**   peach   **II.3**
duro(a)   hard   **I.4,** II.6

E

e *(before i/hi)*   and   **I.4,** IV.1
echar   to throw   **IV.3**
la **ecología**   ecology   **IV.3**
la **economía**   economics   **I.5,** I.9

el **ecuador**   equator   **II.1**
la **edad**   age   **I.1,** I.3
el **edificio**   building   **II.1,** III.2
la **educación física**   physical education   **I.5,** I.9
efectivo (en…)   cash   **IV.2**
egoísta   selfish   **I.2,** II.2
el **ejemplo**   example   **I.1,** I.1
el   the   **I.1,** I.2
el (lunes)   on (with days)   **II.5,** I.9
él   he   **I.5,** I.1
El gusto es mío   The pleasure is mine   **I.1,** I.2
la **electricidad**   electricity   **IV.3**
el/la **electricista**   electrician   **I.2**
eléctrico(a)   electric   **I.5,** III.5
el **elefante**   elephant   **I.5,** I.6
eliminar   to eliminate   **IV.3**
ella   she   **I.5,** I.1
ellas   they *(f.)*   **I.5,** I.2
ellos   they *(m.)*   **I.1,** I.2
el/la **embajador(a)**   ambassador   **I.2,** II.6
embarazada   pregnant   **IV.4**
el **embrague**   clutch   **IV.5**
la **emoción**   emotion   **I.3**
empeorarse   to worsen   **IV.4**
empezar (ie)   to begin   **III.1**
en   in, on, at   **I.1,** I.1
en caso (de) que   in case   **IV.5**
en caso de   in case of   **IV.1**
en el medio de   in the middle of   **II.1**
en vez de   instead of   **II.1,** IV.5
enamorado(a) (de)   in love (with)   **I.3,** III.1
enamorarse (de)   to fall in love (with)   **III.2**
el **encaje**   lace   **II.2**
encantado(a)   delighted   **IV.4**
encantar   to adore   **II.3**
encender (ie)   to light   **III.1**
el **encierro de los toros**   roundup of the bulls   **III.3**
encima de   on top of   **II.1,** III.2
encontrar (ue)   to find, to meet   **III.1**
el **encuentro**   encounter   I.l
encurtido(a)   pickled   **II.3**
la **energía**   energy   **IV.3**
enero   January   **I.1,** I.9
enfermarse   to get sick   **IV.4**
la **enfermedad**   illness   **IV.4,** I.4
el/la **enfermero(a)**   nurse   **I.2,** I.4
enfermo(a)   sick   **I.3,** III.1
enfrente (de)   opposite   **II.1,** III.2
enojado(a)   angry   **I.3,** III.1
enojarse   to get angry   **III.2**
la **ensalada**   salad   **II.3,** I.6
la **ensaladera**   salad bowl   **II.3**
la **enseñanza**   schooling, teaching   **II.5,** IV.4

enseñar   to teach   **II.5**
ensuciar   to dirty   **II.2**
entonces   then   **II.5**, II.1
la **entrada**   entrance   **IV.5**
entrar (en)   to enter, to go into   **IV.5**, IV.4
entre   between   **II.1**, III.2
el **entremés**   appetizer   **II.3**, IV.2
entusiasmado(a)   excited   **I.3**, IV.6
el **envenamiento con comida**   food poisoning
   IV.4
enviar   to send   IV.6
envolver (ue)   to wrap   **III.5**, IV.2
envuelto(a)   wrapped   **III.5**
la **enyesadura**   cast   **IV.4**
el **equipaje**   luggage   **IV.1**
equivocarse   to make a mistake   **III.2**
esa   that   **I.4**, I.5
la **escalera**   stairs   **II.1**, I.7
los **escalofríos**   chills   **IV.4**
el **escape**   exhaust   **IV.3**
la **escoba**   broom   **III.3**
escocés(esa)   plaid   **II.2**
escoger   to choose   **II.3**
el **escondite**   hide and seek   **III.1**
escribir   to write   **I.1**, I.10
escribir a máquina   to type, to input   IV.4
escrito(a)   written   **III.5**
el **escritorio**   desk (of a teacher)   **I.4**, I.8
escuchar   to listen (to)   **II.5**, I.10
la **escuela**   school   **I.4**, I.3
la **escuela primaria**   elementary school   **I.5**
ese   that   **I.4**, I.5
esencial   essential   **IV.3**
eso   that (indefinite)   **I.4**, I.5
esos(as)   those   **I.4**, I.5
los **espaguetis**   spaghetti   **II.3**
la **espalda**   back (of the body)   **I.3**, I.4
España   Spain   II.3
español(a)   Spanish   **I.1**, I.1
el/la **español(a)**   Spaniard   II.3
la **especia**   spice   **IV.3**
especial   special   **IV.5**
especialmente   especially   **II.5**, IV.5
el/la **especialista**   specialist   **IV.4**
el **espejo**   mirror   **III.4**, IV.5
el **espejo retrovisor**   rearview mirror   **IV.5**
esperar   to hope to, to wait for   **II.5**, IV.2
las **espinacas**   spinach   **II.3**
la **esponja**   sponge   **III.4**
la **esposa**   wife   **I.2**, I.3
el **esposo**   husband   **I.2**, I.3
los **esposos**   married couple   **I.2**, I.3
el **esqueleto**   framework, skeleton   **III.3**, II.1
esquiar   to ski   **II.4**, I.10

la **esquina**   corner   III.2
esta   this   **I.4**, I.4
la **estación**   station   **IV.1**, III.2
la **estación de gasolina**   gas station   **II.1**, III.2
la **estación**   season   **II.1**, I.5
el **estacionamiento**   parking place   **IV.5**
estacionar   to park   **IV.5**
el **estado**   state   **I.3**, III.3
los **Estados Unidos**   United States   II.3
el/la **estadounidense**   someone of or from the
   United States, American   II.3
estampado(a)   print   **II.2**
la **estampilla**   stamp   **III.1**
el **estante**   bookshelf   **I.4**, I.8
estar   to be (condition)   **I.3**, I.1; to be
   (location)   **I.3**, I.3
la **estatua**   statue   **III.3**
este   this   **I.4**, I.4
el **este**   east   **II.1**, III.3
el **estéreo**   stereo   **I.5**, I.8
el **estetoscopio**   stethoscope   **IV.4**
la **estirofoma**   Styrofoam   **IV.3**
esto   this (indefinite)   **I.4**, I.4
el **estómago**   stomach   **I.3**, I.4
estornudar   to sneeze   **IV.4**
estos(as)   these   **I.4**, I.4
estrecho(a)   narrow   **I.4**, I.7
el **estreñimiento**   constipation   **IV.4**
la **estrella**   star   II.3
el/la **estudiante**   student   **I.1**, II.5
estudiar   to study   **II.5**, I.10
la **estufa**   stove   **III.4**
estúpido(a)   stupid   **I.2**
evidente   evident   **IV.4**
el **examen**   exam   **II.5**, IV.4
examinar   to examine   **IV.4**
el **exceso**   excess   **IV.5**
exigir   to demand, to require   **IV.3**
exótico(a)   exotic   I.6
la **expresión**   expression   **I.1**, I.1
extranjero(a)   foreign   **I.5**, IV.4

F

la **fábrica**   factory   **II.1**, III.2
fácil   easy   **I.4**, III.3
fácilmente   easily   **II.5**, IV.5
facturar   to check (luggage)   **IV.1**
la **falda**   skirt   **II.2**, I.5
faltar   to lack, to need   **II.3**, IV.4
la **familia**   family   **I.2**, I.3
famoso(a)   famous   **I.2**, II.5
el **fantasma**   ghost   **III.3**
fantástico(a)   great   **I.2**, II.2

la **farmacia**   pharmacy   **II.1,** III.2
el/la **farmacista**   pharmacist   **I.2,** II.5
el **farol delantero**   headlight   **IV.5**
el **farol trasero**   taillight   **IV.5**
  fascinar   to fascinate   **II.3**
  favor de + *infinitive*   please + *verb*   **I.1,** III.6
  favorito(a)   favorite   I.5
  febrero   February   **I.1,** I.9
la **fecha**   date   **I.1,** I.9
  feliz   happy   **I.2,** II.2
  felizmente   happily   **II.5,** IV.5
  feo(a)   ugly   **I.2,** II.1
  feroz   ferocious   **a,** III.6
el **ferrocarril**   railroad   **IV.5**
el **fertilizante**   fertilizer   **IV.3**
  festivo(a)   festive   **III.3**
la **fiebre**   fever   **I.3,** I.4
el **fieltro**   felt   **II.2**
la **fiesta**   party   **III.5,** I.5
la **fila**   row   **I.4,** III.2
el **filete**   filet   **II.3**
el **fin**   end   III.4
  finalmente   finally   **II.5,** IV.5
la **física**   physics   **I.5,** IV.4
  físico(a)   physical   **I.2,** II.1
el **flan**   custard   **II.3,** IV.2
la **flauta**   flute   **III.1**
la **flor**   flower   **II.1,** III.2
la **florería**   flower shop   **II.1,** III.2
el **fluorocarburo**   fluorocarbon   **IV.3**
la **forma**   shape   **I.4,** I.7
el **formulario de seguro**   insurance form   **IV.4**
el **fosfato**   phosphate   **IV.3**
la **foto(grafía)**   photograph   **III.5,** IV.1
la **fractura**   fracture   **IV.4**
la **frambuesa**   raspberry   **II.3,** IV.2
el **francés**   French (language)   **I.5,** II.3
  Francia   France   II.3
la **franela**   flannel   **II.2**
  frecuente   frequent   **II.5**
  frecuentemente   often, frequently   **II.5,** II.1
el **fregadero**   sink (kitchen)   **III.4**
  fregar   to scrub   **III.4**
el **fregasuelos**   mop   **III.4**
  freír (i, i)   to fry   **II.3,** IV.2
el **freno**   brake   **IV.5**
el **frente**   front   **I.4,** III.2
la **frente**   forehead   **I.3,** III.1
la **fresa**   strawberry   **II.3,** IV.2
  fresco(a)   cool   **II.1,** I.5; fresh   **II.1,** IV.6
los **frijoles**   beans   **II.3,** IV.2
el **frío**   cold   **I.3,** I.5
  frito(a)   fried   **II.3,** I.6
la **frontera**   border   **II.1,** III.3

la **fruta**   fruit   **II.3,** I.6
el **fuego**   fire   **III.3,**
los **fuegos artificiales**   fireworks   **III.3**
  fuera de   outside of   **II.1,** III.2
  fuerte   strong   **I.2,** II.1
  fumar   to smoke   **II.3**
  funcionar   to work (machines)   **IV.5**
el **funeral**   funeral   **IV.1**
la **furgoneta**   van   **IV.5**
el **fútbol**   soccer, football   **III.1,** I.10
el **fútbol norteamericano**   football   **III.1,** II.6
el **futuro**   future   **II.5,** II.1

G

las **gafas de sol**   sunglasses   **II.2**
la **galleta**   cracker   **II.3,** IV.2
la **galletita dulce**   cookie   **II.3,** IV.2
la **gallina**   hen   **I.5,** I.6
el **gallo**   rooster   **I.5,** I.6
la **gamuza**   suede   **II.2**
  ganar   to earn, to win   **III.1,** I.10
el **garaje**   garage   **II.1**
la **garganta**   throat   **I.3,** I.4
la **gasolina**   gasoline   **IV.1**
el/la **gasolinero(a)**   gas station attendant   **IV.5**
  gastar   to spend (money)   **IV.2,** I.10
el **gasto**   usage   **IV.3**
el **gato**   cat   **I.5,** I.6
la **gelatina**   gelatin   **II.3**
la **gemela**   twin sister   **I.2,** II.4
el **gemelo**   twin brother   **I.2,** II.4; cufflink   **II.2**
  generosamente   generously   **II.5**
  generoso(a)   generous   **I.2,** II.2
la **gente**   people   **I.2,** IV.6
la **geografía**   geography   **I.5,** III.3
la **geometría**   geometry   **I.5,** IV.4
el/la **gerente**   manager   **I.2,** II.5
el **gimnasio**   gymnasium   **IV.2**
  girar   to turn (in traffic)   **IV.5**
el **giro completo**   U-turn   **IV.5**
el **globo**   globe   **I.4,** I.8; balloon   **I.5,** III.5
la **glorieta**   traffic circle   **IV.5**
el **gobierno**   government   **III.2**
el **golf**   golf   **III.1**
la **goma**   rubber   **IV.3**
la **goma (de borrar)**   eraser (pencil)   **I.4,** I.8
  gordo(a)   fat   **I.2,** II.1
el **gorila**   gorilla   **I.5,** III.6
el **gorro**   cap   **II.2,** I.5
la **gota**   drop   **IV.4**
  gozar (de)   to enjoy   **II.3**
la **grabadora**   tape recorder   **I.4,** I.8

Gracias   Thank you   **I.1,** I.1
las **gracias**   thanks   IV.1
el **grado**   grade (in school)   II.6
la **graduación**   graduation   **III.5**
graduarse   to graduate   **III.2**
grande   big   **I.2,** I.7; large   **I.2,** II.1
la **granja**   farm   **I.5,** III.6
gratis   free (no charge)   IV.4
la **gripe**   flu   **I.3,** I.4
gris   gray   **I.4,** I.7
el **guante**   glove   II.2
la **guantera**   glove compartment   **IV.5**
guapo(a)   good-looking, handsome   **I.2,** II.1
el **guardabarros**   fender   **IV.5**
el **guardapolvo**   duster (feather)   **III.4**
guardar   to keep, to save   **IV.3**
guardar cama   to stay in bed   **IV.4**
la **guardería**   nursery school   IV.4
el **guisado**   stew   II.3
los **guisantes**   peas   **II.3,** IV.2
la **guitarra**   guitar   **I.5,** I.10
gustar   to be pleasing, to like   **I.5,** I.6
gustar más/menos   to like more/less   II.6
gustar mucho   to like a lot   II.4
el **gusto**   pleasure   **I.1**

H

haber + *past participle*   to have + *verb*   **III.5**
había   there was, there were   **I.4,** II.6
el/la **habitante**   inhabitant   **I.2,** III.3
hablador(a)   talkative   **I.2,** II.2
hablar   to speak, to talk   **II.5,** I.10
habrá   there will be   **I.4,** II.6
hace *(+ time)*   ago   **II.5,** II.1
hacer   to do, to make   **II.5,** I.10
hacer (buen) tiempo   to be (nice) weather   I.5
hacer una cita   to make an appointment   **IV.4**
hacer cola   to stand in line   **II.5**
hacer ejercicio   to exercise   **III.1**
hacer investigaciones   to research   **II.5**
hacer jogging   to jog   **III.1**
hacer la maleta   to pack a suitcase   **IV.1,** IV.6
hacer sol   to be sunny   I.5
hacerse   to become   **III.2**
hallar   to find   **IV.2,** IV.1
hambre (tener...)   to be hungry   **I.3,** III.5
la **hamburguesa**   hamburger   **II.3,** I.6
hasta   to (up to), until   **I.1,** IV.4
Hasta la vista   See you later   **I.1,** I.1
Hasta mañana   See you tomorrow   **I.1,** I.1
hasta que   until   **IV.5**
hay   there is, there are   **I.4,** I.3
hay que   must, one must   **II.5**

hecho(a)   done, made   **III.5**
el **hecho**   fact   **II.5,** IV.4
la **heladería**   ice cream store   **II.1,** III.2
el **helado**   ice cream   **II.3,** I.6
el **hemisferio**   hemisphere   **II.1**
la **hermana**   sister   **I.2,** I.3
la **hermanastra**   stepsister   **I.2,** I.3
el **hermanastro**   stepbrother   **I.2,** I.3
el **hermano**   brother   **I.2,** I.3
los **hermanos**   siblings   **I.2,** I.3
hervido(a)   boiled   **II.3**
hervir (ie)   to boil   **II.3**
hidroeléctrico(a)   hydroelectric   **IV.3**
el **hielo**   ice   **I.5,** III.5
el **hígado**   liver   **I.3,** III.1
la **hija**   daughter   **I.2,** I.3
la **hijastra**   stepdaughter   **I.2**
el **hijastro**   stepson   **I.2**
el **hijo**   son   **I.2,** I.3
los **hijos**   children   **I.2,** I.3
el **hinchazón**   swelling   **IV.4**
el/la **hipócrito(a)**   hypocrite   **I.2**
el **hipopótamo**   hippopotamus   **I.5,** III.6
la **historia**   history   **I.5,** I.9
el **hockey sobre hielo**   ice hockey   **III.1**
la **hoja**   leaf   **III.4**
la **hoja clínica**   medical history   **IV.4**
Hola   Hello, Hi   **I.1,** I.1
el **hombre**   man   **I.2,** I.2
el **hombre de negocios**   businessman   **I.2,** II.5
el **hombro**   shoulder   **I.3,** III.1
la **hora**   hour   **I.1,** I.9
la **hora punta**   rush hour   **IV.5**
el **horario**   time schedule   **IV.1**
la **hormiga**   ant   **I.5,** III.6
horneado(a)   baked   **II.3**
hornear   to bake   **II.3**
el **horno**   oven   **III.4**
el **horno de microondas**   microwave oven   **III.4**
el **hospital**   hospital   **II.1,** III.2
el **hotel**   hotel   **II.1,** III.2
hoy   today   **I.1,** I.9
hubo   there was, there were   **I.4**
el **hueso**   bone   **IV.4**
el **huevo**   egg   **II.3,** I.6
los **huevos de colores**   colored eggs   **III.3**
húmedo(a)   humid   **II.1,** I.5
el **humo**   smoke   **IV.3**
¡Huy!   Wow!   I.7

I

ida y vuelta (viaje de...)   round trip   **IV.1**
la **iglesia**   church   **II.1,** I.10

igual   equal   **I.1**
Igualmente   Same here, Likewise   **I.1**, I.2
ilegal   illegal   **IV.5**
impares (los números...)   odd numbers
   I.1, I.10
impedir (i, i)   to prevent   **III.1**
el **impermeable**   raincoat   **II.2**, IV.6
imponer   to impose   **III.5**
importante   important   **IV.3**
importar   to matter   **II.3**
imposible   impossible   **IV.4**
improbable   improbable   **IV.4**
impuesto(a)   imposed   **III.5**
incluir   to include   **IV.3**
incorrectamente   incorrectly   **II.5**, IV.5
incorrecto(a)   incorrect   **II.5**, IV.5
increíble   incredible   **IV.4**
el/la **indio(a)**   Native American   **III.3**
la **infección**   infection   I.3, III.1
influir   to influence   **IV.3**
la **información**   information   **IV.1**
la **informática**   computer science   I.5, IV.4
la **infracción**   infraction, break   **IV.5**
el/la **ingeniero(a)**   engineer   **I.2**, II.5
Inglaterra   England   II.3
el **inglés**   English (language)   **I.1**, I.1
inmediatamente   immediately   **II.5**, IV.5
inmediato(a)   immediate   **II.5**
el **inodoro**   toilet   **III.4**
el **insecticida**   insecticide   **IV.3**
el **insecto**   insect   I.5, III.6
insistir en   to insist on   **II.5**, IV.2
el **insomnio**   insomnia   **IV.4**
instalar   to install   **IV.5**
la **instrucción**   instruction   **II.4**
el **instrumento**   instrument   **III.1**, I.10
intelectual   intellectual   **I.2**
inteligente   smart   I.2, II.2
inteligentemente   intelligently   **II.5**
interesante   interesting   I.2, II.2
interesar   to interest   **II.3**
la **intermitente**   turn signal   **IV.5**
introducir   to introduce   **IV.3**
las **investigaciones**   research   IV.4
el **invierno**   winter   **II.1**, I.5
la **invitación**   invitation   III.5, IV.1
el/la **invitado(a)**   guest   III.5, IV.1
invitar   to invite   **II.5**, IV.1
la **inyección**   injection, shot   **IV.4**
ir   to go   **I.1**, I.8
ir a + *infinitive*   to be going to + *verb*
   II.5, I.10
ir de compras   to go shopping   **IV.2**, IV.6
irritar   to irritate   **IV.4**

irse   to go away   **III.2**, IV.5
la **isla**   island   **II.1**, III.3
el **italiano**   Italian (language)   I.5, IV.4
la **izquierda**   left (direction)   **II.1**, III.2

J

el **jabón**   soap   **III.4**
la **jalea**   jelly   **II.3**, IV.2
el **jamón**   ham   **II.3**, I.6
el **japonés**   Japanese (language)   I.5, IV.4
el **jarabe**   syrup   **IV.4**
el **jarabe para la tos**   cough syrup   **IV.4**
el **jardín**   garden   **II.1**
el **jardín zoológico**   zoo   **II.1**
el/la **jardinero(a)**   gardener   **I.2**
la **jarra**   pitcher   **II.3**
la **jirafa**   giraffe   I.5, III.6
joven   young   I.2, II.1
el/la **joven**   teenager, young person   **I.2**, I.2
las **joyas**   jewelry   **II.2**
la **joyería**   jewelry store   **II.1**, III.2
las **judías**   string beans   **II.3**, IV.2
el **juego**   game   I.5, I.10
el **juego de damas**   checkers game   I.5, III.5
el **juego de vídeo**   video game   **III.1**
jueves   Thursday   **I.1**, I.9
el/la **juez**   judge   **IV.5**
el/la **jugador(a)**   player   **I.2**, II.5
jugar (ue)   to play (game, sport)   **III.1**, I.10
el **jugo**   juice   **II.3**, I.6
el **juguete**   toy   I.5, III.5
la **juguetería**   toy store   **II.1**, III.2
julio   July   **I.1**, I.9
junio   June   **I.1**, I.9
junto a   next to   **II.1**
juntos(as)   together   III.1

K

el **kilómetro**   kilometer   IV.3

L

la   the   **I.1**, I.2; her, you, it   **I.5**, I.5
el **labio**   lip   **I.3**
lácteo(a)   relating to dairy   IV.2
el **lado**   side   I.4, III.2
el/la **ladrón(ona)**   thief   **I.2**
el **lago**   lake   **II.1**, III.3
lamentar   to regret   **IV.4**
la **lámpara**   lamp   **III.4**
la **lana**   wool   **II.2**
la **langosta**   lobster   **II.3**, IV.2

el **lápiz**   pencil   **I.1**, I.8
largo(a)   long   **I.4**, I.7
las   the   **I.1**, I.2; them, you *(pl.)*   **I.5**, I.5
la **lástima**   pity   **IV.4**, I.1
la **lata**   can (tin)   **IV.3**
el **latín**   Latin (language)   **I.5**, IV.4
el **lavabo**   sink (bathroom)   **III.4**
la **lavadora**   washer   **III.4**
la **lavandería**   launderers, laundry   **II.1**
el **lavaplatos**   dishwasher   **III.4**
lavar   to wash   **II.2**, IV.1
lavar a mano   to wash by hand   **II.2**
lavar a máquina   to wash by machine   **II.2**
lavarse   to wash oneself   **III.2**, IV.5
le   to you, to him, to her   **I.3**, I.4
la **lección**   lesson   **II.5**, I.1
la **leche**   milk   **II.3**, I.6
la **lechería**   dairy store   **II.1**, III.2
la **lechuga**   lettuce   **II.3**, I.6
la **lectura**   reading   **II.5**, IV.4
leer   to read   **II.5**, I.10
la **legumbre**   vegetable   **II.3**, I.6
lejos de   far from   **II.1**, III.2
la **lengua**   language   **I.5**, IV.4
lentamente   slowly   **II.5**, IV.5
los **lentes**   eyeglasses   **II.2**, I.5
los **lentes de contacto**   contact lenses   **II,2**, I.5
el **león**   lion   **I.5**, I.6
el **leopardo**   leopard   **I.5**, III.6
les   to you, to them   **I.3**, I.4
la **letra**   letter (of alphabet)   **I.1**, I.2
levantar (pesas)   to lift (weights)   **III.1**
levantarse   to get up   **III.2**, IV.5
la **ley**   law   **IV.3**
la **librería**   bookstore   **II.1**, III.2
el **libro**   book   **I.1**, I.8
la **licencia**   license   **IV.5**
ligero(a)   lightweight   **I.4**, II.6
el **límite**   limit   **IV.5**
el **limón**   lemon   **II.3**, IV.2
el **limpiador en polvo**   cleanser   **III.4**
el **limpiaparabrisas**   windshield wiper   **IV.5**
limpiar   to clean   **II.2**, IV.1
limpiar en seco   to dry clean   **II.2**
limpio(a)   clean   **I.4**, IV.3
el **lino**   linen   **II.2**
la **linterna de calabaza**   jack-o-lantern   **III.3**
el **líquido**   liquid   **IV.4**
el **líquido limpiaventanas**   window cleaner   **III.4**
listo(a) (estar)   ready   **I.3**, III.3
listo(a) (ser)   clever   **I.1**, II.2
llamar   to call   **I.1**, IV.1
llamarse   to be called, to be named   **I.1**, I.2
los **llanos**   plains   **II.1**, III.3

la **llanta**   tire   **IV.3**
la **llanta de repuesta**   spare tire   **IV.5**
la **llanta desinflada**   flat tire   **IV.5**
la **llave**   key   **I.5**
el **llavero**   keyring   **I.5**
llegar   to arrive   **II.4**, IV.1
llenar   to fill   **IV.1**
lleno(a)   full   **III.3**
llevar   to carry   **II.2**, I.10; to bring (people)   **II.2**, IV.1
llevar (ropa)   to wear (clothing)   **III.5**, I.5
llevarse bien   to get along well   **III.2**
llorar   to cry   **III.2**
llover (ue)   to rain   **III.1**, III.5
llueve   it's raining, it rains   **II.1**, I.5
la **lluvia**   rain   **IV.3**
lo   him, you, it   **I.5**, I.5
lo que   what *(not a question)*   **I.2**, I.10
Lo siento   I'm sorry   **I.1**, I.1
loco(a)   crazy   **I.2**, III.1
lógico(a)   logical   **IV.4**
los   the   **I.1**, I.2; them, you *(pl.)*   **I.5**, I.5
la **lotería**   game (like Bingo)   **III.1**
la **lucha**   wrestling   **III.1**
luchar   to fight   **IV.3**
luego   later, then   **II.5**, II.1
el **lugar**   place   **II.1**, III.2
lunes   Monday   **I.1**, I.9
la **luz**   light (electrical)   **I.4**, III.2

M

los **macarrones**   macaroni   **II.3**
la **madera**   wood   **IV.3**
la **madrastra**   stepmother   **I.2**, I.3
la **madre**   mother   **I.2**, I.3
la **madrina**   godmother   **I.2**, II.4
el **maíz**   corn   **II.3**, IV.2
mal   badly, bad   **II.5**, III.1
el **mal tiempo**   bad weather   **II.1**, I.5
la **maleta**   suitcase   **I.5**, IV.6
malgastar   to waste   **IV.3**
el **malgasto**   to waste   **IV.3**
malo(a) (estar)   sick, ill   **I.3**, I.1
malo(a) (ser)   bad   **I.3**, III.1
mañana   tomorrow   **I.1**, I.1
la **mañana**   morning   **I.1**, I.9
mandar   to send, to order, to command   **IV.3**, IV.1
manejar   to drive   **IV.1**, I.10
la **manga**   sleeve   **II.2**, IV.6
el **mango**   mango   **II.3**
la **manguera**   hose   **IV.5**
la **mano**   hand   **I.3**, I.4

el **mantel**   tablecloth   **II.3**
la **mantequilla**   butter   **II.3,** IV.2
la **manzana**   apple   **II.3,** IV.2
el **mapa**   map   **I.4,** I.8
maquillarse   to put on makeup   **III.3,** IV.5
el **mar**   sea   **II.1,** III.3
marchar atrás   to back up, to reverse   **IV.5**
mareado(a)   dizzy   **IV.4**
marearse   to feel dizzy, to become dizzy   **IV.4**
los **mareos**   dizziness   **IV.4**
la **margarina**   margarine   **II.3**
la **mariposa**   butterfly   **I.5,** III.6
los **mariscos**   seafood   **II.3,** IV.2
marrón   brown (dark)   **I.4,** II.6
martes   Tuesday   **I.1,** I.9
marzo   March   **I.1,** I.9
más   more   **I.1,** I.1;   and, plus (arithmetic) I.3;   most   **I.2,** I.7
más... que   more . . . than   **I.2,** I.7
más de + *number*   more than + *number*   **I.2,** II.6
más que nada   more than anything   III.6
la **masa**   dough   **II.3,** IV.2
la **máscara**   mask   **III.3**
matar   to kill   **IV.3**
las **matemáticas**   math   **I.5,** I.9
la **materia**   subject (class)   **I.5,** IV.4
mayo   May   **I.1,** I.9
la **mayonesa**   mayonnaise   **II.3**
mayor   older   **II.4**
la **mazorca**   corn on the cob   **II.3**
me   me   **I.3, I.5, III.2,** I.4, IV.1, IV.5
me duele(n)...   . . . hurt(s) me   **I.2**
Me llamo...   My name is . . .   **I.1,** I.2
el/la **mecánico(a)**   mechanic   **I.2,** II.5
mediano(a)   medium, average   **I.2,** I.7
la **medianoche**   midnight   **I.1,** I.9
las **medias**   stockings   **II.2,** I.5
el/la **médico(a)**   doctor   **I.2,** II.5
médico(a)   medical   **IV.4**
medio(a)   half   **I.1,** I.9
el **medio**   middle   **II.1,** III.2
el **medioambiente**   environment   **IV.3**
el **mediodía**   noon   **I.1,** I.9
los **medios**   means, method   **II.1**
la **mejilla**   cheek   **I.3,** III.1
mejor   better   **I.3,** III.1;   best   **I.2,** II.5
mejorarse   to get better   **IV.4**
el **melón**   melon   **II.3**
memorizar   to memorize   **II.5,** IV.4
menor   less, minus   **I.1,** I.3;   least   **I.2,** I.7;   younger   **I.2,** II.4
menos... que   less . . . than   **I.2,** I.7

mentir (ie, i)   to tell a lie   **III.1**
el **mentón**   chin   **I.3,** III.1
merendar (ie)   to eat a snack   **II.3**
la **merienda**   snack   **II.3,** I.6
el **mes**   month   **I.1,** I.9
el **mes pasado**   last month   **II.1**
la **mesa**   table   **I.4,** I.8
el/la **mesero(a)**   waiter, waitress   **I.2,** II.5
la **mesita**   table (small)   **III.4**
el **metal**   metal   **IV.3**
mexicano(a)   Mexican   II.3
México   Mexico   II.3
mezclado(a)   mixed   IV.2
la **mezquita**   mosque   **II.1,** III.2
mi   my   **I.1,** I.2
mí   me *(after prep.)*   **II.1,** III.2
la **microonda**   microwave   **III.4**
el **miedo**   fear   **I.3**
miedo (tener...)   to be afraid   **IV.4,** III.5
la **miel**   honey   **II.3**
mientras (que)   while   **II.5,** II.1
miércoles   Wednesday   **I.1,** I.9
mil   (a, one) thousand   **I.4,** I.10
la **milla**   mile   **II.4,** IV.3
el **millón**   million   **I.4,** I.10
mío(a)   (of) mine   **I.1,** I.5
mirar   to look at, to watch   **II.2,** I.10
la **Misa del Gallo**   Midnight Mass   **III.3**
el **mitón**   mitten   **II.2**
los **mocasines**   moccasins, loafers   **II.2**
la **mochila**   backpack, knapsack   **I.4,** I.8
moderno(a)   modern   **I.4,** IV.3
molestar   to bother   **II.3**
el **mono**   monkey   **I.5,** I.6
la **mononucleosis**   mononucleosis   **IV.4**
el **monopatín**   skateboard   **I.5,** III.5
la **montaña**   mountain   **II.1,** III.3
montar   to ride   **III.1**
el **monumento**   monument   **II.1,** III.2
morado(a)   purple   **I.4,** I.7
moreno(a)   brunette, dark-haired   **I.2,** II.1
morir (ue, u)   to die   **III.1,** IV.4
la **mosca**   fly   **I.5,** III.6
el **mosquito**   mosquito   **I.5,** III.6
la **mostaza**   mustard   **II.3**
mostrar (ue)   to show   **III.1**
la **moto(cicleta)**   motorcycle   **II.1,** III.4
mover (ue)   to move   **III.1**
la **muchacha**   girl   **I.1,** I.2
el **muchacho**   boy   **I.1,** I.2
muchas veces   many times   **II.5**
muchísimo(a)   very much   **I.5**
mucho(a)   a lot, much   **I.1,** I.1;   often   **II.5**
Mucho gusto   Pleased to meet you   **I.1,** I.2

la **mueblería** furniture store **IV.2**
los **muebles** furniture **III.4**
 muerto(a) dead, died **III.3**
la **mujer** woman **I.2,** I.2
la **mujer de negocios** businesswoman **I.2,** II.5
la **multa** traffic ticket, fine **IV.5**
 multiplicar to multiply **II.5,** IV.4
 mundial worldwide III.4
el **mundo** world **II.1,** II.2
la **muñeca** wrist **I.3,** III.1; doll **I.5,** III.5
el **murciélago** bat (animal) **I.5,** III.6
el **músculo** muscle **IV.4**
el **museo** museum **II.1,** III.2
la **música** music **I.5,** I.9
 musical musical **III.1**
el/la **músico(a)** musician **I.2,** II.5
 muy very **I.2,** I.1
 muy bien fine, very well **I.1,** I.1
 muy mal very bad **I.1,** I.1

N

el **nabo** turnip **II.3**
la **nacionalidad** nationality II.3
 nada nothing **I.5,** I.1
 nadar to swim **III.1,** I.10
 nadie no one **III.4,** IV.4
los **naipes** playing cards **III.1,** I.10
las **nalgas** buttocks **I.3,** III.1
la **naranja** orange **II.3,** IV.2
la **nariz** nose **I.3,** I.4
 natural natural **IV.3**
la **náusea** nausea **IV.4**
la **Navidad** Christmas **III.3**
 necesariamente necessarily **II.5**
 necesario(a) necessary **IV.3**
 necesitar to need (to) **II.5,** IV.2
 negar (ie) to deny **IV.4**
los **negocios** business **I.5,** II.5
 negro(a) black **I.4,** I.7
 nerviosamente nervously **II.5**
 nervioso(a) nervous **I.3,** III.1
 nevar (ie) to snow **III.1**
 ni nor II.4
 ni... ni neither . . . nor **III.4,** IV.4
la **nieta** granddaughter **I.2,** I.3
el **nieto** grandson **I.2,** I.3
los **nietos** grandchildren **I.2,** I.3
 nieva it's snowing, it snows **II.1,** I.5
la **nieve** snow **III.4,** I.10
el **nilón** nylon **II.2**
la **niña** small girl **I.2,** I.2
 ninguna manera (de...) no way **III.4**
 ninguna parte (en...) nowhere **III.4**

 ninguno(a) none, not any **III.4,** IV.4
el **niño** small boy **I.2,** I.2
 no no, not **I.2,** I.1
 no muy bien not very well **I.1,** I.1
 No sé I don't know I.1
la **noche** evening, night **I.1,** I.1
la **Nochevieja** New Year's Eve **III.3**
la **Nochebuena** Christmas Eve **III.3**
el **nombre** (first) name **I.1,** I.2
el **noreste** northeast **II.4**
el **norte** north **II.1,** III.3
 nos us, to us **I.3,** I.4; each other, ourselves **III.2,** IV.5
 nosotros(as) we **I.5,** I.2
la **nota** grade (on tests, etc.) **II.5,** II.4
 novecientos nine hundred **I.4,** I.10
la **novela** novel **II.5,** IV.4
 noveno(a) ninth **II.4,** IV.3
 noventa ninety **I.1,** I.3
la **novia** girlfriend **I.2,** I.2
 noviembre November **I.1,** I.9
el **novio** boyfriend **I.2,** I.2
 nublado(a) cloudy **II.1,** I.5
 nuclear nuclear **IV.3**
la **nuera** daughter-in-law **I.2,** II.4
 nuestro(a) our, ours **I.2,** I.5
 nuevamente newly **II.5**
 nueve nine **I.1,** I.3
 nuevo(a) new **I.3,** II.6
la **nuez** nut, walnut **II.3,** IV.2
el **número** number **I.1,** I.3
 nunca never **II.5,** II.1

O

 o or **I.4,** I.6
 o... o either . . . or **III.4,** IV.4
el **objeto** object, item **IV.2**
el/la **obrero(a)** worker, laborer **I.2,** II.5
 obtener to get **IV.1**
el **océano** ocean **II.1,** III.3
 ochenta eighty **I.1,** I.3
 ocho eight **I.1,** I.3
 ochocientos eight hundred **I.4,** I.10
 octavo(a) eighth **II.4,** IV.3
 octubre October **I.1,** I.9
 ocupado(a) busy **I.3,** III.1
 ocuparse to be busy **III.2**
 odiar to hate (to) **II.5,** IV.2
el **oeste** west **II.1,** III.3
la **oficina** office **II.1,** II.5
el **oído** ear (inner) **I.3**
 oír to hear **II.4,** IV.6
 ojalá hopefully **IV.5,** IV.3

el **ojo**   eye   **I.3,** I.4
la **ola**   wave (water)   IV.6
la **olla**   pot   **III.4**
once   eleven   **I.1,** I.3
operar   to operate   **IV.4**
el/la **optómetra**   optometrist   **IV.2**
la **oreja**   (outer) ear   **I.3,** I.4
el **orgullo**   pride   **I.3,** IV.4
orgulloso(a)   proud   **IV.4**
el **oro**   gold   **I.4**
la **orquesta**   band, orchestra   **I.5,** I.9
os   you, to you (in Spain)   **I.5,** IV.7
oscuro(a)   dark   **I.4,** I.7
el **osito de peluche**   teddy bear   **I.5,** III.5
el **oso**   bear   **I.5,** I.6
la **ostra**   oyster   **II.3,** IV.2
el **otoño**   autumn   **II.1,** I.5
otra vez   again   **II.5,** II.1
otro(a)   other, another   **I.1,** I.8
el **otro lado de**   the other side of   **II.1**
la **oveja**   sheep   **I.5,** I.6
el **ozono**   ozone   **IV.3**

P

paciente   patient   **I.2,** III.1
el/la **paciente**   patient   **IV.4**
el **padrastro**   stepfather   **I.2,** I.3
los **padrastros**   stepparents   **I.2,** I.3
el **padre**   father   **I.1,** I.3
los **padres**   parents   **I.2,** I.3
el **padrino**   godfather   **I.2,** II.4
pagar   to pay (for)   **II.3,** IV.4
el **país**   country   **II.1,** II.3
el **pájaro**   bird   **I.5,** I.6
la **palabra**   word   II.3
la **palanca de cambios**   gear shift lever   **IV.5**
las **palomitas de maíz**   popcorn   **II.3,** IV.2
el **pan**   bread   **II.3,** I.6
el **pan tostado**   toast   **II.3,** IV.2
la **pana**   corduroy   **II.2**
la **panadería**   bakery   **II.1,** III.2
el **panecillo**   roll   **II.3,** IV.2
el **panqueque**   pancake   **II.3**
el **pantalón de sudadera**   sweatpants   **II.2**
los **pantalones**   pants   **II.2,** I.5
los **pantalones cortos**   shorts   **II.2,** IV.6
los **pantalones vaqueros**   blue jeans   **II.2,** IV.6
la **pantimedia**   pantyhose   **II.2**
el **pañuelo**   handkerchief   **II.2**
la **papa**   potato   **II.3,** I.6
las **papas fritas**   French fries   **II.3,** I.6
la **papaya**   papaya   **II.3**
el **papel**   paper   **I.1,** I.8

el **papel absorbente**   paper towel   **III.4**
la **papelera**   wastepaper basket   **I.4,** I.8
la **papelería**   stationery store   **II.1,** III.2
las **paperas**   mumps   **IV.4**
las **papitas fritas**   potato chips   **II.3,** I.6
para   for, in order to, by   **II.1,** I.6
para que   so that, in order that   **IV.5**
el **parabrisas**   windshield   **IV.5**
el **parachoques**   bumper   **IV.5**
la **parada de autobús**   bus stop   **IV.5**
el **paraguas**   umbrella   **II.2,** IV.6
parar   to stop   **IV.5**
pardo(a)   brown   **I.4,** I.7
¡Pare!   Stop!   **IV.5**
la **pared**   wall   **I.4,** III.2
pares (los números…)   even numbers   **I.1,** I.10
el **parque**   park   **II.1,** III.2
la **parte**   part   III.2
la **parte de atrás**   back (of a room)   **I.4,** III.2
el **partido**   match (sporting)   **III.1**
la **pasa**   raisin   **II.3**
el **pasado**   past   **II.5,** II.1
pasado mañana   day after tomorrow   **I.1,** I.9
el **pasador**   barrette   **II.2**
el **pasaporte**   passport   **IV.1**
pasar   to pass   **III.4,** III.3
pasar tiempo   to spend time   **III.1,** IV.6
pasar por   to pass through   **IV.1**
el **pasatiempo**   pastime   **III.1**
la **Pascua Florida**   Easter   **III.3**
el **paseo**   drive   **II.4,** IV.3
el **pasillo**   hallway   **II.1,** I.7
la **pasta**   pasta   **II.3**
el **pastel**   pastry, pie   **II.3,** III.2
la **pastelería**   pastry shop   **II.1,** III.2
la **pastilla**   pill   **IV.4**
la **patata**   potato   I.10
patinar   to skate   **III.1**
los **patines**   skates   **I.5,** III.5
los **patines de hielo**   ice skates   **I.5,** III.5
los **patines de rueda**   roller skates   **I.5,** III.5
el **patio**   inner courtyard, yard   **II.1,** I.7
el **pato**   duck   **I.5,** I.6
el **pavo**   turkey   **I.5,** III.6
el/la **payaso(a)**   clown   **I.2**
los **peces**   fish (live)   **IV.3,** I.6
el **pecho**   chest   **I.3,** III.1
el **pedido**   request   **I.1**
pedir (i, i)   to ask for   **III,1,** IV.4; to request   **IV.3**
peinarse   to comb   **III.2,** IV.5
la **película**   film   **IV.2**
el **peligro**   danger   **IV.3**

peligroso(a) dangerous **IV.3**
pelirrojo(a) redhead **I.2,** II.1
el **pelo** hair **I.3,** I.4
la **pelota** ball **I.5,** III.5
la **peluquería** beauty salon, barbershop
      II.1, III.2
el **pendiente** earring **II.2**
pensar (ie) to think **II.5,** IV.4
pensar (ie) de to think about (opinion)
      II.5, IV.4
pensar (ie) en to think about (daydream)
      II.5, IV.4
pensar + *infinitive* to plan to **II.4,** IV.4
peor worse **I.3;** worst **I.2**
el **pepino** cucumber **II.3,** IV.2
pequeño(a) small, little **I.2,** I.7
la **pera** pear **II.3,** IV.2
perder (ie) to lose **III.1,** IV.4
perder (ie) tiempo to waste time **III.1**
perdido(a) lost **IV.2**
Perdón Pardon me **I.1,** I.1
el/la **peregrino(a)** pilgrim **III.3**
perezosamente lazily **II.5**
perezoso(a) lazy **I.2,** II.2
perfectamente perfectly **II.5**
la **perfumería** perfume store **IV.2**
el **perico** parrot **I.5,** III.6
el **periódico** newspaper **I.5**
el/la **periodista** journalist **I.2,** II.5
el **periquito** parakeet **I.5,** III.6
la **perla** pearl **II.2**
Permiso (Con...) Excuse me **I.1,** I.1
el **permiso** permit **IV.5**
permitir to permit, to allow **IV.3**
pero but **I.4,** I.6
el **perro** dog **I.5,** I.6
el **perro caliente** hot dog **II.3,** I.6
la **persona** person **I.2,** I.2
la **personalidad** personality **I.2**
las **personas** people **I.2,** I.2
pesado(a) heavy **I.4,** II.6
pesar(se) to weigh (oneself) **IV.4**
las **pesas** weights **III.1**
la **pescadería** fish store **II.1**
el **pescado** fish (to eat) **II.3,** I.6
el/la **pescador(a)** fisherperson **I.2**
pescar to fish **III.1,** IV.6
el **petróleo** petroleum **IV.3**
el **pez** fish (live) **I.5,** I.6
el **piano** piano **III.1,** I.10
la **picazón** itch **IV.4**
el **pie** foot **I.3,** I.4
la **piel** fur **II.2**
la **pierna** leg **I.3,** I.4

la **pieza** part **IV.5**
las **pijamas** pajamas **II.2,** IV.6
la **pila** battery (flashlight) **IV.3**
el **pimentero** pepper shaker **II.3**
el **pimiento** pepper (vegetable) **II.3,** IV.2
la **pimienta** pepper (spice) **IV.2**
pintar to paint **III.1**
la **piña** pineapple **II.3,** IV.2
la **piñata** papier mâché figure **III.3**
el **pisacorbatas** tie bar **II.2**
el **piso** floor **II.1,** IV.3
la **pista** track I.10
la **pista de patinaje** skating rink **IV.2**
la **pistola de agua** water gun **I.5**
la **pizarra** chalkboard **I.1,** I.8
la **pizza** pizza **II.3,** III.2
la **pizzería** pizzeria **II.1,** III.2
la **placa** license plate **IV.5**
planchar to iron **III.4**
planear to plan **IV.1,** IV.1
plano(a) flat **I.4,** I.7
la **planta** plant **IV.3,** II.6
la **planta baja** ground floor **II.1,** I.7
el **plástico** plastic **IV.3**
la **plata** silver **I.4**
el **plátano** banana **II.3,** IV.2
plateado(a) silver **I.4,** II.6
el **platillo** saucer **II.3**
el **plato** plate, dish **II.3,** IV.1
el **plato principal** main dish **II.3**
los **platos** dishes IV.2
la **playa** beach **II.1,** III.2
la **plaza** town square **II.1,** III.2
la **plaza de toros** bullfighting arena **III.3**
el/la **plomero(a)** plumber **I.2**
poco(a) little, few **I.2,** II.1
poco asado rare **II.3**
poder (ue) can, to be able **I.1,** I.10
poder (*preterite***)** succeeded **II.5,** IV.6;
      no poder (*preterite***)** failed **II.5,** IV.6
el **poema** poem **II.5**
la **poesía** poetry **II.5,** IV.4
el/la **policía** police officer **I.2,** II.5
la **policía** the police **I.2,** II.5
el **poliéster** polyester **II.2**
el **pollo** chicken **II.3,** I.6
el **polvo** dust **III.4**
poner to put **I.1,** IV.6
poner la mesa to set the table **III.4**
poner fuego a to set fire to **III.3**
poner una multa to give a ticket **IV.5**
ponerse to put on, to become **III.2,** IV.5
popular popular **I.2,** II.2
por by, for, through **IV.1,** I.3; times **I.4,** I.3

por aquí   around here   **II.1**
por ejemplo   for example   III.2
por eso   therefore   II.2
por favor   please   **I.1,** I.1
por la mañana   in the morning   **II.5,** II.1
por la noche   in the evening   **II.5,** II.1
por la tarde   in the afternoon   **II.5,** II.1
¿Por qué?   Why?   **I.2,** II.3
por supuesto   of course   IV.2
por teléfono   on the phone   III.1, I.10
porque   because   **I.4,** I.7
el **portabilletes**   money clip   **II.2**
el **portaequipaje**   trunk of a car   IV.5
portarse (bien)   to behave (well)   **III.2**
posible   possible   IV.4
posiblemente   possibly   II.5
el **postre**   dessert   **II.3,** I.6
la **práctica**   practice   III.1
practicar   to practice   **II.5,** I.10
el **precio**   price   IV.2
preciso(a)   necessary   IV.4
preferible   preferable   IV.3
preferir (ie, i)   to prefer   **II.5,** IV.4
la **pregunta**   question   II.5
preguntar   to ask (in a question)   **I.1,** IV.4
preocupado(a)   worried   **I.3,** III.1
preocuparse   to worry   **III.2**
la **preparación**   preparation   **II.3,** IV.1
preparar   to prepare   **II.3,** I.10
prepararse   to get ready   **III.2**
presentar   to introduce, to present   **I.1,** I.2
el **presente**   present (now)   **II.5,** II.1
la **presión**   pressure   IV.4
prestar   to lend   IV.1
primario(a)   elementary, primary   **I.5,** IV.4
la **primavera**   spring   **II.1,** I.5
el **primer año**   freshman year   **I.5,** I.5
el **primer piso**   second floor (one floor up)   **II.1,** I.7
primer(o)(a)   first   **I.1,** I.9
el/la **primo(a)**   cousin   **I.2,** I.3
prisa (tener...)   to be in a hurry   **I.3,** III.5
probable   probable   IV.4
probar (ue)   to taste, to try (out)   **III.1**
probarse (ue)   to try on   IV.2
el **problema**   problem   IV.3
producir   to produce   IV.3
el **producto**   product   IV.3
los **productos lácteos**   dairy products   II.3
la **profesión**   occupation   **I.2,** II.5
el/la **profesor(a)**   teacher   **I.1,** II.5
profundamente   deeply   IV.4
prohibido(a)   prohibited   IV.5
prohibir   to prohibit   IV.3
pronto   soon   **II.5**

próximo(a)   next (in order)   **I.5,** II.1
el **proyecto**   project   II.5
la **prueba**   test, quiz   **II.5,** IV.4
la **prueba de sangre**   blood test   IV.4
públicamente   publicly   II.5
pudiera   could   IV.2
el **pueblo**   town   **II.1,** III.3
puedo + *infinitive*   I can + *verb*   I.10
el **puente**   bridge, overpass   IV.5
la **puerta**   door   **I.1,** I.8
el **puerto**   port   IV.1
pues   well, then   II.3
puesto(a)   put   III.5
el **pulgar**   thumb   **I.3,** III.1
pulir   to polish   III.4
el **pulmón**   lung   **I.3,** III.1
la **pulmonía**   pneumonia   IV.4
el **pulpo**   octopus   **I.5,** III.6
el **pulso**   pulse   IV.4
el **puño de la puerta**   door handle   IV.5
el **pupitre**   desk (of a student)   **I.1,** I.8

Q

que   than   **I.4,** I.3; that *(conjunction)*   **I.4,** I.8
¿Qué?   What?   **I.1,** I.1
¿Qué hora es?   What time is it?   **I.1,** I.9
¡Qué lástima!   That's too bad!   **I.1,** I.1
¿Qué pasa?   What's happening?   I.1
¿Qué quiere decir... ?   What does . . . mean?   I.1
¿Qué tal?   How's everything?   **I.1,** I.1
¿Qué tiempo hace?   What's the weather like?   **II.1,** I.5
¿Qué tienes?   What's the matter?   **I.3,** III.1
quedar   to keep   II.3
quedarse   to stay, to remain   **III.2,** IV.5
los **quehaceres**   chores   **III.4,** IV.5
quejarse   to complain   **III.2**
quemado(a)   burnt   II.3
quemar   to burn   II.3
querer (ie)   to want   **I.1,** IV.4
querer (ie) a   to love   **III.1,** IV.4
querer *(preterite)*   tried   **III.3,** IV.6;
   no querer *(preterite)*   refused   **III.3,** IV.6
querido(a)   dear   **III.3,** II.2
el **queso**   cheese   **II.3,** IV.2
¿Quién?   Who?   **I.2,** I.2
¿Quiénes?   Who?   **I.2,** II.3
la **química**   chemistry   **I.5,** IV.4
los **químicos**   chemicals   IV.3
quince   fifteen   **I.1,** I.3
quinientos   five hundred   **I.4,** I.10
quinto(a)   fifth   **II.4,** IV.3
quisiera   would like   IV.2

quitar   to remove   **III.4,** IV.2
quitarse   to take off   **III.2,** IV.5
quizás   maybe   **IV.5**

R

el **rábano**   radish   **II.3,** IV.2
el **radiador**   radiator   **IV.5**
el **radio**   radio (set)   **I.5,** I.8
la **radio**   radio (program)   **I.5**
la **radiografía**   X ray   **IV.4**
el/la **radiólogo(a)**   radiologist   **IV.4**
el **ramillete**   bouquet   **III.2,** IV.1
la **rana**   frog   **I.5,** III.6
la **ranchera**   station wagon   **IV.5**
rápidamente   rapidly   **II.5,** IV.5
rápido(a)   fast   II.6
raramente   rarely   **II.5,** II.1
raro(a)   rare   **IV.4**
el **rascacielos**   skyscraper   **II.1,** III.2
el **raso**   satin   **II.2**
la **rata**   rat   **I.5,** III.6
el **ratón**   mouse   **I.5,** I.6
la **Raza**   Hispanic people   **III.3**
razón (no tener...)   to be wrong   **I.3,** III.5
razón (tener...)   to be right   **I.3,** III.5
la **reacción**   reaction   **IV.4**
la **rebanada**   slice   **II.3,** IV.2
el/la **recepcionista**   receptionist   **IV.4**
recetar   to prescribe   **IV.4**
recibir   to receive   **II.5,** I.10
reciclado(a)   recycled   **IV.4**
reciclar   to recycle   **IV.3**
el **recogedor de polvo**   dust pan   **III.4**
recoger   to collect   **III.4,** IV.6
recoger las hojas   to rake leaves   **III.4**
recomendar (ie)   to recommend   **III.1**
recordar (ue)   to remember   **III.1,** IV.4
rectangular   rectangular   **I.4,** II.6
el **recuerdo**   memory, souvenir   **IV.1,** IV.6
el **recurso**   resource   **IV.3**
redondo(a)   round   **I.4,** I.7
reducir   to reduce   **IV.3**
el **refresco**   soft drink   **II.3,** I.6
los **refrescos**   refreshments, beverages   **III.5,** IV.1
el **refrigerador**   refrigerator   **III.4**
regalar   to give as a gift   **III.3**
el **regalo**   gift, present   **II.2,** I.9
la **regla**   ruler   **I.4,** II.6
regresar   to return   **II.5,** IV.6
regular   normal, OK   **I.1**
regularmente   regularly   **II.5**
la **reina**   queen   II.2
el **reloj**   clock   **I.4,** I.8

el **reloj (de) pulsera**   wristwatch   **I.5,** I.5
la **relojería**   clock store   **II.1,** III.2
el **remedio**   remedy   **IV.4**
la **remolacha**   beet   **II.3,** IV.2
el **remolque**   trailer   **IV.5**
la **reparación**   repair   **IV.5**
reparar   to repair   **II.2**
repente (de...)   suddenly   **II.5,** II.1
repetir (i, i)   to repeat   **I.1,** IV.4
la **res (carne de...)**   beef   **II.3,** IV.2
reservar   to reserve   **IV.1**
resolver (ue)   to solve, to resolve   **III.1**
respirar   to breathe   **IV.4**
restar   to subtract   **II.5,** IV.4
el **restaurante**   restaurant   **II.1,** III.2
el **resuelto**   result   **III.5**
el **retrete**   lavatory   **IV.2**
el **retroproyector**   overhead projector   **I.4,** II.6
reunirse   to meet   **IV.2**
reverso(a)   reverse   **IV.5**
revisar   to check   **IV.5**
los **Reyes Magos**   Wise Men   **III.3**
rico(a) (estar)   delicious   **I.3,** III.1
rico(a) (ser)   rich   **I.3,** III.1
ridículo(a)   ridiculous   **IV.4**
el **rincón**   corner (inside)   **I.4,** III.2
el **rinoceronte**   rhinoceros   **I.5,** III.6
el **río**   river   **II.1,** III.3
la **rodilla**   knee   **I.3,** I.4
rogar (ue)   to beg   **IV.3**
rojo(a)   red   **I.4,** I.7
romántico(a)   romantic   **III.3**
el **rompecabezas**   puzzle   **I.5,** III.5
romper   to break   **III.5,** IV.2
la **ropa**   clothing, clothes   **II.2,** I.5
la **ropa interior**   underwear   **II.2,** IV.6
la **ropería**   clothing store   **II.1,** III.2
rosado(a)   pink   **I.4,** I.7
el **rosbif**   roast beef   **II.3,** I.6
la **rosquilla**   doughnut   **II.3,** IV.2
roto(a)   broken   **III.5,** III.1
la **rubeola**   three-day measles   **IV.4**
rubio(a)   blond   **I.2,** II.1
la **rueda**   wheel   **I.5,** III.5
ruidoso(a)   noisy   **IV.3**
el **ruso**   Russian (language)   **I.5,** IV.4
la **ruta**   route   **IV.1**

S

sábado   Saturday   **I.1,** I.9
la **sábana**   sheet (for a bed)   **III.4**
saber   to know (a fact);   **I.1,** IV.1;
    (how)   **III.3,** IV.6
saber (*preterite*)   found out   **I.4,** IV.6

el **sacapuntas** pencil sharpener **I.4,** II.6
sacar to take out **I.1,** IV.1
sacar fotos to take pictures **III.5,** IV.1
sacar la lengua to stick out one's tongue **IV.4**
sacar la nieve to shovel snow **III.4**
sacar una A to get an A **II.5,** IV.4
el **saco** sports coat **II.2,** IV.6
sacudir to shake **III.4**
la **sal** salt **II.3,** IV.2
la **sala** living room **II.1,** I.7
la **sala de emergencia** emergency room **IV.4**
la **sala de estar** family room, den **II.1,** I.7
la **salchicha** sausage **II.3,** IV.2
el **salero** salt shaker **II.3**
la **salida** exit **II.4**
salir to go out, to leave **II.4,** IV.6
salir bien to turn out well **II.5**
el **salmón** salmon **II.3**
la **salsa picante** hot sauce **II.3,** IV.2
la **salud** health **I.1,** I.4
¡Salud! *(for a sneeze)* Bless you! I.4
saludar to greet **III.5,** IV.1
el **saludo** greeting **I.1,** I.1
salvaje wild, untamed **I.5,** III.6
salvar to save **IV.3**
las **sandalias** sandals **II.2,** IV.6
la **sandía** watermelon **II.3,** IV.2
el **sándwich** sandwich **II.3,** I.6
la **sangre** blood **IV.4**
sano(a) healthy **IV.4**
el **sapo** toad **I.5,** III.6
el **sarampión** measles **IV.4**
el **sarpullido** rash **IV.4**
la **sartén** frying pan **III.4,** IV.2
el **saxofón** saxophone **III.1**
se one, you, they *(impersonal)* **III.2,** I.1; each other, yourself, himself, herself, yourselves,themselves **III.2,** IV.5
sé I know **I.1,** I.1
la **secadora** dryer (clothes) **III.4**
secar to dry **III.4**
secarse to dry oneself **III.2**
el/la **secretario(a)** secretary **I.1,** II.5
secundario(a) secondary **I.5,** IV.4
sed (tener…) to be thirsty **I.3,** III.5
la **seda** silk **II.2**
seguir (i, i) to continue, to follow **II.4,** IV.4
segundo(a) second **II.4,** IV.3
el **segundo año** sophomore year **I.5**
el **segundo piso** second floor (third floor up) **II.4**
la **seguridad** security **IV.1**
seguro(a) (estar) sure, certain **I.3,** III.1
seguro(a) (ser) safe **I.3,** IV.3

seis six **I.1,** I.3
seiscientos six hundred **I.4,** I.10
la **selva** forest, jungle **I.5,** III.3
el **semáforo** traffic light **II.4**
la **semana** week **I.1,** II.1
la **semana pasada** last week **II.1**
la **señal** sign **IV.5**
la **señal de unión** merge sign **IV.5**
el **señor (Sr.)** Mr., Sir **I.1,** I.2
la **señora (Sra.)** Mrs., Ma'am **I.1,** I.2
la **señorita (Srta.)** Miss, Ms. **I.1,** I.2
sentarse (ie) to sit down **I.1,** IV.5
sentir (ie, i) to regret, to be sorry **III.2,** IV.4
sentirse (ie, i) to feel **III.2**
separarse to separate **III.2**
septiembre September **I.1,** I.9
séptimo(a) seventh **II.4,** IV.3
el **sepulcro** grave **III.3**
ser to be *(identity)* **I.1,** I.2; to be *(characteristics)* **I.1,** II.1
serio(a) serious **I.2**
la **serpiente** snake **I.5,** III.6
el **servicio** service **IV.2**
los **servicios** lavatories **IV.2**
la **servilleta** napkin **II.3**
servir (i, i) to serve **III.1,** IV.4
sesenta sixty **I.1,** I.3
setecientos seven hundred **I.4,** I.10
setenta seventy **I.1,** I.3
sexto(a) sixth **II.4,** IV.3
si if **I.4,** II.3
sí yes **I.1,** I.1
la **sicología** psychology **I.5,** IV.4
el **SIDA** AIDS **IV.4**
siempre always **II.5,** II.1
la **sierra** mountain range **II.1,** III.3
la **siesta** nap **III.1,** IV.2
siete seven **I.1,** I.3
el **siglo** century **III.3**
el **silbato** whistle **I.5,** III.5
el **silenciador** muffler **IV.5**
el **silencio** silence **I.1**
la **silla** chair **I.4,** I.8
el **sillón** chair (large) **III.4**
simpático(a) nice **I.2,** II.2
sin (que) without **II.1,** I.2
sin embargo however, nevertheless **I.4**
sin escalas nonstop (flight) **IV.1**
la **sinagoga** synagogue **II.1,** III.2
sinceramente sincerely **II.5**
sincero(a) sincere **I.2,** II.2
sino but, but rather **I.4**
el **síntoma** symptom **IV.4**
sobre over **II.1,** III.2

sobrepasar   to pass (car)   **IV.5**

la **sobrina**   niece   **I.2,** II.4

el **sobrino**   nephew   **I.2,** II.4

sociable   social   **I.2,** IV.4

la **soda**   soda, pop   **II.3**

el **sofá**   sofa   **III.4**

el **sol**   sun   **II.1,** I.5

sol (hacer...)   to be sunny   **II.1,** I.5

solamente   only   **II.5,** II.3

solar   solar   **IV.3**

el **soldado**   soldier   **I.2,** III.5

el **soldado (de juguete)**   (toy) soldier   **I.5,** III.5

soler (ue)   to be accustomed to   **III.1**

sólido(a)   solid   **II.2**

sólo mirar   to browse, to just look   **IV.2**

la **solución**   solution   **IV.3**

el **sombrero**   hat   **II.2,** I.5

son (=)   equal(s) (=)   **I.4,** I.3

sonar (ue)   to sound   **III.1**

sonarse la nariz   to blow one's nose   **IV.4**

soñar con   to dream about   **III.1**

la **sopa**   soup   **II.3,** I.6

sorprender   to surprise   **IV.4**

la **sorpresa**   surprise   **III.5**

el **sótano**   basement   **II.1,** I.7

su   your, his, her, their   **I.2,** I.3

subir   to go up   **II.4,** IV.3

subirse   to get on   **IV.4**

subtraer   to subtract   **II.5**

sucio(a)   dirty   **I.4,** IV.3

la **sudadera**   sweatshirt   **II.2**

la **suegra**   mother-in-law   **I.2,** II.4

el **suegro**   father-in-law   **I.2,** II.4

el **suelo**   floor   **I.1,** III.2

sueño (tener...)   to be sleepy   **I.3,** III.5

suerte (tener...)   to be lucky   **I.3,** III.5

el **suéter**   sweater   **II.2,** I.5

suficiente   enough   **I.5,** I.5

sufrir   to suffer   **II.5,** IV.3

sugerir (ie, i)   to suggest   **III.1**

sumar   to add (arithmetic)   **II.5,** IV.4

el **supermercado**   supermarket   **II.1,** III.2

el **sur**   south   **II.1,** III.3

el **suroeste**   southwest   **II.4**

suspender   to fail   **II.5,** IV.4

sustituir   to substitute   **IV.3**

suyo(a)   yours, his, hers, its, theirs   **III.4,** I.5

T

el **tablero de anuncios**   bulletin board   **I.4,** II.6

la **tableta de chocolate**   chocolate bar   **II.3,** IV.2

tacaño(a)   stingy   **I.2**

el **tacón**   heel (of a shoe)   **II.2,** IV.6

los **tacones altos**   high heels   **II.2**

el **tafetán**   taffeta   **II.2**

tal vez   maybe, perhaps   **IV.5**

los **tallarines**   noodles   **II.3**

el **talón**   heel (of a foot)   **I.3,** III.1

el **tamaño**   size   **I.4,** I.7

también   also, too   **III.4,** I.3

el **tambor**   drum   **I.5,** III.5

tampoco   either, neither   **III.4,** III.6;
   not at all   **III.4,** IV.5

tan   as   I.7

tan... como   as . . . as   **I.2,** I.7

el **tanque**   tank   **IV.1**

el **tanque de gasolina**   gas tank   **IV.5**

tanto(a)   as much   **I.5,** I.3

tantos(as)   as many   **I.5,** I.3

el **tapacubos**   hubcap   **IV.5**

el **tapete**   rug, throw rug   **III.4**

la **taquigrafía**   shorthand   **I.5,** IV.4

tarde   late   **II.5,** IV.1

la **tarde**   afternoon   **I.1,** I.1

la **tarea**   homework   **I.1,** IV.4

la **tarjeta**   card (greeting)   **III.3,** IV.6

la **tarjeta de crédito**   credit card   **IV.2**

la **tarjeta postal**   postcard   **IV.1,** IV.6

el **taxi**   taxi   **II.1,** III.4

la **taza**   cup   **II.3,** III.1

te   you, to you   **I.3,** I.4: yourself   **III.2,** IV.5

Te quiero   I love you   **II.2,** II.2

el **té**   tea   **II.3,** I.6

el **teatro**   theater   **II.1,** III.2

el **techo**   ceiling, roof   **I.4,** III.2

teclear   to input (keyboard)   **II.5,** IV.4

el **tecleo**   keyboarding   **I.5**

tejido(a)   knit   **II.2**

la **tela**   fabric   **II.2**

telefonear   to telephone   **III.5**

el **teléfono**   telephone   **I.5,** I.8

la **televisión**   television program   **III.1,** I.10

el **televisor**   television set   **I.5,** I.8

el **tema**   theme   **II.5,** IV.4

temer   to fear   **IV.4**

la **temperatura**   temperature   I.5

el **templo**   temple   **II.1,** III.2

temprano   early   **II.5,** IV.1

el **tenedor**   fork   **II.3**

tener   to have   **I.3,** I.3

tener... años   to be . . . years old   **I.1,** III.5

tener calor   to be warm   **I.3,** III.5

tener celos   to be jealous   **I.3**

tener cuidado   to be careful   **I.3,** III.5

tener frío   to be cold   **I.3,** III.5

tener ganas de + *infinitive*   to feel like + *verb*
   II.5, IV.2

tener hambre   to be hungry   III.5
tener miedo   to be afraid   III.5
tener prisa   to be in a hurry   III.5
tener que + *infinitive*   to have to + *verb*
  II.5, IV.2
tener razón   to be right;   **no tener razón**
  to be wrong   **I.3,** III.5
tener sed   to be thirsty   **I.3,** III.5
tener sueño   to be sleepy   **I.3,** III.5
tener suerte   to be lucky   **I.3,** III.5
el **tenis**   tennis   **III.1,** I.10
tercer(o)(a)   third   **II.4,** IV.3
el **tercer año**   junior year   **I.5**
el **terciopelo**   velvet   **II.2**
terminar   to end, to finish   III.3
la **ternera**   veal   **II.3,** IV.2
la **tetera**   teapot   **II.3**
ti   you *(after prep.)*   **II.1,** III.2
la **tía**   aunt   **I.2,** I.3
el **tiburón**   shark   **I.5,** III.6
el **tiempo**   weather   **II.1,** I.5;   time   **IV.3,** I.5
la **tienda**   store   **II.1,** I.8
la **tierra**   Earth   **IV.3**
el **tigre**   tiger   **I.5,** I.6
las **tijeras**   scissors   **I.4,** II.6
tímido(a)   shy, timid   **I.2,** II.2
la **tintorería**   dry cleaners   **II.1,** III.2
el **tío**   uncle   **I.2,** I.3
el **tipo**   kind, type   III.6
el **títere**   puppet   **I.5,** III.5
el **título**   title   **I.1**
la **tiza**   chalk   **I.4,** I.8
la **toalla**   towel   **III.4**
el **tobillo**   ankle   **I.3,** III.1
el **tocador**   bureau, dresser   **III.4**
tocar   to play (music)   **III.1,** I.10
toca (te...)   it's your turn   I.1
el **tocino**   bacon   **II.3,** IV.2
todavía   still, yet   **II.5,** II.1
todavía no   not yet   **II.5,** II.1
todo(a)   all, whole   **II.5,** I.9
todo derecho   straight ahead   **II.4**
todo el mundo   everyone   **I.2**
todos los (días)   every (day)   **II.5,** II.1
tomar   to drink, to take   **II.3,** I.10
tomar apuntes   to take notes   **II.5,** IV.4
tomar una prueba   to take a quiz   **II.5**
tomarle el pulso   to take one's pulse   **IV.4**
tomarle la presión arterial   to take one's
  blood pressure   **IV.4**
tomarle la temperatura   to take one's
  temperature   **IV.4**
el **tomate**   tomato   **II.3,** IV.2
tonto(a)   foolish   **I.2,** II.2

la **torcedura**   sprain   **IV.4**
el **toro**   bull   **I.5,** I.6
la **toronja**   grapefruit   **II.3,** IV.2
la **torta**   cake   **II.3,** I.6
la **tortilla**   flat bread (Mexico)   **II.3**
la **tortuga**   turtle   **I.5,** III.6
la **tos**   cough   **I.3,** III.1
toser   to cough   **IV.4**
la **tostadora**   toaster   **III.4**
trabajador(a)   hardworking   **I.2,** II.2
trabajar   to work   **II.5,** I.10
el **trabajo**   job, work   **III.1,** I.3
traducir   to translate   **IV.3**
traer   to bring (things)   **III.3,** IV.6
tragar   to swallow   **IV.4**
el **traje**   suit   **II.2,** I.5
el **traje de baño**   swimsuit   **II.2,** IV.6
tranquilo(a)   calm   **I.3,** III.1
el **tránsito**   traffic   **IV.5**
el **transporte**   transportation   **II.1**
el **trapo**   rag   **III.4**
tratar   to treat   **IV.4**
tratar de   to try to   **II.5,** IV.2
el **trébol**   cloverleaf   **IV.5**
trece   thirteen   **I.1,** I.3
treinta   thirty   **I.1,** I.3
el **tren**   train   **I.5,** III.4
tres   three   **I.1,** I.3
trescientos   three hundred   **I.4,** I.10
triangular   triangular   **I.4,** II.6
el **triciclo**   tricycle   **I.5,** III.5
el **trigo**   wheat   **II.3,** IV.2
la **trigonometría**   trigonometry   **I.5,** IV.4
triste   sad   **I.2,** II.2
tristemente   sadly   **II.5,** IV.5
el **trombón**   trombone   **III.1**
la **trompa francesa**   French horn   **III.1**
la **trompeta**   trumpet   **III.1**
tropical   tropical   **IV.3**
tu   your   **I.1,** I.2
tú   you   **I.1,** I.1
la **tuba**   tuba   **III.1**
el **tubo de escape**   exhaust pipe   **IV.5**
turquesa   turquoise   **I.4,** II.6
tuyo(a)   yours   **III.4,** I.5

U

u *(before o/ho)*   or   **I.4**
la **ubicación**   location   **II.1**
último(a)   last (in order)   III.3
un(a)   a, an, one   **I.2,** I.2
un poco   a little bit   **II.1**
una vez   once   **II.5,** II.1

la **unidad**   unit   **I.**1

la **universidad**   university   **I.**5, IV.4

uno(a)   one   **I.**1, I.3

unos(as)   some   **I.**2, I.2

la **uña**   fingernail   **I.**3, III.1

urgente   urgent   **IV.**3

la **urticaria**   hives   **IV.**4

usar   to use   **I.**1

usted (Ud.)   you   **I.**1, I.1

ustedes (Uds.)   you *(plural)*   **I.**5, I.2

la **uva**   grape   **II.**3, IV.2

V

la **vaca**   cow   **I.**5, I.6

las **vacaciones**   vacation   **IV.**1, IV.6

vacío(a)   empty   **IV.**5

la **vainilla**   vanilla   **II.**3, I.6

vale (más…)   it's better   **IV.**4

valer   to be worth   **IV.**4

la **valle**   valley   **II.**1, III.3

vamos a + *infinitive*   let's + *verb*   **IV.**3, IV.1

la **vaquera**   cowgirl   **I.**2, II.1

el **vaquero**   cowboy   **I.**2, II.1

la **varicela**   chicken pox   **IV.**4

el **vaso**   glass (drinking)   **II.**3

Vaya(n)   Go *(formal command)*   **I.**1

Ve   Go *(familiar command)*   **I.**1

el **vecino(a)**   neighbor   **I.**2, IV.1

veinte   twenty   **I.**1, I.3

la **vela**   candle   **III.**3

la **velocidad**   speed   **IV.**5

vender   to sell   **II.**3, IV.2

venir   to come   **II.**1, IV.3

venta (de…)   for sale   **IV.**2

la **ventana**   window   **I.**1, I.8

la **ventanilla**   window of a car   **IV.**5

ver   to see   **II.**4, IV.6

el **verano**   summer   **II.**1, I.5

¿verdad?   right?, true?   **I.**2, II.2

verde (estar)   green (unripe)   **I.**3, III.1

verde (ser)   green (color)   **I.**3, I.7

el **verso**   verse   **III.**3

el **vestido**   dress   **II.**1, I.5

vestirse (i, i)   to dress   **III.**2, IV.5

el **vestuario**   costume   **III.**3

la **vez (veces)**   time(s), occurrence   **II.**5, II.1

la **vía**   way   **IV.**5

viajar   to travel   **IV.**1, I.10

el **viaje**   trip   **IV.**1, IV.6

el/la **viajero(a)**   traveler   **IV.**1

la **vida**   life   **II.**3, IV.5

el **vídeo**   video   **IV.**2, III.4

la **videocasetera**   videocassette recorder   **I.**4, II.6

el **videojuego**   video game   **III.**1

el **vidrio**   glass   **IV.**3

viejo(a)   old   **I.**2, II.1

el **viento**   wind   **II.**1, I.5

viernes   Friday   **I.**1, I.9

el **villancico**   carol   **III.**3

violeta   violet   **I.**4, II.6

el **violín**   violin   **III.**1

el **virus**   virus   **IV.**4

la **visita**   visit   **IV.**4

visitar   to visit   **IV.**1, I.10

visto(a)   seen   **III.**5

vivir   to live   **II.**4, I.7

vivo(a) (estar)   alive   **I.**3

vivo(a) (ser)   lively   **I.**3

el **vocabulario**   vocabulary   **I.**1, I.1

la **vocal**   vowel   **I.**1

el **volante**   steering wheel   **IV.**5

volar (ue)   to fly   **III.**1

el **vólibol**   volleyball   **III.**1

volver (ue)   to return   **III.**1, IV.4

vomitar   to vomit   **IV.**4

vosotros(as)   you *(plural)* (in Spain)   **I.**2, II.6

la **voz alta**   aloud, loud voice   **II.**5

la **voz baja**   low voice   **II.**5

el **vuelo**   flight   **IV.**1

vuelto(a)   returned   **III.**5

vuestro(a) *(possessive)*   your *(plural)* (in Spain)   **I.**2

Y

y   and   **I.**1, I.1

ya   already   **II.**5, II.1

ya no   no longer   **II.**5, II.1

el **yerno**   son-in-law   **I.**2, II.4

yo   I   **I.**5, I.1

el **yogur**   yogurt   **II.**3, IV.2

el **yoyo**   yo-yo   **I.**5, III.5

Z

la **zanahoria**   carrot   **II.**3, IV.2

la **zapatería**   shoe store   **II.**1, III.2

el/la **zapatero(a)**   shoe repairperson   **IV.**2

la **zapatilla**   slipper   **II.**2, IV.6

el **zapato**   shoe   **II.**2, I.5

los **zapatos tenis**   tennis shoes   **II.**2, IV.6

la **zona**   zone   **IV.**5

el **zorro**   fox   **I.**5, III.6

Vocabulary

This glossary contains all the vocabulary introduced in **Compañeros, Spanish for Communication, Books 1 and 2.** The reference number in bold following each entry indicates the unit and lesson in which each word or expression first appears in Book 2. The second number indicates the unit and lesson in which each word or expression first appears in Book 1.

A

a un(a) **I.2,** I.2
a little un poco **I.2,** II.1
a lot mucho(a) **I.1,** I.1
to be **able** poder (ue) **I.1,** I.10
about de **II.1,** II.4
to **accelerate** acelerar **IV.5**
accelerator el acelerador **IV.5**
to **accept** aceptar **III.5,** IV.1
accident el accidente **IV.5**
accordion el acordeón **III.1**
accountant el/la contador(a) **I.2,** II.5
to be **accustomed** soler (ue) **III.1**
ache el dolor **I.3,** III.1
Achoo Achís I.4
acid ácido(a) **IV.3**
across (from) a través de **II.1,** III.3
acting el drama **I.5**
activity la actividad **I.1,** IV.1
actor el actor **I.2,** II.5
actress la actriz **I.2,** II.5
to **add** añadir **II.3,** IV.2
to **add (arithmetic)** sumar **II.5,** IV.4
to **add to** aumentar **IV.3**
address la dirección **II.4,** IV.3
to **admire** admirar **II.2**
to **adore** encantar **II.3**
to **advise** aconsejar **IV.3**
advisor el/la consejero(a) **II.5**
aerosol el aerosol **IV.3**
affectionately cariñosamente II.2
to be **afraid** tener miedo **IV.4,** III.5
after después (de) (que) **II.1,** II.1
afternoon la tarde **I.1,** I.1
again otra vez, de nuevo **II.5,** II.1
against contra **II.1**
age la edad **I.1,** I.3
agency la agencia **IV.5**
agent el/la agente **I.2,** II.5
ago hace *(+ time) + preterite* **II.5,** II.1
AIDS el SIDA **IV.4**

air el aire **IV.3,** IV.6
airplane el avión **II.1,** I.8
airport el aeropuerto **II.1**
alarm clock el despertador **I.5,** IV.5
algebra el álgebra *(f.)* **I.5,** IV.4
alive vivo(a) (estar) **I.3**
all todo(a) **II.5,** I.9
all at once de una vez **II.5,** II.1
allergic alérgico(a) **IV.4**
allergy la alergia **IV.4**
to **allow** dejar, permitir **IV.3**
aloud, loud voice la voz alta **II.5**
alpaca la alpaca **II.2**
alphabet el alfabeto **I.1,** I.2
already ya **II.5,** II.1
also también **III.4,** I.3
although aunque **IV.3,** IV.3
altitude la altura III.3
aluminum el aluminio **IV.3**
always siempre **II.5,** II.1
ambassador el/la embajador(a) **I.2,** II.6
ambitious ambicioso(a) **I.2,** II.2
ambitiously ambiciosamente **II.5**
American el/la americano(a),
el/la estadounidense II.3
amphibian el anfibio **I.5,** III.6
amusement la diversión **III.3**
ancient (old, former) antiguo(a) **I.4,** IV.3
and y **I.1,** I.1; e *(before i/hi)* **I.4,** IV.1
angry enojado(a) **I.3,** III.1
animal el animal **I.5,** I.6
ankle el tobillo **I.3,** III.1
anniversary el aniversario **III.5**
to **annoy** disgustar **II.3**
another otro(a) **I.1,** IV.6
to **answer** contestar **I.1**
ant la hormiga **I.5,** III.6
antacid el antiácido **IV.4**
antibiotic el antibiótico **IV.4**
antibiotic el antibiótico **IV.4**
apartment el apartamento **II.1,** I.7
appendicitis la apendicitis **IV.4**
appetizer el entremés **II.3,** IV.2

499

apple la manzana **II.3,** IV.2
appointment la cita **IV.4**
April abril **I.1,** I.9
aquatic acuático(a) **I.5,** III.6
arcade la arcada de vídeos **IV.2**
archery la arquería **III.1**
architect el/la arquitecto(a) **I.2,** II.5
to **argue** discutir **III.1,** IV.3
arithmetic la aritmética **I.5**
arithmetic (to do…) calcular **II.5,** IV.4
arm el brazo **I.3,** I.4
around alrededor de **II.1,** III.2
to **arrange** arreglar **III.2**
to **arrive** llegar **II.4,** IV.1
art el arte *(f.)* **I.2,** I.9
artist el/la artista **I.2,** II.5
as como I.3; tan **I.2,** I.7
as … as tan… como **I.2,** I.7
as a child de niño(a) **II.5,** II.1
as an old person de viejo(a) **II.5,** II.1
as if como si **IV.2**
as many tantos(as) **I.5,** I.3
as much tanto(a) **I.5,** I.3
to **ask a question** preguntar **I.1,** IV.4
to **ask for** pedir (i, i) **III.1,** IV.4
aspirin la aspirina **IV.4**
asthma el asma **IV.4**
at a **I.1,** I.9
At what time? ¿A qué hora? **I.1**
athletic atlético(a) **I.2,** II.2
to **attend** asistir (a) **II.5,** IV.3
attendant el/la ayudante **I.2**
attic el desván **II.1,** I.7; la azotea **II.1**
August agosto **I.1,** I.9
aunt la tía **I.2,** I.3
automobile el automóvil **IV.1,** II.2
autumn el otoño **II.1,** I.5
avenue la avenida **II.4,** IV.3
average mediano(a) **I.2,** I.7
avocado el aguacate **II.3**

B

baby el/la bebé **I.2,** I.2
to **babysit** cuidar de los niños **III.1,** I.10
back la parte de atrás **I.4,** III.2
back (in…) atrás **III.1**
back (of the body) la espalda **I.3,** I.4
to **back up** marchar atrás **IV.5**
backpack la mochila **I.8**
bacon el tocino **II.3,** IV.2
bad malo(a) (ser) **I.3,** III.1
bad weather el mal tiempo **II.1,** I.5
badly mal **II.5,** III.1
badminton el badminton **III.1**

to **bake** hornear **II.3**
baked horneado(a) **II.3**
bakery la panadería **II.1,** III.2
balcony el balcón **II.1**
bald calvo(a) **I.2,** II.1
ball la pelota **I.5,** III.5
balloon el globo **I.5,** III.5
ballpoint pen el bolígrafo **I.4,** I.8
banana el plátano **II.3,** IV.2
band (music) la orquesta **I.5,** I.9
bank el banco **II.1,** III.2
banker el/la banquero(a) **I.2,** II.5
barber el/la barbero **I.2**
barbershop la peluquería **III.2**
barley la cebada **II.3**
barrette el pasador **II.2**
baseball el béisbol **III.1,** I.10
basement el sótano **II.1,** I.7
basket la canasta **III.3**
basketball el básquetbol I.10;
  el baloncesto **III.1**
bat (animal) el murciélago **I.5,** III.6
bat (baseball) el bate **I.5,** III.5
to **bathe** bañarse **III.2,** IV.5
bathroom el baño **I.1,** I.7;
  el cuarto de baño **II.1**
bathtub la bañera **III.4**
battery la batería **IV.5**
battery (flashlight) la pila **IV.3**
to **be** *(condition)* estar **I.3,** I.1
to **be** *(location)* estar **I.3,** I.3
to **be** *(characteristics)* ser **I.1,** II.1
to **be** *(identity)* ser **I.1,** I.2
beach la playa **II.1,** III.2
beans los frijoles **II.3,** IV.2
bear el oso **I.5,** I.6
beard la barba **I.3,** III.1
beauty salon la peluquería **II.1,** III.2
because porque **I.4,** I.7
to **become** hacerse, ponerse **III.2**
to **become engaged** comprometerse **III.2**
bed la cama **III.4**
bedroom la alcoba **II.1,** I.7
bee la abeja **I.5,** III.6
beef la carne de res **II.3,** IV.2
beet la remolacha **II.3,** IV.2
before antes (de) **II.1,** II.1
before antes de que **IV.5**
to **beg** rogar (ue) **IV.3**
to **begin** comenzar (ie), empezar (ie) **III.1,** IV.1
to **behave well** portarse (bien) **III.2**
behind atrás III.1; detrás de **II.1,** III.2
to **believe** creer **IV.4,** I.8
belt el cinturón **II.2,** IV.6
bench el banco **II.1,** III.2

beside   al lado de   **II.1,** III.2
best   el/la mejor   **I.2,** II.2
better   mejor   **I.3,** III.1
better (it is…)   más vale   **IV.4**
between   entre   **II.1,** III.2
beverage   la bebida   **II.3,** IV.2
bicycle   la bicicleta   **I.5,** I.8
big   grande   **I.2,** I.7
biodegradable   biodegradable   **IV.3**
biology   la biología   **I.5,** IV.4
bird   el pájaro   **I.5,** I.6
birthday   el cumpleaños   **I.1,** I.9
black   negro(a)   **I.4,** I.7
Bless you! *(for a sneeze)*   ¡Salud!   I.4
block (city)   la cuadra   **II.4,** IV.3
block (of wood)   el bloque   **I.5,** III.5
blond   rubio(a)   **I.2,** II.1
blood   la sangre   **IV.4**
blood test   la prueba de sangre   **IV.4**
blouse   la blusa   **II.2,** I.5
to **blow one's nose**   sonarse (ue) la nariz   **IV.4**
blue   azul   **I.4,** I.7
blue jeans   los pantalones vaqueros   **II.2,** IV.6
blueberry   el arándano   **II.3,** IV.2
to **board**   abordar   **IV.1**
boat   el barco   **II.1,** III.4
body   el cuerpo   **I.3,** I.4
to **boil**   hervir (ie, i)   **II.3**
boiled   hervido(a)   **II.3**
bone   el hueso   **IV.4**
book   el libro   **I.1,** I.8
bookshelf   el estante   **I.4,** I.8
bookstore   la librería   **II.1,** III.2
boot   la bota   **II.2,** IV.6
border   la frontera   **II.1,** III.3
bored   aburrido(a) (estar)   **I.3,** III.1
boring   aburrido(a) (ser)   **I.2,** II.2
to **bother**   molestar   **II.3**
bottle   la botella   **IV.3**
bouquet   el ramillete   **III.3,** IV.1
bowl   la cuenca   **II.3**
bowling   los bolos   **III.1**
box   la caja   **III.3,** IV.2
boy   el muchacho   **I.1,** I.2
boyfriend   el novio   **I.2,** I.2
bracelet   el brazalete   **II.2**
brain   el cerebro   **I.3,** III.1
brake   el freno   **IV.5**
bread   el pan   **II.3,** I.6
to **break**   romper   **III.5,** IV.2
breakfast   el desayuno   **II.3,** I.6
to **breathe**   respirar   **IV.4**
bricklayer   el/la albañil   **I.2**
bridge   el puente   **IV.5**
briefcase   la cartera   **I.4,** I.8

to **bring (people)**   llevar   **II.2,** IV.1
to **bring (things)**   traer   **III.3,** IV.6
broccoli   el brócoli   **II.3**
to **broil**   asar   **II.3**
broiled   asado(a)   **II.3**
broken   roto(a)   **III.5,** III.1
broken down   descompuesto(a)   **IV.5**
bronchitis   la bronquitis   **IV.4**
broom   la escoba   **III.3**
brother   el hermano   **I.1,** I.3
brother-in-law   el cuñado   **I.2,** II.4
brown   pardo(a)   **I.4,** I.7
brown (dark)   marrón   **I.4,** II.6
to **browse**   sólo mirar   **IV.2**
brunette   moreno(a)   **I.2,** II.1
to **brush**   cepillarse   **III.2,** IV.5
bucket   el cubo   **III.4**
buffalo   el búfalo   **I.5,** III.6
buffet   el aparador   **III.4**
building   el edificio   **II.1,** III.2
bull   el toro   **I.5,** I.6
bulletin board   el tablero de anuncios
    I.4, II.6
bullfighting arena   la plaza de toros   **III.3**
bumper   el parachoques   **IV.5**
bureau   el tocador   **III.4**
to **burn**   quemar   **II.3**
burnt   quemado(a)   **II.3**
bus   el autobús   **II.1,** I.8
bus stop   la parada de autobús   **IV.5**
business   el comercio   **I.5,** IV.4; los negocios
    I.5, II.5
businessman   el hombre de negocios   **I.2,** II.5
businesswoman   la mujer de negocios
    I.2, II.5
busy   ocupado(a)   **I.3,** III.1
to be **busy**   ocuparse   **III.2**
but   pero   **I.4,** I.6;   **but rather**   sino   I.4
butcher shop   la carnicería   **II.1,** III.2
butter   la mantequilla   **II.3,** IV.2
butterfly   la mariposa   **I.5,** III.6
buttocks   las nalgas   **I.3,** III.1
button   el botón   **II.2**
to **buy**   comprar   **II.2,** I.10
by   por   **IV.1,** I.3
Bye!   ¡Chau!   **I.1,** I.1

C

cabbage   el col   **II.3**
cabinet   el armario   **I.4**
cafeteria   la cafetería   **II.5,** IV.2
cake   la torta   **II.3,** I.6
calculator   la calculadora   **I.4,** I.8
calculus   el cálculo   **I.5,** IV.4

calendar   el calendario **I.1**, I.9
to **call**   llamar **I.1**, IV.1
to be **called**   llamarse **I.1**, I.2
calm   tranquilo(a) **I.3**, III.1
camel   el camello **I.5**, III.6
camper   la caravana **IV.5**
can   poder (ue) **I.1**, I.10
can (tin)   la lata **IV.3**
can opener   el abrelatas **III.4**
to **cancel**   cancelar **IV.4**
cancer   el cáncer **IV.4**
candle   la vela **III.3**
candlestick   el candelero **II.3**
candy   los dulces **II.3**, IV.2
candy store   la dulcería **II.1**, III.2
cap   el gorro **II.2**, I.5
capital city   la capital **II.1**, III.3
capsule   la cápsula **IV.4**
car   el auto, el carro **II.1**, I.8; el coche **I.5**, I.8
carburetor   el carburador **IV.5**
card (greeting)   la tarjeta **III.3**, IV.6
cardboard   el cartón **IV.3**
cards (playing)   los naipes **III.1**, I.10
career   la carrera **I.2**, IV.4
to be **careful**   tener cuidado **I.3**, III.5
carefully   cuidadosamente **II.5**
Carnaval (Mardi Gras)   el Carnaval **III.3**
carol   el villancico **III.3**
carpenter   el/la carpintero(a) **I.2**
carpet   la alfombra **III.4**
carrot   la zanahoria **II.3**, IV.2
to **carry**   llevar I.10
cash   en efectivo **IV.2**
cashier   el/la cajero(a) **I.2**
cashmere   el casimir **II.2**
cassette   el casete **I.4**, II.6
cast   la enyesadura **IV.4**
cat   el gato **I.5**, I.6
to **catch (an illness)**   contraer **IV.4**
cauliflower   la coliflor **II.3**, IV.2
caution   el cuidado **I.3**
ceiling   el techo **I.4**, III.2
to **celebrate**   celebrar **III.5**, IV.1
celery   el apio **II.3**, IV.2
cemetery   el cementerio **III.3**
center   el centro **II.1**, III.3
century   el siglo **III.3**
cereal   el cereal **II.3**, IV.2
certain   cierto(a) **IV.4**
chain   la cadena **II.2**
chair   la silla **I.4**, I.8
chair (large)   el sillón **III.4**
chalk   la tiza **I.4**, I.8

chalkboard   la pizarra **I.1**, I.8
chandelier   el candelabro **III.4**
to **change**   cambiar **III.4**
characteristic   la característica **I.2**
to **chat**   charlar **III.5**, IV.1
to **check**   revisar **IV.5**
to **check (luggage)**   facturar **IV.1**
checkered   a cuadros **II.2**
checkers game   el juego de damas **I.5**, III.5
cheek   la mejilla **I.3**, III.1
cheerful   alegre **I.2**, II.2
cheese   el queso **II.3**, IV.2
chef   el/la cocinero(a) **I.2**
chemicals   los químicos **IV.3**
chemistry   la química **I.5**, IV.4
cherry   la cereza **II.3**, IV.2
chess   el ajedrez **III.1**
chest   el pecho **I.3**, III.1
chest of drawers   la cómoda **III.4**
chewing gum   el chicle **II.3**
chicken   el pollo **II.3**, I.6
chicken pox   la varicela **IV.4**
children   los hijos, los niños **I.2**, I.3
chills   los escalofríos **IV.4**
chin   el mentón **I.3**, III.1
china closet   el chinero **III.4**
Chinese (language)   el chino **IV.4**
chocolate   el chocolate **II.3**, I.6
chocolate bar   la tableta de chocolate **II.3**, IV.2
to **choose**   escoger **II.3**
chop   la chuleta **II.3**, IV.2
chores   los quehaceres **III.4**, IV.5
Christmas   la Navidad **III.3**
Christmas Eve   la Nochebuena **III.3**
church   la iglesia **II.1**, I.10
circular   circular **I.4**, I.7
circus   el circo **III.3**, IV.2
citizen   el/la ciudadano(a) **III.3**
city   la ciudad **II.1**, I.5
clam   la almeja **I.5**, III.6
clarinet   el clarinete **III.1**
class   la clase **I.5**, I.9
classmate   el/la compañero(a) I.2
classroom   el aula (*f.*) **I.4**, I.8
clean   limpio(a) **I.4**, IV.3
to **clean**   limpiar **II.2**, IV.1
cleanser   el limpiador en polvo **III.4**
clear   claro(a) **II.1**, I.5
clever   listo(a) (ser) **I.2**, II.2
clinic   la clínica **IV.4**
clock   el reloj **I.4**, I.8
clock store   la relojería **II.1**, III.2
to **close**   cerrar (ie) **I.1**, IV.4

closet   el armario   **I.4,** I.8
clothes   la ropa   **II.2,** I.5
clothing   la ropa   **II.2,** I.5
clothing store   la ropería   **II.1,** III.2
cloudy   nublado(a)   **II.1,** I.5
cloverleaf   el trébol   **IV.5**
clown   el/la payaso(a)   **I.2**
clutch   el embrague   **IV.5**
coal   el carbón   **IV.3**
coast   la costa   **II.1,** III.3
coat   el abrigo   **II.2,** I.5
cockroach   la cucaracha   **I.5,** III.6
coffee   el café   **II.3,** I.6
coffeepot   la cafetera   **II.3**
cold   el frío   **I.3,** I.5
to be **cold**   tener frío   **I.3,** III.4
cold (headcold)   el catarro   **IV.4,** I.4
to **collect**   recoger   **III.4,** IV.6; coleccionar
    III.1,
color   el color   **I.4,** I.7
colored eggs   los huevos de colores   **III.3**
to **comb**   peinarse   **III.2,** IV.5
to **come**   venir   **II.1,** IV.3
to **come out well**   salir bien   **II.5**
comfortable   cómodo(a)   **I.3,** IV.5
comfortably   cómodamente   **II.5,** IV.5
compact disc   el disco compacto   **I.5,** I.8
competition   la competencia   **IV.4**
to **complain**   quejarse   **III.2**
to **compose**   componer   **III.5**
composed   compuesto(a)   **III.5**
computer   la computadora   **I.4,** I.8
computer science   la computación; la
    informática   **I.5,** IV.4
concert   el concierto   **III.1,** IV.6
condiments   los condimentos   **II.3**
condition   la condición   **IV.4**
condominium   el condominio   **II.4,** IV.3
to **confess**   confesar (ie)   **III.1**
to **conserve**   conservar   **IV.3**
content   contento(a)   **I.3,** III.1
to **consult**   to consult   **II.5**
to **consume**   consumir   **IV.3**
consumption   el consumo   **IV.3**
contact lenses   los lentes de contacto   **II.2,** I.5
container   el contenedor   **IV.3**
content   contento(a)   III.1
continent   el continente   **II.1**
to **continue**   seguir (i, i)   **II.4,** IV.4
to **contribute**   contribuir   **IV.3**
convertible   el descapotable   **IV.5**
cook   el/la cocinero(a)   **I.2**
to **cook**   cocinar   **II.3,** I.10

cooked   cocido(a)   **II.3**
cookie   la galletita dulce   **II.3,** IV.2
cool   fresco(a)   **II.1,** I.5
corduroy   la pana   **II.2**
corn   el maíz   **II.3,** IV.2
corn on the cob   la mazorca   **II.3**
corner (outside)   la esquina   **II.4,** III.2;
    (inside) el rincón   **I.4,** III.2
correct   correcto(a)   **III.5,** IV.5
correctly   correctamente   **II.5,** IV.5
to **cost**   costar (ue)   **III.1,** IV.4
costume   el disfraz, el vestuario   **III.3**
cotton   el algodón   **II.2**
cough   la tos   III.1
to **cough**   toser   **IV.4**
cough syrup   el jarabe para la tos   **IV.4**
could   pudiera   **IV.2**
to **count**   contar (ue)   **III.1,** IV.6
country   el país   **II.1,** II.3
countryside   el campo   **II.1,** III.3
courteous   amable   II.2; cortés   **I.2**
courtesy   la cortesía   **I.1**
cousin   el/la primo(a)   **I.2,** I.3
to **cover**   cubrir   **III.5**
covered   cubierto(a)   **III.5**
cow   la vaca   **I.5,** I.6
cowboy   el vaquero   **I.2,** II.1
cowgirl   la vaquera   **I.2,** II.1
crab   el cangrejo   **I.5,** III.6
cracker   la galleta   **II.3,** IV.2
cramps   los calambres   **IV.4**
crazy   loco(a)   **I.2,** III.1
cream   la crema   **II.3,** IV.2
creamer   la cremera   **II.3**
credit card   la tarjeta de crédito   **IV.2**
to **cross (a street)**   atravesar (ie)   **III.1**
to **cry**   llorar   **III.2**
cucumber   el pepino   **II.3,** IV.2
cufflink   el gemelo   **II.2**
cup   la taza   **II.3,** III.1
Cupid   Cupido   **III.3**
to **cure**   curar   **IV.4**
curious   curioso(a)   **I.2**
curtain   la cortina   **III.4**
custard   el flan   **II.3,** IV.2
customs   la aduana   **IV.1**
to **cut**   cortar   **II.3**

D

dairy (of or relating to)   lácteo(a)   IV.2
dairy   la lechería   **II.1,** III.2
damage   el daño   **IV.3**
to **damage**   deshacer   **III.5**

dance el baile **III.3**
to **dance** bailar **III.5,** I.10
danger el peligro **IV.3**
dangerous peligroso(a) IV.3
dark oscuro(a) **I.4,** I.7
dark-haired moreno(a) **I.2,** II.1
date la fecha **I.4,** I.9; la cita **IV.4**
daughter la hija **I.2,** I.3
daughter-in-law la nuera **I.2,** II.4
day el día **I.1,** I.1
day after tomorrow pasado mañana **I.1,** I.9
day before yesterday anteayer **II.5,** I.9
dead muerto(a) **III.3**
dear querido(a) **III.2,** II.2
December diciembre **I.1,** I.9
to **decide** decidir **IV.1,** IV.6
deep profundamente **IV.4**
deer el ciervo **I.5,** III.6
delicious rico(a) (estar) **I.3,** III.1
delighted encantado(a) **IV.4**
to **demand** exigir **IV.3**
den la sala de estar I.7
denim el dril **II.2**
dentist el/la dentista **I.2,** II.5
to **deny** negar (ie) **IV.4**
department store el almacén **II.1,** III.2
depressed deprimido(a) **IV.4**
to **describe** describir **II.4**
described descrito(a) **III.5**
description la descripción II.1
desert el desierto **II.1,** III.3
to **desire** desear **II.5,** IV.1
desk (of a student) el pupitre **I.1,** I.8
desk (of a teacher) el escritorio **I.4,** I.8
dessert el postre **II.3,** I.6
destination la destinación **IV.1,** IV.6
to **destroy** destruir **IV.3;** deshacer **III.5**
destruction la destrucción **IV.3**
detergent el detergente **III.4**
diabetes la diabetes **IV.4**
diagnosis el diagnóstico **IV.4**
diarrhea la diarrea **IV.4**
dictionary el diccionario **I.4,** I.8
to **die** morir (ue, u) **III.1,** IV.4
difficult difícil **I.4,** III.1
dining room comedor **II.1,** I.7
dinner la cena **II.3,** I.6
direction la dirección **II.4**
dirty sucio(a) **I.4,** IV.3
to **dirty** ensuciar **II.2**
discourteous descortés **I.2**
to **discover** descubrir **III.5**
discovered descubierto(a) **III.5**
to **discuss** discutir **II.5,** IV.3

dish el plato **II.3,** IV.1
dishes los platos IV.2
dishwasher el lavaplatos **III.4**
to **disobey** desobedecer **IV.5**
to **displease** disgustar **II.3**
ditch la cuneta **IV.5**
to **divide** dividir **II.5,** IV.4
divided by dividido(a) por **I.4,** I.3
dizziness los mareos **IV.4**
dizzy mareado(a) **IV.4**
to **do** hacer **II.5,** I.10
to **do arithmetic** calcular **IV.4**
doctor el/la médico, el/la doctor(a) **I.2,** II.5
dog el perro **I.5,** I.6
doll la muñeca **I.5,** III.5
dollhouse la casa de muñecas **I.5,** III.5
domestic doméstico(a) **I.5,** III.6
dominos los dominós **III.1**
done hecho(a) **III.5**
donkey el burro **I.5,** I.6
door la puerta **I.1,** I.8
door handle el puño de la puerta **IV.5**
to **doubt** dudar **IV.4**
doubtful dudoso(a) **IV.4**
dough la masa **II.3,** IV.2
doughnut la rosquilla **II.3,** IV.2
downtown el centro **II.1,** III.3
drama el drama **I.5**
drape la cortina **III.4**
to **draw** dibujar **III.1,** I.8
to **dream about** soñar con **III.1**
dress el vestido **II.2,** I.5
to **dress** vestirse (i, i) **III.2,** IV.5
dresser el tocador **III.4**
to **drink** beber **II.3,** I.6; tomar **II.3,** I.10
drive el paseo **II.4,** IV.3
to **drive** manejar **IV.1,** I.10; conducir **IV.1**
driver el/la conductor(a) **I.2**
drop la gota **IV.4**
drum el tambor **I.5,** III.5
to **dry** secar **III.4**
to **dry clean** limpiar en seco **II.2**
dry cleaners la tintorería **II.1,** III.2
to **dry oneself** secarse **III.2**
dryer (clothes) la secadora **III.4**
duck el pato **I.5,** I.6
dust el polvo **III.4**
dust pan el recogedor de polvo **III.4**
duster (feather) el guardapolvo **III.4**

E

each cada III.4
each other nos, se **III.2,** IV.5

ear   la oreja **I.3,** I.4; **inner . . .**   el oído I.3
early   temprano **II.5,** IV.1
to **earn**   ganar **III.1,** I.10
earring   el pendiente **II.2**
earth   la tierra **IV.3**
easily   fácilmente **II.5,** IV.5
east   el este **II.1,** III.3
Easter   la Pascua Florida **III.3**
easy   fácil **I.4,** III.3
to **eat**   comer **II.3,** I.6
to **eat a snack**   merendar (ie) **II.3**
to **eat breakfast**   desayunar **II.3,** IV.2
to **eat dinner**   cenar **II.3,** IV.2
to **eat lunch**   almorzar (ue) **II.3,** IV.2
ecology   la ecología **IV.3**
economics   la economía **I.5,** I.9
egg   el huevo **II.3,** I.6
eight   ocho **I.1,** I.3
eight hundred   ochocientos **I.4,** I.10
eighth   octavo(a) **II.4,** IV.3
eighty   ochenta **I.1,** I.3
either   tampoco **III.4,** III.6
either . . . or   o… o **III.4,** IV.4
elbow   el codo **I.3,** I.4
electric   eléctrico(a) **I.5,** III.5
electrician   el/la electricista **I.2**
electricity   la electricidad **IV.3**
elementary   primario(a) **I.5,** IV.4
elementary school   la escuela primaria **I.5**
elephant   el elefante **I.5,** I.6
elevator   el ascensor **II.1**
eleven   once **I.1,** I.3
to **eliminate**   eliminar **IV.3**
embarrassed   avergonzado(a) **IV.4**
embroidered   bordado(a) **II.2**
emergency room   la sala de emergencia **IV.4**
emotion   la emoción **I.3**
empty   vacío(a) **IV.5**
encounter   el encuentro I.1
end   el fin III.4
to **end**   terminar III.3
to **endanger**   amenazar **IV.3**
endangered   amenazado(a) **IV.3**
energy   la energía **IV.3**
engineer   el/la ingeniero(a) **I.2,** II.5
England   Inglaterra II.3
English (language)   el inglés **I.1,** I.1
to **enjoy**   gozar (de) **II.3**
to **enjoy oneself**   divertirse (ie, i) **III.1,** IV.5
enough   suficiente, bastante **I.5,** I.5
to **enter**   entrar (en) **IV.5,** IV.4
entrance   la entrada **IV.5**
environment   el medioambiente **IV.3**
equal   igual **I.1**

equal(s) (=)   son (=) **I.4,** I.3
equator   el ecuador **II.1**
eraser (chalkboard)   el borrador **I.4,** I.8
eraser (pencil)   la goma **I.4,** I.8
especially   especialmente **II.5,** IV.5
essential   esencial **IV.3**
even numbers   los números pares **I.1,** I.10
evening   la noche **I.1,** I.1
evening meal   la cena **II.3,** I.6
every   todos(as) **II.5,** II.1
everyone   todo el mundo **I.2**
evident   evidente **IV.4**
exam   el examen **II.5,** IV.4
to **examine**   examinar **IV.4**
example   el ejemplo **I.1,** I.1
excess   el exceso **IV.5**
excited   entusiasmado(a) **I.3,** IV.6
Excuse me   Con permiso, Perdón **I.1,** I.1
to **exercise**   hacer ejercicio **III.1**
exhaust   el escape **IV.3**
exhaust pipe   el tubo de escape **IV.5**
exit   la salida **II.4**
expensive   caro(a) **I.4,** II.6
expression   la expresión **I.1,** I.1
expressway   la autopista **II.4**
eye   el ojo **I.3,** I.4
eyebrow   la ceja **I.3**
eyeglasses   los lentes **II.2,** I.5

F

fabric   la tela **II.2**
face   la cara **I.3,** I.4
fact   el hecho **II.5,** IV.4
factory   la fábrica **II.1,** III.2
to **fail**   suspender **II.5,** IV.4; no poder
 (preterite) **II.5,** IV.6
to **faint**   desmayarse **IV.4**
faintness   el desmayo **IV.4**
fairly, quite   bastante **I.2,** I.7
to **fall in love (with)**   enamorarse (de) **III.2**
family   la familia **I.2,** I.3
family room   la sala de estar **II.1,** I.7
famous   famoso(a) **I.2,** II.5
fanbelt   la correa del ventilador **IV.5**
far from   lejos de **II.1,** III.2
farm   la granja **I.5,** III.6
farmer   el/la agricultor(a) **I.2,** II.5
to **fascinate**   fascinar **II.3**
fast   rápido(a) II.6
fast food   la comida rápida **IV.2**
to **fasten**   abrocharse **IV.5**
fat   gordo(a) **I.2,** II.1
father   el padre **I.1,** I.3

father-in-law el suegro **I.2,** II.4
favorite favorito(a) I.5
fear el miedo **I.3**
to **fear** temer **IV.4**
February febrero **I.1,** I.9
to **feed** alimentar **IV.6**
to **feel** sentirse (ie, i) **III.2**
to **feel dizzy** marearse **IV.4**
to **feel like + *verb*** tener ganas de + *infinitive* **II.5,** IV.2
felt el fieltro **II.2**
fender el guardabarros **IV.5**
ferocious feroz III.6
fertilizer el fertilizante **IV.3**
fever la fiebre **I.3,** I.4
few poco(a) II.1
fifteen quince **I.1,** I.3
fifth quinto(a) **II.4,** IV.3
fifty cincuenta **I.1,** I.3
to **fight** luchar **IV.3**
file cabinet el archivador **I.4,** I.8
filet el filete **II.3**
to **fill** llenar **IV.1**
film la película **IV.2**
finally finalmente **II.5,** IV.5
to **find** hallar **IV.2,** IV.1; encontrar (ue) **III.1**
to **find out** saber (*preterite*) **III.3,** IV.6
fine muy bien I.1
finger el dedo (de la mano) **I.3,** I.4
fingernail la uña III.1
to **finish** terminar III.3
fire el fuego **III.3**
firefighter el/la bombero(a) **I.2,** II.5
fireworks los fuegos artificiales **III.3**
first primer(o)(a) **I.1,** I.9
fish (live) el pez **I.5,** I.6
fish (to eat) el pescado **II.3,** I.6
fish store la pescadería **II.1**
to **fish** pescar **III.1,** IV.6
fisherperson el/la pescador(a) **I.2**
five cinco **I.1,** I.3
five hundred quinientos **I.4,** I.10
to **fix** arreglar **IV.5**
to **fix up (oneself)** arreglar(se) **III.2**
flag la bandera **I.4,** I.8
flannel la franela **II.2**
flat plano(a) **I.4,** I.7
flat bread (Mexico) la tortilla **II.3**
flat tire la llanta desinflada **IV.5**
flight el vuelo **IV.1**
flight attendant el/la aeromozo(a) **I.2**
float el carro alegórico **III.3**
floor el suelo **I.1,** III.2; el piso **II.1,** IV.3
floral centerpiece el centro de flores **II.3**

flower la flor **II.1,** III.2
flower shop la florería **II.1,** III.2
flu la gripe **I.3,** I.4
fluorocarbon el fluorocarburo **IV.3**
flute la flauta **III.1**
fly la mosca **I.5,** III.6
to **fly** volar (ue) **III.1**
to **fold** doblar **III.4**
to **follow** seguir (i, i) **II.4,** IV.4
food la comida **II.3,** I.6; el alimento **IV.2**
food poisoning el envenamiento con comida **IV.4**
foolish tonto(a) **I.2,** II.2
foot el pie **I.3,** I.4
football el fútbol norteamericano **III.1,** II.6
for por **IV.1,** I.3; para **II.1,** I.6
for example por ejemplo III.2
forehead la frente **I.3,** III.1
foreign extranjero(a) **I.5,** IV.4
forest la selva **I.5,** III.3; el bosque **I.5,** III.6
fork el tenedor **II.3**
former antiguo(a) **I.4,** IV.3
forty cuarenta **I.1,** I.3
found out saber (*preterite*) **IV.6**
four cuatro **I.1,** I.3
four hundred cuatrocientos **I.4,** I.10
fourteen catorce **I.1,** I.3
fourth cuarto(a) **II.4,** IV.3
fox el zorro **I.5,** III.6
fracture la fractura **IV.4**
framework el esqueleto **II.1**
France Francia II.3
free (no charge) gratis IV.4
to **freeze** congelar **II.3**
French (language) el francés **I.5,** II.3
French fries las papas fritas **II.3,** I.6
French horn la trompa francesa **III.1**
frequent frecuente **II.5**
frequently frecuentemente **II.5**
fresh fresco(a) **II.1,** IV.6
fresh water el agua dulce (*f.*) **IV.3**
freshman year el primer año **I.5,** I.5
Friday viernes **I.1,** I.9
fried frito(a) **II.3,** I.6
friend el/la amigo(a), el/la compañero(a) **I.2,** I.2
friendly amistoso(a) **I.2,** II.2
frightened asustado(a) **I.3**
frog la rana **I.5,** III.6
from de **I.1,** II.3
from (time) desde **II.1,** IV.4
from the del (de + el) **I.2,** I.2
from time to time de vez en cuando **II.5,** II.1
front el frente **I.4,** III.2

frozen   congelado(a)   **II.3**
fruit   la fruta   **II.3**, I.6
to **fry**   freír (i, i)   **II.3**, IV.2
frying pan   la sartén   **III.4**, IV.2
full   lleno(a)   **III.3**
fun   divertido(a)   **I.2**
funeral   el funeral   **IV.1**
funny   chistoso(a)   **I.2**
fur   la piel   **II.2**
furniture   los muebles   **III.4**
furniture store   la mueblería   **IV.2**
future   el futuro   **II.5**, II.1

G

game   juego   **I.5**, I.10
game (like Bingo)   la lotería   **III.1**
garage   el garaje   **II.1**
garbage   la basura   **III.4**
garbage can   el basurero   **IV.3**
garden   el jardín   **II.1**
gardener   el/la jardinero(a)   **I.2**
garlic   ajo   **II.3**, IV.2
gas station   la estación de gasolina   **II.1**, III.2
gas station attendant   el/la gasolinero(a)   **IV.5**
gas tank   el tanque de gasolina   **IV.5**
gasoline   la gasolina   **IV.1**
gear shift lever   la palanca de cambios   **IV.5**
gelatin   la gelatina   **II.3**
generous   generoso(a)   **I.2**, II.2
generously   generosamente   **II.5**
gentleman   el caballero   **IV.2**
geography   la geografía   **I.5**, III.3
geometry   la geometría   **I.5**, IV.4
German (language)   el alemán   **I.5**, II.3
Germany   Alemania   II.3
to **get**   conseguir (i, i)   **II.5**; obtener   **IV.1**
to **get along well**   llevarse (bien)   **III.2**
to **get an A**   sacar una A   **II.5**, IV.4
to **get angry**   enojarse   **III.2**
to **get better**   mejorarse   **IV.4**
to **get bored**   aburrirse   **III.2**
to **get divorced**   divorciarse   **III.2**
to **get married**   casarse   **III.2**
to **get off**   bajar (de)   **II.4**
to **get on**   subirse   **IV.4**
to **get ready**   prepararse   **III.2**
to **get sick**   enfermarse   **IV.4**
to **get tired**   cansarse   **III.2**
to **get up**   levantarse   **III.2**, IV.5
to **get worse**   empeorarse   **IV.4**
ghost   el fantasma   **III.3**
gift   el regalo   **II.2**, I.9
giraffe   la jirafa   **I.5**, III.6

girl   la muchacha   **I.1**, I.2
girlfriend   la novia   **I.2**, I.2
to **give**   dar   **II.2**, I.10
to **give a gift**   regalar   **III.3**
to **give a ticket**   poner una multa   **IV.5**
to **give thanks**   dar las gracias   **III.3**, IV.1
glass (material)   el vidrio, el cristal   **IV.3**
glass (drinking)   el vaso   **II.3**
globe   el globo   **I.4**, I.8
glove   el guante   **II.2**
glove compartment   la guantera   **IV.5**
Go (*formal command*)   Vaya(n)   **I.1**
Go (*familiar command*)   Ve   **II.4**
to **go**   ir   **I.1**, I.8
go ahead   adelante   I.2
to **go away**   irse   **III.2**, IV.5
to **go down**   bajar   **II.4**, IV.3
to **go into**   entrar (en)   **IV.5**, IV.4
to **go out**   salir   **IV.6**
to **go shopping**   ir de compras   **IV.2**, IV.6
to **go to bed**   acostarse (ue)   **III.2**, IV.5
to **go to sleep**   dormirse (ue, u)   **III.2**, IV.5
to **go up**   subir   **II.4**, IV.3
goat   la cabra   **I.5**, III.6
goblet   la copa   **II.3**
goblin   el duende   **III.3**
goddaughter   la ahijada   **I.2**, II.4
godfather   el padrino   **I.2**, II.4
godmother   la madrina   **I.2**, II.4
godson   el ahijado   **I.2**, II.4
to be **going to** + *verb*   ir a + *infinitive*   **II.5**, I.10
gold   dorado(a)   **I.4**, II.6
gold   el oro   **I.4**
golf   el golf   **III.1**
good   bueno(a)   **I.1**, I.1
Good afternoon   Buenas tardes   **I.1**, I.1
Good evening   Buenas noches   **I.1**, I.1
Good morning   Buenos días   **I.1**, I.1
Good night   Buenas noches   **I.1**
Good-bye   Adiós   **I.1**, I.1
good-looking   guapo(a)   **I.2**, II.1
gorilla   el gorila   **I.5**, III.6
government   el gobierno   **III.2**
grade (on tests etc.)   la nota   **II.5**, II.4
grade (school year)   el año   **I.1**, I.3;
      el grado   II.6
to **graduate**   graduarse   **III.2**
graduation   la graduación   **III.5**
grandchildren   los nietos   **I.2**, I.3
granddaughter   la nieta   **I.2**, I.3
grandfather   el abuelo   **I.2**, I.3
grandmother   la abuela   **I.2**, I.3
grandparents   los abuelos   **I.2**, I.3
grandson   el nieto   **I.2**, I.3

grape   la uva   **II.3,** IV.2
grapefruit   la toronja   **II.3,** IV.2
grave   el sepulcro   **III.3**
gray   gris   **I.4,** I.7
gray-haired   canoso(a)   **I.2,** II.1
great   fantástico(a)   **I.2,** II.2
green (color)   verde (ser)   **I.3,** I.7
green (unripe)   verde (estar)   **I.3,** III.1
to **greet**   saludar   **III.3,** IV.1
greeting   el saludo   **I.2,** I.1
ground floor   la planta baja   **II.1,** I.7
ground meat   la carne molida   **II.3,** IV.2
guest   el/la invitado(a)   **III.5,** IV.1
guitar   la guitarra   **I.5,** I.10
gumdrops   los dulces de goma   **III.3**
gymnasium   el gimnasio   **IV.2**

H

hair   el pelo   **I.3,** I.4
half   medio(a)   **I.1,** I.9
Halloween   el Día de las Brujas   **III.3**
hallway   el pasillo   **II.1,** I.7
ham   el jamón   **II.3,** I.6
hamburger   la hamburguesa   **II.3,** I.6
hand   la mano   **I.3,** I.4
handkerchief   el pañuelo   **II.2**
handsome   guapo(a)   **I.2,** II.1
to **hang up**   colgar (ue)   **III.4**
happily   felizmente   **II.5,** IV.5
happy   feliz   **I.2,** II.2; contento(a)   **I.3,** III.1
to be **happy**   alegrarse (de)   **III.2**
hard   duro(a)   **I.4,** II.6
hardworking   trabajador(a)   **I.2,** II.2
hat   el sombrero   **II.2,** I.5
to **hate (to)**   odiar   **II.5,** IV.2
to **have**   tener   **I.1,** I.3
to **have + *past participle***   haber + *past participle* **III.5**
to **have a good time**   divertirse (ie, i)   **III.2,** IV.5
to **have fun**   divertirse (ie, i)   **III.1,** IV.5
to **have just**   acabar de   **II.5,** IV.2
to **have to + *verb***   tener que + *infinitive* **II.5,** IV.2
he   él   **I.5,** I.1
head   la cabeza   **I.3,** I.4
headlight   el faro delantero   **IV.5**
health   la salud   **I.1,** I.4
healthy   sano(a)   **IV.4**
to **hear**   oír   **II.4,** IV.6
heart   el corazón   **I.3,** I.4
heart attack   el ataque al corazón   **IV.4**
heat   el calor   **I.3,** I.5; **heating (in a building)**   la calefacción   **IV.3**

heavy   pesado(a)   **I.4,** II.6
heel (of a foot)   el talón   **I.3,** III.1
heel (of a shoe)   el tacón   **IV.6**
height   la altura   **III.3**
Hello   Hola   **I.1,** I.1
to **help**   ayudar (a)   **II.1,** IV.1
hen   la gallina   **I.5,** I.6
her   su   I.3; la   **I.5,** I.5
here   aquí   **I.1,** I.3; **around . . .** por aquí   **II.1**
hers   suyo(a)   I.5
herself   se   IV.5
Hi   Hola   **I.1,** I.1
hide and seek   el escondite   **III.1**
high   alto(a)   **I.1,** I.7
high heels   los tacones altos   **II.2**
high school   el colegio   **I.5**
highway   la carretera   **II.4**
hill   la colina   **II.1**
him   le   I.4; lo   **I.5,** I.5
himself   se   IV.5
hippopotamus   el hipopótamo   **I.5,** III.6
his   su   I.3; suyo(a)   I.5
Hispanic people   la Raza   **III.3**
history   la historia   **I.5,** I.9
hives   la urticaria   **IV.4**
holiday   el festivo   **III.3**
home (to go)   a casa   **II.4**
homemaker   el ama de casa *(f.)*   **I.2,** II.5
homework   la tarea   **I.1,** IV.4
honey   la miel   **II.3**
hood (of a car)   la capota   **IV.5**
to **hope**   esperar   **IV.3,** IV.2
hopefully   ojalá   **IV.5,** IV.3
horn (of a car)   el claxón, la bocina   **IV.5**
horse   el caballo   **I.5,** I.6
hose   la manguera   **IV.5**
hospital   el hospital   **II.1,** III.2
host, hostess   el/la anfitrión(ona)   **III.5**
hot dog   el perro caliente   **II.3,** I.6
hot sauce   la salsa picante   **II.3,** IV.2
hotel   el hotel   **II.1,** III.2
hour   la hora   **I.1,** I.9
house   la casa   **II.1,** I.3
housekeeper   el/la criado(a)   II.5
How?   ¿Cómo?   **I.1,** I.1
How are you?   ¿Cómo estás?, ¿Cómo está Ud.?   **I.1,** I.1
How do you say . . . ?   ¿Cómo se dice… ?   **I.1,** I.1
How do you spell . . . ?   ¿Cómo se escribe… ?   **I.1,** I.2
How is . . . ?   ¿Cómo está… ?   **I.1,** I.1
How many?   ¿Cuántos(as)?   **I.1,** I.3

How much?   ¿Cuánto(a)?   **I.2,** II.3
How old are you?   ¿Cuántos años tienes?
   I.1, I.3
How's everything?   ¿Qué tal?   **I.1,** I.1
however   sin embargo   **I.4**
hubcap   el tapacubos   **IV.5**
hug   el abrazo   **III.2,** I.1
to **hug**   abrazar   **III.2**
humid   húmedo(a)   **II.1,** I.5
hundred   cien(to)   **I.1,** I.10
to be **hungry**   tener hambre   **I.3,** III.5
to **hurt**   doler (ue)   **I.3,** I.4
hurt(s) me   me duele(n)   I.2
husband   el esposo   **I.2,** I.3
hydroelectric   hidroeléctrica   **IV.3**
hypocrite   el/la hipócrita   **I.2**

I

I   yo   **I.5,** I.1
I am   soy   I.1
I can + *verb*   puedo + *infinitive*   I.10
I (don't) know   (No) sé   I.1
I love you   Te quiero   **II.2,** II.2
I think that . . .   Yo creo que…   II.5
I'm sorry   Lo siento   **I.1,** I.1
ice   el hielo   **I.5,** III.5
ice cream   el helado   **II.3,** I.6
ice cream store   la heladería   **II.1,** III.2
ice hockey   el hockey sobre hielo   **III.1**
ice skates   los patines de hielo   **I.5,** III.5
if   si   **I.4,** II.3
illegal   ilegal   **IV.5**
illness   la enfermedad   **IV.4,** I.4
immediate   inmediato(a)   **II.5**
immediately   inmediatamente   **II.5,** IV.5
important   importante   **IV.3**
to **impose**   imponer   **III.5**
imposed   impuesto(a)   **III.5**
impossible   imposible   **IV.4**
improbable   improbable   **IV.4**
in   en   **I.1,** I.1
in . . . (months)   en… (meses)   **II.5,** II.1
to be **in a hurry**   tener prisa   III.5
in case   en caso (de) que   **IV.5**
in case of   en caso de   **IV.1**
in fact   de hecho   III.3
in front of   delante de   **II.1,** III.2
in love (with)   enamorado(a) (de)   **I.3,** III.1
in order to   para   **II.1,** I.6
in spite of   a pesar de   **IV.1**
in the afternoon   por la tarde   **II.5,** II.1
in the evening   por la noche   **II.5,** II.1
in the front of   en el frente de   III.2

in the middle of   en el medio de   **II.1**
in the morning   por la mañana   **II.5,** II.1
to **include**   incluir   **IV.3**
incorrect   incorrecto(a)   **II.5,** IV.5
incorrectly   incorrectamente   **II.5,** IV.5
incredible   increíble   **IV.4**
inexpensive   barato(a)   **I.4,** II.6
infection   la infección   **I.3,** III.1
to **influence**   influir   **IV.3**
information   la información   **IV.1**
infraction   la infracción   **IV.5**
inhabitant   el/la habitante   **I.2,** III.3
injection   la inyección   **IV.4**
inner courtyard   el patio   **II.1,** I.7
to **input (keyboard)**   teclear   **II.5,** IV.4
insect   el insecto   **I.5,** III.6
insecticide   el insecticida   **IV.3**
inside of   dentro (de)   **II.1,** III.2
to **insist on**   insistir en   **II.5,** IV.2
insomnia   el insomnio   **IV.4**
to **install**   instalar   **IV.5**
instead of   en vez de   **II.1,** IV.5
instruction   la instrucción   **II.4**
instrument   el instrumento   **III.1,** I.10
insurance form   el formulario de seguro   **IV.4**
intellectual   intelectual   **I.2**
intelligently   inteligentemente   **II.5**
to **interest**   interesar   **II.3**
interesting   interesante   **I.2,** II.2
intersection   la bocacalle, el cruce   **IV.5**
to **introduce**   presentar   **I.1,** I.2; introducir   **IV.3**
invitation   la invitación   **III.5,** IV.1
to **invite**   invitar   **II.5,** IV.1
to **iron**   planchar   **III.4**
to **irritate**   irritar   **IV.4**
island   la isla   **II.1,** III.3
issue   la cuestión   **IV.3**
it   lo, la   I.5
Italian (language)   el italiano   **I.5,** IV.4
itch   la picazón   **IV.4**

J

jack-o-lantern   la linterna de calabaza   **III.3**
jacket   la chaqueta   **II.2,** I.5
jail   la cárcel   **II.1**
January   enero   **I.1,** I.9
Japanese (language)   el japonés   **I.5,** IV.4
jealous   celoso(a)   **I.3,** III.1
jealous (to be . . .)   tener celos   I.3
jeans   los pantalones vaqueros   **II.2**
jelly   la jalea   **II.3,** IV.2
jewelry   las joyas   **II.2**
jewelry store   la joyería   **II.1,** III.2

job   el trabajo   **III.1**, I.3
to **jog**   hacer jogging   **III.1**
joke   el chiste   **III.5**
journalist   el/la periodista   **I.2**, II.5
judge   el/la juez   **IV.5**
juice   el jugo   **II.3**, I.6
July   julio   **I.1**, I.9
jump rope   la cuerda   **I.5**
June   junio   **I.1**, I.9
jungle   la selva   **I.5**, III.3
junior year   el tercer(o) año   **I.5**

K

kangaroo   el canguro   **I.5**, III.6
to **keep**   guardar   **IV.3**; quedar   **II.3**
ketchup   el catsup   **II.3**
key   la llave   **I.5**
keyboarding   el tecleo   **I.5**
keyboarding (class)   la clase de tecleo   IV.4
keyring   el llavero   **I.5**
to **kill**   matar   **IV.3**
kilometer   el kilómetro   IV.3
kind   el tipo   III.6
kind   amable   **I.2**, II.2
kiss   el beso   **III.2**, I.1
to **kiss**   besar   **III.2**
kitchen   la cocina   **II.1**, I.7
kite   la cometa   **I.5**, III.5
knapsack   la mochila   **I.4**, I.8
knee   la rodilla   **I.3**, I.4
knife   el cuchillo   **II.3**
knit   tejido   **II.2**
to **know (be acquainted with)**   conocer   **III.3**, IV.6
to **know (a fact)**   saber   **I.1**, I.1; **(how)**   IV.6

L

laborer   el/la obrero(a)   **I.2**, II.5
lace   el encaje   **II.2**
to **lack**   faltar   **II.3**, IV.4
lady   la dama   **IV.2**
lake   el lago   **II.1**, III.3
lamb   el cordero   **II.3**, IV.2
lamp   la lámpara   **III.4**
lane   el carril   **IV.5**
language   la lengua   **I.5**, IV.4
large   grande   **I.2**, II.1
last (in order)   último(a)   III.3
last month   el mes pasado   II.1
last name   el apellido   **I.1**, I.2
last week   la semana pasada   II.1
last year   el año pasado   **I.1**, II.1

late   tarde   **II.5**, IV.1
later, then   luego   **II.5**, II.1
Latin (language)   el latín   **I.5**, IV.4
laundry (room)   la lavandería   **II.1**
lavatories   los servicios   **IV.2**
lavatory   el retrete   **IV.2**
law   la ley   **IV.3**
lawn   el césped   **III.4**
lawyer   el/la abogado(a)   **I.2**, II.5
lazily   perezosamente   **II.5**
lazy   perezoso(a)   **I.2**, II.2
leaf   la hoja   **III.4**
to **learn**   aprender   **II.5**, I.10
least (the . . .)   el/la menos   **I.2**, I.7
leather   el cuero   **II.2**
to **leave**   salir   **II.4**, IV.6
lecture   la conferencia   **II.5**, IV.4
left (direction)   la izquierda   **II.1**, III.2
left of (to the . . .)   a la izquierda de   **II.1**, III.2
leg   la pierna   **I.3**, I.4
lemon   el limón   **II.3**, IV.2
to **lend**   prestar   IV.1
leopard   el leopardo   **I.5**, III.6
less   menos   **I.1**, I.3
less . . . than   menos... que   **I.2**, I.7
lesson   la lección   **II.5**, I.1
to **let**   dejar   **IV.3**
let's   vamos a + *infinitive*   **IV.3**, IV.1
letter (mail)   la carta   **I.5**, I.8
letter (of alphabet)   la letra   **I.1**, I.2
lettuce   la lechuga   **II.3**, I.6
library   la biblioteca   **II.1**, I.8
license   la licencia   **IV.5**
license plate   la placa   **IV.5**
life   la vida   **II.3**, IV.5
to **lift (weights)**   levantar (pesas)   **III.1**
light (electrical)   la luz   **I.4**, III.2
light (in color)   claro(a)   **I.4**, I.7
light (in weight)   ligero(a)   **I.4**, II.6
to **light**   encender (ie)   **III.1**
like   como   **II.2**, I.3
like (would . . .)   quisiera   **IV.2**
to **like a lot**   gustar mucho   II.4
to **like more/less**   gustar más/menos   II.6
Likewise   Igualmente   **I.1**, I.2
limit   el límite   **IV.5**
linen   el lino   **II.2**
lion   el león   **I.5**, I.6
lip   el labio   **I.3**
liquid   el líquido   **IV.4**
to **listen (to)**   escuchar   **II.5**, I.10
little   pequeño(a)   I.7
little bit   un poco   II.1
to **live**   vivir   **II.4**, I.7

lively   vivo(a) (ser)   **I.3**
liver   el hígado   **I.3**, III.1
living room   la sala   **II.1**, I.7
loafers   los mocasines   **II.2**
lobster   la langosta   **II.3**, IV.2
location   la ubicación   **II.1**
locker   el armario   **I.4**, I.8
logical   lógico(a)   **IV.4**
long   largo(a)   **I.4**, I.7
to **look at**   mirar   **II.2**, I.10
to **look for**   buscar   **III.5**, IV.1
to **lose**   perder (ie)   **III.1**, IV.4
lost   perdido(a)   **IV.2**
loud   alto(a)   **I.1**, I.1
to **love**   querer (ie) a   **III.1**, IV.4
low   bajo(a)   **I.2**, I.7
low voice   voz baja   **II.5**
to **lower**   bajar   **IV.3**
to be **lucky**   tener suerte   **I.3**, III.5
luggage   el equipaje   **IV.1**
lunch   el almuerzo   **II.3**, I.6
lung   el pulmón   **I.3**, III.1

M

macaroni   los macarrones   **II.3**
Ma'am   señora   **I.2**
made   hecho(a)   **III.5**
mail carrier   el/la cartero(a)   **I.2**
main dish   el plato principal   **II.3**
main meal   la comida   **I.6**
to **make**   hacer   **II.5**, I.10
to **make a mistake**   equivocarse   **III.2**
to **make an appointment**   hacer una cita   **IV.4**
to **make a turn**   dar una vuelta   **IV.5**
to **make fun of**   burlarse de   **III.2**
mall   el centro comercial   **II.1**, III.2
man   el hombre   **I.2**, I.2
manager   el/la gerente   **I.2**, II.5
mango   el mango   **II.3**
map   el mapa   **I.4**, I.8
marbles   las canicas   **I.5**, III.5
March   marzo   **I.1**, I.9
margarine   la margarina   **II.3**
married   casado(a) (estar)   **I.3**, III.1
married couple   los esposos   **I.2**, I.3
mask   la máscara   **III.3**
match (sporting)   el partido   **III.1**
math   las matemáticas   **I.5**, I.9
to **matter**   importar   **II.3**
mattress   el colchón   **III.4**
May   mayo   **I.1**, I.9
maybe   quizás, tal vez   **IV.5**

mayonnaise   la mayonesa   **II.3**
me   me   **I.3, I.5**, I.4, IV.1
me *(after prep.)*   mí   **II.1**, III.2
meal   la comida   **II.3**, I.6
mean (not nice)   antipático(a)   **I.2**, II.2
means   los medios   **II.1**
measles   el sarampión   **IV.4; three-day . . .**
   la rubeola   **IV.4**
meat   la carne   **II.3**, IV.2
meatball   la albóndiga   **II.3**
mechanic   el/la mecánico(a)   **I.2**, II.5
medical   médico(a)   **IV.4**
medical history   la hoja clínica   **IV.4**
medical office   el consultorio   **II.1**, III.2
medium   mediano(a)   **I.7**
to **meet**   encontrar (ue)   **III.1; reunirse IV.2**
to **meet for the first time**   conocer *(preterite)*
   III.3
melon   el melón   **II.3**
to **memorize**   memorizar   **II.5**, IV.4
memory   el recuerdo   **IV.6**
merge   la señal de unión   **IV.5**
metal   el metal   **IV.3**
Mexican   mexicano(a)   II.3
Mexico   México   II.3
microwave   la microonda   **III.4**
microwave oven   el horno de microondas
   III.4
midday meal   la comida   **II.3**, I.6
middle   el medio   **II.1**, III.2
midnight   la medianoche   **I.1**, I.9
Midnight Mass   la Misa del Gallo   **III.3**
mile   la milla   **II.4**, IV.3
milk   la leche   **II.3**, I.6
million   el millón   **I.4**, I.10
mine   mío(a)   **I.1**, I.5
minus   menos   **I.1**, I.3
mirror   el espejo   **III.4**, IV.5
Miss, Ms.   señorita (Srta.)   **I.1**, I.2
mitten   el mitón   **II.2**
to **mix**   mezclar   **II.3**
mixed   mezclado(a)   **IV.2**
modern   moderno(a)   **I.4**, IV.3
Monday   lunes   **I.1**, I.9
money   el dinero   **IV.1**, I.10
money clip   el portabilletes   **II.2**
monkey   el mono   **I.5**, I.6
mononucleosis   la mononucleosis   **IV.4**
month   el mes   **I.1**, I.9
monument   el monument   **II.1**, III.2
mop   el fregasuelos   **III.4**
more   más   **I.1**, I.1
more than anything   más que nada   **III.6**
more . . . than   más. . . que   **I.2**, I.7

more than + *number*   más de + *number*
  I.2, II.6
morning   la mañana   **I.1**, I.9
mosque   la mezquita   **II.1**, III.2
mosquito   el mosquito   **I.5**, III.6
most (the . . .)   el/la/los/las más…   **I.2**, I.7
mother   la madre   **I.2**, I.3
mother-in-law   la suegra   **I.2**, II.4
motorcycle   la moto(cicleta)   **II.1**, III.4
mountain   la montaña   **II.1**, III.3
mountain range   la sierra   **II.1**, III.3
mouse   el ratón   **I.5**, I.6
mouth   la boca   **I.3**, I.4
to **move**   mover (ue)   **III.1**
movie theater   el cine   **II.1**, I.10
Mr.   señor (Sr.)   **I.1**, I.2
Mrs.   señora (Sra.)   **I.1**, I.2
much   mucho(a)   **I.1**, I.5
muffler   el silenciador   **IV.5**
to **multiply**   multiplicar   **II.5**, IV.4
mumps   las paperas   **IV.4**
muscle   el músculo   **IV.4**
museum   el museo   **II.1**, III.2
music   la música   **I.5**, I.9
musical   musical   **III.1**
musician   el/la músico(a)   **I.2**, II.5
must (one . . .)   hay que   **II.5**
mustache   el bigote   **I.3**, III.1
mustard   la mostaza   **II.3**
my   mi   **I.1**, I.2
My name is . . .   Me llamo…   **I.1**, I.2
myself   me   **III.2**, IV.5

N

nail (finger)   la uña   **I.3**, III.1
name   el nombre   **I.1**, I.2
to be **named**   llamarse   **I.1**, I.2
nap   la siesta   **III.1**, IV.2
napkin   la servilleta   **II.3**
narrow   estrecho(a)   **I.4**, I.7
nasal congestion   la constipación   **IV.4**
nationality   la nacionalidad   **II.3**
Native American   el/la indio(a)   **III.3**
natural   natural   **IV.3**
nausea   la náusea   **IV.4**
near   cerca (de)   **II.1**, III.2
necessarily   necesariamente   **II.5**
necessary   necesario(a)   **IV.3**; preciso   **IV.4**
neck   el cuello   **I.3**, I.4
necklace   el collar   **II.2**
to **need**   faltar   **IV.4**
to **need (to)**   necesitar   **II.5**, IV.2
neighbor   el/la vecino(a)   **I.2**, IV.1

neighborhood   el barrio   **II.4**, IV.3
neither   ni   **III.4**, IV.4
neither . . . nor   ni… ni   **III.4**, IV.4
nephew   el sobrino   **I.2**, II.4
nervous   nervioso(a)   **I.3**, III.1
nervously   nerviosamente   **II.5**
never   nunca   **II.5**, II.1
nevertheless   sin embargo   **I.4**
new (brand . . .)   nuevo(a) (ser)   **I.3**, II.6
new (to be like . . .)   nuevo(a) estar   **I.3**
New Year   el Año Nuevo   **III.3**
New Year's Eve   la Nochevieja   **III.3**
newly   nuevamente   **II.5**
newspaper   el periódico   **I.5**
next (in order)   próximo(a)   **I.5**, II.1
next to   al lado de   **II.1**, III.2; junto a   **II.1**
nice   simpático(a)   **I.2**, II.2
nice weather   el buen tiempo   **II.1**, I.5
to be **(nice) weather**   hacer (buen) tiempo   I.5
niece   la sobrina   **I.1**, II.4
night   la noche   **I.1**, I.1
nightgown   el camisón   **II.2**
nine   nueve   **I.1**, I.3
nine hundred   novecientos   **I.4**, I.10
ninety   noventa   **I.1**, I.3
ninth   noveno(a)   **II.4**, IV.3
no   no   **I.2**, I.1
no longer   ya no   **II.5**, II.1
no one   nadie   **III.4**, IV.4
no way   de ninguna manera   **III.4**
noisy   ruidoso(a)   **IV.3**
none   ninguno(a)   **III.4**, IV.4
nonstop   sin escalas   **IV.1**
noodles   los tallarines   **II.3**
noon   el mediodía   **I.1**, I.9
nor   ni   **II.4**
normal   regular   **I.1**
north   el norte   **II.1**, III.3
northeast   el noreste   **II.4**
nose   la nariz   **I.3**, I.4
not any   ninguno(a)   **III.4**, IV.4
not   no   **I.2**, I.1
not at all   tampoco   **III.4**, IV.5
not well   no muy bien   **I.1**, I.1
not yet   todavía no   **II.5**, II.1
notebook   el cuaderno   **I.4**, I.8
notes (information)   los apuntes   **II.5**, IV.4
nothing   nada   **I.5**, I.1
novel   la novela   **II.5**, IV.4
November   noviembre   **I.1**, I.9
now   ahora   **II.5**, I.3
nowhere   a/en ninguna parte   **III.4**
nuclear   nuclear   **IV.3**
number   el número   **I.1**, I.3

nurse   el/la enfermero(a)   **I.2**, I.4
nursery school   la guardería   IV.4
nut   la nuez   **II.3**, IV.2
nylon   el nilón   **II.2**

O

oats   la avena   **II.3**, IV.2
object (item)   el objeto   **IV.2**
to **obtain**   conseguir (i, i)   **II.5**
occupation   la profesión   **I.2**, II.5
ocean   el océano   **II.1**, III.3
October   octubre   **I.1**, I.9
octopus   el pulpo   **I.5**, III.6
odd numbers   los números impares   **I.1**, I.10
of   de   **I.1**, II.4
of course   claro   I.10; por supuesto   IV.2
of the   del (de + el)   **II.1**, I.2
office   la oficina   **II.1**, II.5
office (medical)   el consultorio   **II.1**, III.2
often   frecuentemente   II.1; a menudo, mucho   **II.5**
oil   el aceite   **IV.5**
OK   regular   I.1; Bueno   I.9
old   viejo(a)   **I.2**, II.1
older   mayor   **I.2**, II.4
on   en   **II.1**, I.1
on (with days)   el (lunes)   **II.5**, I.9
on foot   a pie   **II.1**, III.4
on the phone   por teléfono   **III.1**, I.10
once   una vez   **II.5**, II.1
one   uno   **I.1**, I.3
one story (of a building)   un piso   **II.4**
one *(impersonal)*   se   **III.2**, I.1
onion   la cebolla   **II.3**, IV.2
only   solamente   **II.5**, II.3
to **open**   abrir   **I.1**, IV.3
open(ed)   abierto(a)   **III.5**
to **operate**   operar   **IV.4**
opposite   enfrente (de)   **II.1**
optometrist   el/la optómetra   **IV.2**
or   o   **I.4**, I.6; u *(before o/ho)*   I.4
orange (color)   anaranjado(a)   **I.4**, I.7
orange (fruit)   la naranja   **II.3**, IV.2
orchestra   la orquesta   I.9
to **order**   mandar   **IV.3**
other   otro(a)   **I.1**, I.8
other side of (on the . . .)   al otro lado de   **II.1**
ought to + *infinitive*   deber + *infinitive*   **II.5**, IV.2
our, ours   nuestro(a)   **I.2**, I.5
ourselves   nos   **III.2**, IV.5
outside of   fuera de   **II.1**, III.2
oven   el horno   **III.4**

over   sobre   **II.1**, III.2
overhead projector   el retroproyector   **I.4**, II.6
overpass   el puente   **IV.5**
to **owe**   deber   IV.2
oyster   la ostra   **II.3**, IV.2
ozone   el ozono   **IV.3**

P

to **pack a suitcase**   hacer la maleta   IV.1, IV.6
pail   el cubo   **III.4**
pain   el dolor   **IV.4**, I.4
to **paint**   pintar   **III.1**
paisley   la cachemira   **II.2**
pajamas   las pijamas   **II.2**, IV.6
pancake   el panqueque   **II.3**
pants   los pantalones   **II.2**, I.5
pantyhose   la pantimedia   **II.2**
papaya   la papaya   **II.3**
paper   el papel   **I.1**, I.8
paper towel   el papel absorbente   **III.4**
papier mâché figure   la piñata   **III.3**
parade   el desfile   **III.3**
parakeet   el periquito   **I.5**, III.6
Pardon   Perdón   **I.1**, I.1
parents   los padres   **I.2**, I.3
park   el parque   **II.1**, III.2
to **park**   estacionar   **IV.5**
parking place   el estacionamiento   **IV.5**
parrot   el perico   **I.5**, III.6
part   la pieza   **IV.5**
party   la fiesta   **III.5**, I.5
to **pass**   pasar   **III.4**, III.3
to **pass a car**   sobrepasar   **IV.5**
to **pass (a test, quiz, etc.)**   aprobar (ue)   **II.5**, IV.4
to **pass through**   pasar por   **IV.1**
passport   el pasaporte   **IV.1**
past   el pasado   **II.5**, II.1
pasta   la pasta   **II.3**
pastime   el pasatiempo   **III.1**
pastry   el pastel   **II.3**, III.2
pastry shop   la pastelería   **II.1**, III.2
patent leather   el charol   **II.2**
patient   paciente   **I.2**
patient   el/la paciente   **IV.4**, III.1
pattern   el diseño   **II.2**
to **pay (for)**   pagar   **II.3**, IV.4
peach   el durazno   **II.3**
peanut   el cacahuete,   **II.3**, IV.2; el maní   **II.3**
peanut butter   la crema de maní   **II.3**
pear   la pera   **II.3**, IV.2

pearl   la perla **II.2**
peas   los guisantes **II.3,** IV.2
pencil   el lápiz **I.1,** I.8
pencil sharpener   el sacapuntas **I.4,** II.6
people   las personas **I.2,** I.2; la gente
    I.2, IV.6
pepper (vegetable)   el pimiento **II.3,** IV.2
pepper (spice)   la pimienta **II.3,** IV.2
pepper shaker   el pimentero **II.3**
perfectly   perfectamente **II.5**
perfume store   la perfumería **IV.2**
permit   el permiso **IV.5**
to **permit**   permitir **IV.3**
person   la persona **I.2,** I.2
personality   la personalidad **I.2**
petroleum   el petróleo **IV.3**
pharmacist   el/la farmacista **I.2,** II.5
pharmacy   la farmacia **II.1,** III.2
phosphates   los fosfatos **IV.3**
photograph   la foto(grafía) **III.5,** IV.1
physical   físico(a) **I.2,** II.1
physical education   la educación física
    I.5, I.9
physics   la física **I.5,** IV.4
piano   el piano **III.1,** I.10
pickup truck   la camioneta **IV.5**
pickled   encurtido(a) **II.3**
picture   el cuadro **I.4,** II.6
pie   el pastel **II.3,** IV.2
pig   el cerdo, el puerco **I.5,** I.6
pilgrim   el/la peregrino(a) **III.3**
pill   la pastilla **IV.4**
pillow   la almohada **III.4**
pin   el broche **II.2**
pineapple   la piña **II.3,** IV.2
pink   rosado(a) **I.4,** I.7
pink eye   la conjuntivitis **IV.4**
pitcher   la jarra **II.3**
pity   la lástima **IV.4,** I.1
pizza   la pizza **II.3,** III.2
pizzeria   la pizzería **II.1,** III.2
place   el lugar **II.1,** III.2
place setting   el cubierto **II.3**
plaid   escocés(esa) **II.2**
plains   los llanos **II.1,** III.3
to **plan**   planear **IV.1,** IV.1
to **plan to**   pensar + *infinitive* **II.4,** IV.4
plant   la planta **IV.3.** II.6
plastic   el plástico **IV.3**
plate   el plato **II.3,** IV.1
to **play (a game)**   jugar (ue) **III.1,** I.10
to **play (music)**   tocar **III.1,** I.10
player   el/la jugador(a) **I.2,** II.5
please   por favor **I.1,** I.1

please + *verb*   favor de + *infinitive* **I.1,** III.6
Pleased to meet you   Mucho gusto **I.1,** I.2
Pleasure is mine (The . . .)   El gusto es mío
    I.1, I.2
to be **pleasing**   gustar **I.5,** I.6
plumber   el/la plomero(a) **I.2**
plus   y, más I.3
pneumonia   la pulmonía **IV.4**
pocket   el bolsillo **II.2**
poem   el poema **II.5**
poetry   la poesía **II.5,** IV.4
police   la policía **I.2,** II.5
police officer   el/la policía **I.2,** II.5
to **polish**   pulir **III.4**
polka dots   los bolitos **II.2**
to **pollute**   contaminar **IV.3**
pollution   la contaminación **IV.3**
polyester   el poliéster **II.2**
popcorn   las palomitas de maíz **II.3,** IV.2
popular   popular **I.2,** II.2
pork   el cerdo IV.2
port   el puerto IV.1
possible   posible **IV.4**
possibly   posiblemente **II.5**
postcard   la tarjeta postal **IV.1,** IV.6
post office   el correo **II.1,** III.2
pot   la olla **III.4**
potato   la papa **II.3,** I.6; la patata I.10
potato chips   las papitas fritas **II.3,** I.6
practice   la práctica **III.1**
to **practice**   practicar **II.5,** I.10
to **prefer**   preferir (ie, i) **II.5,** IV.4
preferable   preferible **IV.3**
pregnant   embarazada **IV.4**
preparation   la preparación **II.3,** IV.1
to **prepare**   preparar **II.3,** I.10
to **prescribe**   recetar **IV.4**
present (gift)   el regalo **II.2,** IV.1
present (time)   el presente **II.5,** II.1
to **present**   presentar **I.1**
pressure   la presión **IV.4**
pretty   bonito(a) **I.2,** II.1
to **prevent**   impedir (i, i) **III.1**
price   el precio **IV.2**
pride   el orgullo **I.3,** IV.4
print   estampado(a) **II.2**
probable   probable **IV.4**
problem   el problema **IV.3**
to **produce**   producir **IV.3**
product   el producto **IV.3**
to **prohibit**   prohibir **IV.3**
prohibited   prohibido(a) **IV.5**
project   el proyecto **II.5**
proud   orgulloso(a) **IV.4**

provided   con tal de **IV.1**
provided that   con tal (de) que **IV.5**
psychology   la sicología **I.5,** IV.4
publicly   públicamente **II.5**
pulse   el pulso **IV.4**
pumpkin   la calabaza **III.3**
pupil   el/la alumno(a) **I.2**
puppet   el títere **I.5,** III.5
purple   morado(a) **I.4,** I.7
purse   la bolsa **II.2,** IV.6
put   puesto(a) III.5
to **put**   poner **I.1,** IV.6
to **put on**   ponerse **III.2** IV.5
to **put on makeup**   maquillarse **III.2,** IV.5
puzzle   el rompecabezas **I.5,** III.5

Q

quarter   cuarto(a) **I.1,** I.9
queen   la reina **II.2**
question   la pregunta **II.5**
quiet   callado(a) **I.2,** II.2
to be **quiet**   callarse **III.2**
quite   bastante I.7
quiz   la prueba **II.5,** IV.4

R

rabbit   el conejo **I.5,** I.6
radiator   el radiador **IV.5**
radio (set)   el radio; **(program)** la radio
   I.5, I.8
radiologist   el/la radiólogo(a) **IV.4**
radish   el rábano **II.3,** IV.2
rag   el trapo **III.4**
railroad   el ferrocarril **IV.5**
railroad crossing   el cruce de ferrocarril **IV.5**
rain   la lluvia **IV.3**
to **rain**   llover (ue) **III.1,** III.5
rainbow   el arco iris **II.1**
raincoat   el impermeable **II.2,** IV.6
rains, it's raining   llueve **II.1,** I.5
raisin   la pasa **II.3**
to **rake leaves**   recoger las hojas **III.4**
rapidly   rápidamente **II.5,** IV.5
rare   raro(a) **IV.4;** poco asado(a) **II.3**
rarely   raramente **II.5,** II.1
rash   el sarpullido **IV.4**
raspberry   la frambuesa **II.3,** IV.2
rat   la rata **I.5,** III.6
raw   crudo(a) **II.3**
reaction   la reacción **IV.4**
to **read**   leer **II.5,** I.10
reading   la lectura **II.5,** IV.4

ready   listo(a) (estar) **I.3,** III.3
to **realize**   darse cuenta **III.2**
rearview mirror   el espejo retrovisor **IV.5**
to **receive**   recibir **II.5,** I.10
receptionist   el/la recepcionista **IV.4**
to **recommend**   recomendar (ie) **III.1**
record store   la discotería **IV.2**
rectangular   rectangular **I.4,** II.6
to **recycle**   reciclar **IV.3**
recycled   reciclado(a) **IV.3**
red   rojo(a) **I.4,** I.7
redhead   pelirrojo(a) **I.2,** II.1
to **reduce**   reducir **IV.3**
refreshments   los refrescos **III.5,** IV.1
refrigerator   el refrigerador **III.4**
to **refuse**   no querer *(preterite)* **III.3,** IV.6
to **regret**   sentir (ie, i) **III.2,** IV.4;
   lamentar **IV.4**
regularly   regularmente **II.5**
to **remain**   quedarse **III.2,** IV.5
remedy   el remedio **IV.4**
to **remember**   recordar (ue) **III.1,** IV.4
to **remove**   quitar **III.4,** IV.2
repair   la reparación **IV.2**
to **repair**   reparar **II.2**
to **repeat**   repetir (i, i) **I.1,** IV.4
request   el pedido **I.1**
to **request**   pedir (i, i) **IV.3**
to **require**   exigir **IV.3**
research   las investigaciones IV.4
to **research**   hacer investigaciones **II.5**
to **reserve**   reservar **IV.1**
to **resolve**   resolver (ue) **III.1**
resource   el recurso **IV.3**
to **rest**   descansar **III.1,** IV.1
restaurant   el restaurante **II.1,** III.2
result   el resuelto **III.5**
to **return**   volver (ue) **III.1,** IV.4
to **return (home)**   regresar **II.5,** IV.6
to **return (something)**   devolver (ue) **III.1**
returned   devuelto(a) **III.5;**
   vuelto(a) **III.5**
reverse   reverso(a) **IV.5**
to **reverse**   marchar atrás **IV.5**
rhinoceros   el rinoceronte **I.5,** III.6
rice   el arroz **II.3,** IV.2
rich   rico(a) (ser) **I.3,** III.1
to **ride**   montar **III.1**
ridiculous   ridículo(a) **IV.4**
right   la derecha **II.1,** III.2
right of (to the . . .)   a la derecha de
   II.1, III.2
to be **right**   tener razón **I.3,** III.5
right?, true?   ¿verdad?, ¿no? **I.2,** II.2

ring   el anillo   **I.5**
to **rip**   desgarrar   **II.2**
river   el río   **II.1**, III.3
road   el camino   **II.4**, IV.3
roast beef   el rosbif   **II.3**, I.6
robe   la bata   **II.2**
rocking horse   el caballo balancín   **I.5**, III.5
roll   el panecillo   **II.3**, IV.2
roller skates   los patines de rueda   **I.5**, III.5
romantic   romántico(a)   **III.3**
roof   el techo   **IV.5**, III.2
room   el cuarto   **I.4**, I.7
rooster   el gallo   **I.5**, I.6
round   redondo(a)   **I.4**, I.7
round neck   el cuello redondo   **II.2**
round trip   ida y vuelta   **IV.1**
roundup of the bulls   el encierro de los toros   III.3
route   la ruta   **IV.1**
row   la fila   **I.4**, III.2
rubber   la goma   **IV.3**
rude   descortés   **I.2**
ruler   la regla   **I.4**, II.6
to **run**   correr   **III.1**, I.10
rush hour   la hora punta   **IV.5**
Russian (language)   el ruso   **I.5**, IV.4

S

sad   triste   **I.2**, II.2
sadly   tristemente   **II.5**, IV.5
safe   seguro(a) (ser)   **I.3**, IV.3
said   dicho(a)   **III.5**
salad   la ensalada   **II.3**, I.6
salad bowl   la ensaladera   **II.3**
sale (for . . .)   de venta   **IV.2**
salesperson   el/la dependiente(a)   II.5
salmon   el salmón   **II.3**
salt   la sal   **II.3**, IV.2
salt shaker   el salero   **II.3**
Same here   Igualmente   **I.1**, I.2
sand   la arena   **I.5**, III.5
sandals   las sandalias   **II.2**, IV.6
sandbox   el cajón de arena   **I.5**, III.5
sandwich   el sándwich   **II.3**, I.6
satin   el raso   **II.2**
Saturday   sábado   **I.1**, I.9
saucer   el platillo   **II.3**
sausage   la salchicha   **II.3**, IV.2
to **save**   guardar, salvar   **IV.3**
saxophone   el saxofón   **III.1**
to **say**   decir   **III.3**, IV.6
to **say good-bye**   despedirse (i, i)   **III.2**, IV.5
scale   la balanza   **III.4**

scarf   la bufanda   **II.2**
school   la escuela   **I.4**, I.3
schooling   la enseñanza   **II.5**, IV.4
science   la ciencia   **I.5**, I.9
scientist   el/la científico(a)   **I.2**
scissors   las tijeras   **I.4**, II.6
to **scrub**   fregar   **III.4**
sea   el mar   **II.1**, III.3
seafood   los mariscos   **II.3**, IV.2
season   la estación   **II.1**, I.5
seasonings   los condimentos   **IV.2**
seat   el asiento   **IV.5**
seat belt   el cinturón de seguridad   **IV.5**
second   segundo(a)   **II.4**, IV.3
second floor (one floor up)   el primer piso   **II.1**, I.7
secondary   secundario(a)   **I.5**, IV.4
secretary   el/la secretario(a)   **I.2**, II.5
security   la seguridad   **IV.1**
to **see**   ver   **II.4**, IV.6
See you later   Hasta la vista   **I.1**, I.1
See you tomorrow   Hasta mañana   **I.1**, I.1
seen   visto(a)   **III.5**
selfish   egoísta   **I.2**, II.2
to **sell**   vender   **II.3**, IV.2
to **send**   mandar   **IV.3**, IV.1; enviar   IV.6
senior year   el cuarto año   **I.5**
to **separate**   separarse   **III.2**
September   septiembre   **I.1**, I.9
serious   serio(a)   **I.2**
servant   el/la criado(a)   **I.2**, II.5
to **serve**   servir (i, i)   **III.1**, IV.4
services   los servicios   **IV.2**
to **set fire to**   poner fuego a   **III.3**
to **set the table**   poner la mesa   **III.4**
seven   siete   **I.1**, I.3
seven hundred   setecientos   **I.4**, I.10
seventh   séptimo(a)   **II.4**, IV.3
seventy   setenta   **I.1**, I.3
to **sew**   coser   **II.2**, IV.2
to **shake**   sacudir   **III.4**
shape   la forma   **I.4**, I.7
shark   el tiburón   **I.5**, III.6
to **shave**   afeitarse   **III.2**, IV.5
she   ella   **I.5**, I.1
sheep   la oveja   **I.5**, I.6
sheet (bed)   la sábana   **III.4**
shell   la concha   **IV.6**
shirt   la camisa   **II.2**, I.5
shoe   el zapato   **II.2**, I.5
shoe repairperson   el/la zapatero(a)   **IV.2**
shoe store   la zapatería   **II.1**, III.2
shopping (to go . . .)   ir de compras   **III.1**
shopping mall   el centro comercial   **II.1**

short (in height)   bajo(a)   **I.4,** I.7
short (in length)   corto(a)   **I.4,** I.7
shorthand   la taquigrafía   **I.5,** IV.4
shorts   los pantalones cortos   **II.2,** IV.6
should   deber + *infinitive*   **II.5,** IV.2;
   debiera   **IV.2**
shoulder (body)   el hombro   **I.3,** III.1
shoulder (road)   el arcén   **IV.5**
to **shovel snow**   sacar la nieve   **III.4**
to **show**   mostrar (ue)   **III.1**
to **shower**   ducharse   **III.2,** IV.5
shrimp   los camarones   **II.3,** IV.2
shy   tímido(a)   **I.2,** II.2
siblings   los hermanos   **I.2,** I.3
sick   enfermo(a)   **I.3,** III.1
to be **sick**   estar malo(a)   **I.3,** I.1
side   el lado   **I.4,** III.2
sign   la señal   **IV.5**
silence   el silencio   **I.1**
silk   la seda   **II.2**
silver   plateado(a)   **I.4,** II.6
silver   la plata   **I.4**
since   desde   **II.1,** IV.4
sincere   sincero(a)   **I.2,** II.2
sincerely   sinceramente   **II.5**
to **sing**   cantar   **III.5,** I.10
sink (bathroom)   el lavabo   **III.4**
sink (kitchen)   el fregadero   **III.4**
sir   el señor   **I.1,** I.2
sister   la hermana   **I.2,** I.3
sister-in-law   la cuñada   **I.2,** II.4
to **sit down**   sentarse (ie)   **I.1,** IV.5
six   seis   **I.1,** I.3
six hundred   seiscientos   **I.4,** I.10
sixth   sexto(a)   **II.4,** IV.3
sixty   sesenta   **I.1,** I.3
size   el tamaño   **I.4,** I.7
to **skate**   patinar   **III.1**
skateboard   el monopatín   **I.5,** III.5
skates   los patines   **I.5,** III.5
skating rink   la pista de patinaje   **IV.2**
skeleton   el esqueleto   **III.3,** II.1
to **ski**   esquiar   I.10
skirt   la falda   **II.2,** I.5
skull   la calavera   **III.3**
skyscraper   el rascacielos   **II.1,** III.2
to **sleep**   dormir (ue, u)   **III.1,** I.10
to be **sleepy**   tener sueño   **I.3,** III.5
sleeve   la manga   **II.2,** IV.6
slice   la rebanada   **II.3,** IV.2
slip   la combinación   **II.2**
slipper   la zapatilla   **II.2,** IV.6
slowly   despacio   **I.1,** I.1; lentamente
   II.5, IV.5

small   pequeño(a)   **I.2,** I.7
small boy   el niño   **I.2,** I.2
small girl   la niña   **I.2,** I.2
smart   inteligente   **I.2,** II.2
smoke   el humo   **IV.3**
to **smoke**   fumar   **II.3;** **(food)** ahumar   **II.3**
snack   la merienda   **II.3,** I.6
snack food   el bocadito   **II.3**
snake   la serpiente   **I.5,** III.6
to **sneeze**   estornudar   **IV.4**
snow   la nieve   **III.4,** I.10
to **snow**   nevar (ie)   **III.1**
snows, it's snowing   nieva   **II.1,** I.5
so   así   **I.1,** I.1
so that   para que   **IV.5**
soap   el jabón   **III.4**
soccer   el fútbol   **III.1,** I.10
sociable   sociable   **I.2,** IV.4
socks   los calcetines   **II.2,** I.5
soda pop   la soda   **II.3**
sofa   el sofá   **III.4**
soft   blando(a)   **I.4,** II.6
soft drink   el refresco   **II.3,** I.6
solar   solar   **IV.3**
soldier (toy)   el soldado (de juguete)   **I.2,** III.5
solid   sólido(a)   **II.2**
solution   la solución   **IV.3**
to **solve**   resolver (ue)   **III.1**
some   unos(as)   **I.1,** I.2; alguno(a)
   III.4, IV.4
some time   alguna vez   **II.5**
some way   de alguna manera   **III.4**
someone   alguien   **I.1,** IV.4
something   algo   **II.5,** I.10
sometimes   a veces   **II.5,** I.5; algunas veces
   II.5, II.1
somewhere   alguna parte   **III.4**
son   el hijo   **I.2,** I.3
son-in-law   el yerno   **I.2,** II.4
song   la canción   **III.5,** I.10
soon   pronto   **II.5**
sophomore year   el segundo año   **I.5**
to be **sorry**   sentir (ie, i)   **III.2,** IV.4
to **sound**   sonar (ue)   **III.1**
soup   la sopa   **II.3,** I.6
south   el sur   **II.1,** III.3
southwest   el suroeste   **II.4**
souvenir   el recuerdo   **IV.1,** IV.6
spaghetti   los espaguetis   **II.3**
Spain   España   II.3
Spaniard   el/la español(a)   II.3
Spanish   español(a)   **I.1,** I.1
spare tire   la llanta de repuesta   **IV.5**
spark plug   la bujía   **IV.5**

to **speak**   hablar   **II.5,** I.10
special   especial   **IV.5**
specialist   el/la especialista   **IV.4**
speed   la velocidad   **IV.5**
to **spend (money)**   gastar   **IV.2,** I.10
to **spend time**   pasar tiempo   **III.1,** IV.6
spice   la especia   **IV.3**
spider   la araña   **I.5,** I.6
spill   el derrame   **IV.3**
spinach   las espinacas   **II.3**
sponge   la esponja   **III.4**
spoon   la cuchara   **II.3**
sport   el deporte   I.10
sport   deportivo(a)   **II.2,** IV.6
sports coat   el saco   **II.2,** IV.6
sprain   la torcedura   **IV.4**
spring   la primavera   **II.1,** I.5
square   cuadrado(a)   **I.4,** I.7
squirrel   la ardilla   **I.5,** I.6
stairs   la escalera   **II.1,** I.7
stamp   la estampilla   **III.1**
to **stand in line**   hacer cola   **II.5**
star   la estrella   **II.3**
to **start**   comenzar (ie)   **III.1,** IV.1
state   el estado   **I.3,** III.3; **(geography)**
    el estado   **II.1,** II.3
station   la estación   **IV.1,** III.2
station wagon   la ranchera   **IV.5**
stationery store   la papelería   **II.1,** III.2
statue   la estatua   **III.3**
to **stay**   quedarse   **III.2,** IV.5
to **stay in bed**   guardar cama   **IV.4**
steak   el bistec   **II.3**
steamed   al vapor   **II.3**
steering wheel   el volante   **IV.5**
stepbrother   el hermanastro   **I.2,** I.3
stepdaughter   la hijastra   **I.2**
stepfather   el padrastro   **I.1,** I.3
stepmother   la madrastra   **I.2,** I.3
stepparents   los padrastros   **I.2,** I.3
stepsister   la hermanastra   **I.2,** I.3
stepson   el hijastro   **I.2**
stereo   el estéreo   **I.5,** I.8
stethoscope   el estetoscopio   **IV.4**
stew   el guisado   **II.3**
to **stick out one's tongue**   sacar la lengua   **IV.4**
still   todavía   **II.5,** II.1
stingy   tacaño(a)   **I.2**
stockings   las medias   **II.2,** I.5
stomach   el estómago   **I.3,** I.4
stop   alto (street sign)   **IV.5**
to **stop**   parar   **IV.5**
store   la tienda   **II.1,** I.8
story   el cuento   **II.5,** IV.4
stove   la estufa   **III.4**

straight ahead   adelante, todo derecho   **II.4**
strawberry   la fresa   **II.3,** IV.2
street   la calle   **II.4,** IV.3
string beans   las judías   **II.3,** IV.2
striped   a rayas   **II.2**
stroke   el derrame cerebral   **IV.4**
strong   fuerte   **I.2,** II.1
student   el/la estudiante   **I.1,** II.5
to **study**   estudiar   **II.5,** I.10
stupid   estúpido(a)   **I.2**
Styrofoam   la estirofoma   **IV.3**
subject (class)   la materia   **I.5,** IV.4
to **substitute**   sustituir   **IV.3**
to **subtract**   restar   **II.2,** IV.4; subtraer   **II.5**
suburbs   las afueras   **II.1,** III.3
to **succeed**   poder *(preterite)*   **III.3,** IV.6
suddenly   de repente   **II.5,** II.1
suede   la gamuza   **II.2**
to **suffer**   sufrir   **II.5,** IV.3
sugar   el azúcar *(f.)*   **II.3,** IV.2
sugar bowl   la azucarera   **II.3**
to **suggest**   sugerir (ie, i)   **III.1**
suit   el traje   **II.2,** I.5
suitcase   la maleta   **I.5,** IV.6
summer   el verano   **II.1,** I.5
sun   el sol   **II.1,** I.5
to **sunbathe**   broncearse   **III.1,** IV.6
Sunday   domingo   **I.1,** I.9
sunglasses   las gafas de sol   **II.2**
to be **sunny**   hacer sol   **II.1,** I.5
supermarket   el supermercado   **II.1,** III.2
supper   la cena   **II.3**
sure, certain   seguro (estar)   **I.3,** III.1
surgeon   el/la cirujano(a)   **IV.4**
surprise   la sorpresa   **III.5**
to **surprise**   sorprender   **IV.4**
surrounding   alrededor de   **II.1,** III.2
to **swallow**   tragar   **IV.4**
sweater   el suéter   **II.2,** I.5
sweatpants   el pantalón de sudadera   **II.2**
sweatshirt   la sudadera   **II.2**
to **sweep**   barrer   **III.4**
sweet potato   la batata   **II.3,** IV.2
swelling   el hinchazón   **IV.4**
to **swim**   nadar   **III.1,** I.10
swimsuit   el traje de baño   **II.2,** IV.6
swing   el columpio   **I.5,** III.5
symptom   el síntoma   **IV.4**
synagogue   la sinagoga   **II.1,** III.2
syrup   el jarabe   **IV.4**

T

table   mesa   **I.4,** I.8
tablecloth   el mantel   **II.3**

taffeta   el tafetán   **II.2**
tailgate   la compuerta trasera   **IV.5**
taillight   el farol trasero   **IV.5**
to take   tomar   **II.3,** I.10
to take a bath   bañarse   **III.2**
to take a pulse   tomarle el pulso   **IV.4**
to take a quiz   tomar una prueba   **II.5**
to take blood pressure   tomarle la presión   **IV.4**
to take care of   cuidar   **III.1,** I.10
to take notes   tomar apuntes   **II.5,** IV.4
to take off   quitarse   **III.2,** IV.5
to take out   sacar   **I.1,** IV.1
to take pictures   sacar fotos   **III.5,** IV.1
to talk   hablar   **II.5,** I.10
talkative   hablador(a)   **I.2,** II.2
tall   alto(a)   **I.2,** I.7
tan (color)   crema   **I.4,** II.6
tank   el tanque   **IV.1**
tape   la cinta   **I.4,** I.8
tape recorder   la grabadora   **I.4,** I.8
to taste   probar (ue)   **III.1**
taxi   el taxi   **II.1,** III.4
tea   el té   **II.3,** I.6
to teach   enseñar   **II.5**
teacher   el/la profesor(a)   **I.1,** II.5
teaching   la enseñanza   **IV.4**
teapot   la tetera   **II.3**
to tear   desgarrar   **II.2**
teaspoon   la cucharita   **II.3**
teddy bear   el osito de peluche   **I.5,** III.5
T-shirt   la camiseta   **II.2,** IV.6
teenager   el/la joven   **I.2,** I.2; el/la chico(a)   **I.2**
telephone   el teléfono   **I.5,** I.8
to telephone   telefonear   **III.5**
television program   la televisión   **III.1,** I.10
television set   el televisor   **I.5,** I.8
to tell   decir   **III.3,** IV.6
to tell a lie   mentir (ie, i)   **III.1**
to tell a story   contar (ue)   **III.1,** IV.6
temperature   la temperatura   **I.5**
temple   el templo   **II.1,** III.2
ten   diez   **I.1,** I.3
tennis   el tenis   **III.1,** I.10
tennis shoes   los zapatos tenis   **II.2,** IV.6
tenth   décimo(a)   **II.4,** IV.3
test   la prueba   **II.5,** IV.4
than   que   **I.1,** I.3
Thank you   Gracias   **I.1,** I.1
thanks   las gracias   **IV.1**
Thanksgiving   el Día de Acción de Gracias   **III.3**
that   ese(a)   **I.4,** I.5
that (conjunction)   que   **I.4,** I.8
that (far away)   aquel(la)   **I.4,** III.3

that (indefinite)   eso   **I.4,** I.5; aquello   **I.4,** III.3
That's the way it is!   ¡Así es!   I.1
That's too bad!   ¡Qué lástima!   **I.1,** I.1
the   el, la, los, las   **I.1,** I.2
theater   el teatro   **II.1,** III.2
their   su   I.3
theirs   suyo(a)   I.5
them   los, las   **I.5,** I.5
theme   el tema   **II.5,** IV.4
themselves   se   IV.5
then   entonces, luego   **II.5,** II.1
there   allí   **I.1,** I.3
there is, there are   hay   **I.4,** I.3
there was, there were   hubo   **I.4**
there was, there were   había   **I.4,** II.6
there will be   habrá   **I.4,** II.6
therefore   por eso   II.2
these   estos(as)   **I.4,** I.4
they   ellos, ellas   **I.1,** I.2
they (impersonal)   se   I.1
thief   el ladrón   **I.2**
thin   delgado(a)   **I.2,** II.1
thing   la cosa   **I.4,** I.8
to think   pensar (ie)   **II.5,** IV.4
to think about (daydream)   pensar (ie) en   **II.5,** IV.4
to think about (opinion)   pensar (ie) de   **II.5,** IV.4
third   tercer(o)(a)   **II.4,** IV.3
third floor   el segundo piso   **II.4**
to be thirsty   tener sed   **I.3,** III.5
thirteen   trece   **I.1,** I.3
thirty   treinta   **I.1,** I.3
this   este(a)   **I.4,** I.4
this (indefinite)   esto   **I.4,** I.4
those   esos(as)   **I.4,** I.5; aquellos(as)   **I.4,** III.3
thousand   mil   **I.4,** I.10
threatened   amenazado(a)   **IV.3**
three   tres   **I.1,** I.3
three hundred   trescientos   **I.4,** I.10
throat   la garganta   **I.3,** I.4
through   por   **IV.1,** I.3
to throw   echar   **IV.3**
throw rug   el tapete   **III.4**
thumb   el pulgar   **I.3,** III.1
Thursday   jueves   **I.1,** I.9
ticket   el billete   **IV.1,** IV.6; el boleto   **IV.1**
tie   la corbata   **II.2,** I.5
tie bar   el pisacorbatas   **II.2**
tie tack   el alfiler de corbata   **II.2**
tiger   el tigre   **I.5,** I.6
time   el tiempo   **IV.3,** I.5
time schedule   el horario   **IV.1**

time(s) (occurrence)   la vez (veces) **II.5,** II.1
times (x)   por **I.4,** I.3
timid   tímido(a) **I.2,** II.2
tire   la llanta **IV.3**
tired   cansado(a) **I.3,** III.1
title   el título **I.1**
title of respect   don, doña **I.1,** I.2
to   a I.9
to (up to)   hasta **I.1,** IV.4
to her   le **I.3,** I.4
to him   le **I.3,** I.4
to me   me **I.3,** I.4
to the   al (a + el) **II.1,** III.4
to them   les **I.3,** I.4
to us   nos **I.3,** I.4
to you   le, les, te **I.3,** I.4
toad   el sapo **I.5,** III.6
toast   el pan tostado **II.3,** IV.2
toaster   la tostadora **III.4**
today   hoy **I.1,** I.9
toe   el dedo del pie **I.3,** I.4
together   juntos(as) **III.1**
toilet   el inodoro **III.4**
tomato   el tomate **II.3,** IV.2
tomorrow   mañana **I.1,** I.1
tonsillitis   la amigdalitis **IV.4**
too much   demasiado **I.5**
tooth   el diente **I.3,** I.4
top (on . . . of)   encima de **II.1,** III.2
towel   la toalla **III.4**
town   el pueblo **II.1,** III.3
town square   la plaza **II.1,** III.2
toy   el juguete **I.5,** III.5
toy soldier   el soldado de juguete **I.5**
toy store   la juguetería **II.1,** III.2
track   la pista **I.10**
traffic   la circulación, el tránsito **IV.5**
traffic circle   la glorieta **IV.5**
traffic light   el semáforo **II.4**
traffic ticket (fine)   la multa **IV.5**
trailer   el remolque **IV.5**
train   el tren **I.5,** III.4
to **translate**   traducir **IV.3**
transportation   el transporte **II.1**
to **travel**   viajar **IV.1,** I.10
traveler   el/la viajero(a) **IV.1**
traveler's check   el cheque de viajero **IV.1**
to **treat**   tratar **IV.4**
tree   el árbol **III.3,** IV.5
triangular   triangular **I.4,** II.6
tricycle   el triciclo **I.5,** III.5
trigonometry   la trigonometría **I.5,** IV.4
trip   el viaje **IV.1,** IV.6

trombone   el trombón **III.1**
tropical   tropical **IV.3**
truck   el camión **I.2**
trumpet   la trompeta **III.1**
trunk   el baúl **IV.5**
trunk of a car   el portaequipaje **IV.5**
to **try**   querer (*preterite*) **III.3,** IV.6
to **try on**   probarse (ue) **IV.2**
to **try out**   probar (ue) **III.1**
to **try to**   tratar de **II.5,** IV.2
tuba   la tuba **III.1**
Tuesday   martes **I.1,** I.9
tunafish   el atún **II.3**
turkey   el pavo **I.5,** III.6
to **turn**   doblar **II.4**
to **turn (in traffic)**   girar **IV.5**
to **turn off**   apagar **IV.3**
to **turn off the water**   cortar el agua **IV.3**
turn (It's your...)   Te toca I.l
turn signal   la intermitente **IV.5**
turnip   el nabo **II.3**
turquoise   turquesa **I.4,** II.6
turtle   la tortuga **I.5,** III.6
turtleneck   el cuello alto **II.2**
twelve   doce **I.1,** I.3
twenty   veinte **I.1,** I.3
twice   dos veces **II.5,** II.1
twin brother   el gemelo **I.2,** II.4
twin sister   la gemela **I.2,** II.4
two   dos **I.1,** I.3
two hundred   doscientos **I.4,** I.10
two-way   la doble vía **IV.5**
type   el tipo **III.6**
to **type**   escribir a máquina **IV.4**
typing   la mecanografía **I.5**

U

U-turn   el giro completo **IV.5**
ugly   feo(a) **I.2,** II.1
umbrella   el paraguas **II.2,** IV.6
uncle   el tío **I.2,** I.3
under   debajo (de) **II.1,** III.2
undershorts   los calzoncillos **II.2**
to **understand**   comprender **I.1,** I.1
underwear   la ropa interior **II.2,** IV.6
to **undo**   deshacer **III.5,** IV.6
undone   deshecho(a) **III.5**
unit   la unidad I.1
United States   los Estados Unidos **II.3**
university   la universidad **I.5,** IV.4
unless   a menos que **IV.5**
untamed   silvestre **IV.3,** II.6
until   hasta **II.1,** IV.4; hasta que **IV.5**

upon   al + *infinitive*   **II.1**
upset   agitado(a)   **I.3**, III.1
urgent   urgente   **IV.3**
us   nos   **I.3**, I.4
usage   el gasto   **IV.3**
to use   usar   **I.1**

V

V-neck   el cuello en V
vacation   las vacaciones   **IV.1**, IV.6
vacuum cleaner   la aspiradora   **III.4**
valley   la valle   **II.1**, III.3
van   el combi, la furgoneta   **IV.5**
vanilla   la vainilla   **II.3**, I.6
veal   la ternera   **II.3**, IV.2
vegetable   la legumbre   **II.3**, I.6
velvet   el terciopelo   **II.2**
verse   el verso   **III.3**
very   muy   **I.2**, I.1
very bad   muy mal   **I.1**, I.1
very much   muchísimo(a)   **I.5**
very well   muy bien   I.1
vest   el chaleco   **II.2**
video   el vídeo   **IV.2**, III.4
videocassette recorder   la videocasetera   **I.4**, II.6
violet   violeta   **I.4**, II.6
violin   el violín   **III.1**
virus   el virus   **IV.4**
visit   la visita   **IV.4**
to visit   visitar   **IV.1**, I.10
vocabulary   el vocabulario   **I.1**, I.1
volleyball   el vólibol   **III.1**
to vomit   vomitar   **IV.4**

W

waffle   el barquillo   **II.3**
wagon   la carreta   **I.5**, III.5
to wait for   esperar   **II.5**, IV.2
waiter   el mesero   **I.2**, II.5; el camarero   **I.2**
waitress   la mesera   **I.2**, II.5; la camarera   **I.2**
to wake up   despertarse (ie)   **III.2**, IV.5
to walk   caminar   **IV.2**, I.10
to walk (to go for a . . .)   dar un paseo   **III.1**, IV.6
wall   la pared   **I.4**, III.2
wallet   la cartera   **II.2**, IV.6
walnut   la nuez   **II.3**, IV.2
to want   desear   **II.5**, IV.1; querer (ie)   **I.1**, IV.4
to be warm   tener calor   **I.3**, III.5
to warn   advertir (ie, i)   **IV.3**
to wash   lavar   **II.2**, IV.1

to wash by hand   lavar a mano   **II.2**
to wash by machine   lavar a máquina   **II.2**
to wash (oneself)   lavarse   **III.2**, IV.5
washer   la lavadora   **III.4**
waste   el desperdicio, el malgasto   **IV.3**
to waste   malgastar   **IV.3**
to waste time   perder tiempo   **III.1**
wastepaper basket   la papelera   **I.4**, I.8
to watch   mirar   **II.2**, I.10
water   el agua (*f.*)   **I.5**, I.6
water gun   la pistola de agua   **I.5**
watermelon   la sandía   **II.3**, IV.2
wave (water)   la ola   **IV.6**
way   la vía   **IV.5**
we   nosotros(as)   **I.5**, I.2
weak   débil   **I.2**, II.1
to wear   llevar   **III.5**, I.5
weather   el tiempo   **II.1**, I.5
wedding   la boda   **IV.1**
Wednesday   miércoles   **I.1**, I.9
week   la semana   **I.1**, II.1
to weigh (oneself)   pesar(se)   **IV.4**
weights   las pesas   **III.1**
well   bien   **I.1**, I.1
well, then   pues   **II.3**
west   el oeste   **II.1**, III.3
whale   la ballena   **I.5**, III.6
what   lo que   **I.2**, I.10, II.5
What?   ¿Qué? ¿Cuál?   **I.1**, I.1
What does . . . mean?   ¿Qué quiere decir… ?   I.1
What time is it?   ¿Qué hora es?   **I.1**, I.9
What's happening?   ¿Qué pasa?   I.1
What's the matter?   ¿Qué tienes?   **I.3**, III.1
What's the weather like?   ¿Qué tiempo hace?   **II.1**, I.5
What's your name?   ¿Cómo te llamas?, ¿Cómo se llama Ud.?   **I.1**, I.2
wheat   el trigo   **II.3**, IV.2
wheel   la rueda   **I.5**, III.5
When?   ¿Cuándo?   **I.1**, I.5
Where?   ¿Dónde?   **I.2**, I.3;
Where (to)?   ¿Adónde?   **II.1**, I.8
Where is . . . from?   ¿De dónde es… ?   II.3
Which?   ¿Cuál?   I.2
while   mientras   II.1; al + *infinitive*   **II.1**; mientras (que)   **II.5**
whistle   el silbato   **I.5**, III.5
white   blanco(a)   **I.4**, I.7
Who?   ¿Quién?   **I.2**, I.2; ¿Quiénes?   **I.2**, II.3
whole (the . . . day)   todo(a) (el día)   **II.5**, I.9
Whose?   ¿De quién?   I.5
Why?   ¿Por qué?   **I.2**, II.3
wide   ancho(a)   **I.4**, I.7

wife   la esposa   **I.2**, I.3
wild   salvaje   **I.5**, III.6
to **win**   ganar   **IV.2**, I.10
wind   el viento   **II.1**, I.5
window   la ventana   I.8
window (of a car)   la ventanilla   **IV.5**
window cleaner   el líquido limpiaventanas   **III.4**
windshield   el parabrisas   **IV.5**
windshield wiper   el limpiaparabrisas   **IV.5**
winter   el invierno   **II.1**, I.5
wire   el alambre   **IV.5**
Wise Men   los Reyes Magos   **III.3**
to **wish**   querer (ie)   **I.1**, IV.4
witch   la bruja   **III.3**
with   con   **I.3**, III.2
with me   conmigo   **II.1**, III.2
with you   contigo   **II.1**, III.2
without   sin (que)   **II.1**, I.2
woman   la mujer   **I.2**, I.2
wood   la madera   **IV.3**
wool   la lana   **II.2**
word   la palabra   II.3
work   el trabajo   **III.1**, I.3
to **work**   trabajar   **II.5**, I.10
to **work (machines)**   funcionar   **IV.5**
worker   el/la obrero(a)   **I.2**, II.5
world   el mundo   **II.1**, II.2
worldwide   mundial   III.4
worried   preocupado(a)   **I.3**, III.1
to be **worried**   preocuparse   **III.2**
worse   peor   **I.3**
to **worsen**   empeorarse   **IV.4**
worst   el/la peor   **I.2**
to be **worth**   valer   **IV.4**
Wow!   ¡Huy!   I.7
to **wrap**   envolver (ue)   **III.5**, IV.2
wrapped   envuelto(a)   **III.5**
wrestling   la lucha   **III.1**
wrist   la muñeca   **I.3**, III.1
wristwatch   el reloj (de) pulsera   **I.5**, I.5

to **write**   escribir   **I.1**, I.10
written   escrito(a)   **III.5**
to be **wrong**   no tener razón   **I.3**, III.5

X

X ray   la radiografía   **IV.4**

Y

yard   el patio   **II.1**, I.7
year   el año   **I.1**, I.3
to be **... years old**   tener... años   **I.1**, III.5
yellow   amarillo(a)   **I.4**, I.7
yes   sí   **I.1**, I.1
yesterday   ayer   **II.5**, I.9
yet   todavía   **II.5**, II.1
yield   ceder el paso   **IV.5**
yogurt   el yogur   **II.3**, IV.2
you   tú, usted (Ud.)   **I.1**, I.1; ustedes (Uds.) **I.1**, I.2
you *(after prep.)*   ti   **II.1**, III.2
you *(impersonal)*   se   I.1
you (in Spain) *(subject)*   vosotros(as)   **I.2**, II.6
you, to you   te, lo, la, los, las, le, les   **I.3**, I.4
you, to you (in Spain) *(plural)*   os   **I.5**, IV.7
You're welcome   De nada   **I.1**, I.1
young   joven   **I.2**, II.1
young person   el/la joven   **I.2**; I.2
younger   menor   **I.2**, II.4
your   tu   **I.1**, I.2; su, vuestro(a)   **I.2**, I.3
yours   tuyo(a), suyo(a)   **III.4**, I.5
yourself, yourselves   te, se   **III.2**, IV.5
yo-yo   el yoyo   **I.5**, III.5

Z

zebra   la cebra   **I.5**, III.6
zero   cero   **I.1**, I.3
zone   la zona   **IV.5**
zoo   el jardín zoológico   **II.1**

Index

Note: Structures new to Book 2 are identified with a large dot. Those items without a dot were introduced in Book 1 and are being reintroduced for review, new learning, or relearning. Many of these previously introduced concepts have been expanded in Book 2. New vocabulary topics introduced in Book 2 are also identified with a large dot. Previously introduced vocabulary may also have been expanded.

⤳ Structure ⤳

Vocabulary

Culture